Media and society

Critical perspectives

Second edition

Graeme Burton

Open University Press

Open University Press
McGraw-Hill Education
McGraw-Hill House
Shoppenhangers Road
Maidenhead
Berkshire
England
SL6 2QL

email: enquiries@openup.co.uk
world wide web: www.openup.co.uk

and Two Penn Plaza, New York, NY 10121-2289, USA

First published 2005
Reprinted 2005, 2007
First published in this second edition 2010

Copyright © Graeme Burton 2010

A catalogue record of this book is available from the British Library

ISBN-13: 978-0-33-522723-5
ISBN-10: 0-33-522723-6

Library of Congress Cataloging-in-Publication Data

Typeset by Aptara Inc.
Printed and bound by CPI Group (UK) Ltd, Croydon, CR0 4YY

Fictitious names of companies, products, people, characters and/or data that
may be used herein (in case studies or in examples) are not intended to
represent any real individual, company, product or event.

The **McGraw·Hill** Companies

Media a

Secon

Contents

Figures and illustrations

Acknowledgements

Writing a book is hard work. It needs a mental space to hear the words that want to be written. And life has a habit of crowding that space. It needs time to start up the engine. So I am grateful to my wife Judy for understanding these things. So too I appreciate the forbearance of my editors as deadlines slip. They have been unfailingly civil and patient, where those in other media industries might have been abrasive.

And then there is nothing like teaching and discussion for challenging the sense of one's views and explanations. So thank you also to students and colleagues at the University of Teesside.

I want to acknowledge the contribution of Stuart Allan, who started this particular project – though even he probably didn't anticipate the first edition getting to Beijing before the Olympics! (I refer to a translation into Chinese.)

Finally I want to acknowledge my mother, who died soon after the first edition came out. I don't think she ever read anything that I wrote. But her evident pride in receiving the copies has been a powerful motivator.

Introduction

This book is intended to help student readers on degree courses and modules which are concerned with media studies, and, to some extent, with the study of cultures. I want to offer a few remarks about the position that I am coming from, and where I hope you may go to through using this text.

I take a holistic and dynamic view of *the relationships between media and society*. That is to say, while I present a range of views and debates about the media in this book, I do not really subscribe to pessimistic opinions about the influence of media on society. Nor do I go along with what I regard as over-optimistic views about audience autonomy and power. It seems to me that the media exist in an evolving and difficult relationship with their audiences, and indeed with institutions of the state. The relationship is dynamic in that it is evolving and changing. I also believe that it is possible for different critical positions to coexist. It is possible to be sceptical about the motives and behaviours of economically powerful media institutions. At the same time, it is possible to be optimistic about the effects of regulatory control in Britain, and about the capacity of audiences and society to resist the forces of commodification, and to generate a culture as much as to have it imposed on them.

I feel much the same way about how we should understand and use *key concepts*. The book is (fairly traditionally) predicated on the importance of institution, text and audience. But I see ideas about ideology, discourse, hegemony, mythologies, genres – to mention only a few examples – as coexisting in the space of 'meaning production'. You will find that this book keeps returning to these concepts, and develops ideas about the relationship between them. It seems to me that every kind of analysis keeps returning one to ways in which ideas and meanings are generated, and then to ideas about the power of these meanings. The media industries are meaning producers. All acts of communication produce meanings. It is the power of these meanings, what we do with them, that shapes relationships, exercises influence, models reality, generates behaviours of domination and feelings of subordination. So major concepts may be equally significant, and exist within a network of relationships with each other.

Media texts are full of **representations**. Media institutions exist, when it comes down to it, to manufacture representations (and their ideas) which they then turn into cash in a process of material exchange. But, of course, as we consume comics or television programmes, we are also part of a process of cultural exchange. The exchange is indeed one of ideas about the world and about ourselves. In a **dynamic model**, these keep developing and shifting and moving around. Some ideas are more persistent than others (stereotypes). But it is an exciting world out there, where the media keep generating, recombining, repeating ideas, even if this is mainly in the cause of commerce.

I take a similarly holistic view of the 'big ideas' about connections between the media and us. I have tried to give a fair if condensed view of a range of such critical positions. You will find boxed summaries of critical approaches and of some important critical thinkers in Chapters 1 and 2. In many ways I subscribe to a **political economy model** because it seems to me unarguable that, in the West, we have gone down what is called a capitalist road. Economic factors dominate media institutions, most of all in the ubiquitous presence of marketing. Profitability, competition and other values of the marketplace drive the production of media texts and behaviours in what we call **globalization**. In this respect I also feel that the outcomes of Marxist rationales and the validity of the notion of **ideology** are both important and not to be argued away. But because I am suggesting that ideas exist within a model, I am also saying that, for example, one cannot simply assert that notions of **pluralism** are nonsense. Yet, on balance, I certainly do not think that they prevail. It is important to me as the writer that you as readers take on different views, and think through your own beliefs for yourselves. It is, indeed, part of the development of critical skills not only to evaluate the validity of arguments, but to be able to hold in one's head a variety of arguments and ideas, all of which may have some merit, and all of which may stand in some relationship to one another.

This idea of dynamic relationships also applies to *academic disciplines*, with which you are involved. No one discipline 'owns' the media, including media schools. So you could be a student of social sciences, with an interest in the media. Because the media are also engines of cultural production you may have an interest in the media among other objects of cultural study. Certainly you will find reference in this book to cultural perspectives and ideas – such as those around **identity** – which I do not believe should be ring-fenced in some kind of discipline ghetto. One could approach the media through many disciplinary interests, from economics to anthropology. So I hope that in reading what follows you will find some sense of reference outwards and across subjects and disciplines. I have tried to delineate and control areas of inquiry, without seeming to circumscribe some absolute object called media study.

In terms of *the structure of this book*, you should know that the first three chapters are intended as an overview – of texts, institutions and audiences, and their co-relationship. The remaining chapters are kinds of 'case study', which exemplify and develop issues, concepts and debates. They are still predicated on those three central terms, and on concerns about the production of meaning and the exercise of power. Although these later chapters can stand alone to some extent, you should realize that reading the whole book is meant to be a process of reinforcement and development. In particular, and apart from key terms such as discourse, you will find that chapters return to ideas about technologies, gender, representations and globalization. So I think you have to make decisions about using the book in three possible ways:

- As a whole and developing text, from which you learn by going from beginning to end.
- As a case study resource in which you can get some ideas and further reading about the given chapter topic by using it on its own.
- As a topic resource in which you plunder the index for references across the book to the given topic that you want to find out more about.

What I would say is that no book can be the last word on a subject, especially one like this, which has a lot of ground to cover. It is meant to give you an overview, mixed with some more in-depth studies of particular topics. But you will need to read more widely. The chapter reading references and the collated bibliography will give you a lot to follow up.

So far as websites are concerned, I take a mixed view of their usefulness. The more specific your object of inquiry, the more useful they are likely to be. But in most cases, the examples that I have given you are meant to be helpful starting points. You need to use your tutors and your learning resource centre for information about sites that are specific to assignments and services such as LexisNexis to which your library will be subscribed. One thing I would say is that I am cautious about the value of the ubiquitous Wikipedia, which students love to use because it is online and easy to get at. Although many entries are excellent, others are not, depending as they do on the selective views of the contributor. It is not always a reliable source of information or of critical views, when used in isolation.

You will see that illustrations have a small amount of text with them, explaining why they are in the book, and perhaps inviting you to think about some issues which they raise. You might like to reflect on the fact that it can be difficult finding such illustrations, and getting copyright at a viable cost. This book and the pictures in it are texts themselves and **commodities**. They too have a market value, and the producers have to operate within the constraints of market forces that I write about.

I have included what I call major questions near the beginning of each chapter for two reasons. One is that they raise problems and issues for discussion around the chapter topics. The other is that they then inform what follows. However, they are not simply an implied list of topic headings for the sections of the chapter. Discussion of such major questions may take place throughout the chapter. Indeed, these questions, especially those from earlier chapters, will be taken on across chapters, as ideas are developed. Ideas about representations, for example, are developed from Chapter 1 into Chapter 9 about sport.

Chapter 1 starts with what I hope is already familiar ground for many media students. It examines media texts in general, with some emphasis on their deconstruction in order to tease out meanings. I also deal with narratives, representations, realism and genres, which are major areas of study in their own right. These features of text are important to understanding the nature of engagement with the audience, as well as the point at which meanings are produced – meanings which frame how we think about the world, how we conduct social interactions, how we understand our individual and collective identities. Chapter 2 goes straight into comments about critical perspectives on media institutions, on the grounds that these produce the texts which engage the audience, and that there are common concerns about media power when one looks at views on the relationship between media and society. I start with a political economy perspective on this relationship, contrasted with ideas about pluralism and the free market. I have tried to incorporate a reasonable amount of information, as background to the chapters which follow. Indeed, this chapter prefigures later material – for example, on audiences, new technology and advertising. Chapter 3 then goes on to look at ourselves as audiences for texts and for the media. I will look at the idea of interaction with the text once more, and take a critical view of assumptions about the effects of media on audiences and on society.

In raising such questions, explaining key terms and laying out issues around the media, I have tried to represent a fair range of established views. These may be alternative, they may coexist, or they may conflict. But overall, the idea is to get you thinking, to encourage you to ask your own questions. I stand responsible for the nature of my explanations, and especially for interpretations, comments and views of my own. But you are responsible for your own learning. Writers and tutors are there to help that happen, but never to hand to you answers on a plate. I hope that you will find much or the whole of this book useful for your studies. I hope that you find at least some of it interesting – or better still, provoking. But most of all, I hope that it will support you in thinking for yourself, and make you want to find out more about the topics and ideas which you are investigating.

Graeme Burton
North Yorkshire
2009

1

Media texts
Features and deconstructions

texts are important as a result of their ubiquity and because there is widespread belief that they contribute to the production of our 'common sense' understandings of the world. As such, media texts are thought to affect, in a very real sense, the way in which we understand ourselves/others and the way we lead our lives.

Briggs, A. and Cobley, P. (eds) (2002) *The Media: An Introduction*, 2nd edn. Harlow: Addison Wesley Longman.

1 Introduction

One may start with media texts because they are a dominant feature of our environment – socially in terms of what we talk about; physically in terms of what we see on our streets; culturally in terms of the time we spend absorbing ideas from screens and pages. The presence of texts is taken for granted and may well be treated uncritically. They are commonplace in both domestic and public environments: music in a department store, or a television set left on at home. Media texts are constantly appearing and changing – street posters come and go. Media texts are continually being produced and renewed. Media texts intend to engage people, to convey some kind of information, and to produce reactions in their audiences which justify their continuing production.

Even when treated as part of the environment they can never be seen as passive in the way that the facade of a building or wallpaper is passive. They are active in their capacity to produce meanings in the minds of the audience. Throughout this book, I want to argue that this production of meaning is what makes media study very important. We live by meanings. This production of meanings happens whether or not we engage intentionally with a text. Even when the text *is* attended to, there are meanings which the reader is conscious of, and yet other meanings which may be produced unconsciously. In this sense the reader of texts is not entirely in control of their engagement with the text. Equally, I am not arguing that the text maker is entirely in control of the production of meaning. The text becomes an interesting place of engagement. Things happen through the text, not all of them predictable or manageable.

What we call 'the text' is not a given thing with given meanings. It means different things to different people at different times. It appears to have a material existence – the DVD, the magazine, even the broadcast live programme. But actually it really exists in an immaterial form, in the mind, and only when it is seen, read or heard. The text that we criticize lies at an intersection between the media producer (institutions) and the media audience. It acts as a stimulus to produce meanings.

5

2 Major questions

Texts

1   In what respects is the media text both a material object or a set of meanings?

2   How far are those meanings determined by the producer or by the reader of the text?

3   How may we use forms of textual analysis to investigate meanings and their influences, especially with relation to ideology?

4   How may we understand the work of conventions in structuring the text and meaning, in relation to narrative, realism and genre in particular?

Representation

5   How are representations constructed, and what do they construct for us?

6   How do representations naturalize ideology?

7   In whose interests do representations work?

8   How do representations link with the construction and expression of identities?

9   Why are representations attractive to the producers of media texts?

Genre

10   What characterizes genres, and gives them significance among texts?

11   In what respects are genre texts attractive to institutions and audiences?

12   What is distinctive about the relationship between genre texts and their audiences?

13   In what respects are genre texts ideological, and the producers of myths?

14   How do genres relate to determinist and pluralist positions, with relation to debates about media and society?

3 What is a text?

In a broad sense, in relation to the study of culture, anything may be described as a text if people can engage with it to produce meanings about themselves, their society and their beliefs. Yet media texts are objects produced with the explicit intention of engaging an audience. In some cases (movies in a theatre) they are transient. Even where they are permanent (e.g. a copy of a magazine), there is a kind of impermanence in the fact that they are continually being produced – the next edition, the next in the series. In this way, media texts comprise a torrent of materials and produce a flood of meanings. They are a moving target, and textual analysis is in some ways an attempt to stem that flow, and subject it to careful attention.

Media texts also have a variety of forms both within media (publishing newspapers or novels) and across media (the front page of a website to the titles of a TV programme). This variety has to be taken into account when one engages with what I take to be the central project when studying text – the production of meaning and the process of influence.

Graddol and Boyd-Barrett (1994) discuss the nature of text, its range and its materiality. They point out that, even in respect of the original definitions of text, an insistence on written forms excluded other, verbal forms and attributes – spoken and non-verbal. But then they also identify two kinds of materiality to the wider range of texts (including media). On one level they refer to 'communicative artefacts', to 'commodities which can enter social and economic relations'; these could be DVDs. On another level they talk about 'semiotic materiality'. In this respect Graddol and Boyd-Barrett (1994) argue that, however **semiotics** seems to be about immaterial meaning, in fact it is also about the material **signifier**. One might refer to the smile of the model on the magazine cover. This then leads on to immaterial factors.

Tolson (1996) talks more about the 'reader' of texts, and about the process of making sense of them: 'meanings are derived from meaning systems to which everyone in our culture has access. The text itself works to structure these meanings', but also the reader 'comes to the text with all sorts of prior knowledge and expectations . . . The modern consumer of the media is a reader of many different kinds of text, which inter-relate and feed off one another.'

The constructed text

The familiarity of texts in our lives can divert attention from the fact that they are made objects. This is important because one must then ask questions about who made the text and with what intentions. In whose interest is the existence of the text and its apparent meanings?

Some of the remarks on analysis which follow – especially those which draw on kinds of **structuralist** approach – do try to explain the nature of the construction. But one always needs to go beyond the descriptive to the interpretive. A clock is not to be understood by an account of its parts and their workings. It is the idea of 'clock-ness' and of time which matters. It is the effects on our social relations of *having* clocks which are important.

4 Texts and meanings

The connection between text and meanings is also about the relationship between media and audiences, or between media and society. One kind of model tends to assume that the text is a vehicle for meaning. Early effects theory (the hypodermic theory), or deterministic media – society models (classic **Marxist models**), and at least some structuralist analysis, all assume that the text carries messages which are either conveyed into the consciousness of the audience and/or do something to the receiver.

Another kind of model sees the text as a kind of stimulus at the interface between producer and audience. The stimulus may be designed to achieve certain kinds of response, yet may also achieve unexpected reactions. In this respect one may cite Barthes' notion of **writerly and readerly texts**. The readerly text is one in which familiar features (see conventions) make it 'easy' for the reader to make sense of it. It is undemanding. Barthes identifies a **narrative** feature of such texts – the **hermeneutic code** – which closes down the reader's ability to look for choices of meaning. Genre material, with its strong conventions, and assumptions about how it is to be understood, fits this version. The writerly text is one in which conventions and predictability do not figure so boldly, and the text may stimulate reflection and alternative meanings for the reader, who in effect becomes a writer of meanings.

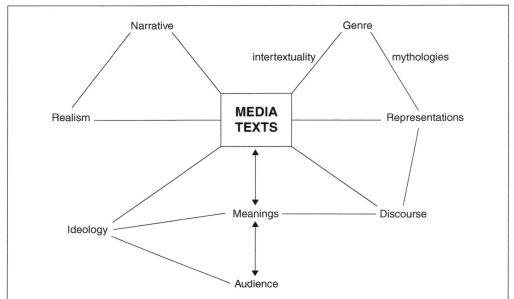

Figure 1.1 The Relationship of Key Concepts
In terms of the production of meaning, the interrelationship between notions of text and of audience is so close that one might equally make audience the focus of this model. In general, you will find that these concepts make sense in relation to one another rather than on their own – rather like the signs in semiotics!

(Graeme Burton 2009)

A third model is one in which the text is seen as a kind of booty to be plundered by the reader. Meanings are there for the taking. This kind of audience-centred and postmodern analysis is represented by writers such as John Fiske (*Television Culture*, 1987) and Henry Jenkins (*Textual Poachers*, 1992).

Clearly it is reasonable to assert that meanings are ideas which exist only in the minds of people – producers or audiences. But what *kinds* of meanings appear in the reader's mind, and why, is another matter. On the one hand, texts are organized, in various ways for various reasons: so it is not possible to argue that they are neutral goods with which readers can do anything that they please. On the other hand, texts are not so absolutely predictive, and audience members not so lacking in the capacity for critical interpretation, that text makers can produce any kind of meaning or interpretation and impose it.

It would seem that a dynamic model is the most plausible one. Some texts for some audience are more able to determine meaning outcomes than others. Halliday (1996), in discussing **sociolinguistics** and text, produces a useful phrase – 'meaning potential'. Media texts have this potentiality. One might argue that media producers have created the potential, and it is the audience that realizes it.

5 Text and contexts

A criticism of some examples of textual analysis is that they operate in isolation. The text is everything. This may be seen partly as a need, for example, to look at the conditions of production that make the text, or at the nature of the audience in relation to what is made of a text. But even as commodities, texts exist in contexts, as do the readers who produce meanings from the text and who may be influenced by it. This sense of context and its influence is complex and far reaching. Any media text exists in the context of all other media texts, especially those which bear particular comparison with it (see Intertextuality). Readers have a residual, even unconscious knowledge of at least some of those other texts. They use them to make sense of the text. They are part of a kind of *conceptual context*.

There is also a *material context* when texts are part of a flow of reading. A news article is a text which is part of larger text – the whole newspaper being read. A TV programme may be part of a flow of programmes in an evening's viewing. There is an *environmental context* in which both text and reader exist. A movie viewed in the home via DVD with others will be viewed differently from the same movie as text viewed individually in a theatre. There is a *social context* which is part of the environment. This is defined in various ways. It is partly a matter of social conventions, in which, if reading a newspaper in a public place, one is not at liberty to turn to a stranger to discuss what is read – as one would be if sitting at home with a partner. It is also a matter of reading conventions, in which one is not expected to engage with a TV programme as intensely in private as one would be in public as part of an audience for a performance of a play. This social context will affect what is attended to and how. There is an *experiential context* which the audience brings to its understanding of media texts. That is to say, we have an ever expanding experience of texts and of ways of understanding them, which we bring to bear unconsciously on any individual text. Then there is an *ideological context*: the dominant values held by the culture which produces and consumes the text. These values inform the text as it is made and the text as it is read. This is a context of ideas.

6 Deconstructing texts

6.1 Textual analysis

The analysis of texts is a process of deconstruction that investigates the operations of texts, their constructions, the ways they produce meanings, what those meanings may be. Deacon et al. (1999) define the approach as one where 'the organization and meaning of the material itself are the major focus of research'. However, they also warn of the dangers of making assumptions about the validity of any one analytic method – for example, assuming 'a transparency between the structures of media texts and the social meanings made of them'. I would add a rider about the obvious limitations of textual analysis – that in isolation it analyses neither the audience as reader of the text nor the institution as producer.

Thwaites et al. (2002), while rather wedded to the methodology of semiotic analysis, make a useful point about texts as 'socially constructed to have certain meanings', and about textual analysis as a way of breaking through a 'façade of naturalness'.

Methods of analysis are various. They have different advantages and disadvantages. They may focus on different features of texts – their conventions of realism, or their endorsement of cultural myths, for example. 'Textual analysis' is a general term which includes various and particular methodologies. For example, *linguistic analysis* might concentrate on the potential effects of style of address. *Content analysis* attends to the repetition and frequency of features, their proportions within the text, and consequent assumptions about significance. The percentage of advertisements of a certain type within a newspaper may, for instance, be significant. *Ideological analysis* of a text would concentrate on meanings about power, and may well seek to reveal contradictions between ideological positions which inform the text. *Narrative analysis* (see following section) has its own kinds of inflection and concerns – structure, or reader positioning. *Discourse analysis* seeks out specific uses of language which signal a certain kind of discourse which has certain kinds of assumed meaning about its subject – the dominant discourse and language of gender, for instance, signalled by such words as 'mankind'.

6.2 Textual codes

The notion of **codes** is one which is especially associated with semiotics and with genres (see below). There is a problem with the rather inconsistent use of the term in critical writing, and it should recognize a set of textual elements that work together according to conventions, which may be loosely understood as kinds of language. The term may be used to describe 'the language' of dress and fashion or the 'technical language' of use of camera, for instance.

What is more helpful in the first place is to grasp the dominant codes or kinds of language which are found in most media texts. These languages speak meanings to us, often working together or striking off one another. They may be summarized as follows:

- *Written language:* the dominant code of this book; this is much less dominant on television.
- *Spoken language:* a dominant code of radio; this is otherwise present in film and TV.
- *Non-verbal language:* a dominant code in the case of all representations of people in the media.
- *Visual language:* a dominant code of all 'image media'; this is the language of images in photography, film and TV, which I take to cover features such as use of camera or of composition.

Clearly this account is not inclusive. It does not refer to important codes of number or of music, for example. But it does foreground major areas of attention in any attempt on textual analysis. These languages speak to us from the text. They are significant in the production of meaning.

6.3 Semiotic analysis

Semiotic analysis regards texts as collections of signs or **paradigms** and possible meanings, operating within the bounds of various codes. Its benefit is that it causes one to attend to the question of what actually generates meaning for the reader – the **sign** – and to the problem of texts having to some degree different meanings for different readers at different times.

A brief survey of key terms and principles now follows, drawn mainly from Barthes' work. The sign is conceived of as having two elements:

- The **signifier**, which classes it as a sign with the potential for meaning.
- The **signified**, which stands for its possible meanings. Because there are many possible meanings, one sign may have many signifieds.

The connection between signifier and signified is arbitrary and not absolute. What tends to tie down the meaning of a sign, to make one meaning more probable than others, is context. This context certainly includes the other signs in the text, and would apply most firmly to genre texts. In such cases readers have a lot of textual experience to go on, which in turn includes repeated conventions and strong expectations.

Figure 1.2 Happy Families on Holiday
In semiotic terms, this image denotes a collection of males and females of various ages in a certain place. However, it connotes ideas about the family, pleasures and holidays. We are positioned as privileged spectators, looking upon this scene. The image represents the family on holiday, and works with other such images, from domestic snapshots to television programmes. The representation works to construct meanings (among others) about how the holiday is an approved cultural activity (rather than a commercial transaction); it is to be equated with happiness and bonding of the family (rather than a time of stress); it is about beaches and sunshine (rather than mountains and walking).

Signs also work on at least two levels, the one more specific, the other more general. This is best understood through example. In written codes, letters are signs which follow rules (conventions) to make up words (rules of spelling). Words may then themselves be described as signs, at a second level. We usually look for meaning in words or strings of words. These strings are themselves bound by conventions of grammar and syntax, to produce phrases and sentences. Similarly, in visual codes the use of colour or camera angle may act as a sign on a primary level. But then the whole image (a collection of primary level signs) may also be described as a sign, on a secondary level. In the case of film and television the image would be a shot, which works in relation to other shots. Where one has a string of words or a string of shots which add up to a meaningful unit of narrative, then in formal semiotic terms these would be called a **syntagm** (see also the work of Christian Metz). Less formally one might talk about a phrase in a novel or a sequence in a movie.

Other books provide effective examples of semiotic analysis, to which you may refer. Among others are Tolson (1996), Bignell (2002) and Thwaites et al. (2002). It is Bignell (2002) who makes the apt comment that 'There is no perfect analytical method for studying the media since different theoretical approaches define their tasks, the objects they study or the questions they ask in different ways.'

I would also refer you to Roland Barthes' own work, not only for examples of analysis, but also for a wider discussion of two categories of sign referred to through the concepts of **denotation** and **connotation**. In effect, denotative signs and their meanings would be at a 'first level' which would, for example, refer to those aspects of an image that refer to a real world. These are elements about which one can make apparently objective statements: 'The person is wearing clothes made of a blue fabric.' Connotations are meanings at a second level, which is more subjective and contestable: 'The clothes are fashionable, suggesting that the person has status and wealth.' Two seminal works of Barthes are *Image, Music, Text* (1977) and *Mythologies* (1973).

6.4 Image analysis

In terms of image analysis, it is important to attend to primary level signs in visual codes, most obviously for examples of still photography. In fact, for all examples of naturalistic imagery, from paintings to advertising images, I would suggest an additional approach to the discussion of textual meaning. This approach categorizes signs in three ways:

- *Position:* refers to signs which tell us where we are placed in relation to the content of the image. Mainly, this is signified through the placing of the camera, which then becomes the location from which the spectator is forced to view the content. We may, for example, be placed at an angle to the subject, behind the subject, viewing the subject as if secretly.

- *Treatment:* refers to those primary signs, often part of the technique of photography, which are about how the image is made. The uses of colour, of focus, of lighting, for instance, will all contribute to the meanings that we make of the image.

- *Content:* refers to objects represented within the image, which may signify to us because of, for example, their symbolic power or because of their composition in relation to each other. For example, one surrealist television advert included the motif of a lion walking through various urban locations – the lion as masculinity and nature. It included a final shot in which a woman is choosing underwear in a department store: the juxtaposition of animal gaze, female gaze and briefs in centre frame creates a whole set of meanings which are greater than the parts of the image.

6.5 *Discourse analysis*

This is about the recognition of discourses at work within a text, and of the features of language which identify those discourses.

The terms 'discourse' and 'discourse analysis' are somewhat complicated by their histories and by their different uses by different disciplines. For example, 'discourse' originally applied to modes of conversation, and in linguistics one deals with 'units of utterance'. Howarth (2000) provides useful discussion of these differences. He talks of a 'relationship between discourses and the social systems in which they function'. Certainly the ways in which the media 'talk about' social systems helps to define them: equally, our social systems provide a kind of framework within which the media operate. Howarth (2000) describes a kind of Marxist inflection to the understanding of discourse (after Fairclough and Wodak 1997), when he writes: 'The task of discourse analysis is to examine this dialectical relationship' – i.e. between discourse and social systems – 'and to expose the way in which language and meaning are used by the powerful to deceive and oppress the dominated.' Whereas, in terms of poststructuralist and post-Marxist perspectives, Howarth (2000) describes a different inflection: 'Discourses constitute symbolic systems and social orders, and the task of discourse analysis is to examine their historical and political construction and functioning.'

What I now propose draws on such views, but (I hope) makes understanding and use of the terms more straightforward. Discourses are linked to ideology and representations, and involve ways of using language – verbal, visual or whatever code – about a subject, so as to produce particular meanings about that subject. Our communication is full of discourses, which shape how we understand our world, how we deal with others, how we make sense of everyday experience. So it is that we talk about parenthood, we talk to parents, we talk as parents, in different terms to those we use towards and about children. Such discourses may well shift from culture to culture, because different cultures think differently about parents and parenting, because they value it in different ways. The essence of a discourse is the 'meanings we have about' its subject. So the discourse of death is not so much about corpses as about 'death-ness'. It is about how we talk dominantly about death; about what death means to most of us in our culture. This talk happens in everyday life, as well as through the media. The meanings that it produces interlock with social practices around death, such as the funeral.

In that the meanings of discourses are about dominant beliefs and values, it follows that discourses are, as it were, ideology in communicative action. Add to this the view that representations do the work of ideology, and you can see how close the connections are between these key terms.

If the discourse lurks within the text, then the language of the discourse is the visible evidence of it – signs which emerge to link us with the invisible discourse and its meanings. To recognize the existence of discourse, the textual reader needs to be conscious that we have 'taken for granted' ways of talking about subjects: this actually means we have 'taken for granted' ways of understanding and thinking about subjects. The selectivity of verbal and visual language can become startlingly obvious if you are able to switch off those assumptions in your head.

For example, the discourse of war is recognizable through language such as 'victory', 'defeat', 'outflank', 'skirmish', 'manoeuvre' and 'troops'. The meanings of the discourse derived from the use of these words refers to ideas about 'aggression', 'conflict' and 'winning'. Now look at ways in which your newspaper talks about politics or economics or football. The odds are that you will find this discourse of war used in an account of a match or of disagreement between political parties. You are so used to it that you do not notice this is happening. But it certainly skews our thinking about the activity called 'sport', or about the process called 'politics'.

The language of discourse is in some ways the word association that we make with the subject – what we think of first – because it is so embedded in the way we talk and think. Gender is a powerful example, in which many words are, for instance, associated with the female subject – 'soft', 'emotional', 'intuitive', 'caring', 'illogical', 'maternal' and so on. Similarly, we take it for granted that images of women may use soft focus, position the lens or viewing eye to look at their breasts, or show women crying. This selective language (selective use of signs) produces selective meanings about how females think about themselves and about how they are thought about by others.

The discourse is also marked by what it is not, by what it is opposed to. Just as war is opposed to peace, so female is opposed to male. The words and images I mention are not used for males. Indeed, they are seen in opposition to being male, to ideas about masculinity.

So texts may also throw up discourses and their meanings if you attend to what are called **binary oppositions**. Textual analysis from the work of Barthes and Lévi-Strauss onwards has referred to patterns of opposing meanings in various ways. Lévi-Strauss noticed that tribal myths contained within stories were often centred on the opposition between characters, and by the association of ideas about what was good as opposed to what was evil. Other narrative analysis has exploited this opposition in terms of motifs, or themes, or dramatic conflict. The approval of a given ideological position may be reinforced through evident disapproval of an opposing view, and vice versa.

So the discourse of war used in political news stories tells us that politics should be competitive. The discourse of masculinity used in the same stories may also tell us that winning is everything, that men are assertive and 'right': conversely that to admit you are wrong is unmasculine and weak.

A given text may contain a number of discourses. Some may oppose one another. And the language of a discourse, however dominant in a culture, may not be entirely consistent. Ideological positions vary. Ideologies are not self-perpetuating, unvarying sets of beliefs, however slowly shifts can take place. So, one kind of text and its discourse about the subject of nature may be dominated by meanings about beauty and sentiment, while another may be dominated by meanings about loss and the need to preserve species. In this case, what is also interesting is, for example, to see how nature is generally talked about now, compared with language about nature used, say, a hundred years ago. Then, nature was about 'plenty', now it is about 'endangered species'; then, it was about 'exploration' and 'adventure', now it is as much about 'conservation' and 'protection'.

Discourse analysis, then, is the analysis of a text through identification of language, so as to reveal its discourses and to comment on their meanings. It is also about the revelation of the ideology behind the text. It is about certain understandings of the subject of the discourse.

Critical thinking: discourse

Michel Foucault
Foucault crosses over areas of philosophy, semiotic analysis, post-Marxism, and even **postmodernism**. His view was that knowledge was power, as were the ways that knowledge was thought about. It may be argued that his ideas are especially useful when he writes about the power of discourses. He distinguishes discourses from ideology, where others would say that the power of ideas carried by discourses is a part of the power of ideology, working for the power of social elites. He would argue that the way we think about any aspect of our society or culture – say, death – creates a kind of truth and reality about that subject. And the way we think about something like death is affected by the social practices and institutions around dying. These practices and institutions reinforce the 'truth' of the beliefs about death. You only have to consider how notions of the afterlife, of heaven, are wound into funeral services to see this. One could also argue that the way a culture thinks about death shapes the way that its social practices and institutions are built up. It is hard to think outside the 'box' of these ideas and practices. For example, Foucault refers to the way in which masturbation became 'demonized' in children for centuries, defined as 'unnatural' by teachers, doctors, parents and psychologists.

Foucault became especially interested in the ways in which certain kinds of behaviour were dealt with, and came to be defined as 'problems' – sexuality, for example. He examined thinking about women and madness, going back to medical practices in the nineteenth century. He looked at the treatment of women for something called hysteria, at the incarceration of women in asylums, at the ways in which women were talked about in terms of intellectual and emotional weakness and instability. His arguments and source materials came together to demonstrate the power of the discourses of subjects such as 'madness'. The ways in which women were thought about, related to the ways that they were talked about (and pictured). Other discourses such as the subject of sexuality were also part of this process. And the ways that they were thought about were made the more 'real' by the ways that hospitals or asylums treated them. All of this conspired to subordinate them. And this working of discourses has a historical dimension in that these ideas – and I would say that they *are* ideological – were established as being 'true' over a period of time. They continue to inform our cultural views of women as 'emotional creatures', as well as, some would say, shape cultural practices within the field of medicine.

Foucault himself talks about 'the problematization of madness and illness arising out of social and medical practices, and defining a certain pattern of "normalization"' (Du Gay et al. 1997: 364, citing Foucault 1987). In the same work Foucault (1987) talks about 'discursive practices' (i.e. discourses) which when analysed show how 'sciences' (institutions and areas of knowledge) come to help define the reality (indeed 'truth') of subjects such as sexuality, madness and criminality.

7 Texts and narration

Media texts tell stories; they have a narrative. Narratives are about storytelling and story meaning. As with previous discussion of meaning, it may be argued that the narrative and its meanings are in the shaping of the text, and then work on the reader. But they are also in the mind of the reader because of what that reader does with the text.

A **structuralist** approach will demonstrate that there are features of a text which present an order, a form, cues to the reader, all of which give shape to that thing called narrative. Those features lead to meanings. A more audience-centred, even cognitive approach, will look at the audience as the active element in the construction of meaning. The audience draws on knowledge of conventions, of other texts, to construct things like storyline and the significance of the narrative. The idea of 'a narrative' is a construct in our minds; it is the product of a set of textual features. Narrative itself is made up of ideas such as place, time, character and relationship. Often the function of narrative is to generate these elements in such a way that engaging with the text is an experience in which a kind of reality is created. Different **modes of narrative** create an illusion of reality for as long as we are textual readers. They do not have to imitate life experience to work. We can go along with flashbacks or jumps in the action, so long as the narrative is consistent to itself – to the rules of the game which it has set up, and with which we are familiar because of our history of reading texts. Most narratives are dominated by two significant features. One is the unfolding of events (plot). The other is the unfolding of emotional states and of ideas (drama), through the representation of characters and relationships, and through the device of the authorial voice.

One needs to take on the idea that there is no such thing as *the* story. There are indeed some texts where readers will probably make pretty much the same story and the same meanings (genres). But there are others where they will not. We tend to assume that the narrative is an object to be uncovered, to which the reader stands in some relation. This is not true. Rather, it is a set of ideas to be put together (by the reader), and the way that they are put together sets up an imagined relationship with the reader. We may feel that there is a story out there, to which we relate differently, for example, if it is autobiographical rather than conventional third person. But there is no story out there. And the sense of authorial voice is just a trick. We are persuaded that we have some position in relation to a truth, but it is an illusion. The sense of a narrative or of a reader relationship gives substance to the illusion of events actually taking place. Indeed this helps create the **diegesis**, or self-contained reality of the story. It kids us that we as individuals have a privileged and intimate view of that reality. It enhances a sense of the truth, of the validity of what we experience – but it is just a story, just a set of representations. In fact the illusion is just another kind of meaning produced by the words and images. A sense of truth and actuality may serve only to convince the reader of other meanings to be drawn from a given narrative – the nobility of the human spirit, the power of love, the rightness of a given social order. Such meanings may in fact equally be arrived at through semiotic analysis or discourse analysis. They are also ideological.

I am not saying that the sense of a narrative, the sense of a reader relationship, the very pleasure of reading, is not significant. The experience may well be valued. But still it is important to establish that a narrative is a conceptual construction, and has no materiality, however it may refer to material objects such as places and people. Narratives are common, in most texts, in all media. Narratives may be read in factual as well as fictional material. They may be read in still images as much as in sequences of images. We tend to think of them as emerging from fictional, naturalistic material – of which there is a lot in the media. But there are very few examples of media communication of which one may say – no one can make a story out of that. A television documentary orders its material to produce a line of argument, to introduce and conclude its subject, perhaps even to impose some dramatic development on the subject. This is no different from a television news item or a drama. We look at still photographs, especially those dominated by human figures, and construct a story around the scene, the people. This narrative may be limited in extent, compared with a whole movie, but it is narrative none the less.

One may argue that people have an inclination to make narrative out of most experiences, not least media experiences: that we take pleasure in following the cues of media material to make narratives. In a sense narrative is a consequence of the particular cognitive skills of our species. We have a sense of time: we conceive before, now and after. We have a sense of place: we conceive here, there, elsewhere. So we conceptualize where and when. We also construct motive: we have a notion of human psychology, of the reasons for and consequences of people's actions. We may not always be right about people. But we do it. Time, place, motive, cause and effect dominate all narratives. The text does not have to supply the narrative. We can do that. A photograph of an old couple sitting on a park bench leads to narrative speculation. What happens next? Why are they there? What is being said about the elderly? The possibilities of narrating are in our heads, not just locked in the text. Narratives – documentary or fiction – are not just artful imitations of some kind of reality. They also signify meanings about their subjects, about society and about the times in which they are created. They are inevitably ideological.

Narrative structures

Narratives have shape and structure. This is much related to order of events and the arrangement of dramatic episodes and resolution. With relation to binary oppositions, I have already referred to one kind of structure. This might emerge through pairs of people, opposing sets of characteristics, pairs of places, and certainly through sets of ideas. The most common narrative structure may be described as mainstream narrative or as the **classic realist text**. It has become a benchmark by which other kinds of narrative and other evocations of reality are measured. This is characterized by a progression of events through time, by conflict between characters, by problems for the protagonist(s), by a series of dramatic moments. Events move forward towards an eventual denouement, a resolution of the problems. Such a narrative structure has **closure** – it is tied up at the end – as opposed to being open-ended. It is the work that the narrative does, as a vehicle for ideas, which makes the structure significant.

Mainstream narrative imitates our lived sense of things moving forward, our beliefs in the linkage between events in our lives, our need to resolve problems. And in this mixing of experience and endorsement of how we feel life is lived, so also such a narrative structure endorses the plausibility of its own ideas. The same may be said of other structures and structural devices. *Circular narratives*, in which the beginning of a story is its end, are a kind of reflection on how we reach points in our lives. The main body of such a narrative is an extended flashback, a disquisition on our belief that our past affects our present. *Parallel narratives* are those in which two or more plot lines are dealt with alternately and eventually brought together. These construct an imitation of our recognition that events coexist in our lives, that coincidences do happen, and that we live within a context of simultaneous and related events and people. Parallel narrative reflects on the significance of one part of our life story to another.

Narrative structures and various features of narrative are largely invisible to the average reader because they are so familiar and conventionalized. The rules or **conventions** by which plot is organized, drama is evoked, time and place are understood, are so well understood by media producers and audiences that the construction called narrative is invisible. It is a corollary of the power of these conventions that narrative which disobeys the usual rules of story development or of keeping the other invisible (for example) may described as 'alternative'. We notice the rules when they are broken. Such conventions may work against an effect of naturalism, against plausibility, against narrative as a reproduction of lived experience. For instance, movies will, by convention, abridge time and place. The story does not move forward at the pace of real time. Bits are 'missed out'. Screen time is not real time. Certain conventions or narrative cues may well help us understand, unconsciously, what is going on. In a movie a character will announce that they have to see someone; then we jump forward to another place and to that meeting. But we do not see that as bizarre or unrealistic because we have been cued to expect it. No more do we crib about the sound of music appearing from nowhere (perhaps to induce emotions that relate to the drama). In fact the music would be described as non-diegetic, or outside the scope of the actual story (the diegesis).

If narrative is also a feature of representation, then we become all the more aware of its constructedness. It is just another way of ordering and evoking meanings. Narrative is so often validated critically in terms of its ability to imitate experience of a physical world, or of the psychology of character and relationships. But in fact what it is really about is comment upon and meanings about our material and conceptual worlds. Analysis of narrative features, and of their significance, leads to meaning and to visions of how the world is.

Reader positioning

Our recognition that there is a construction called narrative depends to an extent on reader positioning. I have already referred to that mode of narrative called autobiography. This addresses the reader directly. It constructs the idea of there being a narrator. It helps authenticate that which is being talked about. It contrasts with the more frequent third person form, in which that which we call 'the story' is apparently told by an invisible narrator, neutrally, as a given thing. But, of course, the idea that there is a narrator is in itself just a device, another aspect of narrative. The narrator is actually a function of the text. The idea that the reader is positioned is more accurately about how the text influences the reader's understanding of what the text means. *Identification* describes the effect of involving the reader with the story, of constructing it as truth. It produces a meaning of truth – a belief in the validity of the text and of all the other meanings that we make from it. *Alienation* is about devices of disengagement from the story – positioning us 'outside' it, as opposed to feeling we are 'inside'. Brechtian alienation in theatrical terms was a self-conscious narrative device intended by the playwright to draw attention to the fact that something called narrative does exist and is manipulative. But alienation may exist only at the level of a degree of detachment for the reader. Such detachment may be useful when, for example, the producers want to moderate the possible effect of emotionally charged material. If one moves the camera (and therefore, the spectator) to an apparently concealed position in some bloody battle scene then this can make violence more bearable.

The positioning to which I refer has spatial, temporal and psychological dimensions. In a movie like *Gladiator* (2002), one may be positioned in relation to the action in the arena, in relation to the Roman times of the story, and in relation to the protagonist and his feelings about combat. Feuer (1995) refers to a level on which this relationship may be seen in terms of a whole medium, as much as the individual text – 'television's foremost illusion is that it is an interactive medium, not that we are peering into a self-enclosed diegetic space' (as is true for many movies). So narrative and the act of narrating is a core feature of many media texts, and this dominates the output of most media.

8 Texts and realism

It may be argued that realism is a function of narrative – the way the story is told – not a separate textual feature. But again it may be argued that where narrative includes content (an account of material elements in some kind of order or relationship with one another), realism is only about form (how that account takes place).

As a notion about the quality and value of some text, of some medium of representation, realism has its own creative and critical history. The nineteenth century, especially in respect of art and the novel, was dominated by aspirations to make paintings 'true to life'. What 'true' and 'life' mean is another matter. As Furst (1992) says, in relation to the novel, 'realism cannot . . . vouchsafe access to an innocent, uncoded or objective experience of an independently existing real world'. Nor is it the case, of course, that all texts even propose manufacturing a 'real world'. Certainly in media studies we would understand that all media are only forms of communication which represent something. That thing may not be life as it is experienced, it may be an experience which is only imagined. And in any case one has to acknowledge the 'problem' of **mediation**, in which the act of communication must in some way transform the 'event' which it seeks to represent.

There are a number of reasons why realism is much discussed in relation to media texts. There is that kind of *material analysis* which is intrigued with the illusion of reality – the kind of text which convinces its reader of the authenticity of character or place – naturalism. The fascination is with language used in such a way as to construct an apparent material or behavioural truth. The discussion is about how it is done.

But then, perhaps along with such analysis, is the validation of the text on the grounds of its qualities of realism – *value analysis*. There has been a strong tradition in Western representational systems of striving after actuality, and of proposing the creative superiority of such texts. The traditions of Victorian naturalistic painting, then of photography, followed by film and television, are all media in which realism as actuality has predominated (though by no means suppressed other modes of realism). In this case the debate is about the merit of what has been achieved – the approval of one mode of representation above others.

Then there is a kind of *philosophical analysis* which is concerned with the very concept of reality, as well as the style of realism which purports to achieve this reality. The quality of seeming real may be as much to do with a sense of truths about human relationships, or about the characteristics of a healthy society, for example, as it is to do with what seems to be authentic or probable. This is about ideas, not form. It is about the representation of an immaterial world. The notion of reality as truth links with the realism that achieves truthfulness. So it may be that a treatment of the text which we describe as surreal, for instance, is as effective in achieving truth as is naturalism. Formalist styles such as Expressionism in the 1920s or film noir in the 1940s may not be 'realistic' but they are about realism. They draw attention to the form of the text, but also point symbolically to truths about the darkness in the human soul, to the truth that evil matters.

If one follows this argument that form links with the ideas within the text, then it is fair to say that to discover the qualities of realism in a text is also to discover meanings about realism. If we say that a scene in some TV drama seems to be realistic because the interaction of the characters is plausible, then we are also saying that one meaning of realism is 'the mimicking of everyday life'. However, another drama in some formalist style might not have naturalistic interaction. But it could still be validated as, for example, 'getting at real truths about how people can play power games with one another'.

This leads one to the idea that one can also talk about something like *ideological realism*, following on from the notion of truth. The audience or reader might well approve the realism of a given text because it expressed what they took to be valid ideological positions. But in ideological terms, that which seems valid often also seems to be the truth because ideology generally works to exclude other ways of looking at its subjects. A narrative which describes a man being manipulated by a woman may be seen as having realism and as expressing a truth about gender behaviour – if the reader believes that view of the world which sees women as being manipulative in relationships and men as being incompetent to deal with such manipulation.

In this respect it may be said that the importance of realism in relation to media texts lies in the views of the world which it endorses. Even a text which is marked by authenticity and naturalism is significant not just for its appearance, its ability to reproduce the physical world (or even the social world). It is significant because it endorses beliefs about that social world, about the value systems behind the material appearance.

So realism is a feature of a text. It is one measure by which that text is validated in its own right. It is a measure by which it may be valued in comparison with other texts. Indeed Hallam (2000) argues that one can define realist styles only by comparison with other styles, given that there is no absolute style of realism to act as a reference point. The criteria for that realism operate both out of what we know of the real world, as well as out of the constructed world of the text. This is realism as 'part of discursive struggle to make sense of our realities' (Hallam 2000).

We may use the real world as a measure for the authenticity of the appearance of objects and places. We may use real-world experience by which to measure the plausibility of human behaviour, or the probability of character motivation. Real-world experience may determine our judgement on the probability of plot and on the nature of coincidence. But those same measures also depend on our experience of the text in question and of other texts. The text being judged can produce its own set of rules, which in turn relate to what we see as its mode of realism, what we should expect. In adventure, action or horror movies we expect some improbability in terms of the real world. But we suspend this relative judgement in the cause of genre pleasures, and go along with what is possible in the film world. In other words, realism is indeed relative, not absolute. Realism may be at work even in texts which on a relative scale of values we might describe as being unrealistic – a number of genre films, such as Horror.

Bordwell (1988) points out that 'intertextual motivation' in genres means that part of their realism for the viewer actually demands that they should include, for example, a stock situation like the shoot-out. But this expectation, this repetition and its satisfaction is in another sense unrealistic. Similarly, Bordwell's (1988) notion of 'artistic motivation' suggests that the shoot-out can happen in slow motion or with much intercutting. We could expect this and feel that it is consistent to the genre. Yet, in its artifice, in that the medium draws attention to itself, one may say that such a device makes the movie unrealistic. It is only in terms of genre and its own rules that one has a sense of realism.

Other media texts become a measure of realism because they supply us with other information, depictions of other places, or possible patterns of behaviour. We may not have been to Chicago, but, even subconsciously, we will judge the realism of some depiction of Chicago of the basis of other things we have seen or read about the city. Indeed, it may be argued that we are inclined to forget that many sources of information are merely representations, not first-hand experience, and that they can become as 'true' for us as any real-life experience.

It may be said that realism is nothing but a combination of conventions within the text. Some of these combinations form what are called **modes of realism**: they are kinds of category. We may use specific terms to describe these – documentary, fiction, fantasy. This categorization, as with genre, sets up expectations of the nature of the text. Such expectations are useful for media producers – for example in scheduling TV programmes by type, or in marketing books. They also help the reader to make mental adjustments in terms of how they will interpret and value the text. There is a kind of axis of realism, with the most factual material at one end and the most fantastic treatments at the other. On the one hand the real world of social experience and material objects becomes a benchmark. On the other, improbability and impossibility become accepted hallmarks.

What we need to remember is that texts are only kinds of representation. So television news may be relatively more real than a satirical novel about the future. But neither is it reality. Because it brings us real-time images of people and places that does not make its meanings true. Equally, the novel may be unrealistic in a material sense, but truthful in an ideological sense.

The idea of *hyper-reality* (e.g. Baudrillard 1988) in the context of postmodernism proposes the fusion of real life and media life into something new. It proposes that the world of media, of electronic representations, of television in particular, has become as real to people as their everyday social world. Reality shows on television are an example of how the medium short circuits distinctions between the two realities. The ordinary citizen (e.g. the late Jade Goody) can become a celebrity. Celebrities become familiar through their appearances on the screen in the home. The Royle family on television are actors who become celebrities because of their pastiche of the everyday, of the lives of ordinary people, who as the audience for the programme both live the everyday and elevate its depiction on screen to celebrity status.

9 Texts, representations, ideology, identity

The idea of representation is central to understanding the production of meaning through texts. Texts are nothing but representations in both a material and an ideological sense. In the material sense the text is a made thing, a product of technology, an image on a screen, a set of marks on the page. In semiotic terms, the signs stand for what is represented, objects or ideas. But they are not the thing itself. In an ideological sense, texts do indeed represent ideas. The reader interacts with the text. The interaction produces the ideas, perhaps preferred by the producer, perhaps more critically manufactured through the mental work of the reader.

The car in a magazine advert is a mental construct produced via a process of perception, using representational features such as hue, shade and outline. And, of course, that construct includes concepts represented about the nature of the car, the desirability of the car, its place in our lives.

Debates about representation in part centre around alternative notions of reflection or of construction. With visual media there is a temptation to follow the 'mirror of reality' approach because of iconographic nature of images in photography, film and television. The pictures look like what they are meant to refer to in the real world (see the idea of denotation). Such 'reflectionist' arguments also link with certain notions of realism. The visual text may be praised for its invocation of physical authenticity (an aesthetic judgement). The text may also be 'approved' of for its representation of, for example, 'natural' social behaviour, or for the 'truth' of lifestyles and attitudes. This kind of value judgement is still very apparent in press reviews of film and television. As Sturken and Cartwright (2001) say: 'Despite the subjective aspects of the act of taking a picture, the aura of machine objectivity clings to mechanical and electronic images.'

Barsam (1974) is part of the critical history of this approach when he speaks approvingly of the qualities of free cinema or of cinema verité documentary film movements – 'the camera work is intimate, often giving the viewer the immediate sense that he is "there"' – and of a particular film – 'a beautiful study of ordinary people in ordinary jobs'. But of course representation is anything but ordinary. The 'constructionist approach' emphasizes the illusion of the representation, and falsity of a number of the ideas which it may propose about people and society.

Corner (1996) robustly critiques the idea of documentary as a 'referential record'. He talks of a critique 'interested in questions of representational form' 'which aims to "uncouple" the relationship between putative reality, pro-filmic reality and screened reality which much documentary depends upon'.

Stereotypes and ideologies

When representation is discussed in terms of social groups and images of people, its significance is not simply about appearance. It is about the substance of ideas invoked about that group. This is in no way to dismiss the significance of stereotypes, or the examination of images of people. But one does need to get beyond discussion of things like physical characteristics or even patterns of behaviour for their own sake, and get to the ideas that are represented. For instance, the femme fatale as a female type goes back to texts from the beginning of the twentieth century, to Georg Pabst's 1920s film vamp, Lulu, for example. But in examining such a type it is inadequate merely to catalogue features such as dark hair or dark clothes; to identify characteristic behaviours such as a seductive manner; or even to describe conventional plot functions such as temptation of the hero. What matters is the representation of ideas about women, perhaps especially in the context of the era in which the text is made.

These ideas are ideological. Representations give substance to ideology. Textual analysis reveals ideology in action. The femme fatale is about gender and power. It is about the male fear of being 'unmanned' by the sexual power of the woman, a fear of 'losing control'. In the 1950s, representations of such a type would include condemnation (sexuality was allied with murderous tendencies) and retribution (such characters were likely to die or to end up alone, without a man). By the 1990s, the films of John Dahl, for example *The Last Seduction* (1994) or *Red Rock West* (1993), represent the femme fatale as strong, and the male often as weak or indecisive or pointlessly violent. The woman is not necessarily punished, sometimes not even for a crime.

Representations tend to reflect the ideological positions of the times in which they are created. They tend to be most conservatively ideological in genre material. Sometimes those reflections are of contradictions between one ideological position and another, or of kinds of challenge to the ideological status quo. Considering the contradictions between the various role expectations of women, it would not be surprising if media representations reflected good examples of those contradictions – e.g. woman as passive beauty object versus woman as active earner. 'Ideological analysis is . . . about recognizing the semiotic and discursive contradictions and tensions within a representation . . . at the core of these contradictions and tensions is the potential to challenge particular power relations and concepts of identity' (Ferguson 1998).

Gunter (1995a) says of the representation of women on television:

> there is a gross under-representation of women in action-drama shows in terms of actual numbers relative to the presence of men; . . . even when women do appear, they tend to be portrayed only in a very narrow range of roles.
>
> (Gunter 1995a: 4)

These comments suggest that representations reveal their negative ideological credentials through who is presented (or not), and how they are shown. The contradictions between the world on screen and the world as we experience it, reveal ideology at work, display a partial view of social relations and dispositions of power.

Social types

Representations of people involve a typology of repeated surface characteristics – appearance and behaviour – that through repetition reinforce ideas about the type and/or group depicted. This typology falls into three main categories, marked by the intensity of recognition, and depth of cultural history: archetypes, stereotypes and types.

Archetypes are characters which are recognizable across genres, have few but very dominant features and characteristics. They are in effect a distillation of ideas about gender, or possibly about well-known occupations. For instance, the heroic male adventurer who is physically powerful and irresistible to women repeatedly emerges in popular texts. He is Caucasian in appearance and marked by loyalty in male bonding and persistence in pursuing quests. His provenance is legendary – Theseus or King Arthur. Such archetypes tend to emerge in texts set in a more fantasy mode of realism. But the impact of the ideas is no less significant for this. Notably he appears in novels and films made from novels – James Bond, Luke Skywalker, *Total Recall* (1990), *Lord of the Rings* (2001), *Die Hard* (1988). The heroic male adventurer is almost always a protagonist, rather than a supporting character. He very much links with genre myths and with a cultural idealization of masculinity.

Stereotypes are equally recognizable, but rather less mythic. They tend to belong to genres rather than to cross them. They may distil the characteristics of specific social roles, or of more contemporary occupations. But they also generate meanings about the stereotype which come out of conservative and dominant aspects of ideology. The stereotypical barmaid has big boobs and a big heart. What she stands for are ideas about sex without danger for the man, listening without criticism, the boosting of self-esteem, and above all a woman who knows her place in a male universe.

Types are the least distinctive category, perhaps because they are also the most sketchily drawn, the least represented and so the least reinforced. They are supporting players. One must acknowledge a degree of subjectivity in how characters are judged in this respect. But examples might be the stupid gang member, as parodied in *Bugsy Malone* (1976), the bucolic farm worker, as represented in a television adaptation of H.E. Bates' *The Darling Buds of May* (1991), or the sharp young party-goer, who appears in material such as *Bridget Jones's Diary* (2001).

In terms of meanings about social groups being constructed through representations, it is worth noting that what is *not* said about the type may be significant. It could be said that these 'meanings by omission' also emerge through analysis which looks for binary oppositions. So racism may emerge in texts first through roles which the subject is not given: how many actors from non-white groups appear in mainstream television drama? Barnard (2000) comments that even in a non-visual medium, 'it is the lack of black and Asian voices on mainstream, daytime radio that reflects least kindly on British radio's representation of non-white listeners'.

Second, this kind of prejudice by default could be shown through representations of race in association with crime: if, say, black comes to equal criminal through representations, then what it does not equal, by implication, is 'law-abiding'.

It will have become apparent that much concern about textual representation is about its negativity. Travellers are often constructed as feckless and deviant. Such constructions also imply the opposing **norms** of behaviour and belief. Again, one is looking at ideological statements. To be nomadic is to be deviant, to be settled is to be normal. To have no fixed address means one can evade some state controls: this is threatening to the state.

Naturalization

The notion of norms also links to the idea that representations are given force through a process of **naturalization**. This means that it is seen as natural that a given social group should be represented in a certain way. It is seen as natural that the representation should carry particular ideas about that group – and not other ideas. It makes negative ideas seem normal and unchallengeable. In fact it makes those ideas invisible. This naturalization also underpins hegemony and the uncritical acceptance of the attitudes and values of the dominant ideology. Indeed one may also hear appeals to 'nature' in terms of genetic inheritance when even casual social judgements are made. Women, so goes the popular myth, are 'known' not to be good drivers; they cannot park a car properly, which has to do with their lack of spatial awareness. To represent women in this way ignores three things. Parking a car is not 'natural' but a learnt skill. The premise about spatial awareness is a false one. Good driving is defined in many other ways; for example, women generally drive more carefully than men, because they are less inclined to take risks.

Media representations of social groups purport to show to others what those groups are 'really' like. They also in fact show to members of the subject group both how they may be seen by others and how they 'should' be seen. This could mean that black teenagers

- are seen as being likely involved with crime and drugs
- believe that they are seen by others as being so involved
- believe that it is normal to be seen like this.

Subjects of representation

Finally one needs to recognize that the subjects of representation are not simply social groups. The term applies to a much wider range of subjects. At its most basic, representation is 'construction of ideas about a subject' through some means of communication. One can talk about representations of institutions or even of social practices. So TV hospital dramas such as *ER* in the USA or *Holby City* in Britain represent not only an occupational group called nurses, but also the institution of the hospital, and the collection of practices known as medicine. Investigative documentaries and news reports will, for example, contribute to the accumulative process of representation, as much as fiction drama. There has been *The Trust* (Channel 4, 2002) about the institution of a large British regional health authority and its hospitals, or *How to Build a Human* (BBC2, 2002) about genetics and the possibilities of medicine. And the range of media that construct representations such as the one whose subject is medicine, extends beyond television, for example newspaper articles on the health service and advertisements for 'health products'. There is a symbiotic relationship between representation and discourse, in which the former takes on a range of discourses to help make meanings about its subjects – nursing or hospitals or medicine – just as it may be said that the discourses contribute to the representation. For instance, whatever the subject of hospitals (and their representation) means to us includes discourses of gender, technology and sickness – to mention only three. Discourses are kept alive through the continued use of language which rehearses their meanings.

Identities through texts

Representations of social groups help create identities for their subjects. The concept of identity is one that is often examined within the sphere of cultural studies. However, at least some comment is appropriate at this point. One can start from the point that representations create meanings not only for the media audience as onlookers, but also for the audience as individuals and as subjects of the representation. Representation is something that is about us, not just about other people. It constructs a sense of identity for us individually, as well as about others. Identity has many dimensions beyond that of mere appearance. I have already referred to characteristic behaviours – what is inferred as being typical, and those which are characterized *for* the group – what is assigned as typical, whether that is true or not. Then there are the 'meanings about' which refer to assumptions about personality, emotional make-up and attributes, such as the mean, dour Scotsman with a liking for whisky! There are the 'meanings about' which refer to beliefs, attitudes and values. This point intersects with ideology. Our Scot believes in being frugal, has contempt for Sassenachs and is very patriotic.

But more than these dimensions are those which focus on a sense of common culture, of belonging, of being distinctive and different. These aspects of identity are those felt by the subject, not by others. They are taken on by the Scot as subject – not assigned by others, because others cannot feel the force and meaning of such identity dimensions. For the Scot, one might be talking about things like a Presbyterian background; a sense of place (Highlands or 'classical' Edinburgh); a feeling for clan; a sense of history (awareness of the Highland clearances or of emigration pressures); a sense of class.

So identity has a number of dimensions. It may be about a sense of place – belonging to a community in a certain city or country. It may be about history – having a certain shared background of events and experiences. These may go back to the past of previous generations – being a New Yorker, or being a Polish person in New York. It may also be about family and history – the stories around a dead grandmother and where she came from. It may be about cultural practices – from the observance of religious occasions to the rituals of family holidays. It may be about role and relationship – taking on the experiences and obligations of fatherhood. It could be about occupation. It is most likely to be about a combination of some or all of these factors.

Most intangibly, identity has been described in terms of being part of a **diaspora** – a sense of belonging to cultural practices and an ethnic background which seems to transcend place and time. One might talk about a Jewish diaspora to which many people, not necessarily practising Jews, feel spiritually attached.

The notion of identity is linked to ideas about personality. There is a debate around the traditional view of a core personality (or fixed identity) and the opposing view that personality and identity is much more mobile. It is unfixed or flexible. Chris Barker (1999) talks about 'the de-centred subject, the self as made up of multiple and changeable identities'.

There may be dominant personality traits, but otherwise personality is actually a response to different social situations. The idea of a fixed identity has attractions because it is securing, it provides a stable view of people. But in truth all we know of people is to do with their behaviour. Personality and identity is to do with their inner lives. These are ideas which we construct from the evidence of behaviour. Identity is something which we feel we have, it is to do with how we see ourselves, but it is also something which is ascribed to us by others. The identity which others believe we have may not be the kind of identity which we ourselves believe in. Representations are very much about ascribing identities to others.

The terms in which one talks about representation and identity continue to overlap in many respects. One may feel positive or negative about one's sense of identity and difference. The onlooker may see the identity in a positive or negative light. Much critical work focuses on negative constructions, not least in trying to explain prejudice, social divisions, or social conflict. But this negativity should be qualified by recognition of all the positive views of identities, in which people take pride in their culture, take pleasure in their sense of place, place value on their own social practices. It is not always true that social groups or ethnic groups see themselves as being diminished and less worthy by comparison with some other dominant culture (and dominant ideology). It could be argued that the media notably add to the possibility of feeling diminished because they carry the images, information and ideas of powerful cultures. They diminish global isolation, yet make more possible global comparisons – perhaps to the disadvantage of some cultures. Yet it is possible to have celebration as much as denigration. The multiplying channels of broadcasting make it very possible to present multicultural material and to address a range of audiences. In Britain there are, for instance, satellite channels that address Asian communities.

Gilroy (1996) talks about there being a high profile to identity issues and identity politics because of the proliferation of media material. He refers to

> the increased saliency of identity as a problem played out in everyday life, and . . . identity as it is managed and administered in the cultural industries of mass communication that have transformed understanding of the world and the place of individual possessors of identity within it.
>
> (Gilroy 1996)

It remains true that in critical studies the concepts of **difference** and of *otherness* are often used to emphasize the negative: 'sameness and difference are marked both symbolically through representational systems, and socially through the inclusion or exclusion of certain groups of people' (Woodward 1997).

The concern is that the representation constructs detrimental ideas about the difference of the subject from others: constructs feelings of being 'other' in the sense of being less. When the subject is looked upon it is seen as the other and not as worthy or 'normal' as the onlooker and their identity. The gay person and the state of being gay is often represented in this negative way. This may be done crudely by exaggerating the appearance and mannerisms of the opposite gender in the subject: to emphasize the idea of not-man or not-woman. It may be done through the representation of relationships, in which the subject is shown to be unhappy with their sexuality or unable to have a happy same-sex relationship. It may be done through narrative resolutions in which the gay character ends up alone or hurt in some way. Of course, by implication, all this says a lot about what one 'should' be like in gender terms, how one should behave, how one will achieve a happy life. It implies the absent opposite – those cultural norms which 'should' prevail.

It is possible to celebrate difference and to challenge norms by in effect exposing the discourses. So it is that black activists of the 1970s used the slogan 'Black is Beautiful', and gay rights activists of the 1990s publicized the phrase 'Proud to be Gay'. Campaigning drew attention to social inequality. How far such slogans caused most people to think again about difference in its negative sense is less certain. But such public **campaigns** and debates about the status of given identities does take one into the area of what is called *identity politics*. These may relate to geography – Jewish and Palestinian assertions about their identity being bound up with certain places. They may relate to spirituality – the claims by Australian Aboriginal people for return of the bones of their ancestors from British museums. They may relate to history – the various arguments put forward by Native Americans about the rights that historical treaties should give them, not least to land. In fact these examples, not surprisingly, can be seen as being about all three aspects of identity; about political issues centring on the importance of having a sense of identity and of worth, as expressed by beliefs, origins, backgrounds.

10 Genre texts

Genre texts dominate media output. Some genres have enjoyed a lot of attention – most obviously news. Film studies has been seminal in exploring the characteristics of certain genres – the western or film noir – and in exploring their ideological implications. There is a fair range of material on TV genres such as soaps and crime thrillers. In general, there is a lot said about the features of genres, and to some extent about what these repeated features may signify. But not so much is written on ideas about genre as a concept, not so much development of the idea of genre itself.

Genre texts are in fact very interesting because they clearly yoke institution and audience around text. Genre texts satisfy the market interests of media institutions, as well as the private interests and pleasures of audiences. They can be intensely conservative in ideological terms, and yet sometimes adroitly subversive of the dominant ideology. They run against that Western tradition of individual artistic achievement as mass product, and yet can occasionally achieve originality. They raise the hackles of those supporting an aesthetic valuation of texts, because they are seen as the creatures of commerce. And yet those same self-interested commercial enterprises have sometimes nurtured genre texts which have been acclaimed as something called Art. They work on principles of repetitive conventions, and yet much of the time manage to reinvent themselves before reader exhaustion sets in. They would appear to resist social change and yet can provide a map of this, as well as sometimes exploring the possibilities for that change.

10.1 The formula

We have already established that genres are full of representations, with all that implies about the production of meaning. The repetitious nature of genre elements is at one with the repetition of types in genres.

Many accounts of genre start by establishing repetition, conventions and the formula. I am assuming that this is largely familiar to the reader, probably in terms of particular genre examples. It is worth emphasizing the idea of formula, which transcends genres, and which provides a perspective on the building blocks of narrative. I am talking about the elements of hero and villain; stock characters; stock situations; iconic objects, characters and background features; mainstream narrative plot structure. The idea of formula is the idea of an overarching blueprint. This blueprint – remembering structuralist approaches – does seem to pivot on opposing elements where oppositions have to be resolved, and on a developmental narrative in which progression, learning and the classic Todorovian equilibrium have to be achieved (for an account of Todorov's ideas about narrative and generic structures, see Hawkes 1977).

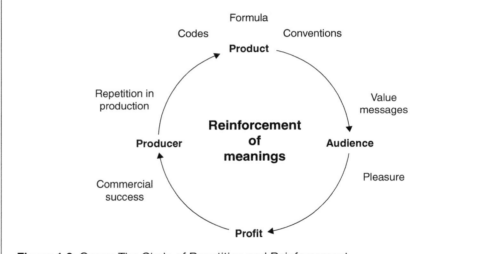

Figure 1.3 Genre: The Circle of Repetition and Reinforcement
Pleasures for the audience and profits for the institutions help maintain a continuous relationship between the two, as well as reinforcing both conventions and their meanings.
(Burton, G. (2000) *Talking Television: An Introduction to the Study of Television*.
London: Arnold)

Of course the exact nature of the elements and of their combination is so varied that the formula can be satisfied (and the audience), without the progress and outcome being entirely predictable. The formula is dominated by fictional examples, but is not peculiar to fiction. The very existence, the life of the formula is prolonged and made known to the audience precisely because the media use it so much. Even game shows work to this formula: the quiz master is a narrator; the contestants are protagonists in opposition to one another; the studio set is iconic; sometimes the contestants (personalities who return week after week) become stock characters; the plot line resolves with one team winning but everyone going away as friends.

The formula and its patterns satisfy in the audience a need for predictability, for security: variations on the formula satisfy a need for some excitement, for risk and the unexpected within a safe framework. Neale (1995) emphasizes the point that the formula creates repetition, yet also frees up a genre creatively so that it can be different: 'genres are best understood as processes. These processes may, for sure, be dominated by repetition, but they are also marked fundamentally by difference, variation and change.'

Problems of genre

The formula becomes a way of identifying a genre – perhaps where this is not immediately obvious. It links to Barthes' readerly texts, where textual patterns and meaning are, at least in the first place, familiar and easy for the reader. Implicitly it identifies those texts which are not genres: the writerly texts where the audience has to work harder on the material to produce meanings. What is not useful, I suggest, is to engage in debates of the 'when is a genre not a genre' variety. I happen to think that film noir is a style, to be found in a range of genres, but mainly linked with crime thrillers. Similarly, I would argue that melodrama can most easily be seen as a mode of realism and as a matter of style. It is not formulaic in the way that a soap is. I find it confusing when people talk about autobiography as a genre, when it has only one dominant feature, or about children's programmes, which have nothing predictable in common. They are generic in terms of being a category, but not a genre as such. But in the end, what we define as genre formulaic material is significant for *what* it is, rather than for *how* it is. What matters is what genres reveal about industrial practices, about the process of audience reading, about its representations of social reality, about its relationship to ideas such as hegemony or identity.

These comments pick up some of the 'problems' of genre study. As Feuer (1992) points out, much genre study has been partly an exercise in taxonomy, partly a critical attempt to promote the value of one genre, or of certain examples of genre texts above others. Film criticism in particular has a tradition of talking up the worth of popular genre material (e.g. Warshow 1970; Sobchack 1988; Maltby 1995) and its industrial origins, in opposition to an aesthetic tradition which (put simply) valued the art film and the work of the auteur.

Feuer (1992) usefully summarizes three approaches to genre study:

- 'The aesthetic approach includes all attempts to define genre in terms of a system of conventions that permits artistic expression.'
- 'The ritual approach sees genre as an exchange between industry and audience, an exchange through which a culture speaks to itself.'
- 'The ideological approach views genres as an instrument of control ... genres are ideological insofar as they serve to reproduce the dominant ideology.'

There is also the question of genre critiques which are inflected either by the medium analysed, or by the critical approach imported to inform that criticism. So, one may argue that looking at TV genres is not the same as looking at film because of the different nature of the industries involved and because of the different nature of the audience – text relationship. Similarly, it matters if one uses a specific critical approach through which to analyse a given TV genre.

For example, Mary Ellen Brown (1990) writes of soap operas first in terms of their generic characteristics as a product of TV in particular, 'whereas traditional literary narratives have a beginning, a middle and an end, soap opera consists of an ever-expanding middle'. But then Brown chooses to interrogate the genre in terms of feminine discourse and the notion of 'carnival'. Among other points, she concludes that whereas dominant discourse represents the position of mothers in society as unproblematic, in soaps the feminine discourse 'plays with conventions' and recognizes problems. Bakhtin's (1968) ideas about 'carnival' are invoked in relation to an argument that female viewers are invited to 'participate' in the world of the soaps, and perhaps to challenge the conditions of the world in which they live.

Brown (1990) is interested in texts as they are 'read', not in isolation. This is also the case for Gauntlett and Hill (1999), in a piece on gender and television. What is interesting is their reference to 'history' and to 'change', for both TV genres and their audiences. One is not talking about a static form:

> the soap operas that were largely shunned by 1970s men were clearly different in content from the soap formulas which have become relatively popular with men today. Therefore the percentage of 'men who watch soap operas' actually has *a different meaning*.
>
> (Gauntlett and Hill 1999)

The writers argue that a study of gender representations from a TV genre text broadcast many years ago does not have much relevance to a contemporary study, least of all in respect of influence and gender formation. In this sense, genre study must be ongoing and updated.

10.2 Expectations

Producers and audience are linked by their knowledge of the formula. Sometimes this relationship is even self-conscious, as with the Wes Craven series of *Scream* movies (1996–2000), which partly depend on viewer knowledge of other horror movies and of what has gone before in the series.

Expectation becomes a creative advantage when the producers know that there are some things they do not have to explain. So the formula is both a cage within which the producer must operate and a framework within which the producer can build different versions. It is both a trap for the imagination of the reader and a structure on which that imagination can build. It closes down some meanings, yet opens up others. It depends on producing preferred readings about the genre in general, but allows for oppositional readings. So in the case of a film like *Black Hawk Down* (2002), expectations are ideologically satisfied in terms of reading ideas about masculinity, heroism and patriotism. But, oppositionally, military authority and the state behind it may be read as being seriously incompetent.

Expectation turns into a commercial tool when marketing campaigns are designed to raise hopes and tap into prior knowledge, to create anticipation of fresh pleasures to come on the basis of past pleasures enjoyed. Expectation satisfied through the text, through the anticipation of the formula and the challenge of the unexpected, turns into an audience pleasure that depends on the fact of the material being genre.

10.3 *Conventions*

What is expected are the conventions which rule the construction of the genre. The elements of the formula are conventions: the ways that they are used can also be called conventions. So not only is the car chase a conventional piece of content, of plotting, in a crime thriller, but also its use in showing off the quality of the hero, or pitting hero against villain, is a convention. In addition, one may argue that creating the excitement of the chase by using the squeal of tyres on the soundtrack is a convention of form.

So this prior knowledge of the 'rules' of genre helps the reader anticipate what will happen and how. It helps the reader to make sense of the text. It not only closes down meanings but also gives the producer a clear foundation on which to compose the text. The operation of conventions in genres is comparable to the formal definition of conventions within semiotics – rules about the combination and use of signs which help make sense of them. It opens up the same debates about how far textual meaning is predictable and can be the preference of the producer (a closed text), and how far texts may be genuinely **polysemic** and open to the preferences of the reader (an open text). Conventions have to be strong enough that some meaning is possible, and so that a degree of social sharing of meaning is possible. Genres take this sharing on to a central area of common ground, where beliefs and values as meanings have a pretty wide currency. There is, as it were, an ideological consensus which is appealed to and reaffirmed, about such subjects as masculinity, heterosexuality, loyalty, social roles. But also from this common ground, from the security of this consensus, genres are also able to question and re-evaluate some subjects.

Conventions are powerful in the way that they frame meaning and make some meanings predictable. They give power to the producer to play games with the audience's understanding of the text. They give power to the producer as a marketer of texts: conventional and iconic elements of genres tap into beliefs and pleasures of the reader. So they are part of the influence of the marketing devices which sell novels or movies by referring to these elements. Audiences are brought to want to consume the text because they want to revisit the emotional turmoil of a battle scene or of a love affair, for instance.

They also give a kind of power to the reader, the power to predict some of the meanings that the text will propose. The reader can predict some content and narrative development, and is left freer to attend to how these things are handled. This position on reader power implicitly says that media producers do not absolutely dominate just because they make the texts in which the conventions appear. The idea of conventions, the idea of 'genre-ness', is something which lives in a cultural space. It is not an object like a spring washer, to be copyrighted and controlled by the source of production, and which can only be used in a particular way. Convention is more like a force which producer and reader can tap into. At the same time, one has to accept that the relationship between producers and readers is unequal, in that this force is contained by the producers in the first place, within the construction called the text. Reader power depends on accessing the force of conventions and reusing it.

Critical approaches: postmodernism

This approach has been used in particular to explain some changes in the characteristics of some media texts since around 1980. But it has also been used more generally to explain and describe social and cultural changes. By definition postmodernism contrasts itself with modernism (see below). But the idea that we have entered a completely new era in terms of society and the media is a false one. It is marked by the following:

- A recognition of some fragmentation of social structures and social institutions
- Interest in the ways that at least some texts have come to privilege form and style, play games with realism, but let go of narrative structures
- A recognition of uncertainty and fluidity in terms of people's sense of identity, of what we may call 'real', and in terms of the intermixing of cultures (also related to globalization)
- An emphasis on expressions of **popular culture**
- An emphasis on very specific studies – of audience **consumption**, of textual characteristics.

In terms of media studies postmodernism is characterized by a reaction against modernist interests in structures, in the big picture, in broad effects analysis. The view taken is that any possible relationship between media and society as a whole is so complex in its range of variables that nothing meaningful can be said about it. It is proposed that what relationships there are, work on a tighter level. The text and the audience are predominant. It isn't really possible to talk about a postmodernist perspective on the relationship between media and society. Postmodernism rejects teleology, or certainties about how society works; there are no absolute truths.

In terms of texts, this critical approach tends to privilege ideas about form and style, about irony, referentiality and **intertextuality**, about text as a manifestation of popular culture. In terms of audience, the approach explores them as players with cultural texts and artefacts, as much as consumers. These players channel hop, Net skip, put together their media experience from a changing variety of sources. They incorporate media texts within their identities, but also use ever-changing fashions to fluid and hybrid identities. *Bricolage* describes the plundering and recombining of source material for entertainment, for making music, for the very clothes on one's back.

Postmodernism sees identities and realities as having become fragmented. **Hyper-reality** blurs the boundaries of the media world and real life so that the audience sees both as being equally valid. Nothing is certain. Everything is relative. A painting of ideas using elephant dung is as good as a painting of a person using oils. Politicians can appear in the news and in quiz shows. An African fashion model can come to earn thousands in the fashion industry while her former neighbours are earning pennies.

Audiences are seen as making sense of texts in ways which suit them and which give them pleasure. There is a sense in which postmodernism has been a celebration of audience power, perhaps to be contrasted with post-Marxism's anxieties about institutional power. But political economy approaches would contest this celebration.

This 'power to the people' approach is probably best exemplified in the work of John Fiske, and certainly represents a view opposed to those which seek to privilege study of the power of media institutions (often tied in with a belief in the power of ideology).

But it does not have to be an 'either-or' situation. Popular culture is of course a legitimate object of study, as are the ways in which cultural texts are lived out through the lives of audiences and social players. But it does not make institutions go away and it does not strip them of their power.

Certainly postmodernism has been criticized for kinds of woolliness, for making everything relative, for skimming over the possibility of media influence, for avoiding the 'realities' of media power in relation to social inequalities. Philo (1999) says: 'This focus on the text and the negotiation of meaning has reduced the ability to study the real and often brutal relationships of power which form our culture.' The Glasgow University Media Group, of which he is a part, are firm in their use of content, semiotic and discourse analysis of television texts in order to expose the working of ideology as it reinforces inequalities based on class, gender, race in our society. So you may see postmodernism as being another critical approach to media, with a certain set of preoccupations.

It is closely bound up with what is called a cultural studies approach. It is about ideas and their implications, as much as having an analytic method like semiotics. With cultural studies, it has helped open up fields of criticism in respect of gender, ethnicity and sexual orientation. It is part of other kinds of social, textual and cultural shift, identified through study areas such as postfeminism, or postcolonialism.

10.4 Intertextuality and postmodernism

The idea of the reader using the text, even playing with it, is one part of postmodern views on genres. In one sense, this idea has been around for some time through, for example, material like the murder mystery thriller series or the action hero comics. In these cases, the 'writers' know that they have a fan base which enjoys being teased by thwarted expectations, which enjoys meeting familiar characters. The fans write in to the producers about questions of continuity, probability, scientific possibility. This exchange cannot take place in real time because of the nature of the medium, the mechanics of production and distribution. But there is an intensity about the relationship, through the genre material, which pushes towards the quality of a live, real-time conversation. The writer plays with the reader: the reader knows that the writer is doing this, and the writer knows that the reader knows. The writer invites the reader to enjoy their shared world.

In this shared world (as with a soap opera) one text about Inspector Morse or Spider-man is understood with reference to another. This cross-referencing is what intertextuality is about. It works on many levels of generality or particularity. It works both on an unconscious level in the mind of the reader, but also consciously, as with the example just given. Unconsciously, one may cross-refer an archetypal protagonist in one genre with the hero in another genre. One may understand the importance of a chase scene in a road movie with reference to a similar scene in a spy thriller. But then the references may operate within the genre – kinds of robot in science fiction. The references may operate temporally, when scenes or characters refer back to earlier examples. This intertextuality, it is argued, has a special intensity in defining postmodern texts. Pam Grier was used as an actress in Tarantino's film *Jackie Brown* (1997) partly because she had previously appeared in Blaxploitation thrillers of the 1960s and 1970s. Another example is Colin Firth, who played Mr. Darcy in the BBC's *Pride and Prejudice* (1995) and was later cast as the arrogant *Mark Darcy* in *Bridget Jones's Diary* (2001).

Not all postmodern texts are genres, but genre has always depended on referentiality. So it lends itself to this intertextual intensity, where form and style lead over content and structure. Even back in the late 1970s a film like Walter Hill's *The Driver* (1978) was a distillation of other heist/crime movies. This film self-consciously did not name its characters because they referred to generic types in other movies. And if the quality of irony includes a certain cynicism about the world, plus juxtaposition of characters and events to create this ambience, then again genre films lend themselves to this quality of postmodernism. A film like Hill's *Last Man Standing* (1996) is intertextual in its debt to Akira Kurosawa's movie

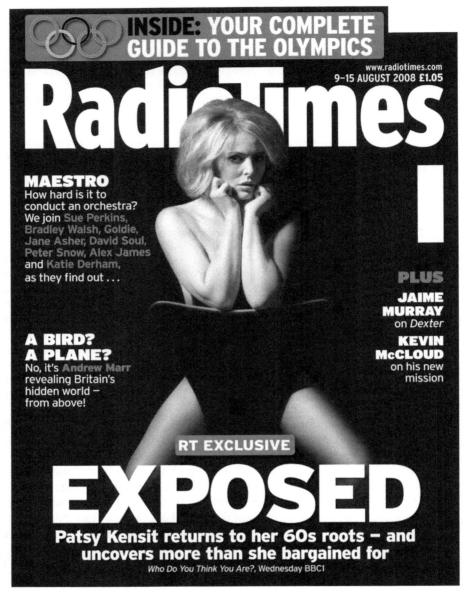

INSIDE: **YOUR COMPLETE GUIDE TO THE OLYMPICS**

www.radiotimes.com
9–15 AUGUST 2008 £1.05

RadioTimes

MAESTRO
How hard is it to
conduct an orchestra?
We join Sue Perkins,
Bradley Walsh, Goldie,
Jane Asher, David Soul,
Peter Snow, Alex James
and Katie Derham,
as they find out . . .

**A BIRD?
A PLANE?**
No, it's Andrew Marr
revealing Britain's
hidden world –
from above!

PLUS

**JAIME
MURRAY**
on *Dexter*

**KEVIN
McCLOUD**
on his new
mission

RT EXCLUSIVE

EXPOSED

**Patsy Kensit returns to her 60s roots – and
uncovers more than she bargained for**
Who Do You Think You Are?, Wednesday BBC1

Courtesy of Radio Times Magazine

Figure 1.4 *Radio Times* Cover: Exposed
This image of the actress Patsy Kensit is a good example of referentiality (and the postmodern text). Her pose on the chair mimics that of Christine Keeler in the 1960s. Keeler
was involved in a much reported sex scandal which included a leading politician. The
chair pose has become iconic, and has been copied by others.

- Can you think of your own examples of a media text in which full understanding of it
  requires the audience to pick up on various references?
- What questions does all this raise about the way in which meaning is taken from a
  text?

Yojimbo (1961); it also contains ironic comment on the quality of heroism and the lack of integrity in human nature.

Intertextual qualities can reduce a text to an anorak's game of 'spot the reference'. But they can also add resonance and layers of meaning. Genres lend themselves to intertextuality because the audience already knows the essentials of plot and character. It is also true that at least some of the audience for a given genre form a committed fan base, and this means that they have the intensive knowledge of, say, gothic horror or romantic melodrama which is there to be woven into the text.

Critical thinking: postmodernism

Jean-François Lyotard

Lyotard brings out a number of points about postmodernity, mainly in *The Postmodern Condition* (1984). He develops the idea that such a reaction against modernity has been around for a long time, and does not simply follow some firmly definable period of modernity. He also rejects the idea of some grand narrative behind all texts, previously pursued through the analytic work of writers such as Vladimir Propp and Christian Metz. He is interested in the smaller narrative structures and devices within texts, not least in those twentieth-century novels which challenge a nineteenth-century model of realist narration (see also the classic realist text in film studies). Put simply, Lyotard's view of texts and social relations is one in which there is complexity and contradiction, rather than simple explanations. He would say that events and experiences can be interpreted, but not explained by any grand designs for society or science or politics.

But Lyotard also argues that significant changes may occur, and interrupt or change anything from politics to art. The worldwide outbreak of demonstrations by the Left and young people in 1968, and in protest against the Vietnam War in particular, is taken to be an example of this. But such events cannot be read as being part of a pattern of history. There is no history and, as Francis Fukuyama said, history is at an end.

Lyotard suggested that the time of absolute truths – the belief in the possibility of these – was over. He thought that the important position of science, as a place where objectivity and truth could be relied upon, was finished. We no longer know what we think we know. One can deal only in the particular, in detail, in specific examples, because general beliefs and critical principles have collapsed.

John Fiske

Fiske celebrates the pleasure of the text, the power of the reader to enjoy material. In fact the idea of enjoyment in engaging with a text or narrative is one that goes back once again to the writing of Roland Barthes. Fiske (1989) has a great deal to say about audience pleasures in a postmodernist world, and in relation to popular culture.

Again, one needs to recognize that he draws on the writing of others: for example, the work of Pierre Bourdieu (1984) in suggesting that there are class distinctions in the way that audiences deal with texts. This might be summed up as being about a more detached relationship of the middle-class audience with cultural texts, in which *appreciation* is a dominant response, contrasted with involvement and *participation* for the working-class audience engaging with popular culture texts. This could be said to be the difference between one kind of response to a Jane Austen novel dramatized on television, and another response to a TV game show.

Fiske has written for instance about how audiences engage with wrestling or dating programmes on TV, as well as the promotion of jeans as a cultural commodity. He refers to the importance of intertextuality, the play of references and of styles, to understanding how audiences respond to popular media material.

He is not interested in general models of the media–society relationship so much as the audience–text relationship as it illuminates audience power. He would discard notions that media simply impose on the audience. Nick Stevenson (1995) says that for Fiske 'the act of consumption always entails the production of meaning'. You read it, you make sense of it. He criticizes Fiske for ignoring the dimensions of institution and ideology. He suggests that Fiske inserts his own readings of popular texts, as much as he acknowledges the kinds of reading which are actually reported by audiences.

Jean Baudrillard

Baudrillard probably best known for his proposition that hyper-reality has replaced the real. His argument is that media reality has become indistinguishable from experiential reality. The experience of the media has become as valid as other 'real' experience. Famously he argued that the Gulf War (1990) did not happen other than in the media construction of it (Baudrillard 1995). The media construction is a *simulacrum* – a copy of war events on screen. I suggest that he was making a point about how much of our lives and our knowledge of the world are lived through the media. It isn't that he would deny that tanks rolled across the Iraqi desert, or that lives were lost. But that wasn't our experience. All we really knew was the version constructed by the press and by broadcasters.

Baudrillard sees us as consumers of signs, of representations, to the extent that we have lost a proper sense of what the sign refers to. Image is everything. Television has consumed public space and has made private spaces public property (e.g. programmes like *Changing Rooms*). Stevenson (1995) explains it in terms of how 'the real relations of production and consumption have been replaced by a sign system'. Form predominates over substance. The consumer need is not so much for objects as for social meaning, for a sense of difference. You can see this in all those ads which desperately try to persuade you that you are going to buy individuality along with the product.

Baudrillard saw Disneyland as a metaphor for what is happening in the USA in respect of the merging of social reality and another reality dominated by the media, but extending into leisure worlds like Disneyland (and, we might say, Center Parcs). He would even argue that these alternative realities have become *the* reality for many people. He might say that while such leisure worlds suggest that there is another adult world where people do not play like children – in fact this is not true either. His postmodernist vision is that we are being encouraged to live in a leisure world, a media fantasy world, *all* of the time. This would be a world of TV screens, of shopping malls, of being cool on the streets, of holidays.

(It should be said that others would argue against this position, as exaggerating the lived experience of what certainly are cultural and economic changes. Even the well-to-do middle classes can't afford an escape into alternative realities all of the time. And those who are poor and who have rioted, whether in the suburbs of Paris or of Los Angeles, certainly know that they are not living solely in a world of style, of celebrity, of infantilization. This counter-view would maintain that citizens can still tell the difference between media reality and social reality. Films like *The Matrix* raise this ancient question about, 'how do we know what is real, and whether we are we living in reality or not?')

Certainly Baudrillard identified a change in which economics are mixed up with representations and with ideology. We now live in a world where to produce anything means it has to be sold. Selling is mixed up with celebrity. Economic activity demands the production of representations. Representations produce ideas, they manufacture ideologies.

Films are promoted in the same way as cars. Painters are promoted in the same way as media personalities. Where Fiske's view of postmodernism tends to celebrate popular culture texts as having a kind of integrity, especially when the audience appears to control their meanings, Baudrillard's view seems to be more pessimistic, seeing culture as eating itself, losing any sense of value and distinctiveness, and collapsing into a swamp of relativity where nothing is original, nothing seems to matter.

Baudrillard wrote about the ways in which the idea of an original production, an original car, or an original copy of a work of art, has been blown away. On the one hand he is right to point out that much of our art, our popular culture, is all about 'simulacra' – copies. Your DVD, your pair of trousers, may be exactly the same as mine. This is about the development of technology and mass production. On the other hand, one can also say that he is wrong to imply that the idea of an 'original', of ownership, has been lost. On the contrary, multi-nationals, or book writers, have fought through the courts to maintain the idea of copyright. This is about ownership (and sometimes the production) of the original of something.

10.5 Myths, discourses and ideologies

Generic texts are at the heart of popular culture. They have become generic because they are popular. The TV presentation of a football match works to a formula, as much as a magazine for young women. They are popular because they tell the stories we want to hear. They give us characters we can fit into our view of the world. They give us a view of relationships, motivation, a moral universe, a structure of beliefs which also fits his view of the world. In fact, they give us a view of the world. More than this, they have already given us such a view: we grow up with genres. So if genres contain ideas about who we are, how we should live, what kind of moral and social structure we should inhabit, then they have generated, repeated and reinforced those ideas. Genres are not, of course, the only influence on people as they develop. But, in the context of information about time spent on viewing and reading genre material, then they are at least significant in helping form the ideas by which we live. The very fact of repetition and reinforcement, the inclination to consume genres and their ideas because they are pleasurable, makes them significant among other texts.

Genres are ideological because, for instance, they naturalize ideas about social role, they endorse ideas about social, economic and political power, they promote ideas about what is true and what is false. They are central to a dynamic relationship between media and society in which genre reflect and promote ideological positions. One might say that they draw on what is 'out there' and reshape it to some extent. At the same time, society consumes genres and draws on their representations in a process of reinforcing its ideas (but also evaluating them to some extent). There is a complexity to this view of exchange and transformation – dynamic interaction. A simple model of media reflecting society or of a helpless society being shaped by the media will not do.

In the Mafioso television series *The Sopranos*, Tony Soprano is on the one hand a traditional model for the audience of masculine physicality, aggression, social power and paternalism. On the other hand, the motif of his visits to the psychiatrist (with his own reflections on his behaviour), come from a social world in which masculine identity is being questioned. The dynamic, the uncertainty, plays off the genre framework. Traditionally the Mafiosi were certain of their place in the world, of the rightness of their values. Tony is both certain and uncertain at the same time. The genre framework gives a point of reference from which the questioning can begin. *The Sopranos* is about ideological divisions. If genres are ideological then they are also full of discourses. In *The Sopranos* these are dominant discourses of gender, family and crime. And discourses help construct myths.

Borderlands/Alamy

Figure 1.5 Che Guevara on a Bag
The image of Guevara's face has become iconic in our culture. It is also mythic because it has acquired meanings beyond the facts of his life and death. He has come to stand for rebellion and youth, as much as for revolution and politics. The repetition of the image and myth reinforces meanings in the same way that genres reinforce our expectations and understanding of what they are about.

● How do you think that this image, reproduced on a bag, relates to ideas about commodification, referred to elsewhere in this book?

Myths are dominant ideas produced by discourses, about culture and society. Myths centre around dominant ideological positions on their subject, and may be focused through characters and roles. For example, the 'whore with the heart of gold' focuses the myth (also seen in other kinds of female character) that there are women 'out there' who are into sex for its own sake; can give (the man, of course) sex without responsibility; and will also be kind and non-judgemental. This kind of myth is altogether convenient for and unthreatening to the male.

Myths have deep cultural roots and are part of the history of a given genre. Dracula is clearly a figure of masculine power (the ravisher) yet also an expression of deeper fears about general cultural invasion – evil taking over the world. *Star Trek* draws on the myth of frontiers and discovery, of uncomplicated codes of conduct, beliefs in order and loyalty – a world where everyone knows their place, and in the end assimilates the universe into that world. 'Myths and genres are universal forms . . . they represent "the way in which a particular culture has embodied both mythical archetypes and its own preoccupations in narrative form"' (Real 1989).

One should be clear that here one is talking about something that is partly to do with Barthean mythologies in semiotics, but which is also to do with wider definitions of mythologizing. Cultural myths structure the text, yet are concealed within it – made invisible by the language of discourse, which naturalizes views about its subject so that one cannot think about them in any other way. So any media text may refer to myths. In Barthean terms one might refer, for instance, to the fact that it is quite common for advertisements to invoke the myth of status linked to the acquisition of certain goods or commodities. As a myth it is merely an idea. Part of its falsity lies in the fact that, for example, wearing a Rolex watch is not a guarantee of status. The myth of status may well be invoked in a piece of genre material, but genres go further into mythologizing, through their repetitions and the development of their histories. They create 'stories about' social roles, gender roles, ways of living. They promote myths favourable to the dominant ideology and to a culture's view of itself. A collection of such myths in American culture has been about how 'we won the West', 'we won the war', 'we are winning the fight against crime'.

What should also be apparent is that myths are about illusion and falsity, while not necessarily being simply invalid. We want to believe the ideas that form the myths in genres, even if they are not true. Part of the popularity of genres is precisely because they contain this quota of wish-fulfilment. Romantic novels perpetuate the possibility of the caring, sensitive male – not to mention the primacy of lifelong, committed relationships. There is nothing invalid about either of these ideas. What is mythological is the romantic world in which this man, this relationship, is idealized and out of step with the messy and problematic realities of the world which the reader actually inhabits.

History

These comments remind us that genres do indeed have a history, on which producers and audience may also draw for understanding. It is a history in which the genre develops its repertoire of conventions and renews itself (or not), perhaps be creating new subgenres. But that history is not a matter of truth and document. War films like *Saving Private Ryan* (1998) may be about actual events, and may indeed be praised for their verisimilitude. But that genre also has its own history of manufacturing heroes, of revisionism in the cause of favouring Western ideology, of negative representations of real or imagined former enemies. Similarly, the history of US gangsters is 'rewritten' through the development of the genre to explore the anti-hero, to exploit violence, to investigate the line between legitimate enterprise and illegitimate crime. Facts are changed and personalities are mythologized as the genre develops. And some genres do not have even the semblance of historical fact to secure their narrative. Notably, the horror film draws on cultural myths and seminal texts (usually novels) to build a fictional history that makes yet more myths out of the original fantasies. So the history of genres can tell us a lot about the times in which the texts were made, but not about historical 'truth' as such.

Genres often fall into groups of films – cycles in their history – which in retrospect represent prevailing concerns and beliefs of the period in which they were made. Television series such as *The Sweeney* or *Starsky and Hutch* from the 1970s represent an implied contemporary desire to find action heroes who would deal boldly with crime. Crime was seen as more violent and more of a problem than it was in, say, the 1950s.

'Genre serves as a barometer of the social and cultural concerns of cinema-going audiences' (Hayward 2000). As a 'barometer' of society, genres cannot help but be profoundly ideological. They may have the power to subvert or challenge, within their traditional form and structure; but they also have that tradition. It would not strike a chord with the audience if it was not about established ways of understanding the world. So, much genre material reinforces traditional gender roles, reinforces traditional ideas about maintaining order in society. Indeed many story lines are about ideological differences, about threats to the status quo and about the restoration of order.

> Different genres possess ... their own ways of resolving the ideological issues with which they deal. The science fiction film is set in the future and deals with the intrusion of 'others'; the gangster film is set in the present and deals with the contradictions that stem from striving for social and financial success; and the western is set in the past and deals with the ethics of violence.
>
> (Neale 2000)

It should also be said that Neale (2000) balances ideas about ideologically determinist readings of genres with comment on the variety of genre material, and on the complexity of genre background – history and industrial processes. In other words, not all genres are simply vehicles for a dominant ideology.

10.6 Genre and the political economy

Genre material is not only attractive to audiences because of its pleasures and its approvable ideological positions, but also attractive to institutions because of its predictability and because of its economies of scale.

The fact of the formula means that the production side of genre material is relatively predictable. The production team has at least some prior understanding of how schemes may be handled, what materials may be used, how the elements may be put together. Its predictability means that it is easier to budget for costs. Its predictability means that it is more possible to predict success in the marketplace; this applies to generic forms such as the series, the serial and the sequel, as well. The familiar profile of genre material, especially iconic elements, means that it is easier to market than one-off, individual texts. It is no quirk of fashion the British television broadcasts fewer original single dramas than it did in the early 1990s, but produces far more examples of genres and of series.

Of course, the drive for success (profit and beating the competition), sharpened by the considerable cost of production (in movies most of all) means that economic imperatives favour genres, yet do them no favours. This means that the 'play safe' syndrome favours another series of the television soap *Neighbours* so long as the ratings hold up, but is reluctant to take a risk on a pilot for an unknown series (even one that is within a known genre). This means that more and more genre material is needed. This is especially true for television, where the number of channels continues to expand. What cannot be bought is the creative impulse which produces new versions of genres. What has happened is that economic imperatives undermine genre when they exhaust them.

Genres become the weapons of the global corporations as they fight in the marketplace for audience share and for the approval of the advertisers. Syndication, spin-off products and different media versions of the text add to the economic lustre of the original, successful genre text.

It may also be argued that, with reference to politics and **regulation**, that genres are often ideologically conservative or, if subversive, they cloak their opposition with the familiarity of the formula. Not that I am suggesting that genres are always uncontroversial. But the controversy usually relates to sex, violence and 'bad language'. Government seeks to regulate this in the public interest, but institutions seek to exploit it in the interests of marketing. Controversy can become free publicity. The two great institutions of media and government dance around one another, negotiating their interests. Government invokes criteria of 'taste', media invoke criteria of realism or of creative freedom. But neither seriously challenges what some might see as the tyranny of the marketplace, which to a fair extent denies the audience alternative texts. So one might argue that the depiction and presence of violence in many genre texts is not so much a 'problem', as is, for example, the implicit endorsement of to whom the violence is done. The idea of regulating out of texts violence done to women, or to other nationalities, or even to criminals, would become a lot more controversial because it is ideological.

10.7 *Genre and the illusion of pluralism*

The commercial success of generic forms multiplies the amount of media material in circulation. Genres such as news, and looser categories such as children's programmes, now occupy whole channels of broadcasting. But there is little or no evidence that this expansion of material brings about exploration of the form. We have news or children's programmes done in much the same way as before, only there are more of them. This is not consumer choice, nor is it pluralism except by numbers. If pluralism is to mean anything then it must involve plurality of forms for a plurality of audiences. It should mean plurality of points of view. It should serve minorities as well as majorities.

A successful genre text in any medium is likely to produce replications of the text or spun-off additions based on the core text. But again, more is the same. Similarly, a successful text will induce imitations with the same characteristics. The novel *Longitude* (Sobel 1995) was followed by any number of dramatized science factual stories. This is not to argue that all imitations are without merit, but that the extension of generic forms produces only an illusion of pluralism.

The debate about what constitutes pluralism takes an interesting twist when one reflects that the commercial response to criticism is, 'it is what people want, and it sells, and it keeps some people in work'. Such a material argument neatly avoids any reflection on questions such as: Why do people want such material? How do they come to have such wants? Which people don't want it? Which people might enjoy texts that are denied production support? How does anyone know what they want if they can't see what might be on offer? Who really decides what we do or don't want, anyway?

In terms of genres, one might say that a media model in which the market rules, produces false pluralism – economies of production, targeting of the most profitable audiences (of whatever size), play-safe production decisions, repetition of formulaic material. A model in which there is disinterested regulation and the protection of experimental and challenging producers and texts, should produce some exploratory and innovative genre material. Genre can provide a shelter under which some ideological goosing of dominant views and of the establishment can take place. Genre formulas can provide a reference point for experiments with form or with the representation of character types. This would be the kind of pluralistic environment in which choice and variety is not just an illusion.

The question is, how may we create that kind of environment, in which multinationals do not determine our choice of texts, and in which we may easily obtain that choice of texts and those points of view which indeed serve a multicultural and varied society?

Textual features: contrasting the modern and postmodern

Modernism	Postmodernism
Emphasizes structure (organization of content)	Emphasizes form and style (sense of irony and ambivalence)
Emphasizes narrative direction structure (see also closure)	Fractures and downplays narrative
Ideological certainties	Uncertainty and ambiguity about what is right and true
Moral certainties	Challenges views on morality and taste
Classic realist text	Reality is blurred – *hyper-reality*
Conceals its artifice	Exposes its construction
Self-contained	*Intertextuality*/referentiality (also about other texts)
Art is often equated with high culture	Emphasis on popular culture texts
Emphasizes the original work and the boundaries of convention	Celebrates plagiarism and blending of texts and genres: plays with retro – *bricolage*
Seeks appreciation and a contained audience	Seeks pleasures, even through excess, for any kinds of audience

---

11 Discussion extract

Content analysis makes some claims to being a 'scientific' method of textual analysis and seeks generally to reduce messages to quantifiable elements – elements that can be clearly delineated in media output and then counted or measured. Often this is to enable a comparison between one text or series of texts and another, or perhaps to make comparisons between 'messages' and reality, and it is often the case that the research seeks to find the 'truth' – the true meaning of the text.

Alternative ways of understanding texts draw on constructivist or structuralist understandings of communication and assume that there is no single 'message' encoded into media outputs but that communication is one of the ways human beings seek to make sense of the world, and that texts construct meaning rather than carry meaning. In this view, meaning is produced by the interaction of texts and their reader through pre-existing structures. One purpose of textual analysis is to uncover the structures (the rules that govern the system of communication) that produce texts. Going further, the purpose of textual analysis might then be to uncover the potential meanings produced by an individual text. From this perspective meanings are always potential, to be negotiated between the text and the reader of the text.

Sometimes the analyst is interested in the operations of ideology . . . And, assuming that texts produce and reproduce ideology, is seeking to analyse the text to understand the operation of ideology, a position that may come close to seeking the 'truth' of the text, or to seeing texts as producing 'misleading messages'.

Hughes, P. (2007) Texts and Textual Analysis, in E. Devereux (ed.)
Media Studies: Key Issues and Debates. London: Sage.

1   What is objective or provisional in the approaches to textual analysis outlined in the passage?
2   Is there such a thing as 'the text', without the interaction of reader and text?
3   Is it possible to identify the truth of a text?
4   How do you understand the phrase 'operations of ideology' ?

12 Further reading

Bignell, J. (2002) *Media Semiotics*, 2nd edn. Manchester: Manchester University Press.
Hall, S. (ed.) (1997) *Representation: Cultural Representations and Signifying Practices.* London: Sage/Open University.
Hallam, J. with Marshment, M. (2000) *Realism and Popular Cinema.* Manchester: Manchester University Press.
Lacey, N. (2000) *Narrative and Genre.* Basingstoke: Palgrave.
Thwaites, T., Davies, L. and Mules, W. (2002) *Tools for Cultural Studies*, 2nd edn. Melbourne: Macmillan.

2

Media institutions
Key areas and their implications for understanding media

power will lie with those who own the key building blocks of new communication systems, the rights to key pieces of technology and, even more importantly, the rights to the cultural materials – the films, books, images, sounds, writings – that will be used to put together the new services.

Murdock, G. and Golding, P. (2005) Culture, Communications and Political Economy, in J. Curran and M. Gurevitch (eds) *Mass Media and Society,* 4th edn. London: Arnold.

1 Introduction

In this chapter I want to make connections between elements such as regulation and power, as they relate to the production of meaning through texts, and as they illuminate the relationship between media and society. The nature and workings of media institutions are also examined for the part these play in explaining media power and influence.

Texts and audiences are relatively accessible. Media businesses are not. Information about their policies and financial affairs is hard to come by for reasons of confidentiality. Access to the production needs of their businesses may be denied for the same reason, or because these organizations are suspicious of what academic researchers are going to do and say.

A number of elements of this chapter relate to later chapters and issues raised. For example, matters of power and finance are discussed in Chapter 10 on globalization, as is globalization itself. The place of advertising as the financial engine of media institutions is discussed in Chapter 7. The relationship between institutions and their audiences, as mediated through texts, or conducted through marketing, is discussed in Chapter 3. Most of what needs to be said about institutions and new technologies is dealt with in Chapter 6.

Now picking up on the quotation opening this chapter, it may be said that a political economy perspective on the media would be interested in

- The production of cultural goods by institutions
- Regulation by those institutions and by government
- Media texts with reference to the relationship between representations and the conditions of production and consumption
- Cultural consumption with relation to cultural and social inequalities.

Differing views on the practices and products of media institutions throw up contradictions. For example, if a pluralistic approach proposes diversity of product, then at what point does diversity in fact become cultural fragmentation? May this not simply encourage social fracturing, and work against cultural coherence?

Ralph Negrine (1994) identifies contradictions between statements in support of a free market, and those which then ask for regulation of that market because of the consequences of its becoming 'too free'. He quotes John Keane:

> there is a structural contradiction between freedom of communication and unlimited freedom of the market . . . the market liberal ideology of freedom of individual choice in the marketplace of opinions is in fact a justification of the privileging of corporate speech and of giving more choice to investors than to citizens.

Negrine (1994) talks of a free market which is 'regulated to allow for freedom, albeit a freedom where market forces dominate, and where, crucially, media content is treated as a commodity rather than a public good'.

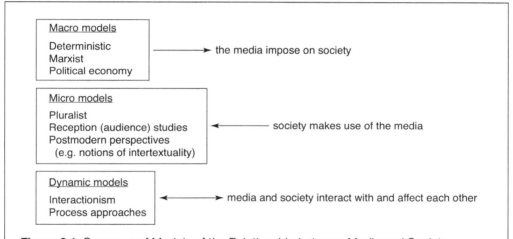

Figure 2.1 Summary of Models of the Relationship between Media and Society
This mapping of broad critiques of the relationship between media and society represents general truths, but needs particular qualifications. For example, some political economists veer towards a dynamic model in accepting that there is a complex relationship, in which economic power does not simply determine cultural change. Similarly, **feminist** critiques embrace a range of positions, both determinist and audience centred.

In terms of the relationship between media and society, these observations raise questions about different critical approaches, as well as about ideological positions. On the one hand, Western beliefs in democracy and freedom of choice support ideas about a free market and about visions of a plurality of media and their materials. On the other hand, the freedom of institutions to produce what they like does not fit other ideological imperatives – to endorse a particular system of social morality and to protect certain social groups, for instance. Nor do such freedoms as are now allowed seem to add up to a genuine freedom of choice for all sections of society. The power of relatively few media institutions to determine what appears in the marketplace equally endorses critiques offered by both neo-Marxists and political economists – that society is not best served by the media, least of all in terms of a free market of ideas.

Doyle (2002) discusses pluralism in terms of diversity, referring to a document emanating from the Council of Europe, which aspires to 'a plurality of independent and autonomous media' (Doyle 2002: 12). She links political pluralism to democracy, and describes cultural pluralism as reflecting social diversity. She talks about 'sustaining representation within a given society for different political viewpoints and forms of cultural expression' (Doyle 2002: 14). But all this depends on diversity of supply of media material. The problem is that 'the market' as we see it in action tends to concentration of supply, to control of distribution, to concentration of the ownership of media content. There is a price on the maintenance of diversity, and it is not clear who is to pay it, let alone sustain the conditions for its existence.

Cottle (2003) argues that there is an opposition between political economy and cultural perspectives on the media. He sets up explanations about media and society as being contrasted in terms of economic determinants in the case of the former view, and in terms of cultural discourse in the case of the latter. I would not agree that the critical positions are mutually exclusive. Indeed this book talks equally about the effects of economy as helping define media businesses and their texts, and about discourse as helping define the sense we can make of the construction and deconstruction of those texts.

Cottle (2003) is helpful in defining the landscape of these critical approaches. He sees political economy as being about media concentration, competition, commodities, the mass market, replication of product, consumerism, as well as the structures, routines and output of media institutions. Whereas he would describe a culturalist approach as being about consumption rather than production, as contesting the nature and importance of ideology; as being interested in the signification of media representations, popular culture, and the generation of meanings within texts. But I suggest that he misrepresents political economy when for example he asserts that it is more interested in class than other social divisions. And again one would have to say that to explore media through either approach will lead a student into ideas and territory supposedly belonging to the other. So while it is useful to gain a sense of the predominant interests in a given critical approach, it is inaccurate to see conceptual walls surrounding each approach. What matters are the ideas – any ideas – which help us make sense of how the media work, why that matters, how they relate to us, and how we may be affected by what we read and see.

Critical approaches: political economy analysis

This approach is generally concerned with how the media operate, why, and with the significance of the how and the why. It is marked by the following:

- *Economic determinism:* the idea that economics determine the behaviour of media institutions and underpin their power
- *Regulation:* the idea that the regulation or control of media behaviour controls their power and is exerted in the main, directly or indirectly by government.

This approach takes on a number of ideas behind post-Marxism. It is concerned with the power of the media and its effects on society: 'political economy tends to concentrate on a specific set of social relations organized around the power or the ability to control other people, processes and things . . . in the face of resistance' (Mosco 1996). Social relations may be about media and society: power may be that of the media and resistance may be that of the audience which wants something other than what it is offered.

The notion of ideology is evidently still important to the approach, whether commentators use the word or not. There is a concern for objectivity in describing and analysing the workings and finances of media institutions. Its proponents tend to see such analysis as supporting a view that institutions exert power over audiences and over the ways those audiences think – about the nature of society and social relations for example. This view largely runs against that aspect of cultural study which has proposed audience power and autonomy in constructing meanings from media texts, and in using cultural objects (such as clothes) to express that autonomy.

More recent critiques within this approach have tried to emphasize a belief that economic and regulatory analysis should be better connected with comment on the effects of power on texts and audiences. Murdock and Golding (2000) refer to approaching textual analysis in terms of how media production structures the discourses which are a part of texts, and which exert power through the meanings that they generate. Much of the relevant literature is about institutions and regulation. Audiences are often talked about as 'citizens'. Media influence is often talked about in terms of 'the public good', and at least some malign effects on choice, the political process and access to knowledge.

This critical approach may also inform writing about globalization and the power of the transnationals. The approach includes the idea of commodification in that media texts are (cultural) goods, and audiences are commodities whose existence and purchasing power underpins the economies of the media.

McQuail (2000) describes political economy as 'a socially critical approach that focuses primarily on the relationship between the economic structure and the dynamics of media industries and the ideological content of media'.

One may also say that there is a concern with the basis of media power, and how this helps explain connections between the nature and conditions of media production and their effects on audience consumption.

---

2 Major questions

1   How may we understand the identity, function and significance of media institutions apart from their role as constructors of media product?

2   In what respects may we understand media institutions as being distinct from or similar to other commercial enterprises?

3   How do we understand the relationship of media institutions to other dominant institutions of our society, especially to the advertising industry?

4   What characterizes the relationship between media and government, especially with reference to the regulation of media?

5   How does media policy affect the position of public service broadcasting (PSB) in particular, as it competes with a free market model?

6   How do media institutions understand their audiences, and what are the implications of this understanding?

7   What do we mean by the phrase 'power of the media'? What is its location, its expression and its significance?

8   How have media institutions changed with the advent of new technology, and with relation to ideas about globalization?

Critical thinking: political economy

Graham Murdock and Peter Golding

Their chapters on political economy in the four editions of *Mass Media and Society* (1977, 1996, 2000, 2005) by James Curran and Michael Gurevitch are central to understanding this critical approach and its development. In the first place they wanted to leave behind classic Marxist concerns with the role of mass communications in the production of class relations. They were not interested in explanations of media power which had conspiracy theory undertones. They wished to objectify the origins of media power. They wanted to explain how 'oppositional values ever emerge' through the media (Curran et al. 1977). It was clear that media are not all powerful and that dissident views on many subjects do emerge through media. Equally, there were (and are) socially inequalities of power, and it could be argued that the media had something to do with this. They were interested in 'the interplay between economic organization and political, social and cultural life' (Curran and Gurevitch 1996). Increasingly, they have proposed the complexity of the relationship between media and society. This is seen as being founded partly on the idea of the production of meaning being an exercise of power by institutions (Curran and Gurevitch 2000). They would look at the audience as playing a part in a power struggle over the production and control of influential ideas – and not always winning. They would look at texts as key locations of meaning, not necessarily as mouthpieces of institutions, but perhaps as repositories of half concealed ideas about how the world should work – and work in ways that suited those institutions.

By the fourth edition of *Mass Media and Society* Murdock and Golding (2005) are writing about a 'critical political economy' which is 'centrally concerned with the balance between capitalist enterprise and public intervention'. They see its work on media power as being able to 'engage with basic moral questions of justice, equity and the public good'. They suggest that what we may think of as a good society is linked to citizens' rights. They argue that a primary task of this approach is to investigate how 'the economic organization of media industries impinges on the production and circulation of meaning and the ways in which people's options for consumption and use are structured by their position within the general economic formation' (Murdock and Golding 2005: 61). They confirm that economic factors are still centrally important to understanding media–society relations. But one also needs to look at a whole process, including the 'commodification of cultural life' (2005: 64).

Robert McChesney

McChesney, writing from a US perspective, is very critical of the failure (as he sees it) of US governments to regulate the media. He tracks the increasing concentration of media financial power and control of distribution in fewer and fewer hands, globally speaking. He argues that a largely unregulated media has acquired more power following the US Telecommunications Act 1996, increasing corporate interests across a wider range of media. He is particularly concerned about what he sees as the collusion of the American political establishment in this process. He would argue that the news agenda has been hijacked by dominant media interests, and that widespread public debate on any issue is largely stifled. He argues that democratic politics are under threat in the USA. His critics would see him as veering towards a 'conspiracy' perspective. But his political economy analysis of the facts of what is happening is based in valid information, and the facts do not encourage optimism – 'the global media and communication market exhibits tendencies not only of an oligopoly, but of a cartel or at least a "gentleman's club"' (Herman and McChesney 1999: 193). For example, the writers refer to a deal in 1996 between the advertisers Proctor & Gamble (P&G) and the media corporations NBC and Viacom in which P&G provide up to 50 per cent of finance for a television series in return for access to advertising time on the show (Herman and McChesney 1999; see also Herman and McChesney 1997).

Nicholas Garnham

Garnham is also concerned with social inequalities and the exercise of power. His focus in explaining the role of the media in shaping an unequal society would be on government and media institutions. The mechanisms of media finance, and what is allowed or disallowed to the media operators in regulatory and financial terms, are crucial in defining the relationship between media and society. He would acknowledge that the media within this critical framework do exert certain kinds of influence on society. But he would not see the audience within that society simply as being victims of the media.

In *Emancipation, the Media and Modernity*, Garnham (2000) reveals pessimism about the state of things, arguing that we are set on a capitalist path from which we can only turn through some kind of catastrophe. His view is that 'the media are worth studying because they raise some very old but central questions in social theory'. Among such questions are those to do with how persuasion and coercion works in our society (see Marxism and Gramsci) and with ways communication has developed as a tool of control (historical dimensions to political economy). Clearly issues of power and influence are there for Garnham, tied in with observations on modernity and specialization. The media partake of that specialization. He is critical of media studies in that (in his view) it 'tends to focus on things rather than the whole social process which lies behind then'. He links the idea of commodification with an economic perspective when he says that 'the media can in part be understood as systems for the economic production and distribution of cultural goods and services'. But he also in effect criticizes cultural studies when he says that 'culture designates everything and thus nothing'. His argument would be that cultural studies and political economy share largely the same interests and origins, for example ideas about 'struggle, empowerment, resistance, subordination and domination' (Garnham 1997: 57). He would claim to be as interested in cultural production as in cultural consumption. He would argue that one cannot ignore the conditions of a capitalist mode of production or the consequences of people depending on work and wages by simply rebadging them as consumers. He would argue that study of cultural practices also depends on understanding the control and disposition of material resources.

3 Defining institutions

3.1 When is an institution?

The media do not of course represent one coherent organization, even if one may talk collectively about 'the institution of the media'. Nor can it be supposed that one is talking just about those organizations which are producers of media material. If one is discussing for example

- questions of power
- the nature of media influence
- media–social relations
- the media as public space

then it is important to realize that the media are about more than the sum of their texts. There may be some things to be inferred about the institution from its texts, but not everything which explains how and why they operate as they do within a social, political and economic context. The production of meaning is about more than the text. Critiques of media – a political economy perspective in particular – are about more than textual production.

Media business covers commercial functions such as finance, distribution, exhibition and retailing, as well as production. The owners of media businesses may be into non-media enterprises. Media institutions may not even be commercial in their foundation; the BBC is the most obvious example of this, as a non-profit-making public service broadcaster with a turnover of millions. Others do not work in a free-for-all market economy. The *Guardian* and *Observer* newspaper group is run by a trust, which denies control to shareholders or to entrepreneurs buying in to those newspapers. Channel 4 television is constrained by its foundation through an Act of Parliament, into providing for minority interests, whatever the commercial implications.

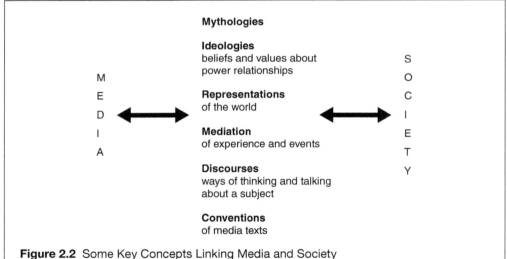

Figure 2.2 Some Key Concepts Linking Media and Society
Media workers and members of society share, for example, ideologies. But media workers have control of technologies through which to mediate experience in the form of texts. The texts construct representations, using discourses, and so promote myths and ideologies.
(Graeme Burton 2004)

Many media institutions are large and wealthy, without being directly in the business of production and exhibition. WPP is a global advertising agency which designs campaigns and commissions adverts. But it does not run the broadcasters or the press that present the ads to us.

Associated Press is a huge press agency that gathers and shapes stories which it sells on to newspapers. The US-owned NTL (rebranded as Virgin Media after a merger in 2007) is, in Britain, a dominant cable operator that distributes the texts made by others. It is a major operator in terms of turnover, and of dominance in its field (though it is still struggling to make a profit). In the USA, AT&T, which also owns the cable operator TCI, is a distributor and a major force in the media. Its name is not on the lips of the public because it does not have high public visibility. But this raises another issue about defining media institutions – what one might refer to as associated industries. With texts in mind, one might not regard telecommunication industries as part of the media. But in their operations as distributors or carriers, they are hugely powerful in bringing media texts to the audiences.

One may argue that their other operations (for example, telephone) are part of mass communications, as distinct from mass media. But again this is a fine distinction to make. The problem with making such a distinction is exemplified by the Net. It is both a carrier of one-to-one communication – email and information from websites – and a distributor of media text – micro cinema or online versions of newspapers. So our object of study is not just about text makers, but also about text enablers and the environment in which text gets made.

The media industries actually comprise interdependent institutions. The links between these are based not least on the outcomes of new technology – about which more later. Even when one considers the interface of texts with audience, there is a tendency to underestimate the scope of the media. So, the sphere of 'the press' is not just about dominant national newspapers but also about the range of regional papers; not just about papers but also about magazines; not just about the public press but also about the trade press; not just about the print press, but also about online newspapers and about e-publishing in general.

Media institutions which we may wish to examine are usually part of larger global corporations. The revenues of these dominant companies are greater than the gross domestic product (GDP) of small companies. In 2003 the following global corporations had the following incomes, described in billions of US dollars: Sony, 71; Time Warner, 39.6; NewsCorp, 29; Disney, 27; Viacom, 26; Bertelsmann, 20.7 (Leiss et al. 2005: 338).

3.2 *Characteristics of institutions*

More accurately one might be talking about the characteristics of dominant media institutions, since the range of business in the media industries in general (see section 3.1) is such that it is not easy to generalize. This also begs the question of what one means by 'dominance'. But for now I will at least refer to dominance in terms of income/turnover/expenditure, volume of product/output, size of audience/consumer base. In this case, one may refer to the following:

- degree of vertical integration
- investment in new technology
- multinationalism
- conglomeration – lateral integration
- diversification.

These features are, significantly, not peculiar to media industries. They mark dominance in other industries. In the British media, they mark out those five market leaders (as well as some others) which typically control some 70 per cent of the market concerned. This is the pattern, whether you look at Bertelsmann in Germany, Murdoch's NewsCorp in the USA, Berlusconi's Fininvest in Italy. This pattern represents a capitalist or market model for business, in which competition, profit and return on investments drive the behaviour of the company. It is difficult not to conclude that most media companies operating on these principles work in the interests of owners – as opposed to the interests of audiences or the community at large. Where there are qualifications to this pattern, it is either because of regulation – the BBC – or because the organization is working in a niche market that is of no interest to bigger commercial players.

Vertical integration refers to the pattern of business ownership in which a company buys or sets up other companies which relate to the core business – say, publishing. In particular, big media organizations tend to try to control production, distribution and exhibition or retailing. So when NewsCorp moved into the USA, it bought Twentieth Century Fox, which is about film production and distribution. These films provide product for Fox TV, which itself was greatly expanded in respect of its production and distribution of TV material. News International also owns a chain of 33 TV stations in major US cities, which gives it some guaranteed exhibition of its product. This integrated power also gives such a media institution the power to cut one-sided deals with apparently independent makers of film and TV.

Multinationalism links to globalization and refers to the fact that the largest media companies do business in different countries, have links across national boundaries (co-productions), distribute product across different countries, and have manufacturing bases in different countries. This can make them more difficult to regulate, less easy to tax and generally more difficult to 'challenge' in national and cultural interests.

Conglomeration refers to a tendency to buy into similar businesses in order to meet competition and to dominate the media sector which a given company is in. So in Britain, during the mergers of the 1990s, Granada Television bought controlling interests in Yorkshire, Tyne Tees and London Weekend television companies, and then merged with the other big player, Carlton, in 2004 to form ITV plc. To take a smaller example, my local newspaper, *The Whitby Gazette*, is run by Yorkshire Regional Newspapers, but is owned by the Johnston Press, which has specialized in buying up local and regional titles. Johnston Press owns 18 regional dailies and 300 local weeklies in the UK, including *The Scotsman* and *The Yorkshire Post*. Since the late 1970s, it has expanded to become one of three groups dominating the UK local press, and is worth around £1 billion. On another scale, the failing French global media business, Vivendi, which owned Universal Pictures, sorted out financial problems (2003–04) by negotiating a merger deal with General Electric, owner of NBC TV, radio and cable.

Lateral integration refers to a company move sideways, buying across different media. The biggest companies, like News International, provide examples of both vertical and lateral integration. An example of lateral strength would be the Walt Disney Company, which in respect of films owns Miramax and Touchstone, as well as Walt Disney Pictures. In television, it owns the ABC network, as well as Touchstone and Buena Vista television, plus a number of cable channels. In radio, it owns ABC radio networks. In music, it owns Walt Disney and Hollywood records. In publishing, it owns, among others, Hyperion books, seven daily newspapers and a variety of magazines.

Croteau and Hoynes (1997) provide good analysis and description of such ownership, including a study of the media conglomerate Bertelsmann, which owns over 350 companies in some 30 countries.

Diversification refers to another version of the lateral process in which a media company is either bought by a business having nothing to do with media, or in which the media company buys into a non-related media business as a way of spreading its financial bets.

It may be argued that these characteristics are linked to economic drivers which in turn may be summarized as seeking

- profitability
- economies of scale
- control of the market
- suppression of competition.

All these commercial practices contribute to the superior market position and power of certain media organizations.

Nicholas Garnham (2000) produces the following definition of media organizations in relation to their economic activity:

- *Editorial model:* individual goods are produced directly for the consumer (such as CDs).
- *Press model:* goods are produced collectively but are also guaranteed repeat sales (such as newspapers).
- *Flow model:* a constant supply of goods is produced (as in broadcasting).

Such models reinforce the idea that media organizations are institutions of commerce, as much as creative sources, cultural enablers or part of a social structure.

However, Hesmondhalgh (2007) also describes them as cultural industries. He argues that since the 1980s significant changes have happened, not least because of deregulation of media and ownership in Western countries. He points out that cultural products know no national boundaries. He points to the expansion into multimedia and global alliances. He refers to the explosion of new technologies and their applications, to the appearance of financially significant niche audiences, to a boom in advertising expenditure, to the extent of changes in all kinds of texts in all media. He argues, perhaps optimistically, that smaller media companies continue to appear and to flourish. One might question whether they flourish in spite of global conglomerates, or because of them. Somewhat contradictorily he describes cooperation between apparent media rivals as 'alliance capitalism'. This might seem to be about cartels by another name, and certainly about concentration of power. But then he does propose that the mega corporations have moved to internal structures where internal 'units' have a fair degree of autonomy in terms of creativity. This, however, cannot reassure one that genuine diversity and pluralism exists.

4 Media institutions and finance

What I want to consider here is where the money comes from, where it goes, and the implications. The remarks which follow refer to institutions which are producers as much as distributors. Grossberg et al. (1998) make a useful general description of how media make sales and derive income

- via direct purchase of the commodity (e.g. the cost of the magazine)
- via a charge for access to the point of distribution or display (e.g. box-office charge at the movie theatre, or an Internet provider charge)
- via indirect financial support, though the commodity is free at the point of sale (e.g. commercial television)
- via indirect financial support, plus a cover cost (e.g. advertising in newspapers).

The account which follows amplifies this model and applies mainly to British media.

The BBC is, exceptionally, funded by a licence fee of £145.50 per annum, payable by all households having a TV set, and bringing in around £2.5 billion a year. In principle it is independent of market forces. In practice it is not. Successive governments, that set the licence fee income of the BBC, have made it clear that the BBC must compete with the commercial sector in terms of quality, ratings and public approval, not to mention adopting commercial practices.

The rest of British media relies a great deal on advertising. Broadcasting almost entirely depends on this. Newspapers and magazines derive between 30 per cent and 70 per cent of their income from advertising. For example, the *Sun* tabloid newspaper, with sales of around 4 million a day, can charge £50,000 for a full page advertisement. However, one should note that books and CDs, for example, have to make their profits on unit sales. There is also a small amount of money that comes from sponsorship; the Cadbury Group sponsors the successful soap, *Coronation Street*, while HSBC Bank sponsors drama series on ITV.

This dependence on advertising reinforces institutional values which are tied in with a market perspective. It means that the interests of the media become closely identified with the interests of other kinds of business. It underpins the view that media goods come to be treated like any other commodity: that if media products are manifestations of culture, then that culture becomes a collection of commodities, where the media are concerned, at least.

Doyle (2002) points out that media industries have especially high startup costs which cause them to look for economies of scale, perhaps in terms of units produced (CDs), or in terms of range of distribution (television). There is a positive incentive for media industries to go for vertical integration in order to achieve efficiency and cost savings. Again, in this respect one is talking the language of commerce and commodities, rather than invoking a discourse of culture and aesthetics. It reminds us of the peculiar position of the media as they combine business and art.

I now want to look at one or two examples of media industries.

The film industry

This is an interesting case in many ways. First, there is no coherent British film industry in the way that radio programmes or books are produced, distributed and sold in Britain. There is a constellation of companies which specialize in things like producing (not making) films, or in support services such as making trailers.

Second and consequently, there is no large film company which can, from its own turnover and backers, finance movies – least of all for distribution on a global scale. Finance for British films is cobbled together from a variety of sources. Predominantly, money comes from the US majors. Television may also provide some funding. Channel 4 has been a relatively significant supporter of low-budget British films, but by 2004 it had pulled out of this activity. The BBC puts only 1 per cent of its budget into film production. The British National Lottery has also given some money, to be administered through the UK Film Council. The most successful British film company is Working Title, with a history of hits such as *Love Actually* (2003) and *Shakespeare in Love* (1998). But even this example reinforces my point that British film is all about cutting deals with US majors for finance and distribution.

Third, what are legally defined as British films (and so eligible for certain tax concessions) may be made largely by British workers, but often are funded by US money – companies such as Miramax.

Fourth, the income of films globally is not derived much from advertising around screening: this goes to the exhibitor, in Britain often one of the US majors once again. As Doyle (2002) puts it: 'The small size of the domestic UK market and the disaggregated structure of the industry prevent the indigenous production sector from growing beyond a cottage industry.'

But in any case, even globally, few films survive solely on box-office receipts. DVD sales are important. So is the income from TV rights – often made in a pre-sales deal which provides cash upfront to pay for the movie being made. And then there are the spin-off product deals – music, games and toys. The fragmented sources of income for movies is partly an expression of the huge sums needed to pay for the most expensive media product of all (if one is considering mainstream film making). Major Hollywood movies cost around US$100 million to make and promote. But one may also say that the huge sums to be made from such a variety of sources also feeds the ballooning cost of making major feature films. It feeds the profit expectations of film companies. It creates a film producing market in which the divide between global and very local and small scale is marked. It creates a film consuming market in which the worst excesses of mass appeal, mass culture can be realized.

The television industry

Though the industry makes a lot of money from spin-offs, programme sales, and syndication, this still has not inflated the economic balloon to the same extent as is true for the film industry. If these three sources disappeared tomorrow, there would still be a British TV industry. However, it is also fair to point out how much TV now depends on co-productions – money from US or European networks – to help pay for the really big drama and documentary series, such as *Life in the Freezer* (2006) on BBC1. And such large-scale internationally targeted productions come about because of the nature of the financial environment in which the media operate. The earlier BBC/Discovery Channel co-production, *Blue Planet* (2002), cost £7 million for eight 50-minute episodes, or £850,000 a programme – serious money for documentaries. BBC TV, apart from its income from the licence fee, also runs a commercial arm, BBC Worldwide, which made a profit of £111 million on a turnover of £810 million in 2007. It has 70 TV channels in 160 countries around the world. It owns 75 per cent of the Lonely Planet travel guide company. BBC America is available in 58 million US homes. It publishes a range of magazines, including the *Radio Times*. It is into digital media services such as iPlayer and Kangaroo (a commercial media player).

In 2002, British TV saw a 6.6 per cent increase in the value of programme sales, most of which were to the USA (worth £148 million) and to Canada (£100 million); this £248 million was about half the value of total sales.

So while media institutions derive some income directly from product sales, it is the case that much of their financing and profit comes indirectly from other sources. This is well illustrated as part of the symbiotic relationship of media with one another – the patterns of cross-media ownership. I am talking about ways in which one medium helps finance another. Newspapers advertise on television; television finances some film production; film and television have created the video market; spin-off computer games pay a percentage to the film producers and pay for advertising in magazines and on TV.

In terms of British commercial television, and in comparison with the BBC and other commercial providers, ITV plc is having a horrendous time (2007–08), as it fails to create product that attracts audiences, and consequently loses advertisers. In the first half of 2008 its balance sheet dropped into the red by £1.54 billion. The current recession has not helped. Commentators are talking about the company being broken up and sold in pieces. The company is negotiating for some relief from its expensive public service licence obligations (costing around £200 million a year). This is a business which 40 years ago was described as a licence to print money.

Book publishing

It is worth remembering that 'old' media are as much affected by globalization and technology as are the apparently more cutting edge visual media. The same production technologies that have transformed the pace and progress of producing and distributing newspapers and magazines have also affected the book trade and its finances. The same process of mergers and global conglomeration has also polarized UK book publishing into mass and niche markets. The UK retailing is similarly dominated by a few players, mainly W.H. Smith and

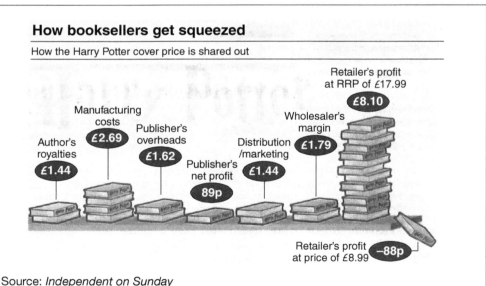

Source: *Independent on Sunday*
Figure 2.3 How Booksellers Get Squeezed: Costs and Profits on Book Sales
This analysis explains how massive discounting of certain books by supermarkets and dominant retailers can be destructive for the average bookshop (and its customers).

Waterstones. Publishing is not such a risk as making a film in Hollywood, but identifying what will be a 'blockbuster' is just as chancy. Promotion has become as essential for the big publishing event as it has for a high-concept Hollywood product. Online purchasing, dominantly through retailers such as Amazon, has benefited some consumers, yet has made the market ever more competitive, with margins being squeezed. Independent booksellers are struggling with the supermarket power of the major retailers (and supermarkets!) to be able to reduce profit margins as they increase volume.

An analysis (see illustration) by the *Independent on Sunday* business section (18 July 2007) shows how on the one hand an average bookseller can in principle get about half the cover price of a (Harry Potter) book, but on the other hand they can actually lose money if the Majors are selling a book as a loss leader.

Radio

UK radio is a very interesting example of an 'old' medium which has reinvented itself in a digital age. Nationally, viewing figures are dominated by the BBC, especially Radio 1 and Radio 2, and the BBC licence fee income pays for the BBC channels. Altogether, the BBC has 56 per cent audience share, and 90 per cent reach into audiences. But locally, some commercial channels challenge their BBC rivals in terms of total listening figures (e.g. XFM in Manchester) and are of course paid for by advertising. Commercial radio is dominated by big players such as Global Radio (Heart FM, Galaxy FM) and GCap (Classic FM [national], Capital FM [London]). Takeovers are happening because it has been a very fragmented industry – 300 stations and 70 owners – with a relatively small annual turnover, £600 million (*Independent on Sunday* 1 July 2007).

What is transforming radio is the arrival of digital. Listener numbers are soaring via media such as digital television and the Net. About one-sixth of all listening is now via digital sources (*Guardian* 29 October 2007). In 2007 4.4 million people listened to radio on their mobile phones (Rajar), 63 per cent of the audience for digital only stations are listening to commercial radio (*Guardian* 5 November 2007). Significantly, spin-off digital only stations (from successful magazines) are doing very well (Smash Hits Radio or Heat Radio). Audiences for other commercial stations are growing (and therefore so are advertising revenues) e.g. The Magic Network or The Hits. Radio is relatively cheap to run, and therefore can afford to expand into niche markets (Gaydar Radio for gay listeners, or Big Blue for Chelsea football club supporters). Advertisers see stations as having a (profitable) close relationship with their listener base. Some 70 per cent of 15–24 year olds have listened to radio via one of the new digital platforms (*Guardian* 5 November 2007). While the spot ad still dominates commercial radio income, there has been a huge growth in kinds of sponsorship, e.g. Heat radio going for brand sponsorship from the likes of Ford.

Cost elements

It follows from the above that, in terms of media expenditure, *advertising and promotion* is a significant part of any budget. Clearly this may not be the case if one is a provider or distributor like Virgin Media (cable), as opposed to being a major manufacturer of product. But even portal and search engine providers for the Net, such as Yahoo!, not only take income from advertisers, but also have to advertise their merits to attract more users and advertisers. The average feature film will spend between a quarter and a half of its production costs again, in order to promote itself. Quality television drama, such as adaptations of the classics, costs between £300,000 and £500,000 for 50 minutes on screen. A psychological crime thriller series such as *Wire in the Blood* (ITV, 2002–09) cost about £750,000 an episode.

Another significant cost element is *labour*, including celebrity performers. Of course, specialist workers may command high salaries, not least in operating new technology. But the really big cost elements are for those media industries where the star, the celebrity, the personality worker is essential for attracting audiences and income. Film and TV are obvious examples. Media products which depend on individual expertise and recognition have a charge attached to them.

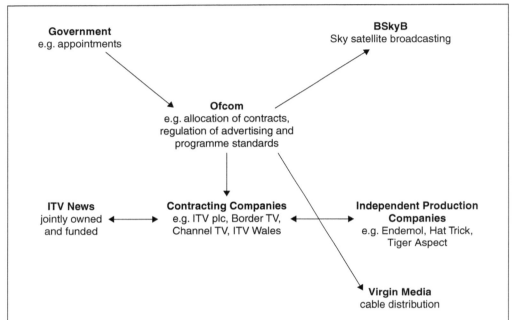

Figure 2.4 Elements of British Commercial Television
The UK government set up Ofcom (Office of Communications) in 2003 to monitor and regulate the output and commercial behaviour of the contracting companies. Mergers have meant that these are now dominated by ITV plc, and essentially it *is* British commercial terrestrial television. It takes at least 25 per cent of its material from independent production companies. It now effectively controls ITV News, although this is legally a separate body.

● Would a model for any one of the media look like this – interdependent organizations, public and private? If so, what are likely to be the consequences for the ways that they operate and for the nature of their media output?

(Graeme Burton 2004)

A third major cost element is that of *new technology* (see Chapter 6). But, in general, there is a huge investment in new technology because it may produce:

● economies of scale
● enhancement of product

- new products or services or reduction of labour.
- and so increase profits and increase competitiveness.

Doyle (2002) asserts that in television there is a considerable correlation between market share and profitability (see also economies of scale). Market share gives the distributor considerable economic leverage over suppliers (production companies) and buyers (of advertising).

The three elements cited above are the most significant for media institutions. But of course there are many other factors which affect different industries in different ways, and for different reasons. For example, the development of new media (especially the Net) which expand the numbers of outlets for advertising and which offer more choices for leisure time activity, has helped reduce TV advertising revenue (and therefore its capacity to spend) over the past few years. Grossberg et al. (1998) report that US Network audience share fell from 91 per cent in 1978–79 to 40 per cent in 1996–97, because of competition from cable and satellite channels. There has been a similar though less marked pattern in Britain. Still, it has been enough to hit ITV viewing figures and to contribute to the reduction in advertising revenue. However, it may be pointed out that the British commercial television system has its own peculiar elements which affect income, costs and profits. In particular, there is the amount that has to be bid in order to get a contract to broadcast in the first place. Then there are taxation costs. In the case of ITV these two cost elements mean that the company pays back to government about 30 per cent of its advertising income. Also, ITV has a public service licence, which means that it is obligated to provide news, regional and minority interest television – which are relatively unattractive to paying advertisers. Regulation comes in various guises, and the free market is not, in these respects, as free as it may seem.

5 Media in relation to other institutions

My remarks in the previous section about other industries remind us that media institutions exist within a context of other powerful organizations. Garnham (2000) makes a criticism of at least certain kinds of approach to media when he says that 'media studies . . . tends to focus on things . . . rather than the whole social process which lies behind them'. Media institutions may have particular qualities and a particular position within commerce, society, culture. But they are not pre-eminent. Government uses political and legal power to modify their sphere of operation. Individuals and groups have recourse to the law in order to contain or even redefine what it is acceptable for the media to do. The police may act for the State in a similar process of containment. Education makes the media an object of study and may question its role.

Cottle (2003) argues that

> media industries are different from most other businesses and organizations in that they characteristically produce or purvey commodities and content that are essentially symbolic in nature – and these symbols enter into the life of society.
>
> (Cottle 2003: 4)

He has a point in talking about the media in effect as 'meanings industries'. But actually they are not unique in this respect – see the fashion industry. And commentators such as Doyle

(2002) talk about the media industries precisely as if they are *similar* to other industries in the ways that they conduct their businesses. In the same vein, McChesney (quoted in Cottle 2003: 27) talks about 'the crucial role of the profit motive in shaping media performance'. If the media are selling culture, emotion, meaning, experiences, then he would say that they are doing it within a capitalist model and within the conventions of market practices.

The media also interact with other institutions – say, the military at a time of war through TV news, or the health service in a time of reorganization through an article. They are neither dominant nor submissive in this interaction. But this interaction, this general context, needs to be accounted for in making models of the relationship between media and society. It suggests that whatever influence media may have, this is qualified and modified.

In whatever ways the media industries are similar to or different from other industries, and whatever their relationship to them, one should be clear that they are economically very significant, let alone in terms of their (contested) influence. Steemers (2004) cites a UK government Mapping Document (Department for Culture, Media and Sport 2001) on the creative industries, which estimates that in that year for Britain they brought in £112.5 billion in revenues, plus £20.3 billion in export earnings. This is not pocket money.

Whether one is taking culturalist or political economy perspectives, it is significant that in both cases one can talk about production and consumption. The production and marketing of cars as lifestyle accessories seems to me to be little different from the same process with television programmes. And the consumption of television programmes as cultural fodder seems little different from the purchase of goods such as curtains and linens for the home.

Critical approaches: cultural studies (culturalism)

This approach – and whole new academic discipline – emerged in the 1980s in association with postmodernism. However, it had its roots in changes that went back a further 20 years, to sources such as the Birmingham Centre for Cultural Studies in the 1960s. It arose partly out of a critical distaste for elitist thinking about what constituted (high) culture, and an interest in examining popular culture – Hollywood movies and television. This new approach also applied structuralist methods such as semiotics to textual analysis, to understanding how power might be expressed through texts, and then to redefining the idea of a 'text' outside of a media 'box'.

There has been a history of critical antagonism between culturalists and those interested in remaining focused on the media. But this should not concern a free thinking student. Culture can refer to the culture of media institutions. Media texts are also cultural texts, though cultural texts may also refer to buildings or to fashion, for example. But again, the study of how we understand what clothes or cathedrals mean to us can hardly be separated from media representations, or the music industry.

The important thing about cultural studies is precisely that it has blurred boundaries between academic disciplines; that one can now talk about cultural geography, identity theory, gender studies. One may say that cultural studies is marked by the following:

- an interest in popular culture texts and their meanings, and generally in the production of culture
- a conception of the audience as consumers
- an interest in the pleasures of consumption
- an interest in **reception studies** and in what audiences may do with texts (cultural practices, audience activity and audience powers)

- the regulation of cultural production
- the representation of identities (and their loss) and how people may be subordinated by these representations
- historical and geographical dimensions of culture and cultural behaviours.

Cultural studies works through the use of concepts such as identity and difference, discourse and ideology, when making analyses of texts. It may be said that in the end it has no boundaries in terms of the scope of its inquiries. One could argue that life is culture, just as During (2005: 38) asserts that 'culture is politics'. It certainly links to understanding how we conceive of ideas such as gender or ethnicity. It certainly relates to subjects such as globalization. It has resisted buying into absolutist views of the media (institutions) as controlling people (see also postmodernism). Yet it is still interested in dispositions of power, in how societies make and express what they call culture – through what happens on the streets, through religions, through political interventions and ministries, through music, through museums. So it is interested in culture and its relationship to social power. It is interested in everyday life. It is interested in the contexts within which culture is generated and consumed.

> cultural criticism offers a distinct way of engaging with culture, and the meanings generated within cultures, which matter in the world today. Without an understanding of what generates the meanings by which both the world, and we in relation to that world, come to be defined, dominant cultural meanings go uncontested in any thorough lasting terms.
>
> (McGowan 2007)

For a discussion of culture and communication, see Burton and Dimbleby (2006: Chapter 4).

6 Media and government

The relationship between the institutions of media and government is one of mutual self-interest, though not entirely one of equals. When the chips are down, it is government that makes law and controls a source of information vital to media (see also Chapter 8 on News). Mechanisms of regulation (see below) are controlled directly or indirectly by government. Nevertheless, the access of media to the audience (citizens) means that government often wants to use media to disseminate policy, to promote initiatives, to release information into the public domain, to test reactions to possible new laws, and most of all to present in a public sphere a favourable view of government work.

The attitude of media institutions to government is partly defined by degrees of interference, which are in turn defined by the terms of regulation for a given media industry. It is also partly defined by the ideological position of given media businesses, or even their proprietors, towards the rights of the state, within their own idea of the media–audience relationship. So marketeers such as Rupert Murdoch refer to the absolute freedom of the press and to the ability of competition in the marketplace to produce the media we want, as providing valid arguments for government keeping out of media business. Congdon (1995) disagrees, and comments with particular relation to news:

Just as there can be little confidence that unregulated commercial broadcasters are much concerned to maintain pluralism in political debate, so there can be no presumption that the free market will give top priority to the truthfulness of the news or seek an appropriate mix of news and other programmes.

Broadcasters, even commercial channels, are more inclined to take **liberal pluralist** positions. Their terms of reference, their executives, their governing bodies, talk more about responsibility and public service. This is built into the statute and charter which allows their existence and which defines the broad terms of their operation. However, although they may chafe at things like restriction on the proportion of cross-media ownership, broadcasters still accept that they should wear the government bridle, if not a muzzle.

One issue which operates at the highest levels is that of mutual self-interest and its consequences for genuinely free media and free opinion. Governments in the West are very conscious of the value of media coverage, of what they assume to be the power of the media to sway public opinion. Yet they also assert the existence of and value of an independent media sector – not least if that independence (such as it may be) validates what the media may say positively about government. And again, there is the need of the media to report and present politicians in order to attract an audience, because it is seen to have access to important authority figures.

So, we are talking about a collusive relationship. The question is whether or not this works to the benefit of the citizen.

7 The regulation of media institutions

> Recognition of the need to safeguard pluralism has historically been the main reason for regulating ownership of the media.
>
> (Doyle 2002)

Any discussion of media regulation raises issues of *freedom and responsibility*. It raises questions about whose freedom and whose responsibilities. From one point of view, any regulation of organizations' right to be media producers, or of what they produce and how, is a curtailment of liberty in a free society. Libertarianism is behind criticisms of the **censorship** of media texts. Yet, knowing what you are against does not necessarily explain what you are for. In any case, it is very clear that not just anyone is free to join the ranks of producers, and it is likely that most people would have some objections to some material that might be produced in a free-for-all.

One progresses then to the notion that institutions and producers have a kind of responsibility to the *public interest*. For pro-regulators, this in turn raises the problem of who defines that interest and how. Media may argue for the public's right to know, when the individual being talked about in the media argues for a right to privacy. Media may argue that public interest requires an article should be printed: government may take the opposite view on the same grounds. In each case one might go on to ask, who is demonstrating what responsibility to whom? Media can purport to serve their audiences, but then we know that in operational practice they serve the interests of their financial backers and of their governing bodies. Governments are at least elected. Yet even here one can easily demonstrate self-interest. For example, in 1991 the US military stopped American reporters from filming flag-draped coffins being brought back from the Gulf War. When British troops were sent to Sierra Leone in 2000 to back that government against rebel incursions, it was suggested that the British government's interest was in the arms industry and the oil industry, not the views of the British public. In 2001 there was a furore because a British civil servant recommended that the terrorist destruction of the World Trade Center should be used as a distraction and an occasion for the release of politically uncomfortable information. Such examples do not inspire confidence in the idea of government as regulator.

Regulation also invokes ideas about censorship. But the word should not be misused in discussion of what happens to the media. Censorship implies overarching and centralized control of media material – such as is usually practised only by government in wartime. The regulatory practices of government on media institutions and their work do not usually emerge in this way. Where the word 'censorship' may seem to be appropriate is if material is removed 'secretly', without this being generally known or understood. So you might consider whether you would describe the practice by TV organizations of cutting films without telling the viewers to be an example of censorship. Similarly, there have been examples where whole programmes have been pulled in response to political pressures. From the 1970s to the 1990s, there were a number of TV programmes about Northern Ireland that were cut or not shown. More trivially, in 2007, the film *Casino Royale* had a scene featuring the Virgin brand tycoon, Richard Branson, cut in response to the demands of British Airways, a product sponsor of the movie. Branson is of course a competitor, the owner of Virgin Airlines. Where is the line between censorship and a response to concerns about taste, or between censorship and the best interests of a healthy political process?

The concept of regulation of media institutions does not only refer to intentional and external forces. If one connects it with the notion of constraints on institutional practices, then there are four main areas in which constraints operate:

- *Law:* respects in which the fear of legal action or actual legal intervention constrains the media from 'publishing' anything they please.

- *Finance/the market:* lack of resources or concern about performance in the market may constrain media from 'publishing'. This constraint may limit or shape the media product, or even simply stop its production.

- *Professional practices:* what media workers have agreed it is OK to 'publish' or not, and in what ways, will in effect constrain what institutions put out, and therefore what we are 'allowed' to have in the public domain.

- *Public responsibility:* is also about the beliefs of media workers acting as a constraint. They will share beliefs about the nature of their responsibility to the public and therefore again about what should be 'published'.

Regulation of British media is generally not exerted through external agencies. For most media there is a process of *self-regulation*. The various categories of media sponsor the collective and voluntary bodies which regulate them, and/or they have internal mechanisms of control. Before one applauds the public-spirited appearance of this condition, it is worth bearing in mind the following points.

- Even self-regulation must be based on institutional values and practices – with which one may not agree, but which one has no control over.

- Part of self-regulation is a response to fear of legal consequences external to the institution.
- Self-regulation is also a response to other external forces:
  - what the audience will accept in the marketplace
  - specific forces such as the government setting the BBC licence fee and therefore their income
  - what it is believed that the government will accept – or even kinds of government intervention. There have been many examples of ministerial pronouncements that have a weighty intervention in some discussion about, for example, TV scheduling.

Examples of British media self-regulating bodies are

- *Movies:* British Board of Film Classification (BBFC)
- *Video:* Video Standards Council
- *Press:* Press Complaints Commission
- *Broadcasting:* Broadcasting Complaints Commission (but also see below)
- *Advertising:* Advertising Standards Authority.

In broadcasting, the BBC operates an internalized system known as 'referral upwards' (if in doubt about material). The BBC Trust establishes policy and standards. But this is hardly a voluntary and internalized system because the charter of the BBC establishes ground rules for its behaviour, and because the Trust members are appointed by the government. Given the fact that a licence is needed to broadcast in the first place (there has been no licence to print since 1697!) it is apparent that radio and television are treated differently from other media.

One major external regulatory body is Ofcom for the broadcasting industries, which took over (December 2003) the work of the former separate regulators: the Independent Television Commission, the Radio Authority (the Radio Communications Agency which manages radio frequency allocations), the Broadcasting Standards Council and Oftel (the telecommunications industries). In particular, Ofcom has regulatory responsibility for commercial broadcasting, having an overview of programming, advertising and its standards, and responsibility for allocating broadcasting contracts. This may moderate any potential for market excesses on the part of commercial contractors.

It could be argued that there is an illusion of freedom for the media, but many practices of regulation by stealth. Government is partly behind this, but then so are the media themselves. Media practices tend to impinge on the material – the editing of films for broadcasting or for video release. One may also question the effectiveness of such regulation. For instance three policy statements from the Press Complaints Commission assert the following:

- Inaccurate and misleading material should not be published.
- There should be a fair 'right to reply'.
- Reporters should not misrepresent who they are in order to obtain material.

Some might say that these 'rules' are broken every week.

The law

The law regulates the activities of media institutions in a variety of ways. Some laws relate to the management and operation of the business, as they would to any company. The Health and Safety at Work Act 1974 protects employees, for example, in respect of the time spent looking at screens. The Companies Act 2006 forces the publication of accounts and a summary of operations, year on year.

It is those laws which affect media material which are seen as being most significant. And it is true that it is the business of media institutions to produce, distribute and publish that material. These regulatory laws are directed at the notion of protection:

- Protection of specific and possibly vulnerable audiences such as children and young people
- Protection of the public interest as in the case of security services
- Protection of the general public as in respect of notions of good taste
- Protection of the process of law in respect of the notion of a fair trial
- Protection of the interests of military operations (which are taken to be carried out in the interests of the people).

Examples of such laws in the UK are:

- *Defamation Act 1996:* covers defamation of character, libel and slander, and is meant to protect the public reputation of individuals. However, it may be argued that the cost of litigation is so great that most people cannot afford to defend their reputation against statements made in the media.

- *Obscene Publications Act 1959:* the purpose of this is obvious, but its effects are contestable. There cannot be an objectifiable definition of obscenity. So in effect the Act denies some institutions access to some audiences: and denies some audiences the right to read and watch some material to which they may not object. The Act was extended to cover broadcasting in 1991.

- *Young Person's Harmful Publications Act 1955:* covers horrific and otherwise harmful material, particularly in comics and magazines. This raises problems to a degree. For example, 'comics' are no longer a format published for young people. Also there is the question of what is harmful; this was raised for instance in 1997 when Members of Parliament (MPs) expressed objections to the new and sexually explicit (if informative) content of magazines for young women, such as *Sugar* and *More*.

- *Official Secrets Act 1989:* in effect covers anything which government decides it does not want known about its security and military operations. The issue of a D notice by someone in the Home Office, covering certain information, is used as a threat merely to invoke the Act. Most obviously this constrains freedom of speech in the press, in broadcast news and documentary. It is the focus of an ideological contradiction between the idea of a free (democratic) society and the practice of state control.

- *Prevention of Terrorism Act 1974:* was originally framed to control information about and reporting of the conflict in Northern Ireland. However, it has also in effect constrained discussion of what is going on there and why. It incorporates assumptions about who is a terrorist which, it may be argued, have extended conflict and made a peace process that much more difficult.

- *Public Order Act 1986:* has sections which forbid the publication of material which incite racial hatred and unrest.

- *Contempt of Court Act 1981:* forbids the publication of anything about a trial in progress which may prejudice its fairness and the outcome. This is why, in particular, that one sees drawings of trial events, not photographs.

- *Video Recordings Act 1984:* restricts what may be hired from video shops, and imposes categories on films available on DVD.

This last example, which clearly is a kind of censorship, does remind us that regulation does not merely raise moral issues or those of national security. It also refers to differences of values and of judgement within society – categorizing material on film and video for consumption by different age groups must ultimately be a matter of individual beliefs and values: regulation is ideological in its implications and operation. Male nudity is censored to a degree and in ways that is simply not true for female nudity. There is a whole history of inequity in the disposition of gender power behind this practice.

In this sense, regulation implies *cultural norms* (which must also be ideological). These norms also change over time. For example, the word 'fuck' was first used on British TV in 1965, when it caused an uproar. There was a valid critical context to the use of the word, but still the BBC bowed to the storm and made a public apology. Or there is the example of the early James Bond films which were originally X rated, but have ended up being shown on prime-time television.

In this discussion of regulation and of related issues one must not lose sight of the thrust of market interests (the large media corporations) towards deregulation. Government is sympathetic to this view, while not entirely agreeing with it. In this context the term 'regulation' is more synonymous with political and economic controls than it is with regulation according to social or cultural norms. The market constructs the term regulation as being opposed to 'freedom' – an evocative and misused term. Such a dichotomy is false. Herbert Schiller (2000) refers with concern to a 'push towards total social unaccountability'. Government remains concerned about accountability, not least if freedom were to undermine governance.

Governments (including the European Commission) tend to regulate media power by controlling what they define as ant-competitive behaviour, rather than by interfering directly with corporate structures (in the UK, see the Competition Commission). The UK operates through non-governmental organizations (quangos); this is government and regulation at arm's length. Broadcasting is regulated through Ofcom, although this body is supported through the terms of broadcasting Acts. So one media owner can, for instance, control up to 20 per cent of national newspaper circulation, up to 15 per cent of radio (though having only one national licence), and up to 15 per cent of television (also by audience share). However, there is some cynicism about the reality of regulation of media ownership, when NewsCorp already controls 40 per cent of UK circulation as well as SkyTV, the near monopoly satellite broadcaster. Doyle (2002) reminds us of what this regulation is all about: 'Restrictions on media ownership provide a way of rationing power over which ideas will circulate (or not circulate) in the public domain.'

The only one of the media to which comments about conventional regulation do not apply is the Net. There is no owner of the system to be regulated. It is possible to apply voluntary controls via computers, for example, to restrict the access of minors to porn sites. Court cases in a number of countries have made some providers and posters of content responsible for what is on the servers, for example via the law of libel. But it is still not clear as to how far any systematic regulation of this medium is technologically viable. In the USA the Digital Millennium Copyright Act 2000 requires website owners such as YouTube to take down copyright material if its owner complains – and to ban those who posted such material if they persistently reoffend. YouTube is owned by Google; in 2008 the media giant Viacom obtained a judgement against Google in respect of video material being posted on YouTube users' sites. Google was forced to agree to provide identity details of such users so that Viacom might pursue them through legal channels. This issue is about regulation as it may protect the intellectual property rights of owners and artists, as opposed to the rights of users and audiences.

Figure 2.5

Ofcom

Ofcom is the UK telecommunications regulator. It is intended to modify and control the power of media institutions.

* To what extent does Ofcom control these institutions and their output?
* Considering what it does, in whose interests does it operate?

---

8 Institutions and power

The existence, nature and exercise of institutional power is an issue in itself. The question is raised about what kind of power, exercised in what ways and with what identifiable effects. One may suggest that whatever this power is about, it operates out of a material base, but has ideological implications. For 'power' to have any meaning one has to identify a process in which some kind of force exerted by a given source (institutions) produces some kind of change in the object of its attention (audience). In this respect we are back to the idea of influence.

The material base and source of institutional power may be identified as

* control of financial resources which fund media distribution and production;
* control of technical resources which manufacture media goods;
* control of human resources which develop relevant technology and make specialist production possible;
* control of legal resources which copyright and control the scope of distribution and production, and which amplify profits;
* control of a management centre which holds the reins of ownership, which produces policy, which directs distribution and production.

The maintenance of this material base depends partly on the ability to generate profit, partly on the production of confidence in the company within the marketplace, partly on the ability to promote the work and products of the media institution concerned. This work

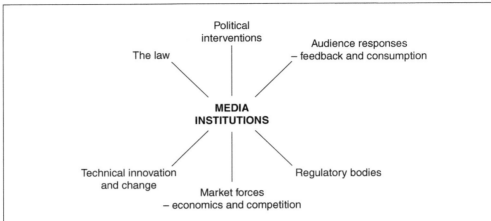

Figure 2.6 The Media: Power Pressures
The media should not necessarily be seen as dispensing influence and exerting power. Media institutions are themselves under pressure from a range of forces, not least those of the varying tastes of their audiences or consumers.

(Graeme Burton 2004)

may directly produce media goods, and it may enable the production of those goods, and it may enable the distribution of those goods.

The symbolic base of this power and the expression of the power of the material is constituted in the media goods and texts which produce meanings and which are the point of contact with the audience. The ideological expression of institutional power is in these meanings. This is the focus of possible change. This is the fulcrum of power. If these meanings change the lives and the thinking of the audience in some way which is to the advantage of the institution and to the disadvantage of the audience members, then power becomes real and it matters.

Garnham (2000) refers to two kinds of power:

- *Structural power:* this is about allocation of resources (see Althusser and allocative control) which operates within the institution.
- *Economic (corporate power):* this operates within structural constraints within the marketplace and in the context of regulation.

Power is both potential and actual. By this I mean that the apparent capacity of media to influence the attitudes of audiences is power enough itself. It is this potential which causes politicians to court media appearances. It is the potential which leads to censorship and regulation – as much as actual examples of the exercise of, or even the abuse of power.

At the same time, it is not reasonable to suggest that media power is simply imaginary. All media industries tend towards monopoly: three newspaper groups control most of the circulation of daily papers in Britain. The same is true for the control of news agencies. ITV plc owns 12 of the 15 commercial television licences in Britain (granted by Ofcom). Globalization and the need for financial muscle to meet competition leads to larger conglomerates which lead to less competition and therefore to less actual choice. The workings of the market contradict aspirations to healthy pluralism. The numbers of newspapers, the variety of content and the range of audience has closed down as the numbers of owners has decreased. Hesmondhalgh (2007) refers to seven major global media corporations, which in 2005 had total revenues of $178.8 billion, and to a second tier of 42 global companies with total revenues of over $1 billion.

The power of media owners although exaggerated by some critics has substance. Rupert Murdoch does cut deals. He has built up an American media empire, including Twentieth Century Fox and Fox TV as a credible fourth network in American television. He bought and expanded Star Channel, which satellite broadcasts to 53 countries through 28 channels and in seven languages across much of Asia and the Middle East. Star broadcasts a channel for British Asians as well. He also owns Sky (BSkyB) satellite television in Britain and Europe, plus Japan's Perfect TV. He controls about one-third of British press circulation, and more than this in Australia. NewsCorp owns 175 titles across three continents, and publishes a total of 40 million newspapers a week, including *The New York Post*, and the *Sun* in Britain. In 2003 he acquired control of the US company DirecTV (satellite and cable), bringing access to 10 million subscribers. He is developing interactive TV. He owns Latin Sky Broadcasting in association with the US telecoms giant AT&T, as well as the major broadcasters Televisa in Mexico, and Globo in Brazil.

David Walker (2000), formerly a journalist with *The Times* in England, talks about his experiences of working under the authoritarianism of editors and owners. He describes a feeling of powerlessness and of alienation among journalists, and talks directly of *The Times* being 'compromised by Murdoch's ownership'.

In an article in the *Guardian* (17 February 2003) Roy Greenslade analyses the 'coincidence' of how all NewsCorp papers worldwide backed the war on Iraq. 'He (Murdoch) has an unerring ability to choose editors across the world who think just like him.' Greenslade refers to articles and editorials, as well as taking direct quotations from Murdoch himself, which construct a consistently pro-war line, behind which one may hear clearly the creak of the levers of power being pulled.

Then as an example in Europe, there is Silvio Berlusconi who is prime minister of Italy, as well as owner of major TV channels in Italy and newspapers across Europe. Through his company MediaSet he controls 48 per cent of Italian television – Canale 5, Italia 1, Retequattro and La 7. In advertising he owns Publitalia. In publishing he has 30 per cent of the Italian book market plus 50 magazines, through Mondadori. His brother owns the leading Italian daily, *Il Giornale*. He has a 19 per cent stake in Albacom, a telecommunications company. Tobias Jones, in his book, *The Dark Heart of Italy* (2003), says:

> It's impossible to move without inadvertently coming up against his influence. If you watch football matches, or television, try to buy a house, or a book, or a newspaper, rent a video, or else shop in a supermarket, the chances are you're somehow filling the coffers of Il Cavaliere (last estimated to be worth $14 billions).

In *Mass Media and Society,* Murdock and Golding (2000) refer to the power of the media moguls:

> In the emerging environment, power will lie with those who own the key building blocks of new communications systems, the rights to the key pieces of technology and, even more importantly, the rights to the cultural materials – the films, books, images, sounds, writings – that will be used to put together the new services . . . the media moguls have

a sizeable advantage since they already own a formidable range of the expressive assets that are central to public culture.

(Murdock and Golding 2000)

Doyle (2002: 177) is in no doubt that this power exists and is exerted, for example in respect of challenging attempts to moderate and regulate the scope of action by major media companies. She refers to 'unhealthy alignments of corporate media power and political power' which impede curbs on concentrated media ownership. She criticizes the Broadcasting Act 1996 as being ill-founded and based on inadequate information gathering: 'powerful corporate media interests triumphed in impressing their wishes onto the design of policy changes'.

There is also a kind of power which is in the hands of media producers, as opposed to the owners who employ them. In respect of production, power exists materially through the technologies and in the expertise of those who use them. But it also exists conceptually in those workers' view of themselves as professionals. The idea of *professionalism* is one which endorses expertise and the right to do things in certain ways. People are reluctant to criticize 'the professional'. The good side of professionalism is its attachment to a certain idea of responsibility towards colleagues and towards clients (audiences). Less attractive is a degree of self-regard which leads to uncritical endorsement of production routines and habitual practices. It is well documented that news workers invoke professionalism as a way of endorsing news values and therefore what they do selectively with news material. In fact professionalism becomes part of news ideology. It is a value position which is behind newswork. It is also an instrument of power which supports the authority of the newsworker, what they do, how and why.

It is the case that a relatively small number of media workers collaborate to represent the world to us. One might say that this is analogous to the small number of political workers in the US Senate and in Congress, who represent a superpower and who also speak for millions. But the media workers are not elected to their positions by even the semblance of a democratic process. They speak to us, but are not entitled to speak for us – though this position, of representing 'the people', is one often adopted by news reporters and newscasters.

For audiences, the immediate exertion of power through ideas is embedded in the texts they consume. We will look more at this in the chapters which follow. This is the power of the production of meaning. The interesting thing is that media material does not have to be overtly politicized to be political, nor does it have to have intentions in order to have effects. Institutions may be blown by the winds of the market economy. This economy may have indirect effects. For instance, in 2001 competitive game shows were proving to be very popular on British television. ITV competed with the BBC for ratings. Its rescheduling of Saturday night programmes had proved to be a failure, and its share of advertising revenue was slipping, so it introduced *Who Wants To Be a Millionaire?*, which proved to be very successful. Similarly, the BBC brought in an equally successful programme, *The Weakest Link*, which it later exported to the USA. More recently (2009), ITV has competed with the BBC's *Strictly Come Dancing*, through presenting another type of reality/celebrity show, *The X Factor*. Such programmes are about fame in a public arena and about turning audiences into cash.

The meanings that will be reinforced through a glut of such game shows are, for example, about the value of being competitive, the stigma of being a loser, the desirability of acquiring material goods. This is ideology at work. These meanings are political because they are ideological. They refer to the power of being a winner – and the disempowerment of 'losers'. But the production of these meanings is not calculated. The institutional imperative is to get people watching and to keep them there. This is what power is about as far as the institution is concerned: the power of attraction and absorption. But then media criticism is concerned with unintended but no less real or significant effects.

Dennis McQuail (2000) suggests that key aspects of media power may be summarized as follows:

- attracting and directing public attention
- persuading in matters of opinion and belief
- influencing behaviour
- structuring definitions of reality
- conferring status and legitimacy
- informing quickly and extensively.

Critical perspectives: post-Marxism

It is difficult to separate clearly any one period of time or one set of people 'owning' a set of ideas from any other period or set of ideas. However, by post-Marxist I wish to refer to those thinkers and ideas which emerged in the second half of the twentieth century. Those ideas are immensely important precisely because they infuse so many other critical perspectives, even though that debt is sometimes denied. For example culturalists and political economists continue to talk about power and inequality even when they go into denial about use of the word ideology. The fact that there is so much drift between the ideas of critical perspectives which appear to be crisply separated by their labels can be confusing to a student. I would say, don't worry. The ideas are more important than academic territory building.

A Marxist perspective on the media–audience relationship makes the assumption that the media do things to people. The media are part of capitalism and its interests, and inevitably promote views of the social elite – the ruling class – and promote the dominant ideology which serves to maintain the power of this elite. Capitalist ideology believes in the production and purchase of goods, for the profit of the owners. (The culturalist variation on this theme would say that consumption has replaced mere purchase. Living through goods has become more important than talking about production.)

Indeed, the Marxist critics Theodor Adorno and Max Horkheimer of the so-called **Frankfurt School**, writing over half a century ago, saw the then developing mass media as, rather, **mass culture**. They talked about the *culture industries*, trying to emphasize how in their view the 'quality' of what they thought of as culture was being turned into nothing but big business, producing goods not art. It should be said that post-Marxism has gradually modified views of 'media' and 'audience' as being collective coherent entities – simply the mass media.

Media programmes or magazines would be examples of cultural goods. Goods may also be called commodities. Belief in materialism, in the importance of commodities, then affects the way that we value everything else in our lives. Even our social relationships could be valued in terms of these commodities. The process of defining social values and relationships in this way is called **commodification**. The energy which is behind capitalist media industries comes from the force of economic determinism – the behaviour of media institutions is determined by economic factors (see **political economy perspectives**; see also pp. 53–9). The economic base of society is founded on the labour of workers. The media are run in the interests of the wealthy and of wealth creation, which remains the privilege of the few. The media may be seen as part of the *superstructure* of society in a Marxist model, where ideology is at work. This ideology affects workers (base structure) and their understanding of the exchange value of their labour and of the goods that they produce.

Marxist ideas relate to the argument that control over the means of production and distribution of goods leads to control over the ideas which are (in the case of media) within those goods. It seems reasonable to argue that such control represents some sort of power and influence. In particular, Marxist criticism produces variations on the idea of *false consciousness*, in which social institutions generate false ideas about social relations. They produce ideas – through representations for instance – about status, power, class, which are made to seem true and valid when they are not. An unequal society is made to seem falsely and yet naturally acceptable.

The manufacture of this false consciousness is part of the invisible exercise of power – or **hegemony.** It springs from a **dominant ideology** – a particular and prevailing view of the world, of how it should be, of its values, of power relations. It maintains and conceals that ideology. Ideology is about a system of beliefs which benefit those who have social, economic and political power, but which work against the interests of those who do not have such power. For example there is a prevailing belief that everyone has the capacity to work, that they should work, that work is good. This belief drives government efforts to question the situations of people with a disability on incapacity benefits or single mothers on social benefits. It makes it hard for some employees to have stress-related illness and nervous breakdowns recognized as being valid or even true. It may invoke a related belief that somehow the retired and low income earners are less worthy citizens than those in full employment.

Critical thinking: post-Marxism

Antonio Gramsci
First one needs to note that Gramsci is actually a contemporary of the Frankfurt School. He spent the 1930s in a Fascist prison, until he died. There he produced *The Prison Notebooks*, which were not generally available until the 1970s. It is still the case that Gramsci's development of Marxist theory most plausibly explains the two problems outlined above. In his view hegemony (the invisible exercise of power), is achieved through coercion and consent. The state exercises coercion through various kinds of institution such as the army and the police – a certain kind of law and social order is enforced through the explicit use of material power. But consent is obtained through less obviously instrumental institutions, such as education or the media.

So we acquire a naturalized and dominant view of how things should be, but indirectly, through formal learning and through media consumption. Gramsci also broke with the earlier models by arguing that in fact there is a continuous struggle for the dominance of one set of ideas over another. It may not even be an equal struggle, but it is there. He also proposed that 'intellectuals' were especially important in the struggle because they generated the ideas which inform ideologies. The media are one site for that struggle.

It also follows that hegemony is there in our everyday lives because ideology (ideas) is ever present in our thoughts. One would have to accept that our perception of media material is filtered through a naturalized view of how the world is and should be. The way we think about social difference and inequality is bound up with hegemony and the ideas in our heads.

Louis Althusser

Althusser's ideas (1969, 1971) came from a revisiting of Marx's original work. He privileged what might be called the scientific arguments of Marx related to materialism, and developed concepts which also have relevance for ideas about media and society. Althusser wanted to explain how capitalist society managed to reproduce dominant institutions and relationships between them. In particular, he proposed that dominant **discourses** frame off how we think about the world. They make unthinkable other explanations about how society might work. Discourses are ideological. And as Grossberg et al. (1998) put it: 'Ideologies . . . set the boundaries on what we are able to understand as possible.'

Althusser put forward the notion of **interpellation** – the hailing of the media consumer in a particular way that draws them into discourses and ideology. He also offered the idea of the **ideological state apparatus** as an explanation of how institutions operate to promote the dominant ideology. Again, one may see the media as an example of such an apparatus (refer back to Gramsci here). Education and the family would be other examples. If the media reproduce certain kinds of social relations, and if media consumers see themselves in those relations, then they also see the ideology behind those relations as being acceptable, and they go along with it.

Fredric Jameson

Jameson would see himself as both a Marxist and as belonging to a postmodernist period. He would likely see my categorizing of critical positions as a suspect modernist project. He exemplifies the difficulty of assigning 'isms' to critical thinkers, and critical thinkers to discrete periods of history. Indeed he himself argues against the notion of homogenous periods of history, and for the persistence of modernism, saying that all cultural production is not postmodern (Jameson 1991). He has written widely on culture, literature, film and architecture.

In terms of Marxism, he admires the work of Adorno. Drawing on Ernest Mandel, he argues for a third stage of capitalism, and for the idea that postmodernism is actually an expression of this (Jameson 1998). This, it might be said, is a stage where commodification is reaching into every area of life and of experience so that (my example) even love and marriage have become the creatures of bridal exhibitions, pre-nuptial agreements, *Hello* magazine features, wedding managers, and so on.

Jameson would see as an important feature of postmodernism something to be described as the loss of individual style. Texts have become all about pastiche. Originality has been lost. A sense of history has been lost. One example of this we can see is the success of the Primark chain of stores, which specialize in making imitations of successful designs created by leading fashion houses – which often themselves plunder ideas from clothes styles of the past.

Jameson (1990) implicitly affirms the importance of history and of 'period' by talking up the influence of context: 'Marxism, like other cultural phenomena, varies according to the socio-economic context.' He goes along with the importance of the transformational effect of 'universal commodification' (Jameson 1992). But he is against dialectics and binary oppositions when they produce what he might call simplistic notions of high culture versus mass culture. Similarly, he would not be happy about that kind of Marxist suggestion which proposes that the only 'real social life' is political and ideological.

In his view, everything is mediated through culture, including for example, our understanding of race and its ideologies. The arrival of a third stage of capitalism is, he suggests, an inevitable consequence of how it works: 'capitalism systematically dissolves the fabric of all cohesive social groups . . . and thereby problematises aesthetic productions and linguistic productions which have their source in group life' (Jameson 1992).

In this case, the only authentic cultural production comes from those groups which have not been penetrated by the market. In terms of the reach of globalization (see Chapter 12), it is difficult to see where those groups are. But then Jameson himself says that the very idea of 'the popular' is now untenable because society and class have become so fragmented – which is another characteristic of postmodernism.

He makes links with postmodernism when he says that one may see it as 'the cultural dominant of the logic of late capitalism'. Postmodernism is, then, a logical development within a Marxist framework: 'Postmodernism is the consumption of sheer commodification as a process' (Jameson 1991). In terms of texts, postmodernism is about irony, nostalgia, the cannibalization of past styles, and the 'universal practice of pastiche'. But Jameson wants to take a totalizing view of postmodernism. For him it is about ways of thinking and living, it is about society and audiences, it is about economics and institutions – not just texts. He does not accept that postmodernism has simply effaced narrative, realism or historicity. In such respects, 'the modern' persists, and the idea of discrete historical periods is again denied.

9 New institutions, new media, new markets

New technology is also capable of using new media in new ways to generate new forms of income. For example, Ticketmaster® has become a pre-eminent site for booking and paying for sports events and concerts, without leaving home or picking up the phone.

New media have given rise to new companies, and have changed the business of old ones. Internet service providers (ISPs) such as Yahoo! and Hotmail are now familiar names. The Sony PlayStation® is a dominant product for a well-established company, but in a fairly new medium – the computer games business. Mobile phones have become such a tool and an icon of the so-called new communications era that in Slovakia they are being buried along with their deceased owners. The Swedish IT company Ericsson saw its fortunes transformed through its commitment to this new media business. DVD discs have changed the film business. Handheld communication devices (e.g. the Blackberry) have transformed the nature of work. Microsoft's dominance of operating systems and standard software which does the business for many homes and institutions has been so great that it has been heavily fined by the European Commission – to stop it tying the manufacturers of hardware to its products.

One needs to take account of the fact that the working life of media institutions has been revolutionized by new technology. One cannot just discuss what the audiences can see, e.g. computer-assisted technology in animation for movies, or live digicam images from news correspondents in war zones. It is the less glamorous and concealed effects of new technology which have changed institutions. Financial forecasting and product development use computer models. Global corporations can function only because of telecommunications. Programme design, even call centres, are outsourced to India. Report writing and financial analysis is outsourced to Germany, while the USA sleeps. Video conferencing enables management discussion and decisions on a global basis. New technology even enables new kinds of industrial espionage through which competitors may be outflanked.

Of course, 'new' does not necessarily mean 'good' or 'effective'. Garnham (2000) refers to the phenomenon of 'path dependency' when he points out that the cost–risk–investments features of new technology may mean that industries do not follow the best path of development. The persistence of the QWERTY keyboard and the MS-DOS operating program on personal computers (PCs) are infamous examples of this problem. But there is no area of media institutions or their work that is not affected by new technology – administration, production, product, distribution, retailing and exhibition. Most of it we rapidly take for granted. We do not notice the electronic retouching of magazine images. Neither do we know when commercials have been electronically edited, unless the graphics make it obvious. We take for granted live reports from half a world away. We do not think about downloading music or image files. We become blasé about the digital interactivity which enables us to choose which camera view we want with our sports programme.

McQuail (2000) defines four main categories of 'new media':

- Interpersonal communication media, such as email.
- Interactive play media, such as computer games.
- Information search media, such as Net search engines.
- Participatory media, such as Net chat rooms.

He also points to the changed experience of using such media, compared with the older product/consumption model:

- *Social presence:* a sense of contact with others when using the medium.
- *Autonomy:* a sense of control over the medium.
- *Interactivity:* with the source.
- *Privacy:* of experience when using the medium.
- *Playfulness:* in respect of the enjoyment gained through using the medium as opposed to merely taking things from it.

New technology has made the media–audience relationship more complex. In some respects its ability to expand the range of textual form while also concealing its own artifice makes the audience more subordinate to institutions. But in other ways, the multiplication of media formats and the greater engagement of audience with text in respect of new media forms, gives the audience more power over knowledge production.

There is a question of how far new technology produces continuity or change for media institutions. On the one hand, Russell Neuman (1991) inclines to an optimistic view about change. He proposes the following:

- New media become less expensive and so more available to the audience.
- New technology changes the audience view of geographical distance.

- New technology increases the speed of communication.
- New technology increases the volume of communication.
- There will be more and more channels of communication.
- There will be more interactive communication.
- There will be more control for users.
- There will be increasing interaction of previously separate forms of communication.

Webster (1999) also acknowledges the considerable weight of criticism which sees continuity and the power base of existing media institutions merely being extended into new media. Neo-Marxists like Schiller or political economists like Garnham would be in this continuity camp. Webster contrasts these views with those which argue for change and a new kind of society. In this case, one might be looking at the postmodernists and critics such as Baudrillard, at those who argue for a new information society and greater public access to that information.

Critical approaches: liberal pluralism

The liberal pluralist approach to understanding the media finds much favour among the media and politicians, but far less credence among academics. The essential pluralist position is that there are many producers, many products, many opinions and many audiences. You pays your money and you takes your choice – but the choice is all out there. Most academics would dispute this, and in varying degrees argue that the evidence points the other way.

Pluralism does not have a rigorous critical tradition. It is wrongly seen by some as merely a defence of capitalism. The classic liberal pluralist view was expounded in *Four Theories of the Press* (Siebert et al. 1956), in which the freedom of the Press was seen as underpinning the variety of positions offered by newspapers to citizens. Pluralist views are usually contrasted with the **determinist** views of the Left and of Marxists. The liberal pluralist position was developed into a further theory of social responsibility, in which the obligation of the press (media) to be responsible for its utterances and its effects was made explicit.

> The principal democratic role of the media, according to the liberal theory, is to act as a check on the state. The media should monitor the full range of state activity, and fearlessly expose abuses of official authority. Only by anchoring the media to the free market, in this view, is it possible to ensure the media's complete independence from government.
>
> (Curran 2000)

In this view, a responsible media fulfils a political function, balancing the power of the state and representing the interests of citizens. This is what might be called a 'watchdog' perspective. This position shows a degree of idealism which is not borne out by the pattern of development of the press in recent years. It could be argued that the proliferation of magazines or of radio channels does represent more choice for more audiences. But it might also be argued that we are ending up with only more of the same: more mags for lads, even more talk radio, yet more soaps on TV. New broadcast channels only write larger the existing genres – channels for sport, movies, news, children's programmes. It could be said that this is false choice, the illusion of plurality. And it is difficult to see how much if any of the pluralist material does in effect monitor state activity or expose abuses of authority.

Pluralism would take an optimistic view of the relationship between media and society, suggesting that the media serve us by providing a variety of information and entertainment which represents a variety of points of view. For pluralists, there is no great problem of media power and influence. Pluralism would not necessarily argue that the media are perfect and need no regulation. But it would generally propose that in serving society, the media also reflect that society (including sections of it) and its needs. We get what we want. This view would also be adopted by those in favour of 'the market', of a free market. It may include that glib argument which says that the market is self-regulating, to the benefit of the consumer.

You can evaluate the validity of this position by examining the nature of media material and the notion of choice. Look at patterns of ownership, mechanisms of control, and their implications, and decide how and whether or not choice can be offered.

Positively, you would have to take account of the existence of magazines for ethnic minorities such as *The Voice*; of the fact that someone like John Sayles can still get funding for alternative, rather uncommercial films in the USA.

Alternatively, you would have to reflect on how plurality of opinion has its limits – in respect of editorial control in broadcasting for example – in respect of what the editor and owners want in the case of newspapers and magazines. There is very little serious critical reflection on the media within the media. There are very limited rights of access by the audience to the media. There are huge financial – and some legal – barriers to starting up a magazine or a radio station. Pluralism as proposed by those running or supporting the media seems to work from a position of assuming that it is naturally right and requiring others to prove their positions, rather than having to prove its own.

There is often an assumption that pluralism and democracy go hand in hand. Pluralism becomes part of a defence of public service broadcasting. This view is typified by the remarks of Green (1995):

> It is vital for a modern liberal democracy that the great majority of citizens have access to a wide range of voices and opinions.

But what is more interesting are Green's concluding remarks which see pluralism as a natural and desirable model for the media, but one which is not guaranteed a life:

> there is no guarantee that the immense power to communicate given to societies and individuals by the digital revolution will lead to greater plurality of expression. The need for Governments to legislate and regulate to protect pluralism will remain.
>
> (Green 1995)

10 The public service debate

When the BBC was established in 1927 it was seen as the only possible broadcaster. Broadcasting was conceived of as a unified *public service*. This stopped being the case in 1954 when ITV started, and commercial imperatives arrived. The single public service model was broken, and the notion of how public service may be defined was necessarily called into question. The unique funding arrangements for the BBC became questionable once there was another channel funded a different way. The financial issue here becomes a question about why all of the public should pay for some of the service when they do not all watch or listen to the BBC. In practical terms the legal underpinnings of the British broadcasting systems insist that a range of those who comprise the public should be offered a range of material. Regional broadcasting, broadcasting for minority interests, broadcasting for children, are all required of broadcasters by Ofcom. So even ITV plc has a public broadcasting remit in return for getting its licence.

Hesmondhalgh (2002) describes public service broadcasting (PSB) systems as being characterized by:

- public accountability
- an element at least of public finance
- regulation of content
- a universal service
- an audience which is addressed as citizens rather than as consumers.

The position of the BBC as an exemplar for independent-minded PSB was made worse in the 1980s when the Conservative government pushed it further into commercial practices, confirming that it should compete in the marketplace for audience figures. In the early days of ITV, BBC's viewing share had collapsed in the face of the populist and genre attractions of the commercial channel, so it had already moved into competitive commercial behaviour to justify its licence fee to Parliament. But things got worse in the 1980s when licence fee rises were held down and when Channel 4 was created. Just as the BBC was not free in practice to offer any 'alternative' material it pleased, so also Channel 4 did not really have to operate in a free market competitive commercial climate. Indeed it was required to serve minority interests – like BBC2. But it was ensured funding because the government creamed this off the ITV1 Channel 3 profits (until 1991).

Broadcasting regulation, described above, means that no broadcaster ever operates in an entirely free climate. It means that some channels are positioned by their licences as being more alternative than others. It means that some element of public service is legislated into the whole system. The more channels that are licensed (including radio) to serve more specific (niche) audiences, the more that any distinction between the BBC as a clear model for wide-ranging public service, and the commercial channels as a model for populist mainstream provision, has been fudged. It has already been questioned as to whether the BBC, in ideological terms, was ever a representative and independent institution as it has been run by establishment figures and had institutionalized values that feed conservative notions of good taste and cultural norms. In its history one can point to the satirical goosing of politicians through programmes such as *That Was The Week That Was* (1963), under the liberal regime of director general Hugh Carleton Greene. Over the years there have been sterling examples of challenging drama, such as *Boys from the Black Stuff* (1982), which said a lot about the effects of government policies on the working class. But then its mainstream tendencies were reinforced by the market culture referred to above, and enacted under the managerialist regime of director general John Birt in the 1990s. To be fair to the BBC (and Birt) there are ideological contradictions at the heart of the debate about PSB, even in the pronouncements of liberal politicians and PSB minded commentators. With deregulation these people wanted a risk-taking, community-serving, creative public service to emerge from a union with market forces. They wanted public service broadcasting to be all things to all people – popular and profitable and yet serving minorities at the same time. The BBC has been damned by some for its commercial partnership with the American Flextech (UK Gold) and with Discovery Channel, and for the considerable profits that it has made from BBC Worldwide. Yet the same people who do not want the BBC to play commercial games with public money because it is in 'public service' are also reluctant to give it money if it loses audience share (perhaps through taking uncommercial risks) and so is not seen to be serving all of 'the public'.

The licence fee itself was renewed in 2006 only after much debate, and was not increased to the level asked for by the BBC, which is making cuts in its provision. The government is keeping its commercial options open with reference to the possibility of BBC funding moving to a kind of commercial subscription system.

It is true that degrees of public service can be enforced through regulation. Such regulation (policed by Ofcom) enforces a degree of service to minorities and communities for all broadcasters; there is the impact of licences awarded to local commercial and BBC radio; these channels do give some voice to local communities and to local issues; they provide local information and discuss some local problems, while also imitating popular genres and models for talk radio. Nationally, Channel 4 has walked a PSB and commercial tightrope quite successfully, not only providing some populist material but also screening some challenging film seasons and documentaries which address minority issues.

This takes one back to the contradictions of public policy, in which deregulation of broadcasting has driven the Broadcasting Acts of 1991 and 1997 in order to achieve more competition. At the same time recognition that free markets do not actually produce freedom of choice has encouraged government to cling on to kinds of regulation. Negrine (1994) discusses this contradiction, partly with reference to the pronouncements of the Peacock Committee on broadcasting (1985): 'regulatory requirements . . . produce not a free market, but one regulated to allow for freedom, albeit a freedom where market forces dominate'.

The structure of media institutions, and the climate within which they operate, can be regulated by government to satisfy some model of what public service entails. But there is no 'natural' base model of PSB offered by commercial broadcasters. Neither is the BBC a naturally dominant model. It is possible to use political mechanisms to allow or disallow whatever kind of institutional model we want. What is difficult to do is to determine the kind of service preferred and for what kind of public. Broadcasting to serve the various communities of people with disabilities, or immigrant communities, or those who want to question government policy, becomes a political issue. There is no coherent 'public' out there, though there may be larger and smaller communities. But it goes against the grain of dominant political and broadcasting visions to have to accept this and do something about it. In a sense the dominant ideology cannot cope with the vision of a diverse public. Nor can it take on the financial consequences of having to find the money to pay for that public's service. In particular, it is not going to pay for a public voice given to views that might undermine this dominance. Equally, it is not reasonable to argue that PSB is only, or even mainly, about giving a voice to radical and oppositional politics.

The public service debate is not confined to Britain. The conduct and effects of media policies across Europe are a cause for concern to broadcasters and citizens who fear for the erosion of a genuine choice of material and of ideas. These fears are focused on the evident expansion of private ownership and its consequences in market terms for broadcasting. France and Italy have both seen formerly central national PSB TV channels turned into commercial broadcasters, with the effect that their output has become trivialized and generalized, and fails to answer the needs of minorities.

Concerns about protecting media so that their output reflects a sense of national identity and serves a real range of audiences takes us back to the beginning of this chapter and to questions about genuine choice for audiences, and about how far we should allow media institutions free rein in a commodified marketplace.

▌11 Discussion extract

The first interest (of media owners) is in maximising the profits, revenues, market share, share price, and so on of their own particular company. . . . In this first respect, companies obviously pursue their own interests. Aiming for profit maximisation, all businesses will try to ensure that expenditure on staff pay and other costs is well below the level of revenues generated. Within this system, some companies will offer higher levels of pay and provide better conditions than others. Some industries will have better working conditions than others. As we have seen, there are specific conditions surrounding the business of cultural production, whereby creative workers have been given greater creative autonomy than is the case in other sectors. However, exploitation is inevitable: the system of capitalist accumulation depends on it. As Miège (1989) pointed out, cultural industry companies subsidise costs by means of pools of reservoir labour and the use of casualised cultural work. Other strategies include moving work overseas to countries where levels of pay are much lower (as is the case for most animation production – see Lent, 1998).

The second type of interest that owners and executives are likely to pursue is that of companies like their own. Obviously, such companies compete with each other, except when they are involved in cartel arrangements, usually forbidden by law. Even within a system of mutual competition, though, companies will affiliate to form trade bodies, lobbying groups and alliances. There is a deeply rooted tendency in advanced capitalism for oligopolies of large companies to form in nearly all industries. These oligopolies are particularly effective at forming lobbying groups, campaigning against what they see as obtrusive government legislation and regulation – much of it, in fact, intended to protect workers and consumers. Such corporate lobbying has been an important feature of cultural policymaking. Oligopolies also come to embody a set of conventions for understanding how best to organise business. Non-profit enterprises and smaller commercial companies, including those aiming at lower profit margins and innovative working practices, will tend to be excluded or marginalised. They may even come to appear naïve or incompetent because of the greater wealth and prominence of companies in the oligopoly.

That companies pursue the interests of owners and executives in these two ways seems to me to be undeniable. The controversies surrounding such a system of self-interested production are mainly ones regarding the wider system of capitalism as whole – principally, whether or not the advantages (such as dynamic growth and the production of greater amounts of total wealth) of economic systems based on such actions outweigh the disadvantages (systematic underpaying of most workers, oligopoly, massive inequality, social fragmentation). Here, of course, questions about business ownership and structure overlap with questions raised above about the role of the cultural industries in society. Examination of actual businesses can more clearly locate agency – that is, who is making things change and how.

There is, however, a third type of potential interest that owners and executives might pursue. Other things being equal, all businesses tend to want conditions in which businesses as a whole can thrive: political and economic stability and lively demand. This means the businesses will, for example, make huge donations to political candidates they think are likely to achieve these general business environment goals. They will oppose reform and the struggle for greater equality if they perceive that such developments might threaten their business interests.

Hesmondhalgh, D. (2005) *The Cultural Industries*, 2nd edn. London: Sage.

1   Define the terms oligopoly and cartel.

2   Give examples of the kinds of trade bodies and campaigns referred to.

3   Why might companies want to maximize profits, revenues and market share?

4   In what respects are the cultural industries different from other industries?

5   What are examples of government regulation designed to protect workers in cultural industries?

6   How might the Confederation of British Industries respond to the three charges made in this extract?

12 Further reading

Cottle, S. (ed.) (2003) *Media Organisation and Production*. London: Sage.

Curran, J. (2002) *Media and Power*. London: Routledge.

Curran, J. and Seaton, J. (1997) *Power Without Responsibility: The Press and Broadcasting in Britain*, 5th edn. London: Routledge.

Doyle, G. (2002) *Understanding Media Economics*. London: Sage.

Hesmondhalgh, D. (2005) *The Cultural Industries*, 2nd edn. London: Sage.

Stokes, J. and Reading, A. (1999) *The Media in Britain: Current Debates and Developments*. London: Macmillan.

Tumber, H. (ed.) (2000) *Media Power, Professionals and Policies*. London: Routledge.

3

Audiences and effects

Defining audiences and exploring their relationships with texts

audiences are complex, elusive, shifting social formations
Gillespie, M. (ed.) (2005) *Media Audiences*. Maidenhead: Open University Press.

1 Introduction

When one conceptualizes the process of media influence – often discussed in the context of audience studies – there is the danger of following a **transmission model** for media. This model sees the media as having unqualified effects on the audience. It assumes a sequence in which institutions generate texts, texts generate meanings, and meanings affect audiences.

Of course it would be nonsense to deny that institutions do produce texts, and that they exert a degree of power in this respect. Institutions control access to the media. They define the terms on which audiences may participate – talk-back programmes or game shows. It is also the case that once members of the public become part of a media text, they are in some way transformed: the beginning at least of a process of manufacturing celebrity.

But in terms of the relationship between the media in general and the audience as members of a society, I would like to advance a **dynamic process model**, the parts of which stand in a more equal relationship with one another. This is a model in which the media industries are simultaneously institutions of society, proposers of information to society, and drawers of material from society. This is a relationship in which, as manufacturers of representations, the media variously and simultaneously remake versions of society, but also are themselves shaped by forces within that society.

Rather than choose between critical positions summarized in terms of 'the media do things to people' or 'people do things with the media', I want to propose that both views are true. You will remember that I have already suggested that while it may be true that institutions produce texts within which certain devices prefer certain kinds of understanding, it is also true that the audience reads the text. The text has the potential for meaning, and perhaps the potential for selective and partial meanings. But this potential is not realized until some process of cognition in the mind of the audience/reader actually 'makes sense' of that text.

I also want to remind you that behind this debate about the relationship between three core concepts is the further debate about the general relationship between media and society. In this case and in connection with ideas about influence, one is referring back to determinist and pluralist positions. I would remind you of issues around these positions.

- Do the media determine the nature of that relationship, and is the operation of the media itself determined by dominant forces such as those of economics?
- Or are the media so plural in their institutions and texts that no such determining influence is possible?
- Does this plurality mean that the relationship is one in which the audience can make choices not only about what it consumes, but also about the meaning it makes from this consumption?

There is a dominant critical tradition within the media–audience debates that assumes an effect on those audiences. But there is also a newer tradition – ethnographic survey and reception analysis – which sidesteps this to examine the relationship between media and audience. I would point out that the nature of relationships affects both elements, so one cannot simply hit the effects debate out of court. But it is true that, even having ideology within one's terms of reference, looking at how things happen, rather than assigning a determining power to the media producer alone, seems to offer a less assumptive, more openly enquiring approach to audience study.

Gillespie (2005: 2) sees three main areas in which issues around which the relationship between audience and media may be raised:

- the power of media relative to the power of audience
- the part played by media in shaping knowledge, values and beliefs
- ways in which changes in media technologies are changing the experience of the audience, perhaps relating to ways in which audiences change over time.

Brooker and Jermyn (2003) consider phases in the development of audience studies, falling very roughly into the sequence of decades, from the 1960s to the 1990s:

- a concern with effects and uses and gratifications theory in particular
- a view of the audience as victim, especially with the notion of **moral panics**
- belief in the active audience and its resistance to media influence
- more specific areas of interest: spectatorship, fans and cults, female audiences, ethnicity.

▌2 Major questions

So major questions about audience in the context of media study which one needs to address are to do with who it is exactly that we are talking about when we use the term 'audience', and with how that audience stands in relation to both media texts and the producers of texts.

1 How do we understand the term 'audience', given the difference between the actuality of the reader as an individual, and the notion of audiences as coherent groups?

2 How should we understand audiences in terms of the marketplace?

3 How may audiences be understood as being 'active' in their engagement with texts, and how far does any such activity give audiences power over the production of meaning?

4   How may we understand the process of audiences reading texts?

5   In respect of visual media, how should we understand the act of looking, in relation to representation, and especially with regard to gender?

6   What do we mean by audience pleasure in the text? In what respects might one validate such pleasures, and in what ways may they be an expression of the producers' hold over the audience?

7   In what ways can we see the audience as having access to a public sphere created by the media, in which debates take place?

8   What are the dominant views of the process of media influence on the audience? What factors modify such views?

9   What evidence is there for various kinds of media effect on the audience? What are the problems with researching such effects?

10   How may we recognize gender differences in audience relationships with given media texts?

3 Concepts of audiences

The term 'audience' is problematic. There are assumptions made about it which do not stand up to examination. For example, the idea of audience as a collection of people experiencing a performance may be true for live theatre, but is not true for magazine readers. There is not even a collection of people in one place at one time. The idea of mass audience is hardly valid, only on a relative scale of numbers. The significance of any audience may lie in its composition as much as in its numbers. The scale may run from tens of thousands to millions. I am not saying that media audiences are insignificant for their size. It is difficult not to assume some process or degree of influence in this case. But it is also difficult to define or prove this influence. Certainly the conditions under which Marxist critiques of mass audience and mass culture were formed, no longer exist. Since the 1950s the number of media and the range of media texts has increased immeasurably. This has not only expanded the numbers of the audience, but also fragmented it. We should not ignore the 15 million or so viewers for peak-time popular TV programmes, but we should also understand that one has moved from the dominance of broadcasting to more **narrowcasting**. In the 1940s, mass media were dominantly the press, cinema and radio, with the music industry rapidly expanding in size. There is no longer this coherence and focus, not least if one considers what new technologies have done to expanding the range of media. The very idea of audience in relation to the Internet or to multifunctional mobile phones is problematic, though not totally invalid. Just as film is no longer all about movie theatres, so music is no longer all about sales of discs. Just as film is no longer dominated by a mass audience attending by the week, so music is no longer about a few dominant genres and mass purchase in specialist stores. This further undermines the notion of audience as a coherent term. Now there are both large and small audiences, general and specialized audiences. There are different inflections on the term audience which imply different views of audience behaviour, or of audience function in relation to media and society: consumer, user, receiver, participant, social being, cultural being, media being. To talk about the 'fan' takes one into the cultural realm of consumption and pleasure. Talking about 'the citizen' implies something about politics and media use.

It is also arguable that the social and cultural coherence of audiences has changed greatly since the 1950s. The demarcation between a working class marked by lack of mobility and dependence on employment in manufacturing, and a middle class with a markedly greater income no longer holds true. Class still exists, but in different terms. And anyway the media industries are interested only in spending power. Now, a school-age person can save up to spend £250 on PlayStation® 3. In the 1950s, they would save to spend the price of a bag of sweets or a cinema ticket – very possibly to see the same film that their parents would go out to see. Now the movie-going audience is fragmented into categories of consumption – youth, family, 'adult', art-cinema goers. For the industries these are niche markets. For the critic this relates to the arrival of 'narrowcasting' – specialist magazines, dedicated channels. Assumptions that the audience is culturally homogeneous no longer hold true.

The more closely one examines the characteristics of those who watch a programme or who read a newspaper, the more differentiated the audience members become. This increasing differentiation also increases the variables in any assessment of effects and influence. The more variables, the less easy it is to say that a given text is likely to affect its audience in a distinctive manner.

But the 'opposite problem' is that, in terms of reception studies, while looking at very specific audiences may reveal the 'truth' of individual response, it undermines the possibility of generalization about influence. This is the disadvantage of detailed ethnographic surveys. 'Much audience theory remains over-concerned with the microscopic worldview of socially dispersed viewers, readers and listener' (Stevenson 2002).

One needs to juggle the quantitative evidence of research into **macro**-audience preferences with the more qualitative evidence of **micro**-audience research into detailed pleasures, responses and behaviours. Knowing how a selected group of women enjoy some soap operas does not prove that women in general are influenced by most soaps. Equally, knowing the viewing figures by age and gender for given soaps says little about the meanings which specific groups of female viewers may construct into their lives.

'Audience' is also complicated by having to allow for, in the case of television, the presence of both primary and secondary audiences. The former would be the studio audience for the chat show, the fans at the outside broadcast of a rock concert, the crowd on screen at a football match; the latter will be the audience at home. The experience of the programme as event is clearly different for each of the primary and secondary audiences. So also the meanings are different. 'Audience' changes according to the media example given and to the analytic approach used in each case. Discussion of 'fan talk' produces an audience with qualitative dimensions. Description of audience through television ratings produces a quantified audience.

It is arguable that audiences have become more participative in their relationship with the media. There is the obvious example of reality television, where the viewer becomes the performer, where viewers may vote such performers out of a given show. There are less obvious examples such as the effects of Web fan sites on media texts. A romantic relationship in the TV show *Grey's Anatomy* was written out of the series after fans made it clear they hated it. The TV show *Heroes* has adjusted to fan feedback: 'you can't completely ignore your audience or they'll stop watching' (*Guardian* 17 November 2008).

Figure 3.1 Family Viewing, As Seen by Viacom

- What point is made by this ad about the 'new' family viewing experience?
- How many intertextual references in the image can you pick up?

4 The commodified audience

> the audience is continuously segmented and differentiated in a search for the qualities sought by particular marketers.
>
> (Ross and Nightingale 2003)

Audiences are defined as commodities by the media because those industries want to objectify their natures and their existence. They want to quantify the idea of audience.

The audience may be fragmented into categories by interest, e.g. for video, sport, 'keep fit', drama, porn. The media industries have a vested interest in validating the idea of audience as a meaningful and coherent term. If they cannot define their audiences in terms which validate investment by backers and expenditure by advertisers, then they do not have a business.

Audiences are measured for purely functional reasons, as Ross and Nightingale (2003) point out:

- to determine programming and pricing decisions
- to plan and evaluate media campaigns
- to schedule and evaluate programme performance
- to help government, the media and financial planners form broadcasting policy, award licences, measure the commercial value of companies.

Audiences are defined and delivered in terms of number – reader figures, circulation figures, box-office figures, viewing figures and so on. These numbers are worth money, not least for those media where their output is sold by the unit (for example, magazines, CDs). Quantity analysis may be refined by such factors as region of sale or time of viewing. It may be further defined as in the case of television where television ratings measure the numbers of the target audience for the programme who are watching at the time of broadcast. This is as distinct from the total audience, and may include features such as gender and occupation.

In such terms the audience itself becomes a commodity to be bought and sold. Indeed it may be argued that the media manufacture audiences: the media do not discover them. These audiences have a value in the marketplace of rate cards, circulation managers and media brokers. The success of the media producer is measured in terms of 'audience as goods' as much as on the basis of any critical estimation.

For the media producer, audiences may be defined as 'audience profile', which is in turn defined by features such as age, gender and disposable income. What matters is the producers' ability to target the audience and its purchasing power. Audiences may also be defined in terms of the product type which they prefer, which in turn relates to their interests. This is why marketing devices such as the National Households Survey are used, to try to define such interests. This is a generic audience – the readers of computer magazines or of romantic fiction. More specifically, one could define audiences by the particular product consumed: the audience for the *Washington Evening Post* or for *Harpers* or for the *David Letterman Show*. Similarly, broadcast channels seek to identify and attract their 'type' of audience. The more specific the material broadcast, the more specific the audience identity is – from Discovery Channel to local radio.

And even where qualitative elements appear in descriptions of audiences by the media, it is always an adjunct to quantity. Lifestyle or psychographic descriptions of audiences' character and social behaviour is ultimately linked to factors such as disposable income, purchasing habits and the numbers in the group so defined. The media want to be able to categorize people, for commercial reasons. This does not mean to say that these categories are valid.

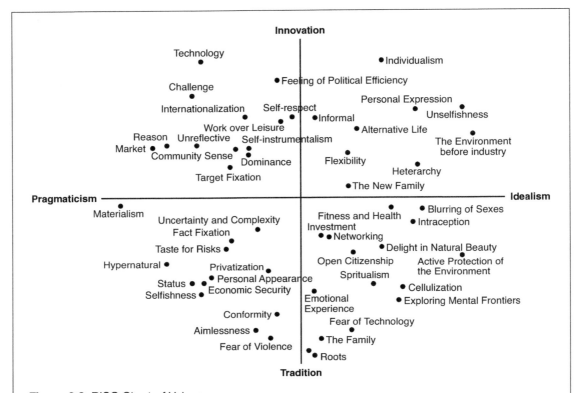

Figure 3.2 RISC Chart of Values
Reproduced by permission of SAGE Publications, London, Los Angeles, New Delhi and Singapore, from Pertti Alasuutari (ed.) (1999) *Rethinking the Media Audience*, London: Sage, copyright © Kim Christian Schrøder, 1999, p. 57.
Research into Social Change attempts to segment people as audience or consumers, according to their preferred life values. Research via interviews and questionnaires may deal with groups as small as a single family. These groups can be placed on the chart and described in terms of the main values they espouse, and in terms of the four key qualities which make up the axes of the chart. The numbers of groups from an area and their placing helps identify a kind of consumer in that target area.
(Reprinted by permission of Sage Publications Ltd from Kim Christian Schrøder (1999) The Best of Both Worlds? Media Audience Research between Rival Paradigms, in P. Alasuutari (ed.) *Rethinking the Media Audience*. London: Sage.

And, of course, all this commodification rides on the back of the related industry of market research. Generally speaking media industries subcontract their audience investigation, description and measurement to others who then also have a vested interest in the commodification of audience and the validity of their findings. In Britain there is the Broad-casters' Audience Research Board or the National Readership Survey.

This commodified audience may be seen as the audience which is 'spoken at' by the institution and through the text. It is in effect addressed as an object, as constructed groups, within the terms of reference of the market. This is the target audience as conceived by the producers, the audience of the advertisers' world. It is not the more complex audience of a real world, as it lives, and as it is studied through critical audience approaches to the media.

It may also be seen as the 'audience in the text'. In this case one has to understand how media texts find ways of putting into themselves the kind of audience at which they are aimed. Generally, one only has to ask 'what is it about the text that causes one to believe that it is aimed at a particular audience, and why?' to identify how that audience is written into that text.

Part of the writing of the audience into the text may be in the representation of the audience as an ideal type within that text. So TV ads for cars aimed at women include a kind of female whom the target audience might like to be – independent, romantic, assertive. A representation is not a reflection but an idealization, a stereotype. It is an idea about the audience which both producer and viewer would like to be true.

There are at least two problems with trying to achieve objectivity and particularity when trying to specify the audience, in the cause of doing business. First, if audiences have a place in a social world, then as communities they have the complexity and variability present in any such group. Second, they are not necessarily communities tied to texts, but are as likely to be committed to a medium. Advertisers struggle to engage with young audiences that surf channels, visit live performances and live through the Net – rather than follow a given programme series, or buy a given magazine regularly.

5 The active audience

This is the audience conceived in terms of how it deals with the media. This is about taking a perspective which starts from the view of the audience, not the view of the institution. It is about how the audience engages with the text. The notion of activity draws attention to the part of the audience in making choices, making sense of the text. It allows for the audience being a producer of meanings. The activity referred to is both about the intellectual work of the audience and about kinds of physical reaction around the text.

For example, in terms of context, audiences do not passively engage with media. They use radio as an adjunct to activities such as driving a car or household work. It has been shown that audiences engage in all sorts of activities while 'watching' television – from playing a musical instrument, to forms of housework. Newspapers and magazines may encourage active engagement with quizzes or crosswords, which have nothing to do with news or reading articles.

It is also true to say that audiences can be active in making choices (channel hopping) and in using technology (selectively recording programmes). Indeed, one form of 'resistance' which audiences can now practise against TV is to buy and use various hard-disk recording devices. These can, for instance, screen out advertisements: not good news for the US networks and for British ITV, both of which are slowly but steadily losing audiences and advertising revenue.

The very act of reading requires a process of cognition – constructive cerebral activity to make sense of the text. Of course this kind of activity may vary in its nature and in its intensity, from emotional response, to analysis and reflection. Sonia Livingstone (1990) warns against idealizing the active reader, and might refer to the 'dangers' of readerly genre texts when she says that 'Activity may refer to . . . the more mindless process of fitting the text into familiar frameworks or habits.'

Postmodernist and audience-centred critiques see the audience as taking charge of the production of meaning and as taking their pleasures from the text. In this respect, they argue against the audience as an unresisting victim of the text. Rather, the audience may resist the underlying commercial intentions of the producer. This again emphasizes the importance of the emotional response to material. In this case one might argue that arousal of emotions may mean that the audience is not disposed to move on to make rational and objective decisions, in relation to arguments about influence. The programme is fun, and is forgotten. Others may argue that emotional pleasures make the audience receptive to views and attitudes implied through the text and its representations.

This critical perspective which allows the audience autonomy in the production of meaning is best exemplified by John Fiske (1987) in *Television Culture*, in which he makes much of the notion of the 'producerly text'. He argues that television texts 'delegate the production of meaning to the viewer–producer'. But against this critical swing to endorsing the power of the audience in the 1980s one must set the evidence of textual analysis which demonstrates that not all TV material is that malleable in terms of meaning. Programmes are not necessarily 'open texts', though some may be more open than others. As Morley (1996b) argues, 'the power of the viewer to reinterpret meanings is hardly equivalent to the discursive power of centralised media institutions to construct the texts which the viewer then interprets'. I have already suggested that one should see the audience more as a kind of collaborator in making meanings. It is not possible to demonstrate that audiences resist all the effects potential of media texts.

Wayne (1994) is also against an uncritical view of audience power:

> Problems within the mass culture tradition are more than balanced by the blind spots of popular traditions which come through strongly in audience studies. Here, there has been a tendency to conceive the popular as a realm of cultural self-making where 'the people' reconstruct their identities and their sense of place in the world at will. Thus questions of power and ideology are suppressed by methods which celebrate audience creativity and/or dissolve the text as an object with any effective-ness.

Uses and gratifications

One fairly traditional perspective on the audience as a user of text (which also is part of the effects debate) is described as the uses and gratifications approach. In this case it has been assumed that people are motivated by kinds of 'need' in their engagement with the text, as with their engagement with others in social interactions. I will summarize these as follows:

- informational needs
- personal needs, such as maintenance of identity
- social needs, not least for forms of interaction
- entertainment needs, including the need for kinds of diversion.

In such cases one might say that a given audience member will take from a text what it says about a personal issue of moral principle, or how it describes social behaviours that are of interest to that individual. The audience is actively selecting aspects of the text for its own use: it is using that material actively to work through interests and concerns. This approach, although it includes the idea of the collective needs of an audience, also tends to emphasize the audience as an individual. This again runs counter to an institutional conception of audiences as coherent, consuming groups.

Although this approach appeals to those critical views which favour at least some autonomy and activity on the part of the audience, commentators such as Ross and Nightingale (2003) express scepticism:

> An undoubted drawback in the 'Uses and Gratifications' approach was the assumption that mass communication is no more than need gratification, and that media effects are demonstrated by people's ability to indicate that their needs have been gratified.

Ethnography – reception studies

The notion of the active audience relates to a tradition of audience-centred media studies, which has, since the 1980s at least, tried to talk up the importance of the interaction of specific audience members with specific texts. We are back to a struggle over the ownership of the power to produce meanings. **Ethnographic** research in particular has been used as a way of addressing the qualitative nature of 'audience'. It investigates reception in its context and as a social activity. This approach may include conversational engagement with respondents rather than questionnaires; Ang (1991) says, 'the ethnographer ... conceptualises media audience-hood as lived experience'.

Again, it is Ross and Nightingale (2003) who comment on the importance of context within this approach – of seeing the act of being an audience as a whole experience, not just being there in some kind media limbo: 'ethnographic studies attempt to situate media consumption within the wider context of personal, social and domestic life'.

Context

This notion of context is important to contemporary audience studies. It can have many facets, referring to place, time, culture, social practices, as well as to what is immediately around a given text. For example, there will be a whole newspaper surrounding one article. The paper may be read on a bus or in a library reading room. It may be part of habitual breakfast rituals. All these kinds of context will affect how the audience member reads, what they may select, how they may concentrate, and of course what sense they make of the given article. Audience can be an abstract concept. But audiences are people, and people live their lives (and consume media) in a variety of ways, in a variety of surroundings.

6 The reading audience

This is the audience in a state of engagement with the text. This conception of audience is about it being engaged in an activity. But audiences as readers are not necessarily understood to be entirely in control of the process of the production of meaning.

Indeed, one approach used by Morley (1989), drawing from Hall (1980) and before that from Parkin's (1972) ideas about three 'meaning systems', describes the audience in terms of three different relationships with the text. In each case the audience has more or less autonomy in terms of the sense they make of the material.

- The **preferred reading** is about that meaning which is preferred by the producer, inscribed in the text, and likely to be taken from the text by the reader because the use of various conventions and devices close down other ways of understanding it.
- The **alternative reading** is one that produces meanings which were not intended by the producer but which do not seriously challenge the dominant meaning.
- The **oppositional reading** is one which does so challenge that dominance, and implies a degree of intellectual autonomy in the reader. This kind of analysis also tends to deal in ideology, so that dominant meanings are also about the dominant ideology.

Taking the popular press coverage of the death of Princess Margaret in Britain in 2002 as an example, one would say that the preferred reading of this event was in terms of an expected but tragic event involving a great public figure. Alternatively, it might have been read as the regrettable passing of a life, but of little relevance to the lives of most British citizens. Oppositionally, a reader might have understood it to be a matter of relief that the death of an old-guard member of an anti-democratic institution (the monarchy) made it a little more likely that the abolition of that institution could take place.

The question remains, to what extent is the audience free to resist preferred readings? The answer seems to have a lot to do with the cultural background of the audience member, and with their particular beliefs, attitudes and values within that cultural nexus. Liebes and Katz (1993) have demonstrated that a text may be understood in different ways by those coming to it with different sets of values and priorities.

Silverstone (1994) comments on their work: 'results suggested that cultural and ethnic identity do provide a significant determinant of different relationships to the texts, differences which are an expression of those groups culturally and politically in the wider society'. However, he also disputes that differences of understanding, of moral judgement for example, necessarily mean that the 'ideological force' of the text is blocked. 'Viewers can be critical but still accept the basic, dominant or structural meanings offered by the text.' Yet again the jury stays out on attempts to demonstrate media influence, though the importance of conditioning factors remains pretty clear.

In the initial flush of a structuralist period of media criticism, Hall (1980) conceptualized 'audience as reader' as decoders of material. We have to recognize the codes and conventions within a text in order to make sense of the text. He was interested in the relationship between producers and audience in terms of the amount of common ground there was between them (or not). They would share for example knowledge of the codes of news. They would share the ideological background to that news. They would even share understanding of the technologies which produce that news – the use of camera or of satellite links. What concerned him was the extent to which that sharing might close down the possible meaning of a text, the extent to which there was a closed circle of encoding and decoding. Again, this concern was ideological in basis. If drama or news encodes crime as a problem with an inflection of race, then what chance is there for the audience to decode crime as perhaps a problem of selective representation, or perhaps as a problem of how police deal with crime?

At the same time as attention was turning from the text alone to the audience, and to what was entailed in reading, there was also recognition of the polysemic nature of visual texts in particular. So again, there was a conceptual struggle between the notion of the text closing down meanings for the reader, and the ambiguities of texts (some more than others) which offer more opportunities for different readers to open up different meanings. By the same token, whatever influence is proposed becomes less certain, less specific, more problematic.

The notion of the 'audience as reader' does at least get rid of early critical notions of audiences as some kind of receptacle into which ideas might be poured by the media. But then, even when one understands that audiences do have some part to play in the production of meaning, still there is the question of how that part is conceptualized. Critical views still tend to fall into the model of audience as either victim or as hero. What we need to remember is that, if texts cannot be neutral – and some may be less neutral than others – so too audiences as readers bring their own experiential and ideological baggage to that process of reading. In saying this, I am not suggesting that there is some kind of absolutely truthful reading out there of the film or magazine. But I am drawing attention to the fact that readers may be 'influenced' by factors other than devices in the text, or their experience of the media in general.

The variability of audience experience and attitudes has been used in what Curran (1996) has called 'New Revisionism', which argues that the media do not influence the audience in any consistent or meaningful way. He cites research by Meyer (1976) as typifying findings about the variability of response to the media: 'different types of children, bringing different beliefs, attitudes and values to the viewing of the show as a result of different socialisation processes, are affected in different ways'. Such evidence has been used to talk down media influence and to talk up the importance of the text and of the 'audience as reader' (not as victim). This approach is about reception analysis, not analysis of influence as such. This kind of analysis has been used to emphasize the power of reading, the possibility of making oppositional readings. It argues for ways in which the reader reuses media materials to affirm cultural identity, to resist subordination to that same material.

However, this kind of use and its immediate context (in micro-studies of audience) is also open to the criticism that it fails to take account of a larger industrial and political context to 'use'. Murdock and Golding (2000) criticize the 'romantic celebration of subversive consumption' (see also section 8 on Taking pleasure).

7 Gazing and looking

The terms gazing and looking are relevant to the nature of the audience's engagement with visual texts. In the first place, some of that engagement may be understood within the context of narrative theory. Ideas about spectator positioning relate not only to the audience to the 'narrative as an idea of story' but also to events depicted on the screen. In this respect positioning is about camera placement, and, therefore, where the spectator is placed spatially in relation to the action. That placement also influences the viewer's understanding to the story. So if one's view of a scene is via a camera placed half behind some object, then one is positioned as some kind of spy. If the subject of that scene is some kind of private moment or romantic encounter, then the spectator is positioned as a voyeur. Indeed, the spectator becomes subjectively involved in that thing called 'the story'. The same thing applies if those conventions of camera and editing are used which cause the viewer to adopt the gaze of, and understanding of, one of the characters in the story (subjective camera). Usually the camera/spectator position is something more neutral, in which one is, as it were, just looking in on the scene, at the characters. This is objective camera or third-person narrative. This kind of spectator position may also be seen in still images. Again, the camera positions the spectator in relation to the subject within the image. This is especially relevant if the subject represents a person. The position helps construct meaning. It is commonplace that a low-angle point of view on a figure produces a sense of the dominance of that figure, especially if that figure is looking down at one, as the viewer.

There is also the matter of the nature of the look. It is not just camera position that causes us to look at certain subjects in certain texts in certain ways. It is to do with the cultural experience that we bring to looking, and to specific media experience which has encouraged certain ways of looking. Looking is not neutral. What we attend to in the image, what sense we make of that image, is an active process. The use of the word 'gaze' in critical theory has intended to replace the falsely neutral sense of the word 'look'. Gaze has been related to gender critiques of media texts in particular. There is the notion that there is a peculiarly male gaze which regards images of woman in a voyeuristic and sexual fashion. It is a gaze which constructs the woman as a sexual being, which objectifies her. This process of objectification may be magnified by camera movement which surveys the woman's body as if it were an object of pleasure, as if it were a man looking. It may be magnified by the selective close-up (common in advertising), which attends to parts of the woman's body, making her less than a whole human being. This male gaze, it is theorized, is one which may even be adopted by the female viewer of the image of a woman. It is the female, as it were, taking the man's part, because she has learned that her 'natural' gender role includes being looked at by men.

> The determining male gaze projects its fantasy onto the female figure, which is styled accordingly. In their traditional exhibitionist role women are simultaneously looked at and displayed, with their appearance coded for strong visual and erotic impact so that they can be said to connote *to-be-looked-at-ness*.
>
> (Mulvey 1989)

This same kind of gender positioning is put forward as a way of making sense of the woman who gazes out of the photograph. Many magazine and advertising images of women look at us, the viewer. It is proposed that the female reader may identify with a woman in the image but, as that person, conceive herself as being looked at by men. In the case of sexually provocative looks, it is clear that the women in the picture are encoding messages for the supposed male viewer. But even in the women's magazine, where the viewer may be assumed to be female, still it is suggested that the viewer sees herself as the picture woman who is seeing herself in terms of the male gaze – a kind of indirect engagement.

> *Men act* and *women appear*. Men look at women. Women watch themselves being looked at. This determines not only most relations between men and women but also the relation of women to themselves. The surveyor of woman in herself is male: the surveyed female. Thus she turns herself into an object – and most particularly an object of vision: a sight.
>
> (J. Berger 1972)

The concept of gaze has also been associated with the idea of an intensity of attention to the image, which is assumed for the film viewing audience in particular. Indeed, John Ellis (1992) coined the term 'glance' to describe how, he believes, television is looked at differently. He argues that television is a less intense experience, in which the audience may be distracted by friends and family, by doing other things at the same time, by practices such as channel hopping. However, I would point out that it has also been shown that audiences watch some television intently, that they are not necessarily very reflective about all movie viewing, and that anyway we gaze upon a wider variety of visual texts. The idea of gaze should be associated not so much with degrees of intentionality, as in terms of how it relates to the production of meaning, the manufacture of identity, and the conduct of social relations.

8 Taking pleasure

The notion of audiences taking pleasure from texts is one which is associated with post-modernism, with feminist critiques and with audience-centred studies. In the first place one may look back to the previous section, in terms of the male gaze and the sexual pleasure of voyeurism. Cinema has provided some notorious examples of this kind of gaze and pleasure, including Brian de Palma's *Dressed to Kill* (1980). This included a shower scene much criticized for lengthy gratuitous shots of the female protagonist victim. But then the shower has become a stock setting in its own right for this kind of gaze and pleasure (see promotional shots in mail-order catalogues).

In terms of postmodernism and popular culture texts, the idea of audience pleasure has been set up as both a kind of gratification from that text, and as a kind of validation of the text. So the idea is not only that pleasure is a valid response, but also that this validity transfers to the text. It may be populist, but that is acceptable because it is enjoyed. In one sense this is partly a reaction against that kind of analysis that has seen the text as worthy only in relation to its seriousness of purpose. It is also something of a reaction against a postmodernist and Marxist analysis which goes for the ideological nature of a text and what it imposes on the audience. So in terms of audience studies, validating pleasure is also a way of winning back power for the audience.

Fiske (1994) discusses the pleasure of 'playing with' the text. The referentiality of post-modern texts encourages this. The construction of computer games like *Monkey Island Two* actually makes this play mandatory. Unless one plays with the choices given and reacts to the 'problems' thrown up, there is no text. Take pleasure, play the game – or there is no game. Fiske (1994) argues that audiences enjoy ways in which texts both confirm that there are rules, but also take the audience along on narrative journeys that challenge and break those rules. We can experience death – but outside the trauma of social reality. This is where genres in particular can 'have it both ways'. They depend on intertextuality for their understanding and enjoyment. But precisely because their base material is so well known, it is possible to work off this, to be inventive and challenging.

The taking of pleasure can work on different levels. In the case of game shows, there is a studio audience that is directly involved with the performance. They can enjoy the spectacle, the challenge, the right to respond, at first hand. But then there is the domestic audience, taking pleasure at a distance. There is pleasure in the ritual of the genre – a ritual which is controlled by that lord of misrule, the host. There is pleasure in the possibility of unruly behaviour: the form is largely unscripted. Fiske (1987) – himself drawing on ideas from Bakhtin about carnival and excess – sees this kind of populist material as resisting the meanings that might have been imposed by the producer through the text. He talks about 'a theory of pleasure that centres on the power to make meanings rather than on the meanings that are made'. However, Bourdieu (1984) argues against this kind of autonomy. He proposes the notion of 'habitus', in which people are predisposed to respond to experiences in certain ways because they have been so culturalized. We are back to questions about what or who shapes the meanings that come from the experience of engaging with any text. We are circling round the notion of ideology, which lurks behind such ideas about predispositions or about kinds of resistance.

I suggest that, however the postmodernist position tries to marginalize and efface either the presence of ideology or the possible influence of textual features, this is not sensible because it does not actually deal with these two factors. In any case, interests in the working of ideology and the working of audiences on texts do not have to be mutually exclusive.

In terms of feminism in particular, there is literature from Radway (1984) through to McRobbie (1994) that speaks for the female audience in various ways. Not surprisingly, this criticism addresses what are known as dominantly female texts – the romantic novel, girls' magazines, television soap operas. The female-ness of the texts and of the pleasures is defined in terms of female subject matter and ways of making sense of this. The pleasure is in, for example, the expression and negotiation of emotion and of relationship within the narrative. The pleasure is in identification with character and situation. In terms of uses and gratifications, the pleasures are about satisfying personal and social needs. Sometimes the pleasure is solitary – Radway's readers escaping domestic duty in the world of the novel. Sometimes it is shared – Silverstone's (1994) soap viewers talking about how problems in the soap world relate to problems in their own lives, working through problems indirectly by talking about the soap. The problem remains as to whether pleasures are taken or given.

Curiously, the notion of pleasure in texts provides an argument for saying that postmodernism eats itself. So there may indeed be pleasures in the ironies and referentiality of postmodernist form, in the fractured or shadowy narratives of a supposedly typical postmodern text. But the most popular texts – murder mystery thrillers or soaps, for example – are still resolutely modernist in their structures. The grand narratives are still with us. Reports of the death of modernism or indeed of realism, have been greatly exaggerated.

9 Audiences and the public sphere

The notion of a public sphere was proposed by Jürgen Habermas and defined in terms of a 'space' where information could be exchanged and public debate could take place. It may be said that this space could be provided by the media. In terms of politics and democracy, the idea becomes attractive as a kind of electronic substitute for the direct interaction between citizens in the agora of the classical Greek city state (my metaphor, not Habermas's). The idea is also an attempt to redefine the functions and activities of the media. That is to say, generally speaking, media have been seen (and set up) as a mechanism for broadcasting to an audience. They distribute material for which people pay. Audience members do not generally interact with one another, even in examples such as stage and movie theatres where they literally inhabit the same space. So if the media could become more interactive and more genuinely plural, then something like a public sphere would be created. Ironically, and since Habermas proposed his ideas, the Internet has offered a new working model for such a sphere. Bulletin boards and chat rooms attached to 'political' websites offer a discussion space for the Net-connected and Net-literate. But this does not include all citizens, and it does not much affect the conduct of conventional politics. In other words, it is a sphere only adjacent to the lives of many citizens and only tangential to the dominant political process.

The problem is that citizens are not in the end equally free to participate in this public sphere, whatever its form may be. Historically, the evidence is that 'public debate' in fact involved a limited range of literate citizens with access to the media of the time. As Gripsrud (2002) says of the nineteenth century: 'Discussions in the public sphere were to aim for *consensus*. The principles of the public sphere were primarily *the bourgeoisie's understanding of itself*.' One could argue that nothing much has changed, looking at the value placed on consensus in the discourse of contemporary news and current affairs in television.

Curran (1996) discusses the work of Newcomb and Hirsch and their analysis of television fiction as 'a forum of normative debate'. He refers to what they say about 'the way in which television fiction potentially informs the collective dialogue of society' (Curran 1996). This is an interesting extension to the scope of the public sphere and the arena of debate. Livingstone (1990) also argues that her research fits in with Newcomb and Hirsch's findings, showing that 'television provides a "cultural forum"'. But as Curran (1996) points out, it is a fallacy to suppose that television 'reflects the full diversity of society' which would make such 'collective dialogue' in such a 'cultural forum' at all meaningful. It is true that some fiction represents some discussion of issues which are of public concern. But the terms of reference of this discussion are another matter. This kind of argument is dangerously like that which proposes that the media reflect society to itself and so everything is right with the world – uncritical pluralism. If there is 'normative debate' in this kind of public sphere, then one would want to ask whose norms are in play, and whose are ruled out, and by whom?

The media which the public dominantly experience – and television is pre-eminent here in terms of hours spent – often purport to speak for the public, but do not often let the public speak. When the public does speak, it is usually under terms and conditions which the broadcasters control. So discussion and current affairs programmes are controlled up-front by personalities. Those who do appear are allowed to do so by producers. Their appearance is allowed in relation to ideas about balance and audience interest. Access to the media, to a public sphere which all might at least switch on to, is not free, is not guaranteed and in fact only takes place according to ground rules defined by the media themselves. Broadcasters always reserve to themselves the power of editorial control. The relevant kinds of programmes are placed in off-peak schedules or minority channels, so that the 'sphere', such as it is, is set up for minorities. Equally, one should not sound too strident a note about lack of audience access to a public sphere constructed by the media, where 'the people' might have a voice. The voice of some people might be less welcome than that of others. There are few of us who would like any person or group to have absolute right of access to the media. This attitude reminds one that the public (who after all are also the audiences under discussion) retain a concern about media influence. Public debate about the extent to which the Labour government was guilty of 'spinning' its policies through the media (in the early years of the twenty-first century) relates to worries about news management in particular. If not expressed in such terms, it also connects with debates about hegemony – who is controlling what agenda that carries what ideas?

Figure 3.3 Media Consumption in a Public Place: The Olympics
Media technologies of entertainment and communication are available everywhere, in public and in private.

- What are the possible consequences of this, in terms of social interactions?
- What other examples of technologies are used to keep audiences in touch with various kinds of sport?

Hesmondhalgh (2002) talks of the 'difficulties of sustaining participatory citizenship in a society where most people get their knowledge of politics from television'. This reminds us that first, there are legitimate concerns about media influence. But second, it reminds us that, despite those views of audiences having some kind of active and critical role, the relationship of the viewer/listener/reader to the media is one where they can deal only with what has been said.

Silverstone (1994) discusses 'a suburbanisation of the public sphere' in which he argues for two things. The first is that there has been (and still is, to an extent) a 'coherence' that broadcasting has offered to 'the community of suburbs'. Second, he suggests that this suburbanized public sphere is fragmenting, as new technologies multiply and divide means of distribution, channels and audiences. He describes the politics of this kind of public sphere as 'a domestic politics of self interest, conformity and exclusion'. But the real power play happens elsewhere. 'Participation of a kind may have been substantially enhanced by the mediation of national and international agendas . . . but the terms of that participation and the possibilities for its realisation are very much in question.'

So in effect the media continue to be consumed in the private sphere of the home for the most part. The material which is distributed is dominantly that of entertainment. Audiences are treated as deindividualized groups of consumers. The dominant pattern of relationship is between audience members and producers. There is a financial charge on that relationship.

Audience members may interact in terms of private discussion about what they have seen in the cinema or have heard on the radio. But this discussion does not take place in a public sphere. The audience is unable to make an impact on the conduct of public affairs, whether these are to do with the management of the media or with the conduct of political decisions. At this point one might remember the issues surrounding a public service model of the media. Who defines what kind of service for what kind of public?

It seems that the service does not include the creation of a genuinely public sphere. This has a particular irony in that the UK Labour government is very fond of proclaiming the need for 'a genuine debate' on given issues of the moment. The problem is that, apart from the floor of the House of Commons, the only place for that debate is in the pages and the programmes of the media. And that sphere remains privatized and commercialized.

There is also an issue as to whether we can identify a clear distinction between public and private spheres, given the place of broadcasting in domestic life. However, this does not deal with the previous question about whether or not there are real debates in whatever public sphere we may have – real interactions between those who move the levers of power, and those who live with the consequences of this leverage. There also needs to be a questioning of what, it is assumed, 'belongs' to each sphere, especially on gender grounds. News practices represent a difference between hard news and soft news: between masculinized reports that bear on power politics and conflict 'out there', and feminized reports that bear on health and family issues, on social relations and celebrity behaviour. But one needs to question the assumptions that refer such feminized reports into a private/domestic sphere. Andrea Press (2000) refers to the 'customary division between these spheres'. With reference to her own work (with Elizabeth Cole) on abortion, she points out that the debates about this do take place out there in a public and politicized arena. An Irish referendum on abortion in 2002 may have reflected on what goes in a private sphere, but the media debate was fierce, and out there in the public sphere, with no sense that the issues had been assimilated into some 'less worthy' feminized soft news reporting.

10 Influences and effects

The final part of this chapter should be read as providing a context for Chapter 4, which discusses particular areas of influence. There is a long-running debate about the possible influence of the media on certain audiences, via certain material, under certain circumstances. There is also a popular mythology around the idea that a range of media effects are proven and that they are pernicious. This is not so, even with relation to the effects of violent material in the media (see section 3 of Chapter 4).

Nevertheless, one finds contrary positions asserted with confidence, though not necessarily with proper evidence. For example, Hesmondhalgh (2002: 3) says confidently: 'the best contributions to such debates suggest the complex, negotiated and often indirect nature of media influence, but of one thing there can be no doubt – the media do have an influence'. I would suggest that the first half of this sentence has to be squared with the second half. On the other hand, Ross and Nightingale (2003) say with equal certitude: 'despite decades of work in which researchers have tried to demonstrate the cause–effect relationship, it has never been actually possible to isolate out the specific influence of media from other factors'. And indeed this does seem to be the case (see the points made within the case study).

One significant source of negative views about media lies intellectually in the work of the Frankfurt School and the writing of members such as Theodor Adorno, Max Horkheimer and Walter Benjamin, in the 1930s and 1940s. Their critique, relating in effect to popular music and cinema, described a new kind of mass culture, generating a new mass audience, and undermining the values of a genuine culture of the people. This 'genuine' culture is conceived as something like 'folk culture'. Indeed Adorno was still reasserting this view many years after his original essay was published: 'The culture industry intentionally integrates its consumers from above. To the detriment of both it forces together the spheres of high and low art' (Adorno 1991).

Another negative and critical impetus appeared in the 1950s, with the arrival of television. Its material was deprecated by a number of critics, including Richard Hoggart of the Birmingham Centre for Cultural Studies, essentially on the grounds that it would undermine and supplant the values of 'high culture' (as Raymond Williams described it). Criticism of violence in such American crime genre series as *Dragnet* followed on this more general argument against television and for its negative effects.

Ironically, the main vehicle for views about the negative influence of the media has been the media themselves. They have been the means by which intellectual and political opinion and debate filters through to the general public. They have been (and still are) the sometime agents of moral panic, which typically might relate to the release of some film or video which supposedly influences the minds of the public at large or of the young in particular. The media, and especially the press, can be said to be motivated in this criticism by two things. One is the urge to create controversy which sells products, the second may be to gain kudos as the champion of public 'safety' by attacking another medium. This would have been especially true in the 1940s through to the 1970s, when television viewing figures rose steadily, as newspaper circulation declined.

All this debate goes back to models of the relationship between media and society, between texts and audiences. The conservative position returns to an argument that the media do things to people, that audiences may be passive, and that the media producers have a power which audiences cannot resist. This book has so far argued that none of these things is true, or has not been conclusively demonstrated. Truth is more complicated.

It may be useful to summarize a few points about media influence, which do seem to hold true.

- Media effects may be benign as much as malign.

- The influence of media is collective rather than operating through any one medium or text.

- The media collectively operate within a range of other cultural and social factors which also condition possible influence.

- The influence of media is conditioned by a range of personal and social factors for the individual audience member, including their social upbringing and their immediate personal circumstances.

- Influence is conditioned by the context of reception.

- Influence is more likely if the media text speaks of attitudes and values already held by the audience.

- One may recognize behavioural response to, for example, a charity campaign: but this does not demonstrate attitudinal change.

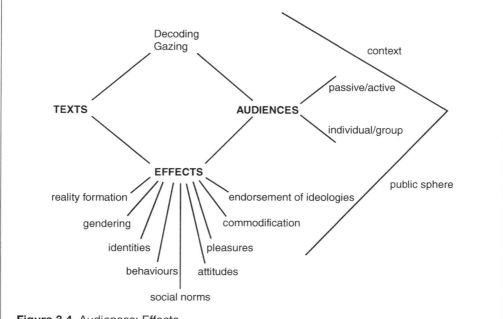

Figure 3.4 Audiences: Effects
The interaction of audiences and texts, within given contexts, produces a range of possible effects.

● Can you give examples, under the categories above, of what the effects could be in practice (e.g. identity – the possibility that young females' sense of who they are is affected by the magazines that they read)?

(Graeme Burton 2009)

So the influence of the media is a subject which most people have opinions about, but which is so hedged about with conditional factors that it may be difficult to sustain those opinions. The kind of influence which invokes most concern relates to attitudinal changes. It is assumed that favourable attitudes are behind people's decision to behave in certain ways. In this case it is not surprising that research and debate weigh most heavily in certain areas: violent behaviour, voting behaviour, purchasing behaviour. The first has to do with public order and the security of the state. The second has to do with the mechanism which transfers power from people to politicians. The third has to do with the consumption on which our capitalist system depends. So there has been a certain emphasis of research resources to the possible benefit of those who exert political and economic power.

Previous discussion of media power and ideology has already suggested that the media may be seen as a site of struggle for the dominance of one set of ideas over another (Gramsci), or as a kind of ideological state apparatus, a Trojan horse for the dominant ideology (Althusser). But propositions about how ideology reproduces itself, or how it exerts consensual control, are only propositions. John Thompson (1990) disagrees with the notion of the ideologically subjugated audience:

It cannot be assumed that the individuals who receive media messages will, by the fact of receiving them, be impelled to act in an imitative and conforming way and thereby be bound to the social order which their actions, and the messages which allegedly impel them, serve to reproduce.

Curran and Seaton (1997) say much the same thing on a broader basis which still reflects on effects and influence: 'there is no adequate vocabulary to describe the relationships between the media, individuals and society'.

Nevertheless, convictions about the effects of the media remain, and research abounds. There are various propositions about effects, how they work and therefore about that relationship between audience and media.

- *Hypodermic effects* propose that the media directly influence people, largely adversely, 'injecting' them with views and behaviours.

- *Copycat effects* propose a variation on this theme, which is about imitation of media behaviours.

- *Inoculation theory* proposes that audiences become desensitized to the adverse qualities of media material through repetitious exposure to that material.

- *Two-step flow theory* proposes that media influence is indirect, mediated through opinion makers in the media and through opinion leaders in the social groups inhabited by a given audience member (see Katz and Lazarsfeld 1995).

- *Uses and gratifications theory* proposes that audience needs influence their choice and use of media material (see above).

- *Cultivation theory* proposes that repetitive consumption of certain kinds of media material accumulatively cultivates certain kinds of attitudes and values.

Ross and Nightingale (2003: 77) also refer to propositions by Perse (2001) that there are four kinds of meaningful models for effects theory:

- direct effects models (e.g. short-term effects)

- conditional models (e.g. suggesting effects on the attributes and belief systems of consumers)

- cumulative effects models (in which repetition of media material is assumed to be influential)

- cognitive-transactional models (in which the audience is 'primed' by some kinds of media content rather than by others).

Propositions about media influence have often been set up along a short-term/long-term axis. Short-term effects are sometimes known as hypodermic theories (above). However, since the 1950s, it has not been shown that media in any area can simply inject people with ideas and behaviours, with immediate results. So most cautious propositions about media influence now hinge on the idea of long-term attitudinal change.

What are also important in this respect are attitudes to a whole range of social groups and social behaviours. One may ask what part the media play, for example, in forming attitudes towards ethnic minorities, or towards situations such as single-parenthood. One may ask whether they have changed or hardened existing attitudes. One could argue that they have failed to bring about change when it needed to happen (for example, in the treatment of gay people in the popular press). It is difficult to believe that the media have nothing to do with the way we view others and construct our beliefs. On the other hand, it is in the end impossible to demonstrate conclusively that this influence is there. This kind of problem is relevant to discussion of negative representations of social groups. It seems reasonable to assert that those representations of young people that treat them as 'a problem' will tend to confirm prejudices, and to help ensure that they are a problem. But, even when respondents in research articulate negative attitudes on the basis of what they have seen or read, still it is hard to connect what some people say they think with what they or others actually do.

It is also the case that there are positive representations around. One can find examples of the media offering a constructive lead in thinking about such subjects as 'race' or 'crime' or 'youth'. So how does this fit into the equation? The most certain thing that research throws up is that people tend to use media material selectively to reinforce what they already believe. But, of course, what they already believe may itself be a product of prior media use.

In terms of outcome – as opposed to the process of effect – there are a number of dominant propositions which dominate conclusions about effects. One version is summarized by McQuail (2000) in terms of the influence on beliefs and opinions held by the audience:

- causes intended change (conversion of views)
- causes unintended changes
- causes minor changes (perhaps in the form of views held, or in their intensity)
- facilitates change of views (whether intended or not)
- reinforces existing views
- prevents a change in views.

His categories refer to whether or not change happens, and in what ways. Media influence may lead to attitude change, not necessarily of great significance or by any calculation on the part of the producers. Equally, it may either reinforce what people already believe, or even work against people shifting their beliefs. So evidence is in some respects contradictory.

Burton (2002) describes influence in terms of types of change, and of broader effects on society and on social groups:

- *Attitude change:* effects on people's orientation towards or against certain ideas or behaviours – what one is for or against.
- *Cognitive change:* effects on people's values and beliefs – how one thinks about a subject.
- *Affective (emotional) change:* effects on the emotional state of the audience: this may include the production of an emotional frame of reference for or against such subjects as social groups or commodities – what one feels about a subject.
- *Agenda setting:* especially through news material, constructing a prioritized set of issues for the public sphere, and denying the importance of other issues.
- *Moral panics:* inducing unfounded anxieties about given social groups, social behaviours or social phenomena.
- *Socialization:* in terms of persuading audiences that certain norms, certain kinds of behaviour, certain kinds of social relationship should be adopted (in preference to any others).

- *Reality formation:* producing a set of ideas about what constitutes 'the real', especially in relation to social reality and social norms.

- *Social control:* acting a mechanism for the production of a consensus about the 'proper' relationship between social groups, between the state and society, with an emphasis on particular ideas about law and order.

- *Endorsement of ideology:* reinforcement of a dominant set of values which add up to a certain way of looking at and thinking about the world: this includes reinforcement of views about power relationships between social grounds and about difference between groups.

Ideas about the process and outcome of effects are themselves dependent on given research methodologies, which are also open to question, for various reasons. One may refer to Gauntlett (1995) for a blunt critique of research methodologies in relation to television (which are much applicable to other media).

A few comments, at least, will indicate the scope of 'the problem'.

- If one is trying to identify attitudinal effects, then one has to find a method and evidence that unambiguously points to that internal state which we call 'attitude'. In particular, surveys are only as good as the questions they ask. They depend on the ability of respondents to express 'truthful' answers, and on the objectivity of the researcher in correlating the comments and information drawn out. Examples here would be the questions asked of and records kept by respondents in research done by the Broadcast Audience Research Board or by National Readership Surveys.

- If one is trying to identify behavioural effects, then one has to be able to describe distinctive behaviours, and distinguish an unambiguous connection between that behaviour and given media material.

- If one is trying to fasten on media material as being the key variable in the context being researched, then it has to be distinguished from possible influences outside the media, from influences of other media, from influences of other material within the medium being examined. This is a tall order.

- If one conducts any 'hands-on' research, then by definition there is a kind of intervention which means that the experience of consumption is no longer 'natural'.

- If one conducts research into textual material alone (e.g. content analysis) then any statements about effect are conjectural (however, they may seem to be probable) because the engagement of audience with text has been ignored. Similarly, correlation studies assume that there is a connection between two exceptional items of statistical information, and they assume that this connection is causal. Neither may be true.

- If one conducts experiments with large audience numbers, then one is likely to come up with generalizations about effects, at best. And these generalizations will appear less true the more one looks at specific sections of the audience.

- If one looks at individuals or small audience groups – ethnographic surveys – then the specific 'information elicited will not necessarily be true for larger audience groups.

11 Gender modelling

There is a quantity of material on audiences, which is concerned with gender differences between and within audiences. This interest attends to audience preferences and audience reading of texts. It looks for ways of modelling these audiences.

Christine Geraghty (1996) has considered ways in which women are constructed as an audience and operate as consumers, in relation to a proposed difference between how the viewing of film has been understood, as opposed to television. In the case of television she points to an emphasis on the context of viewing for the female audience. With regard to film she refers to an emphasis on spectator positions and psychoanalytic discourses. She comments on other critiques which draw attention to the way in which the female viewer of film is often modelled as being passive, whereas the viewer of television is often described as ' "active", "conscious" and "optimistic" '. She discusses the representation of mothers, in particular. There are accounts of various views on the nature of identification with mother characters, for the female audience. Psychoanalytic positions seem to be more pessimistic about women reading disempowering meanings into, for example, melodramas. Whereas a more postmodern analysis is fairly positive about pleasures gained and about a sense of resistance to social strictures being generated. There is also comment on the process of viewing – perhaps a shared experience in the case of TV, in which women will talk about and assimilate material collaboratively.

Such comments on viewing tend to be confirmed by the work of Silverstone (1994) and Morley (1992), for example. They comment on the fact that male viewers of TV prefer not to be interrupted, whereas female viewers may view spasmodically, and prefer to talk about material on screen. On the other hand, their research suggests that males more than females will control the machinery of viewing, and therefore the material that is actually watched. It should also be pointed out that such gendered behaviours and preferences operate in a context – that of family life. Other kinds of media consumption may take place in other contexts, with other implications for gender. For example, males and females will go to see a movie as a shared and social experience, not just for the film. The choice of the film could depend on either male or female preferences.

So the context of that lived experience is not just about the domestic sphere. And even where it is, gender roles may vary from one type of household to another and over a period of time. So, for example, Hobson (1982), like Morley (1992), found that female viewers of the then early evening soap, *Crossroads*, experienced interrupted viewing because they were trying to watch, prepare a meal and deal with children. But 20 years on and more, one would have to say, what about that majority of households that do not contain children? What about the impact of the VCR and then the Skybox, and the possibility of deferred viewing? What about the impact of the microwave and ready meals? What about different households of different socio-economic groups, with different incomes?

So, one might now question the validity of work by people like Morley (1992), on the basis of the comparatively narrow cross-section investigated and of the likelihood that social behaviours and relationships have changed, and are changing. Again, I would argue that UK prime-time TV schedules have changed since the 1980s. They now present a great deal of drama material which contains themes and characters of especial relevance to women's lives, and which is also sometimes treated in what might loosely be termed 'soap style'. A past example was the third series of a drama called *Clocking Off* (2002), based around a northern textiles factory. The storylines focused on both male and female characters, but they are very much concerned with relationships and emotional dilemmas.

In this week of writing I can at random select three examples from September 2008. *Fiona's Story* (BBC1) is about a wife dealing with the discovery that her husband trawls the Net for paedophilic material. *The Children* (ITV) is a three-parter again in a domestic setting, and dealing with a child's murder. *Lost in Austen* (ITV) is a fanciful time travel story based on the conceit that a contemporary young women travels from life to fiction to romance Jane Austen's Mr Darcy.

Similarly, it is noticeable that movie releases contain a fair proportion of material which is clearly aimed at a specifically female audience. *Bridget Jones's Diary* has topped both novel and film best-sellers' lists. The novel and film *About a Boy* (2002) contains male protagonists but appeals to female readers/viewers because of its exploration of emotion and relationship. One also has to be careful about explaining a gendered audience in terms of material supposedly tailored for female viewers. For a start, there will be differences between what younger and older females will prefer. Indeed, the whole notion of a 'female audience' implies a coherence of interest, of background, of gender definition, which hardly stands up to examination, and which is in its own way demeaning. Not much better is the assumption that material supposedly for a female audience contains nothing of interest and value for men. I would also argue that audiences may not and should not be differentiated by gender without good evidence. The audience for David Fincher's *Panic Room* (2002) was as much female as male. Horror material in all media is very attractive to a young female audience. Or a film like *24 Hour Party People* (2002) is sold on its cultural attractions and references, within which gender is largely irrelevant.

Where there has been explicit identification of a female-gendered audience one may argue that it has something to do with those ideological shifts related to feminism, and a lot to do with economic changes that have given women more leisure and more spending power.

12 Discussion extract

In the digital television environment there are more broadcasting channels, and therefore smaller amounts of money per channel and per programme to spend because the audience sizes for programmes are correspondingly smaller than those of conventional terrestrial television. The costs of making programmes are therefore more difficult to recoup from advertisers, and need to be generated from the subscriptions paid by the viewers of interactive digital television channels, or from one-off payments made by viewers to see a particular programme. Subscription and pay-per-view are gradually becoming economically significant in Britain, and it seems likely that these modes of viewing will increase in importance.

Interactivity is bound to change the forms and formats of television programmes. If interactive betting or voting are the primary ways of generating revenue, increasingly programmes will be structured to include opportunities for competition among the people appearing in them, and the possibility of a range of different outcomes within the programmes and at their conclusion, so that viewers are able to gamble or vote for the results. The ways in which audiences view programmes, identify with and relate to people appearing on television and follow storylines would also change.

Some of these changes can already be seen in programmes broadcast on terrestrial television and on cable and satellite in Britain. This is because new developments in technology of any kind are more likely to be adopted when they enhance a service that already exists or offer services that are linked to an established brand or property. As John Storey has argued, people's media use is strongly influenced by their habits and routines, since 'cultural consumption is a practice of everyday life. Cultural commodities are not appropriated or used in a social vacuum; such usage and appropriation takes place in the context of other forms of appropriation and use, themselves connected to other routines, which together form the fabric of everyday life'.

Bignell, J. (2004) *An Introduction to Television Studies*, 2nd edn. Abingdon: Routledge.

1   When might a niche audience generate proportionately more money than the audience for a 'large' channel?

2   Why has interactive voting been the subject of considerable criticism?

3   What other means of viewing films are competing with pay-per-view, and with what effect?

4   What examples are there of new developments being adopted, as referred to in the passage?

5   How do audiences make television part of the routines and the fabric of their everyday lives?

13 Further reading

Alasuutari, P. (ed.) (1999) *Rethinking the Media Audience*. London: Sage.

Brooker, W. and Jermyn, D. (eds) (2003) *The Audience Studies Reader*. London: Routledge.

Gillespie, M. (ed.) (2005) *Media Audiences*. Maidenhead: Open University Press.

Ross, K. and Nightingale, V. (2003) *Media and Audiences: New Perspectives*. Maidenhead: Open University Press.

Ruddock, A. (2001) *Understanding Audiences*. London: Sage.

4

Media – audience – influence

Questions of effects: politics, children, violence

Very few studies have conclusively identified or rejected the possibility of media effects. Part of the problem is its sheer complexity. After all, rarely are comparable institutions such as religion and law analyzed in terms of their effects on individuals (McQuail 1977). These institutions, so we are led to believe, are good for us and do not harm us if we behave accordingly. Media institutions, on the other hand, are bad for us – or at best, equally cursed and blessed.

Laughey, D. (2007) *Key Themes in Media Theory*. Maidenhead:
Open University Press.

1 Introduction

In this chapter I want to lay out some areas of the relationship between media and society which are thought to raise significant concerns around issues to do with *influence*. There will be two examples: children as a subject of concern and the conduct of politics. There will also be a short critique of research methodologies and effects theories, placing some emphasis on the subject of violence. However, there is not the space for extensive analysis of the influence of very specific elements such as campaigns at particular election times, which you may explore further through the reading list.

At the outset one should say that there can be no question of 'buying into' simplistic assumptions about the media doing things to its audience. People do not vote in certain ways, even at election times, simply because they habitually read a newspaper which favours one political party. Children do not become violent because they play some computer games with violence in them. The dynamic relationship between media and society is, on research evidence, too complex to be understood simply in terms of immediate and dominant effects. The context to that relationship is so rich that it is in most instances nearly impossible to say that the media, as opposed to any other influences, has caused something to happen to the behaviour and attitudes of any one part of the audience. The very belief that media are influential, in various ways, is itself just one of the many factors which contextualizes the relationship. Yet it is a belief that is hard to support – even though one can show correlations between for example the 2007/8 Marks and Spencer TV advertising campaign for M&S food, and a rise in sales. Ironically, a rather different effect was found in November 2009, when an M&S campaign comparing some of its products with items in the new Waitrose Essentials range boosted Waitrose sales. Advertising can work, just not always in the way that advertisers expect. 'Effects are difficult to isolate and establish, media texts are complex and contradictory, and audiences are active and influenced by other social and cultural factors' (Davis 2007: 7).

There is a conundrum at the heart of the relationship between society and the media, and with regard to the notion of influence. It is taken for granted that the media do have influence – over attitudes, values, and the terms in which we understand the world. And yet the one thing that critical method tells us is that nothing should be taken for granted. Media effects in isolation simply are not demonstrable, whatever 'taken-for-granted' views may say. So far as they seem to exist they are always contingent on things such as the context of reception, or other influences such as socialization. On the other hand, many people would also say that, for instance, neither does it make sense to allow children to play any kind of computer game that they want to, at any time of the day. It does not make sense to allow any political party uncontrolled access to the media and indeed to any amount of cash.

So one has to steer a course between saying that the media have no influence at all, and accepting that, for instance, research which tries to say that the media influence people into behaving violently does not justify that conclusion. It is not to say that one should not be concerned about that thing called 'media power' – whatever it is exactly. But it is to say that the media audience relationship has many facets, including benign features – website fan communities love to talk about their favourite films or TV programmes or comics. Media have enhanced this pleasure. The fans influence each other, as much as being influenced by the original media texts. Here, influence is not about something disempowering or demeaning.

As a media student you should not succumb to popular assumptions about the media. Test them. For example, is it necessarily true that too much TV watching is bad for children? What do you mean by 'bad'? How does one define 'too much'? If there is some influence, is it the same for any child of any age?

2 Politics

> Political communication – 'a system of dynamic interaction between political actors, the media and audience members, each of whom is involved in producing, receiving and interpreting political messages'.
>
> (Voltmer 2006: 3)

In the first place it is interesting to reflect on how one's choice of words may affect assumptions about what the media–society relationship is, may be, or could be. 'Audience' is a fairly neutral term, though it is still hard to remove that association with passivity – as I have tried to do in Chapter 3. It might be used with relation to party political broadcasts. 'Citizen' carries more political and sociological baggage, implying that each person is a part of a society, has obligations to fellow citizens, and is part of some political process. 'Voter' makes that explicit. It refers to a specific and political act of decision making. It implies allegiance to particular ideological positions. 'Consumer' – of cultural or material goods – implies a role within a certain kind of economic system. It may be argued that all adults are all these things. But discussion of influence in the media–society relationship tends to select such terms to inflect or explain that discussion. In a discussion of the idea of the public sphere, we become citizens, sometimes responsible ourselves for shaping the conduct of political activity. But in a discussion of marketing techniques used by contemporary political parties, we may become consumers, because that is an assumption behind marketing. We are buying into ideas about – a politician, a political programme, the ethos of a political party.

Politics is also a concept that is referenced through certain key terms which are commonly used in political debate or media coverage. For example, 'Parliament' is defined as a seat of legitimate power and of democracy. But one might ask why it matters quite so much when most of its deliberations have no immediate effect on the everyday lives of most British citizens. Its legitimacy seems less valid and more mythical when one reflects that a hotly debated anti-terrorism bill was passed on the back of the nine votes of one minority party (12 June 2008). The very concept of 'party' is embedded in our understanding of politics – that it is OK for politics to be conducted on a group basis where loyalty is everything. In this case politics can mean MPs voting with their party or indeed with their consciences, but ignoring what they may know was preferred by those who voted them into power in the first place. Another key word is 'minister' with its attachments of respect and recognition of power. And yet considerable real power is exercised by senior civil servants or by select committees of Parliament. Finally one might ask what the term 'nation' really means within definitions of politics. The word is often invoked in relation to public service or to pronouncements about what the nation needs. But the coherence of 'nation' is very questionable in the cases of any number of states around the world. Presidential elections show a USA clearly divided by cultural and ethnic differences between its regions. The same is true for the UK. I am trying to draw attention to the fact that we talk of and conceive of politics via terms which carry a baggage of sometimes idealized meanings.

If one is questioning the concept of politics in relation to the media, then one should also understand that it does not just reside in Congressional debates or global news coverage of events in Zimbabwe where in 2008 the president was trying to manipulate adverse election results. Movies are political, not least when, as with *Sex and the City* (2008), they are 'saying' things about the disposition of gendered power in society. Pop songs can be political. Concerts may be political – in support of environmental causes. Tourism becomes political when the Chinese authorities pressure their citizens into boycotting France and French goods (June 2008). Sport is intensely political when it comes to national lobbying over the venue for the next Olympic games.

2.1 *Major questions*

1 What is the nature of the relationship between media and government, media and society, in terms of political activity?

2 Can government influence news media coverage of politics?

3 Can media political coverage influence voting habits?

4 How influential are political campaigns?

5 What is the relationship between media and celebrity politics?

6 In what ways has the arrival of new media, especially the Net, influenced the conduct of politics?

2.2 Media and government

It is 'a relationship of mutual convenience and interdependence . . . between the politicians and the media professionals' (McNair 2007: 25).

One could describe the relationship as being consensual, dynamic and competitive. There is a tacit agreement (a working consensus) that they need each other. Media depend on government as a major source of information, in the case of news operations. Broadcast media are permitted to exist only through Acts of Parliament. In financial terms, the BBC depends on government for most of its income, from the licence fee. The media depend on the goodwill of the government in that Parliament retains the power to regulate media in various ways (see pp. 62–7), not least through the body known as Ofcom.

On the other hand, government would agree that it needs media, not least as a collection of means of communication which can tell audiences what government is doing or proposes to do, and why. Politicians and political parties have come to believe that media can be influential on public opinion. They depend on media as a means of promoting (or marketing) their differing views, most crucially at times of national and local elections.

The relationship is dynamic in that it changes according to the differing views and needs of those involved. Most obviously it changes in respect of what the government allows or disallows through mechanisms of regulation. So, in the 1980s, in the UK, partly as a response to industry lobbying, there was the start of a 20-year process of deregulating broadcasting. Among other things, this process fragmented audiences and expanded the production base. Other changes have less specific causes. The arrival of the celebrity politician is part of the manufacture of celebrity-dom in general within the media – audiences are interested in people and mostly in people who are 'famous'.

The relationship is competitive in that both media and government would like to control its terms. Governments would like media coverage which is always favourable and which suppresses 'inconvenient' news. Media would like pretty much uncontrolled access to stories which 'belong to' government, and would like to decide the nature and extent of political coverage for its collective self.

In the relationship, it does seem that the media at least have a dominant role in defining 'political reality'. We do have access to sources apart from broadcasting and the press, as regards information about what government is doing, e.g. government websites. But the fact is that for most people their view of what 'politics' means, how politics is conducted, what are the key political issues, does come through the former. And it is also agreed that the media create a kind of narrative within which political events are understood. As I write, that narrative contains many references to the 'declining years of an administration'. So the public may get the idea that the Labour government is on the way out, even if it is not. This is much like the negative press that the Conservative government received in 1997, when it lost the election – even though the economy was doing quite well, contrary to 'the narrative'. You need to read Chapter 8 on news and what it has to say about narrative, genre and agenda setting, to add to your understanding of these comments.

In this sphere of politics, one may say that the media and political actors influence one another, not least through a common interest in public opinion, in public responses to their actions, and in the voting habits of citizens. News practices and the practice of politics mesh with one another.

One also has to be aware of that difference between the press and broadcasting, in which the former is allowed to be politically partisan, but the latter must stay impartial, even when programmes are about politics. Of course this requirement creates logical contortions, as in the assumptions about balancing government views with those of *the* Opposition, when in fact there are two opposition parties in the UK. The generality of programming is not supposed to raise political issues – as when (June 2008) the presenter George Lamb (Radio 6) was disciplined for making off-the-cuff partial remarks about the London mayoral elections. But of course programmes cannot but be political – as when reference is made to the loss of community facilities in a programme about the countryside.

2.3 Politics and points of contact between media and society

In political terms the links between media and society are not just about through news and current affairs. They are not just about government press briefings or politicians' media appearances. There are many of what are called 'actors' in the political process. Citizens may also belong to one of these categories, or they may just be onlookers to the activities of such actors. There are pressure groups such as Friends of the Earth. There are trade unions such as Unison, or consumer magazines such as *Which?* There may be lobby groups, perhaps attached to single issues such as abortion. Corporations such as Shell become political actors especially when something like a tanker drivers' strike happens (June 2008). Non-government organizations (NGOs) such as the Red Cross become political actors when there are political arguments surrounding the Burmese government's refusal to let in foreign aid after the disastrous cyclone of 2008. Naming these actors reminds one that politics is not just about the politicians, and it is not just about what happens in Downing Street or Parliament. We may have become a voter apathetic nation, but whether we like it or not we are all involved in politics when we, for example, express opinions about 'benefit scroungers' or maternity rights. Not voting also has political consequences. And of course terrorist groups such as FARC in Venezuela are political actors even if they operate outside the legitimized political process.

In media terms, and apart from the obvious examples of newscasts, the media offer a variety of political activities and points of contact which involve the citizen. Opinion polls, such as those conducted by MORI or YouGov and commissioned by newspapers, express political opinions about their subjects. People are enthusiastic bloggers on the Net, as are a number of journalists. Newspaper readers may write letters to the editor. Television generates debates, such as the programme *Question Time* on BBC1. There are party websites. There is a digital channel screening parliamentary debate, through which media act as a bridge between the process of government and society. Radio talk shows such as *Start the Week* include political material. There are even satirical shows such as *The Thick of It* (BBC) which in spite of its cynical take on the conduct of politics, is still in the 'politics in the media' frame.

So, however important it is, media news is not the only point at which people experience politics, or may be influenced in their understanding of what is on the political agenda, what are political issues arising from these agenda items, and what are the positions that may be taken on the issues.

Perhaps the most significant point of contact is that indirect kind, represented by government created quangos, which are unelected, yet are still creatures of government which affect our daily lives. Health Care Trusts run hospitals, the Learning and Skills Council distributes millions of pounds in support of various education courses. The media will produce coverage about them, e.g. the current and ongoing scare about cleanliness in hospitals. They will use their own public relations to help deal with media coverage.

The BBC, itself a global media player, is also monitored by a kind of quango – the BBC Trust. Politicians play with the illusion that this is an independent body. But such a claim is clearly nonsense, when the Trust members are appointed by government. What we have here is an example of mechanisms of regulation, which may themselves act as a point of contact. The same is true for the regulator Ofcom, the chair of which and half the Board are government appointees, and which oversees all communication media. It is worth pointing out that, although there are party political broadcasts during election campaigns, political broadcast advertising is banned in the UK (Communications Act 2003). This Act stops non-party political groups such as Amnesty International from buying airtime to promote their views. However, Amnesty and others can and do buy display ads in newspapers, or poster space.

So do the media become an organ of publicity for interested political groups? Are they a site of information for an active electorate? Are they even a forum for public discussion (see also ideas about the public sphere)?

2.4 Media, publicity and voting

There are many in the public relations industry who wish to believe that their work can manufacture influence over voter behaviour. The evidence for this is contradictory and sketchy. It is rather more that media promotional activity creates awareness in the public mind, as much as it actually swings votes. The evidence is that many voters have decided on who they will support even before a campaign happens, and certainly before polling day. However, there has also been a rise in the 'floating voter' at whom much of a campaign will be targeted. Many of the 2.5 million floating voters switched from Conservative to Labour between the UK elections of 1992 and 1997 (Stanyer 2007: 25).

As with any kind of research, finding evidence of influence depends on methods, and all methods have some flaws. One can use focus groups to elicit views on political issues, or opinions of proposed political ads. But what people say in these groups and how this translates into their votes are not necessarily connected. One can conduct surveys of voting intentions, but there are sufficient examples of survey results being wrong that it is clear that what people say and what they do (and what they decide at the last minute) are two different things; witness Neil Kinnock's failure to win for Labour in the UK in 1992. Exit polls about the results of elections, conducted as voters leave the booths, are usually quite accurate. But by definition that has little connection with obtaining information that can be used to shape a political campaign. One should of course conduct research experiments which are designed to isolate factors which may dominate people's political and possibly their voting preferences. In practice this is difficult and next to impossible. There are just too many factors. And again, preferences do not necessarily demonstrate behaviours. Of course in voting terms the fact that there is evidence that about 3 per cent of undecided voters can be influenced by the publication of opinion polls, and so could influence the results in marginal constituencies, is something to be considered. But, as with advertising, if someone had clearly defined the publicity gap between attitudes and behaviours, then there would be no need for a marketing industry.

One might listen when an experienced figure in political analysis and marketing argues that there are three influential factors when considering voting behaviour – the image of leadership; the image of policy; the corporate image of the party concerned (Bob Worcester of MORI, quoted in McNair 2007: 32). But that does not tell one how to represent those images successfully, let alone how one can achieve the votes.

Equally, it would be wrong to suggest that all publicity has no influence on voting behaviour and election outcomes. To an extent, the situation is analogous to product advertising, where some campaigns have some effect, in terms of enhanced sales, but no one knows just how or why. We know that in 1996 in the USA 92 per cent of Congressional contests and 88 per cent of those for the Senate were won by the candidates who spent the most money on publicity (Stanyer 2007: 35). But we do not know many fundamental things such as what made the publicity successful, and what part was played by other factors, not least news coverage.

Then again there is no evidence that newspapers lead public opinion or voting behaviour, even when they make claims like the *Sun* in 1997 – 'It Was the Sun Wot Won It'. It is true that the paper backed Labour. But the evidence is that the electorate was tired of the Conservative government and wanted a change anyway. Norris et al. (2007) investigated the behaviour of readers and voters at the time of this election and found little to tie the two together. They do argue that if the *Sun* had stayed supporting the Conservatives, then evidence suggested that more readers would have supported the Conservatives, proportionately, than the numbers of those who did switch to supporting Labour. It is possible that the press mobilized some voters who were already committed to one or other of the parties. But all in all, 'newspapers have but a limited influence on the voting behaviour of their readers' (Norris et al. 2007: 168).

A 1991 MORI poll showed that 71 per cent of *Daily Telegraph* readers voted Conservative. But this does not tell us whether that newspaper influenced voting behaviour, or whether readers chose the paper for its views, and would vote Conservative anyway. Indeed a study of the 1992 election supported the idea that voters had pre-existing values which influenced their choice of newspaper (Street 2001: 86).

In terms of discussing the possible influence of news media on public opinion and voting during political campaigns, one may note that coverage has significantly declined since the late 1980s. In the USA a report found that main network news coverage of presidential campaigns declined between 1988 and 2004 by about 30 per cent. In Britain, the coverage on BBC1 and ITV1 main evening news of elections stories fell by about half between 1992 and 2005. Coverage in the UK tabloid press has fallen significantly (Stanyer 2007: 116). Any news media influence has in this sense been diminished, and certainly dissipated as news coverage for different audiences has been spread across media, not least the Net.

It would seem that, rather than being able to prove media influence in respect of voting habits through election studies, it is more a case of media shaping the view of voters and citizens as to what politics itself is about – a 'suggestion that the effects of media extend beyond the voting decision to the perceptions of, and feelings about, the political process' (Street 2001: 90).

The fact that politics are now conducted through public relations, and campaigns are conducted on principles of marketing, leads to the conclusion that they are also now thoroughly commercialized. Values are invoked, politicians are positioned, and issues are packaged. From this point of view, voting becomes a matter of consumer choice – between different products. The political party becomes a commodity to be sold, as much as the image of, say, a car company. Some would argue that this represents a corruption of the political process. From this view, voters would go for the politician who was convincing, not necessarily able or sincere. They would go for the policies that they were persuaded best fitted their lifestyle, not necessarily policies that are best for society at large.

'Parties are . . . rapidly becoming commercial companies whose raison d'etre is to market a political cause' – 'the reality is a system in which corporate power acts to depoliticize politics, transforming the citizen into the consumer' (Street 2001: 202, 221).

In terms of marketing, Scammell (2003) argues that there is too much emphasis placed on selling leaders or personalities, and not enough attention paid to 'relationship marketing'. In this case the idea is to sell party membership and its values. It is true that the Labour party has lost nearly half its membership since 1997, at a time when its politics have been defined through leading figures in the government. She argues that political interest is alive and well, but party politics is moribund. She points to the rise of NGOs, of grass-roots politics, of single issue politics related to topics such as organics and food, fair trade and goods, cosmetics and testing on animals.

2.5 *Government and news media*

Governments may influence news media political coverage by using public relations strategies and by taking advantage of their control of information. It is inferred that this may shape understanding of political issues and help define the political agenda. But explicit evidence of this is hard to find.

Government news conferences or press releases can be timed so that they fit in with news production schedules, and so are the more likely to be used. It is particularly likely that political parties or actors will influence agenda setting during a campaign because the media have already committed resources to that campaign, because it is a narrative already in the public domain and public consciousness. The media are caught up in the momentum of that narrative.

Governments also use publicists to manage information flow and the spin put on it, to an ever-increasing degree. There are press secretaries in abundance, not to mention spokespersons who are part of publicity departments. In the lobby system, some journalists are allowed by the prime minister's press secretary (in principle it should be the party Whips) to meet with MPs or someone from the press office in the lobby of the House of Commons, to get 'unattributable' briefings (they cannot name names). Ministers are notorious for avoiding the Lobby – so making themselves less accountable for their words and deeds. This frankly iniquitous system of news management has no basis in law. But no one seems able to challenge it or the right of an unelected individual to determine who may (or may not) talk to who.

It has been noted that government will use such devices to 'fly kites' about possible policy developments, to see how they go down with the public when journalists make copy out of these 'rumours'. The idea of the political spin doctor managing news for the government is now perfectly understood by the public. But of course a manipulative relationship of government with news media works against public trust and the credibility of any information released.

It is also difficult to separate government information management from public relations. Not only does government want to put the best possible construction on its information, but also it is in effect engaged in a continuous publicity campaign in order to maintain a favourable image in the minds of the public. Some would argue that the TV information films put out by the Central Office of Information (COI) for the Thatcher government in the 1980s about the privatization of public utilities were designed to do more than inform: they promoted the very idea of privatization. It is notorious that by 1989 the prime minister's press secretary, Bernard Ingham, was running both the COI and the Government Information Service (now Government and Communication Information Service).

Probably the best known of these press secretaries has been Alastair Campbell, who worked for Tony Blair (until 2003), and who became the subject of media coverage in his own right. As McNair (2007: 130) puts it, Campbell 'seduced, cajoled, harried and intimidated the media from behind the scenes into giving his leader the best possible coverage in any given circumstances'.

The government, parties and politicians have websites and offer webcasts. The prime minister offers regular televised press briefings. Radio 4 carries a long interview with a politician in the morning. The BBC has a long-running Sunday morning political talk show. Political issues have become part of soap storylines, supported by information packs from the government. Politicians, especially Tony Blair, have appeared on many talk shows such as *Richard and Judy*. It was Blair's one-time poll adviser Philip Gould who said 'unless you can handle the media well, you cannot govern competently' (in Stanyer 2007: 44).

One consequence of government news management is of course that it is difficult for anyone to get at the truth. Another is that journalists can become 'institutionalized' by their dependence on a controlled access to political information. Some would argue that the politicians and the political journalists are simply two kinds of elite group who collude in a system of information management which works for them (but which may not work for democracy or for the electorate).

2.6 News media and politics

This section complements the more extensive examination of news in Chapter 8. Many commentators talk about the indirect influence of news practices on understanding of political issues, rather than pursuing questions about the direct influence of partisan press views. Such influence has been shown to be very doubtful. People mostly have political views formed before they read newspapers, which in any case they have chosen to read. And broadcast media are not permitted to be partisan – although of course elsewhere this book raises questions about the influence of covert ideological positions represented on television and radio.

Some main factors which work against journalists providing a full and fair reporting of political events and practices are as follows:

- production deadlines
- over-reliance on Web sources and wire sources, and routinized practices in news production (see also pp. 239, 241–2, 245)
- under-resourcing of extended investigations
- over-reliance on specific sources
- dependence on sources
- evidence that political stories do not attract readers, and market pressures to compete and maximize viewers and readership at the expense of content.

As always, and in respect of the idea of influence, one should be concerned about what is not reported as much as about that which is, and how it is reported – 'issues which matter to those who do not consume news become excluded' (Davis 2007: 41). An example of this might be that in the education sphere, skills development and the new diplomas are very important to the lives and futures of a majority of the population. But they get scant coverage in the red tops, or even the middle-ground press like the *Daily Mail*. What does get a lot of coverage, and especially in those papers read by the articulate and affluent middle classes, are stories about the importance of A levels and of protecting them. Similarly, one could say that there is scant coverage of the British membership of the European Union (EU), what people think about it, where they want to go with it. There is a kind of collusion between the journalists and the political elite that this is too contentious an issue to talk about. This is influence (and bias) through absence.

Aeron Davis (2007) quotes the president of the National Union of Journalists, Tim Lezard, March 2006 (see also Nick Davies 2008):

> No longer are reporters given time to go and get stories, to cultivate contacts, and meet the people that make the news ... accountants have decided that a reporter out of the office cannot be writing stories ... so reporters are chained to their desks, ordered to rewrite press releases by large corporations, or to localise a story sent over the wires by the national press agencies.
>
> (Davis 2007: 43)

So the argument here is that journalistic practices have led to reporting and an influence which is about producing social ignorance regarding what is going on in politics. The implication is that issues are not explained properly or thoroughly enough across a range of news media. News media fail to act as a **Fourth Estate,** throwing an informed light on political practices (not just on the behaviour of a few politicians). By extension one might say that a relatively ignorant electorate is then ill equipped to vote, or perhaps is influenced into not bothering to vote. This last point was well illustrated when vox pops on television indicated that Irish voters in a referendum on a revised EU treaty (12 June 2008) the so-called Lisbon treaty – did not understand what they were voting about (they voted to reject it).

Aeron Davis (2007) would argue that the market forces responsible for the change in the conditions of news production (see above) are also then responsible for this situation of political ignorance. Media owners want more output from fewer news workers across a greater range of outlets, to please more people. To this extent the media have had some influence on society – or rather, the market, as practised by media owners has had the effect.

Davis (2007) argues that the market and its competitive forces cause individuals to act in ways that are actually against their interests. Especially where one is talking about elite social groups operating within a limited communication environment, they end up behaving irrationally and in a collective manner. He examines the City and the London Stock Exchange where the 'actors' are so competitively watching each other's backs, and listening to media to which they themselves give the stories, that they can for example talk up stocks beyond their real value (for example, the DotCom bubble of 2000, a phase of intemperate investment in IT ventures). One might see the same error in journalism where journalists talk to each other about what is hot, and what angles should be taken on a given story; where they watch the news that some of them appear on, as well as read the newspapers that they write – with the effect that one ends up with a consensus and an agenda that fails to fairly reflect views, and which again has a malign influence on public understanding: 'rational, self-interested individuals can, collectively, behave in mass, irrational ways, and in response to common sources of media and communication' (Davis 2007: 169).

When one moves away from the search for direct media influence on voting behaviour or the shaping of political attitudes in society, then interesting lateral influences do turn up. Robert Putnam (2000) has demonstrated a correlation between television viewing and civic disengagement. In other words, heavy television viewing causes viewers to spend less time than other citizens on political activity – mainly that which would be at a local community level. This is in fact about politics and influence – in a negative sense – quite as much as the evidence that young people get rapidly bored with media political coverage, and anyway would prefer to get their news from the Net. However, this is most likely to be celebrity news. And where politics are involved sites such as the *Drudge Report* inspire no confidence that the user will get a fair view of a fair range of political issues. Stanyer (2007: 104) points out that newspapers are no longer a main source of news for most people. Television national and local news viewing has declined from 52 million in 1980, to 27 million in 2005. And two-thirds of the audience for newspapers and TV news are over 45. In 2006 the Net was the main source of news for 41 per cent of 18–34 year olds. If news media do have any influence on audiences' perceptions of politics, or on their voting preferences, then this influence must be rather selective by age.

2.7 Political campaigns

Whatever the doubts raised about the influence of political campaigns, through analysis of voting habits and voting change, political parties clearly believe in it. In the UK, parties fielding 50 or more candidates at election time are entitled to broadcast time, as determined by custom and practice and a committee of broadcasters and politicians. Campaigners employ market researchers and consultants. They tend to target relatively few marginal seats and floating voters, since it is accepted that many voters have commitments which will not be easily changed. They want to persuade the target audience into coming off the fence because they acquire a favourable view of party leaders and a favourable feeling about the party itself. To this end political advertising may for example employ the delightfully named 'dog whistle' messages. These are designed to influence the views of specific segments of the electorate on specific subjects, and are embedded in more broadly targeted ads. Only the dog can hear the whistle, which might for instance, alert them to an angle on some contentious issue such as embryo research. They might also use devices such as targeted mail shots or phone calls, or even DVDs, as was the case in the 2005 UK general election campaign for Labour. Photo opportunities are now a commonplace of campaigns and indeed the everyday management of political life. Sometimes they can backfire, as when Prime Minister Blair was barracked by the normally placid Women's Institute in 1999, and lectured on camera in 2001 by the very cross wife of an NHS patient. More recently (October 2009), the now former prime minister was publicly snubbed by the bereaved father of a soldier and told that he had blood on his hands. Blair's intention had been to polish his image as a senior statesman. Politicians are trained in the production of the soundbite – brief because it suits the news structure. Political actors at party conferences have been observed switching from general conference peroration to soundbite mode as soon as they know the cameras are live.

Direct media are very important to campaigns, specially with the arrival of databases linked to devices such as automated personalized phone and text messages and mail or email messages. Belief in the influence of media is most clearly seen in the huge sums of money spent on campaigns. In 2004 in the USA, George W. Bush spent $345 million, John Kerry $310 million. In the UK election spending is capped, and does not have to include television advertising. All the same, in 2005 the parties collectively spent £41.2 million (Stanyer 2007). Politics has become intertwined with public relations. The advocacy of given political views has become professionalized.

Margaret Scammell (2007) argues that the conduct and success of US political campaigning proves that

- Advertising matters
- Repetition does prove influential
- Negative advertising is the most effective ploy.

The influence of a campaign on the minds of the electorate is perhaps not so much about how people vote, even though this is what the money is being spent for. It is also about how citizens are brought to think about the conduct of politics. And in turn this is as much about the coverage of the campaign by the media. Cappella and Jamieson (1997: 33) summarize this coverage in terms of

- stories about winning and losing
- a story that includes performers (politicians), critics and the audience
- personalization – the style, performance of a given candidate, and how they are assessed on this
- the use of language (discourses) of competition, of war, of games and sports
- the importance of polls, not least in relation to assessing candidates.

News media become part of any campaign whether the party managers like it or not. So all they can do is to try to influence this coverage. At the same time, given voter apathy, given the importance of marginals and given the division of news media consumption by age, the conduct of any campaign will itself be highly selective:

> political communicators pursue those who vote, those with disposable income and those who will help them achieve their aims; while these groups become the target of ever more intense investigation and personalized messages, other are ignored.
>
> (Stanyer 2007: 12)

2.8 Net (and IT) politics

> The power of movies and television to speak to a vast public is immensely greater than the diffused reach of the new media, through which many messages can be circulated but few can ensure a hearing.
>
> (Jenkins and Thorburn 2003: 13)

Much has been written about the promise of a brave new world incubated through the Net; the reality is less dramatic, but still interesting a transformative to a degree. Elsewhere I have written about the Net and the public sphere (pp. 197–200).

In this respect we have to accept that it is not practical to construct a system of direct democracy via the Net, any more than one could have a room full of the UK's 50 million voters. Net use has exploded since the late 1990s, in the Western world. But again, there has been no remotely comparable growth in political participation. All the same, the Net has become an indispensable part of political campaigning (targeted emails), and is now essential to lobby groups (websites and YouTube postings). Much has been said about the democratizing power of the Net, and yet there is no sign that it is in some magical way wresting power from elites. Indeed, those who have various kinds of power are themselves moving onto the Net; witness the sites set up by parties and powerful politicians.

> parties, interests, news media, bureaucracies, and public officials who dominate politics in the real world have become more adept at exploiting the Web for political purposes than have their real-world rivals who live outside the mainstream.
>
> (Margolis and Resnick 2007: 313)

Advocates for Net (and new technologies) politics talk enthusiastically about communities and bottom-up politics. But the examples, though important in themselves, are occasional rather than really transformative. Websites and email have been used to organize effective protests at, for example, the climate change summit in Copenhagen in 2009. But the economic servitude of less developed countries has not in fact changed. In 2001 in the Philippines, texting was used to bring together huge crowds protesting at attempts by the authorities to stop the impeachment of the President. The protests worked. In 2002 Jonah Peretti in the USA started a damaging publicity campaign against sweatshop labour employed by Nike. He forwarded to friends his email exchanges when the company refused to honour a commitment to customize their shoes when he asked for the word 'sweatshop' to be stitched onto his purchase. The email exchanges spread to blogs. The blogs were eventually picked up by journalists. The story became mainstream news. But there has been no political intervention against the use of sweated labour.

Stanyer (2007) describes the arrival of blogging and social networking sites as promoting what he calls 'the rise of self-expressive politics'. People have the freedom to talk politics in these cyberspaces. But on the whole they talk about other things. And there is no sign that political expression in these spaces is going to transform the traditional political processes. Stanyer (2007: 174) talks about 'a plurality of voices talking across one another'. Councils and politicians encourage citizens to express their views via websites and email. But if nothing is done with such views, then they have no real part to play in the political process.

Lee (2006: 182) makes much the same point in his study of e-government in Taiwan, where online voting and discussion forums exist. He concludes that citizens may be better informed, but are not really enabled to become politically active.

The Net can enhance the exchange of and access to political information. So far, it does not seem that it will change the conduct of political actions. 'Politicians are more interested in using new media in old ways' (Davis 2007: 115). People live in real space, not cyberspace. The demise of the nation state, with all its political apparatus, has been overhyped. MPs do set up websites and engage in consultations by email. But some of them say that such access has generated a volume of exchanges that they cannot deal with on top of their other duties. And if this represents some adaptation of the political process, it does not affect any process of influence.

While the Net has clearly facilitated the electronic coming together of 'alternative' political groups, it has not transformed mainstream politics. There is no point in its becoming a universal voting system if the voters are no better informed about issues, or indeed are further traduced by political publicity machines. It is not practicable for it to be a real-time talk shop for millions of citizens. But it is possible for it to be an important source of alternative facts and views about politics and politicians, and about whatever it is we mean by democracy: 'there is nothing inherently democratic about Internet technology' (Schuler 2003: 73).

Tim Graham/Alamy

Figure 4.1 Celebrity Politicians: Nicolas Sarkozy and Carla Bruni
This President of France has been well known for leading a celebrity lifestyle. He married a model and singer.

• What may this say about a new style of politics, about the relationship between politicians and media and citizens, and about the process of influence?

2.9 Celebrity politics

Here, one is talking about the use of celebrities in political causes in order to influence public awareness and opinion, and the media (and political party) recreation of politicians as celebrities, so that in effect they become more influential. This is a point at which the lines between political information and practices and entertainment become very blurred.

People like Bob Geldof and Bono have become celebrities twice over – as pop stars and as political activists generating public awareness and funds to combat poverty and hunger in Africa. Bono has spent time with the US president at the White House and with the Pope at the Vatican. The Live8 concert of 2005, entangled with the Make Poverty History campaign, and against the backdrop of the G8 summit meeting of world leaders, is a good example. In terms of political effectiveness and influence here, the central issue would be to do with the gap between celebrity media coverage and hard political action. Politicians are never reluctant to borrow some of the gloss of media celebrities by association. But they are reluctant to respond to attempts to influence their policies or political decisions. Live8 raised a lot of awareness, a fair amount of money and, some would say, no real improvement in the levels of Western aid to poor countries. In this respect celebrity politics becomes no more than a generous puff of dry ice on the political stage.

The USA deals in celebrity politics par excellence. It is not just about Hollywood stars endorsing one presidential candidate or another. They can actually become (celebrity) politicians – Ronald Reagan as US president, Arnold Schwarzenegger as governor of California, Clint Eastwood as mayor of Carmel, CA. Bill Clinton played the saxophone on national TV, rather like Tony Blair posing with his electric guitar. The White House and Downing Street have invited actors and musicians to parties and performances – as if some of the media celebrity gloss would rub off on the politicians – perhaps to suggest, we are all celebrities now.

'Policies are advertised and citizens targeted, parties are branded and politicians hone their image' (Street 2003: 86). Whether politicians like it or not, the shift to soft news and an appetite for personal information about media celebrities has changed their lives and the conduct of campaigns. It has become accepted that people are voting for personalities as much as for policies and programmes of a given party. The personal lives of Hillary Clinton and Barack Obama, in the 2008 US primaries, were closely scrutinized. Episodes such as the one when the supposed 'ball-breaker' Clinton shed a tear on network television were much discussed and clearly influence public response (and votes). The more that our politicians appear on chat shows and let cameras or webcams into their homes, the more this practice of politics becomes normalized. It encourages the placing of the person before their ideas. 'Political actors, both elected and appointed, have moved from being the recognizable distant other to intimate strangers' (Stanyer 2007: 81).

As it does with celebrities in all spheres, politics comes to be about style. The clothes, the behaviour, the photo opportunities, all contribute to the politician's image. Partners and family become part of that style. Michelle Obama's power punch at her husband's victory for presidential nomination in 2008 was noticed and discussed, as much as anything he might have said about the direction of his policies. Audiences sympathize with or identify with the lifestyles of celebrity politicians, perhaps confusing their style with their ideas.

One should be clear that politicians collude in this process of personalization. It is not just about the media being intrusive. The children's programme *Blue Peter* (BBC) was invited into Number 10 Downing Street in 2006, to look round the prime minister's home. The Downing Street website put up its own mini film about the prime minister's life. Political parties want their leading politicians to be celebrities, to be in the public eye. This change of relationship between voter and political leaders has its price. Where Lord George Brown was, in the 1960s, known by the media to have a drink problem, they nevertheless respected his abilities and did not conduct the kind of public 'trial by revelations' that one might expect today. But in 2006 Charles Kennedy was forced to resign as leader of the Liberal Democrats by his own party, because they feared damaging public exposures (and questioned his ability to do his job properly under the circumstances).

One can argue that celebrity politicians are part of the affective relationship that audiences (voters) now have with the media and the version of the world that it constructs. 'The business of political communication is about turning politicians into celebrities in order to organize the sentiments that they want to represent' (Street 2003: 92). If the politicians have influence it would be on this affective (emotional) level. To this extent, this is to propose an argument that politics is no longer dominantly about issues and debates. It is about what citizens feel. It is about the faux relationships that media create between actors and audiences.

This relationship does energize audiences. Corner and Pels (2003: 1) point out that the two finalists for the ITV show *Pop Idol* in 2002 polled more votes than did the Liberal Democrats in the general election of the previous year: 'politics has become more of a "culture industry", increasingly resembling a talent show or popularity contest'.

3 Children

> Older children are both more cynical about television advertising than their younger counterparts but still susceptible to its persuasive messages.
>
> (Gunter et al. 2005: 61)

I am looking at the topic of violence in relation to this audience as well as more generally in this section because it is so often raised by the media about the media, and in rather hysterical terms. The child audience is seen as a special case in terms of influence because it is assumed to be vulnerable. Without contradicting the essence of this special case, I want to draw attention to some mythologies surrounding this audience and the process of influence. For example Buckingham (2003: 7) challenges assumptions about 'children as passive recipients of "external" social forces', and demonstrates that they can think critically for themselves.

There is a context to these mythologies, to research and to received 'wisdom' about childhood and agents of influence. That changing context includes concerns about the changing nature of the family (no longer nuclear); about the issue of child abuse (an ongoing moral panic); about the availability of a range of drugs and more recently weapons (knives and guns). On the one hand, there is a perception that the streets are a dangerous place, where some older children run wild. On the other hand, there is the evident fact that for many children their leisure time and occupations have moved from public spaces to private space at home. In parallel with this there has been a decline in public leisure facilities – fewer local cinemas, fewer sports facilities per head of population.

At the same time this young audience has an ever larger disposable income and has become the target of marketing (see section 3.8). But this does not mean that the audience is simply a victim of media. Adults may be projecting their anxieties onto their children. It can be argued that there is an overemphasis of research into areas such as violence because adults (and the media) are having moral panics about childhood. The panics are an expression of anxiety about violent children (actual or potential) as being

- a threat to social order (for example the current media coverage of knife crimes committed on the young by the young)
- disruptive of our mythologies (can young people who attack adults still be seen as being vulnerable?)
- an expression of our own ideological contradictions – innocence (about sexuality) versus the natural child (with its consequent capacity for sexual expression).

We may be over-concerned with issues around advertising and the representation of violence. There is a need for more attention to be paid to ways in which children incorporate media into their lives; what they do with their media experiences; to other areas of possible influence. For example, new media are changing the way that young people learn to relate to others, diminishing face-to-face interaction. The explosion of available media and the time spent with these suggests that young people have less time on their own. Media public discussion of issues around the environment and our futures may be for adult consumption: but it does not simply disappear when young eyes and ears are trained on this material. It must be shaping the attitudes of the young in some fashion. But how true are such suggestions about these media experiences and their possible influences?

3.1 Major questions

1   What do we actually mean by terms such as 'child' and 'childhood', and what follows from this?
2   What do regulation and programming tell us about assumed views of children and media influence?
3   What do we know about the nature and extent of media use by children?
4   Has the advent of new technologies changed this use and its potential for influence?
5   What can we say about influence on the child audience and areas of special concern such as violence and advertising?

3.2 Defining the child

It may be suggested that how we think about children's relationship with media (and the possibility of influence) rather depends on how one conceptualizes 'childhood' and 'child'. That term itself becomes malleable because young people develop in different ways at different rates, whether one is talking about cognition, identity awareness, emotional intelligence, or other aspects of consciousness.

There is a sense in which media texts themselves have reflexively defined what we understand by the term 'child'. The ways in which children are represented in dramas, or the ways in which they are talked about in news media, flesh out the discourse, construct the meanings.

Buckingham et al. (1999) offer four discourses which frame ways in which we think about children:

- *The vulnerable child:* who is to be protected by media regulation.
- *Child-centredness:* which justifies there being special programming for children.
- *The child as consumer:* which conceptualizes a more active child, and which underpins the toy and clothing markets.
- *The child as citizen:* which also assumes an active role for the child; one in which the child is a social and political actor in waiting.

'Child' is often defined in terms of age. Researchers tend to use the term for those aged up to 12 years, and then to talk about youth or teenagers. There is an underlying assumption about the significance of the 'division' of puberty. But then perhaps research, society and the law is not adjusting to the fact that puberty is occurring earlier and earlier. And even in respect of a pre-pubertal period, can one simply lump together all 'younger' children as a homogeneous group? Clearly not. Again, developmental psychology would define the young in terms of stages that they go through – based on the thinking of Piaget or Erikson, for instance. But people do not develop according to a set of rules, and children are people, not a species to be studied.

The law has other and rather contradictory ideas. Childhood is supposed to stop at 15 in the UK, though not in other countries: it is 12 years in countries such as Spain and Sweden. This means that children cannot be punished as adults because they are assumed to be less responsible for their actions. But then the actual age of majority in the UK is 18, with legal protections up to that age – being sent to young offenders' centres rather than prison, for instance. However, 'children' are old enough to have legal sex at 16, though they cannot vote until they are 18. In other European countries individuals can have sex legally before 16; indeed they can get married. This points to the fact that the notion of 'child' is also culturally subjective. It follows that assumptions about vulnerability and influence will also be relative and movable.

This is not to argue that the term 'child' is meaningless. But it is to argue that we impose meanings and make assumptions, which need to be recognized and tested. It may be dangerous to assume that children have no capacity for evil or no capacity for reasoning.

Even just to talk about 'children' as an audience is to invoke a discourse of childhood, and therefore sets of ideas about what children 'should' be like, how they should behave.

So far as childhood is concerned, this really is a social construct. The notion of the innocent child and of a sacrosanct period called childhood, did not exist much before the Victorian period. Earlier on, children were treated like the potential adults that they are, and were inducted into the world of work at an early age. It was also convictions about education and child employment that created the notion of childhood which we now own. Even playthings were mostly a Victorian creation, especially the manufacture of specific objects called toys. The notion of a child's world built around these toys was also a cultural creation.

As Livingstone (1996) says:

the concern over children and television may reflect cultural pressure towards constructing childhood as a period of innocence, as a private sphere of protected and uncontaminated leisure in which children can acquire the moral strength to deal with society and in which adults can ground their values and ideals.

(Livingstone 1996)

Indeed there is a contradiction and tension between the desire of many young people to achieve adult status, and the ways in which adults deny them this and defer adult rights as the process of education is extended ever later (the UK government proposes to extend the period of compulsory education to age 18). However we frame media for 'children', however young people make sense of media, all has much to do with how we make sense of them, what is assumed about them, what they are allowed.

Livingstone (2002: 7) points out that there are a number of paradoxes embedded in our notions of childhood. One of them is seen in the way that adults surveyed argue for the importance of the family being together. The everyday reality is that the lives of family members are lived apart, perhaps because of parents' work schedules, but to some extent because media consumption is more individualized. Children will not be with parents when they are on Facebook and 'talking' to friends. In this sense, families come to be groups of people who are living together separately.

The broader trend has been towards the multiplication and diversification of media that are largely used individually, according to particular tastes or lifestyles.

(Livingstone 2002: 23)

In some ways adults construct childhood for their own benefit, not for that of their children. Media texts are made by adults. The movie *E.T.* (1982) is a classic example of constructing a mythology of innocence. Even *Forrest Gump* (1994) was a film that celebrated the child in the adult – a kind of nostalgia for an innocent America (that never was).

In what follows, when I use the term child (unless defined differently by the research quoted) I would mean young people up to the age of 12. After that I would use the term teenager to cover those up to age 16.

3.3 Programming and regulation

In practice, media regulation tends to be restrictive, circumscribing (or trying to) children's media experience of the world. Regulation not only implies a view of childhood, but also implies that media are influential. Further, it defines those areas of experience and meaning which it is judged to be inappropriate for children, even in a mediated form. In this sense regulation is indeed ideological. What is disallowed can be as influential as what is seen and read. French media do not regulate the presence of the naked body as much as UK media. The fact that nakedness is less visible to UK children not only stands for the positions which inform its regulation, but also means that regulation reinforces those positions. In effect, in the cause of avoiding one set of (assumed) influences, regulation replaces them with another set. This is much the same as the example of the British Board of Film Classification (BBFC) which censors some US films in respect of violence (for both adult and child viewers), and partially cuts them, even though they have already been edited for the US censors.

In general, children are protected by broadcasters' codes of practice, including those imposed on commercial channels by Ofcom; by the Consumer Protection Act 1988 which is strong on misleading advertising; and through the Broadcasting Advertising Clearance Centre run by the broadcasters themselves. Codes of practice refer to factors such as misleadingness, to harm (i.e. not encouraging the young audience to talk to strangers), and to product category restrictions (i.e. no depiction of dieting, no projectile type guns, no medicines unless clearly used under adult supervision).

Programming has also been based on sets of assumptions about cultural patterns of behaviour and about parents' needs. Very young children have an afternoon slot, after morning school. Older children have an end of afternoon slot, after a full school day. Most children will be put to bed by 9.00 p.m. Children want to watch TV on Saturday mornings. The scheduling is about parenting. The nature of the programmes is about composite views of education and children's entertainment. There are embedded beliefs that material can be influential on children's development, influential on a 'healthy' family life, influential on children's developing sense of what is information and entertainment. Those beliefs are further underpinned by the terms of the various codes of practice. These do, for example, ban ads for female sanitary protection devices before 9.00 p.m., though this seems somewhat perverse when one considers that on average girls from the age of 11 years have a need for these.

But apart from the fact that such beliefs need to be debated, the question of influence is complicated by media changes. The range of media vying for children's time has expanded enormously. Even in the case of TV there are whole digital channels for children, which has made the idea of scheduling rather redundant. The child audience is interested in programmes not programming; there is no clear line between children's programmes and the rest.

More broadly, media regulation makes implicit assumptions about broadcasting being more influential than publications. There is a Young Person's (Harmful Publications) Act 1956 which helps regulate print media. But the degree of intervention is nothing like that for broadcasting.

In the case of the Net, regulators do not appear to know what to do. There is public concern expressed about children's access to pornographic and other 'adult' sites. There is anxiety about cases of children being groomed by paedophiles through social network sites (of course the law can and has prosecuted once these people are caught). But again it seems there is a significant cultural change, in which parents have to take responsibility for regulation, where the state cannot find a reliable technology to achieve this. There has been much made of programmes that can block selective sites, usually via key words. But this medium is interesting because it raises questions of definition (what is 'unsuitable'?); it challenges assumptions about the nature of influence (will children be affected if they download music with 'unsuitable' lyrics?); it questions in effect assumptions about the audience (at what age would you give your child free access to social networking sites?).

3.4 Children and the implications of new technologies

In terms of the idea of influence more generally, it is important to reflect on the effects of developing technologies on young audiences. It has changed what children do with their leisure time. They have more access to more material and more communications devices than their parents ever had. Many of these devices are also more within their control, to some extent because of changing social and parental attitudes – the explosion of televisions and personal computers in children's bedrooms. One also has to bear in mind that – especially for rather older children – they have both technical competence and access to new technologies in the main rooms of households. One immediate implication of all this is that parents carry far more responsibility than they did regarding what their children see and use.

Since the 1980s we have seen the arrival of the following devices (with comment on their implications):

- *VCRs:* children can control their own viewing.
- *Satellite (digital) TV:* children now have a much greater range of channels available, such as Nickelodeon or CBeebies).
- *Personal audio players:* children can carry their own sound culture with them.
- *Cheap DVD players:* children have access to their own films and TV series in their own private space, when they want.
- *Personal computers:* children have access to the Net, to downloading, to an information resource, to emailing, to social networking sites and to computer games.
- *Mobile phones or cell phones:* these have changed children's social relationships, have made them more independent of parents, yet more accessible in terms of parental surveillance.

The experience of being a child has changed fundamentally within a generation. At the same time, one should not ignore the possible influence of traditional (yet changing) children's programming on terrestrial channels. Dramas such as *Grange Hill* (BBC) have been screened for decades now, and refract their own view of school and childhood back to their viewers. The programme raises social issues that some viewers may not have experienced, but others that they have – bullying. The viewer plays with the ideas in such programmes and learns from them, as much as they may do from explicitly educational material.

Concerns about violent video postings on YouTube raise a number of issues in relation to young users. With millions of uploads every year, it is impossible for the site managers to monitor all the material. They rely on complaints being made. Material includes camera phone material celebrating bullying or violent acts, as well as biographical pieces in which there has been false macho posturing involving guns and knives. The nature of the technology makes it impossible for parents or managers to control the age of users in any meaningful way. YouTube has posted guidelines and will delete material. But in effect children (like those allowed to watch TV after the 'watershed') can and do participate in an adult world.

3.5 Children and media use

This only acts as background to propositions about media influence. All the same, Livingstone's (2002: 60ff.) findings challenge some assumptions, even if the information is now ageing.

- Children use television for 147 minutes a day on average.
- About half of children spend time reading books.
- Comics are consumed dominantly by boys.
- Two-thirds of children play computer games in some form.
- Most children spend a lot of time listening to music in any given week.
- Videos and DVDs are viewed mainly by young children.

- One-third of time spent on PCs is for uses other than playing games (one suspects this has changed a lot in the last few years).

- Boys tend to prefer screen media, girls tend to prefer music and print media.

- On average 6–17 year olds spend five hours a day with various media.

- Young respondents often said that watching TV was 'boring' and a time filler. They often wanted or preferred to be out with friends or playing sport – anything to get out of the home.

The concept of media use also links to the idea of the active audience, getting away from old-fashioned assumptions about passivity and influence. Various studies evidence the fact that media are important to young people for individuating them, for differentiating them from others, for contributing to their identity – here the importance of fandom comes in as a cultural experience.

Gunter et al. (2005: 116) refer to research by Thompson and Laing (2003) which indicates that new media are changing the parameters of media use very quickly. They found that young people were, as much as their parents, getting used to the idea of 'window-shopping' on the Net. Again, this is an activity which parents are not monitoring.

A UK government report asks for more parental involvement and for more self-regulation of the Net, not least by ISPs and advertisers (Byron 2008). The report asks parents to assume the same responsibilities for and rights to control their children's use of the Net as they would for any other media. It asks for games to be regulated by the BBFC. There is already a UK Council for Child Internet Safety.

3.6 General points about influence

One area of assumed influence on children by television is in respect of gender roles. But if one looks at the influence of only one medium on any section of the population then one is by definition failing to take into account the influence of all other media. So do ads for toys matter more or less than the images on the toy packaging? Or do the toys themselves actively construct sex roles, for example carpentry sets and prams? Or are the toys inherently neutral, and it is the behaviour of parents and other adults giving toys or commenting on play which gives the objects a gender role spin? Are there not 'gender neutral' toys, or found play objects, such as a stick from the garden, which have nothing to do with gender behaviour?

It is possible to argue that some aspects of some TV programmes and ads for children represent gender differentiation. But then one has to prove that acquired attitudes follow from such representations. Examples include the prevalence of male roles and voiceovers in ads for children and showing females in mainly domestic roles. Gunter et al. (2005: 24) also report research into gendered differences such as the use of soft music and relatively passive behaviour in ads aimed at girls, but louder music and more activity in ads aimed at boys. Research gives cause for concern about influence on young females, with reference to the beauty myth and to dieting. The evidence is that girls with a poor body self-image are the most influenced by ads (Gunter et al. 2005: 8).

Another set of assumptions surrounds the definition of children's media, and specifically children's programmes. Children of *different* ages will read magazines or view programmes that are intended for the child audience in general. Children will read, hear and view material that is not intended for them. Apart from the popularity of 'kidult' programmes such as *Neighbours*, it is known that children view DVDs that are 'outside' their rating, and watch TV programmes in the 'adult slots', not least after the supposed watershed of 9.00 p.m. It is known that females younger than the target audience read magazines such as *More*, with its upfront attitude towards sexuality and relationships. What is not known, because there is no research evidence, is how this 'illegitimate' experience figures in the process of influence, such as it may be.

The 'collateral influence' of television gives rise to concern in a number of areas which are not always directly to do with advertising. Many programmes which children see – including old movies – show the use of tobacco and alcohol in a positive light. There are concerns about the lack of representation of ethnic minorities, and the tendency to over-represent the nuclear family as the natural context for narratives (Gunter et al. 2005).

With all this, there is also an implicit assumption that adults know what is best for children. They produce the media materials which other adults sometimes carp about. This is not arguing for handing over media production to children, but one could argue for their greater involvement in the process of production. It goes back to how one conceptualizes childhood. If this is seen in terms of passivity and disempowerment, then this will have some effect on the nature of texts and on how they are understood.

Among other contextualizing factors which affect the presence of media in the home (and therefore their potential for influence) is that of parental income. Livingstone (2002: 40–9) discusses this and points out that parental income will affect the range of media available, or the presence of satellite TV, computer games consoles and home cinema. But factors such as education come in to influence computer purchase or whether technologies are allowed in the bedroom (more than two-thirds of children and teenagers have TVs in their bedrooms).

3.7 Violence and children

> Despite decades of research, the proof of a connection between violent television and aggressive behaviour is at best weak, and the conclusions so qualified as to be of little value to potential policy makers.
>
> (Buckingham 2003: 6)

There is a lot of difference between a 7-year-old, an 11-year-old and a 15-year-old. Emotional and critical development varies between individuals, and is contingent on various backgrounds and experiences. We are simply not clear as to the effects of various kinds of violent material on these various groups of children. Indeed, it would be impossible to research children's responses to violent material, when legal regulations and cultural rules forbid one to expose children to that material in the first place. We do know that children are disturbed by exposure to kinds of first-hand violence – by experience of war, social aggression and killing in Northern Ireland or Sierra Leone, for example. But then media life is not real life. One is back to that uncertainty about the power of representations.

One has to take account of the real patterns of children's viewing, which, depending on the age of the young person involved, can vary considerably. Hamilton (1998), for example, points out that in the USA children aged 2 to 11 spend an average of 23 hours a week watching TV. But he found that, in a sample of viewing made in 1993, more children watched prime-time sitcoms than programmes for children. He also asserts that considerable numbers of children watch violent material that is not intended for them. For example, he says that the most violent movies shown on prime-time network TV in 1993 were seen by a total audience which included 1.3 million children aged 2 to 11.

Other approaches to long-term effects have looked at children in particular. Some research has suggested that childhood viewing of violence may be related to aggressive behaviour in adulthood. However, the evidence is not conclusive, given the range of socializing influences that may produce such an effect.

These strictures still apply when one is talking about the youth market. Relatives of victims in the case of the Columbine high school shooting (see below) filed a lawsuit against the company which produced the computer game *Doom*, claiming that the young killers had been influenced by this. The case was thrown out in 2002. In another case, a right-wing campaign in the 1990s, directed at an IceT rap track entitled *Cop Killers*, was more successful. The objections were to lyrics which it was argued incited violence against the police. The album was withdrawn, but influence was not proven. Again, arguments put forward by Provenzano (1991, cited in Osgerby 2004: 205) to suggest that video and computer games cause violence and aggression among young players also do not stand up. Lab-based research has inherent disadvantages (see below), and the presence of multiple and social influences was not taken into account.

The relationship of the young to apparently violent texts is complicated, and not simply about subordination and influence. For some young people watching material that is 'too old' for them is a badge of courage, a sign of aspiration towards adulthood. But they will still admit to be frightened by some of this material. The frisson of fear is also one factor which makes the horror genre popular with teenagers. As an effect, a temporary charge of fear is not an influence towards aggression. This emotional charge is part of risk taking, such as going on the most challenging ride at the theme park. The horror text is clearly understood to be just a representation. There is also a dangerous tendency to talk about immaturity as a quality of the young audience, without properly defining the term. Conversely, do we assume that adults are automatically mature? Is the 25-year-old immune to influences which the 15-year-old is necessarily prey to? Children and adults enjoy material which transgresses social and cultural rules.

In assessing influence, adults may project their beliefs onto children. Critics and researchers talk about some cartoons and computer games as being violent. But children do not see it this way (see Buckingham 2000: 132). Buckingham also points out that although short-term emotional effects of some textual experience can be negative (not necessarily visual material), the longer-term effects can be beneficial – the principle of catharsis.

It is also the case that the media sometimes projects false beliefs through its texts onto its audiences (see Chapter 8, section 11.1). There was an episode in 1993 when some among the press asserted that the young killers of James Bulger had been influenced by a horror movie (*Child's Play*, 1991). It was later demonstrated that the two children had not in fact seen the film. The assertion was an invention. Such is the power of what we (or the media) want to believe, as opposed to what is true.

In an article which criticizes the ethics of the latest Batman film, Camila Batmanghelidjh voices objections not so much to the graphic qualities of violence put before 12-year-olds upwards, but rather to a lack of moral vision which might have counteracted the nihilistic violence of the damaged character, the Joker (*Independent on Sunday* 10 August 2008).

This also sounds like a plea for a return to a moral narrative structure, away from the glossy surfaces of postmodern style.

3.8 Advertising and children

Children have always been seen as a special interest group in terms of advertising, because of their assumed vulnerability to its persuasive devices. The Ofcom code of practice and the guidelines of the Advertising Standards Association both give an insight into how Western culture understands children and the concept of childhood. There are implicit beliefs about the innocence of children, and assumptions about their (in)ability to distinguish fact from fantasy at certain ages. In the case of the assumptions, these are, of course, based on some research. In fact, the full range of research suggests that children are much more capable than the advertising regulators give them credit for. Gauntlett (1995), for example, summarizes evidence that some children as young as 3 years are able to distinguish fact from fiction.

Although one can see a reconstruction and idealization of childhood as happening from the late Victorian period, children were not targeted by advertising They might be invoked within images as a selling device (Millais's painting of a boy, *Bubbles*, to sell Pears soap), especially for domestic products aimed at the wife/manager of the household. But the targeting of children, in various age bands, as consumers themselves, took off only when affluence put cash in the hands of young people. Gunter and Furnham (1998) report that in 1997 the then 28 million of American teenagers spent $57 billion of their own money. Gunter et al. (2005: 2) tell us that in 2000 children up to the age of 12 in the USA spent $28 billion, and influenced the spending of a further $250 billion. In terms of so-called pester power, it was estimated that in the UK parents spent an average of £7 more per supermarket shop when they had their children with them. This is serious money, and is about the influence of the child as much as the influence of advertising. It is also worth noting (Gunter et al. 2005) that there is evidence that heavy TV viewing leads to more pestering, but that parental response to and discussion of advertising makes a real difference to how their children evaluate it.

The arrival of the child consumer has meant that she/he is the object of continuous market research. Buckingham et al. (1999) discuss the work of organizations such as Strategic Marketing and Research Consultants (SMRC) Childwise and British Market Research Bureau (BRMB) Youth Target Group Index. But they also make the point vis-à-vis broadcasting research by the Broadcasters' Audience Research Board (BARB) that as the child market is increasingly fragmented by channel choice and researchers' categories, the evidence for preferences and behaviours becomes increasingly dubious. Continuous research is also carried out by channels such as Nickelodeon, which will ask children about their preferences in respect of factors such as story development. There is indeed a lot of research about children, advertising and influence which we simply do not know about because commercial interest means that it never gets into the public arena.

Kline (1993) notes the change that occurred between the 1950s and the later 1960s, when children's TV programmes were initially under-funded simply because they did not represent a viable market for advertisers. But by 1987 US toymakers were spending $350 million a year on TV adverts alone, aimed at children. The toymaker Mattel had a huge success with merchandising which accompanied the hit TV series for children – *He-Man*. For every hour of TV on the US networks, an average of 10 minutes is given over to ads (Gunter et al. 2005). Now television dominates advertising to children in most countries, in terms of the amount spent on it. Half the ads on UK TV top children are for food – often unhealthy foods (in terms of salts and sugars). In general, ads for children focus on toys, cereals and sweets. A survey carried out in 1996 indicated that about £70 million was spent in the UK on advertising chocolate sweets, but £3 million on fresh fruit, vegetables and nuts (Gunter et al. 2005: 17). Advertising is of course time conscious in its focus, reaching peaks around late afternoon and Saturday morning viewing, as well as in the run-up to Christmas. Research in the UK in 1998 found that an average of £250 was spent on each child. The influence of advertising, such as it may be, is not evenly spread; but the financial incentives to advertise are very great. Even Gunter at al. (2005), who retain a cautious approach to evidence of influence, do say that 'it is disingenuous to imply that advertising is ineffective'. But they also say that 'it would be wrong to conclude that television advertising represents a pervasive and insidious influence on children that alone shapes their consumer urges, decisions and behaviours' (Gunter et al. 2005: 11, 116).

We also need to remember that influences on children which may shape their views on toys and other products are manifold. Peer groups, relatives, brochures, the retail experience, all have their parts to play in shaping preferences and attitudes.

Children not only had become a target for advertisers, having money to spend, but also had learned how to spend. As Kenway and Bullen (2001) say, a child who is shopping with adults from a young age 'learns to be a particular sort of child'. They are being inducted into a culture of consumption. Shopping as an experience becomes a dimension of socialization. Even the fact that parents may use the giving or withholding of material goods as forms of reward and punishment, contributes to this consumer socialization.

Toys for the child market can represent not only cultural positions on childhood and adulthood, but also changes in the psychology of marketing. Until the 1950s many toys not only stood for the gender divide – a miniature cookery set for her and some variety of building set for him – but also represented a pragmatic connection between childhood and adulthood, with some emphasis on role playing. But as the market identified consumers, and the adverts had to be targeted, so at least some toys became more completely assimilated into 'a child's world'. The Mattel Corporation's *Barbie* appeared in 1959 on the back of market research which led to the toy being constructed as personality, not just a doll, which led to the marketing of a relationship with the toy. Toys, as Kline (1993) comments, became concepts that were ever more heavily realized through TV commercials. *My Little Pony*, which came round for the second time in 2005, was originally created as the expression of those imaginings which little girls had before they went to sleep (according to the research done by Hasbro).

Advertising and marketing aimed at children has followed many of the patterns of marketing in general. For example, the notion of marketing a suite of related entertainment goods across a range of media goes back to the 1970s and to cinema in particular – merchandising and tie-ins. Similarly, children's toys might be sold on the basis of creating a 'world', of inducing children to buy the inhabitants and infrastructure of this world – GI Joe, Transformers, The Cabbage Patch Dolls.

BBC Worldwide is the 27th richest licensing body in the world (*Guardian* 15 December 2008). Merchandising from properties such as *In The Night Garden* are hugely successful (try the dancing Iggle Piggle!). Of course one has to recognize the even greater success of adult programme spin-offs. For example in 2007 Worldwide, the producer of *Top Gear* and the lead presenter Jeremy Clarkson turned over £8.6 million on the back of that car programme.

Kenway and Bullen (2001) refer to a process in which entertainment for children and advertising to children have converged. TV programmes become like commercials. Commercials are mini-narratives. Product placement suffuses child and adult programmes, especially in the USA. Indeed, they go further, to argue for a convergence between the child and the adult. There is a simultaneous exaggeration and collapsing of adult–child differences. There is a creation of adult-like children (clothing for children), and of childlike adults (the computer gaming PlayStation is for adults as much as for children). Sponsorship has also blurred the lines between ads and other television material. All this, combined with the fact that children will be watching adult programmes and 'adult ads', means that the process and outcomes of influence on children is extremely complex.

Persuasion

In terms of the persuasive powers and influence of advertising directed at children, there are unresolved differences of opinion about the degrees of understanding of the audience and about the deviousness of the advertiser. Kline (1993) asserts that: 'Research has shown that by five years of age about fifty per cent of children understand the persuasive purposes of advertising. By eight, almost all know that advertising is intended to make them buy things.' So does this awareness of children allow them to resist advertising? Advertisers would argue that persuasion works – but then, they would, wouldn't they? Kline (1993) reproduces a trade advert which outlines persuasive devices which, it is said, work on children. Among these are the following (paraphrased):

- Children like stories which involve fantasy or conflict or mystery.
- Children respond to emotional stimuli, perhaps through humour or action or music.
- Children like to see themselves.

To this list Gunter et al. (2005: 20) would add devices such as the use of celebrities, special effects, and appeals to fun, to product performance and to sensory responses. Gunter and Furnham (1998) are sceptical about claims to persuade. They argue that research tends to concentrate on the process of influence, and takes insufficient account of variables such as demographics or parent–child interactions. They suggest that research into exposure to commercials is unreliable in its methodology, saying little about, for example, talk and play during the commercial, or about 'zapping' while commercials are on. They say that below the age of 5, children may well confuse adverts with general programming (see also John 1999: 6). But then, by age 8, most children seem to understand the message of the advert and how this message is being delivered. John (1999: 6) also says that by the age of 8 most children can recognize degrees of bias and deception. Equally, one cannot generalize about child development, least of all in relation to advertising. Gunter and Furnham (1998) would seem to be right when they talk about inconclusive and contradictory evidence. So it is that they conclude that 'the influence of television advertisements on children's consumption behaviour is not greater than that of other factors' and that 'the precise influence of an advert on a child will vary from child to child and from advertisement to advertisement'.

Gunter et al. (2005) refer to research by Gorn and Goldberg (1980), which suggests that repeated exposure to ads can affect brand choice by child viewers, but there is no evidence that this influences purchases or for example the amounts of a given product eaten by children.

Buckingham (2000: 151) is quite robust in questioning the persuadability of children, and asserts that by the ages of 7–8 they are 'well aware of the motivations of advertisers': that 8- to 12-year-olds show awareness and indeed cynicism about the production and intentions of ads. He sees the 'innocent–seducer' model of children's relationship with media as being unfounded. His research indicates that children can distinguish ads from programmes at an early age – certainly around 5 years old. He is not making claims about their judgements, however. He accepts that 'younger children ... are generally least able to remember and understand ads' (Buckingham 2000: 150).

It is one thing for Kline (1993) to assert that the marketing context has become naturalized as a cultural experience for children, it is another to assert what that naturalization may have led to. Young (1990) talks about the effects of TV advertising to children on

- their knowledge, attitudes and values
- their choice of consumption behaviour
- other people (especially parents).

But still it is difficult to make links between advertising and purchasing without, for example, taking into account the influence of the peer group. At one point, Buzz Light Year from the animated film *Toy Story* (2000) was a must-have Christmas present. But there was little actual advertising. Word of mouth, new media reports and the effect of the original movie, all combined to generate a need. In this respect, we also need to achieve a better understanding of the influence of merchandising, where one is not simply talking about advertising. The object of persuasion (toy or clothes for instance) is embedded in a text; it does not float free in the marketplace. And that text will carry all sorts of other possible influences – perhaps to say that 'childhood should be fun', or that 'animals are like people' – neither of which message is valid, and both of which are of as much concern as the possibility that the child will be persuaded to beg for a given plaything.

One might conclude that rather than be concerned about the direct marketing of toys in particular to children, one might have greater concern for more diffuse and long-term effects. Among these effects is culturalization into the marketplace. One might empathize with the concern of Kenway and Bullen (2001) about, for example, the corporate invasion of schools and of the education process. American high schools have contracts with Coca-Cola. More is spent on public relations and promotion to children in the USA than is spent on 'straight' advertising. British secondary schools allow specific banks to sponsor financial information and advice, even to offer 'free' merchandising. The concern is about how children learn to think, rather than about what they buy. It is about how they learn to live, as much as what they play with. It is also about how what is bought (by them or others) to play with may shape how they think, how they choose to live. 'Advertising plays a part in the wider socialization of children in relation to consumerism' (Gunter et al. 2005: 101).

In fact, we may say that these last concerns for children are equally applicable to worries about the functions and effects of advertising on society in general. There are anxieties about how the weaving of advertising into the fabric of everyday life, not just the stuff of the media, subverts our ability to form objective views of the value of both goods on offer and the social relations which are promoted in tandem with those goods.

Figure 4.2 Images of Conflict
Public debates about the effects of violent material tend to show more concern about physical acts of violence, and less about the psychological effects of verbal and emotional violence.

- What do you think about this?

4 Media research methodologies and their problems

It would seem that a general problem with research into media is to do with selectivity of approach and a failure to take whole views of problems, methodologies and the range of work in the field. The following remarks place some emphasis on research concerned with media violence, in order to give them context.

> if research of the 2000s is to better comprehend the import of media violence and achieve more practical results, it must . . . combine teleological understanding and causal explanations, and quantitative and qualitative methodology. It must also leave the simplified notion of 'entertainment violence' aside and realise that the borderlines between fictional and non-fictional media violence are often blurred and sometimes non-existent, and that all kinds of media violence are cultural or symbolic constructions.
>
> (Von Feilitzen 1998)

Every approach to research has its problems which work against drawing absolute conclusions about media influence. Specific audiences are not the same thing as 'society'. Individuals who may be influenced are not separate from the 'audience'. It may well be that as yet we are simply not up to the kind of theorizing needed to argue and prove such effects: 'there is no adequate vocabulary to describe the relationships between the media, individuals, and society' (Curran and Seaton 1997).

Here are some brief critiques of research approaches by way of example.

Content analysis

This depends on assumptions about how one defines violence in a given medium, how one categorizes types of violence and then about how one measures incidents – by number, for example, or by time/space given to them.

The kind of study carried out by Cumberbatch and Howitt (1989) for the BBC used elaborate categories, and in the end indicated that the incidence of violence on television had gone down over the previous ten years, even though this might not have fitted with public perceptions.

The key assumption behind this methodology is that the number of incidents will be significant and necessarily implies an effect on the audience. In fact this does not follow. One might read violent novels all day and every day without this proving anything about how the material is made sense of, or how it affects the reader.

Potter (1999) asserts, among others, the following content findings about TV violence:

- Rates of violence fluctuate across different types of programmes.
- Rates are higher for verbal violence than for physical violence.
- Violent crime is much more frequent on TV than in real life.
- Most perpetrators are white, middle-aged and male.
- A high proportion of violence is committed by 'good' characters.
- Consequences for victims are rarely shown.
- Weapons are often found in violent acts.
- Much of the violence is portrayed in a humorous context.

In elaboration on these points Potter (1999) comments on the fact that white characters are more likely to be portrayed as police officers, whereas African American and Latino characters are more likely to be portrayed as criminal suspects. He refers to the fact that the serious physical, emotional and psychological consequences of violence are rarely portrayed.

The difficulty with assessing influence lies in uncertainty about how various audience members may or may not incorporate such 'facts' within their world views. As Gunter (1985) put it: 'Major problems arise when moving from statements about what the content implies, as assessed by objective analysis of its inherent structures, to how it is actually perceived and interpreted by the audience.'

Laboratory experiments

These are inherently 'unreal' because they take place under artificially controlled conditions. They remove the influence of everyday surroundings and influences – the context of life.

The well-known Bandura experiments of the 1960s with the Bobo doll were said to have demonstrated how violence could be transferred from play to social behaviour in children (and it may be argued that media consumption is a kind of play). However, and apart from the fact that not all the children showed this transfer, the experimental conditions removed normal social constraints on violent behaviour. Also, they arguably set up the children in a frame of mind where they would behave in ways which they could see might please the researchers (Bandura 1973; Bandura et al. 1963).

Field experiments

These are only as effective and significant as the quality of their questions and the reliability of their respondents – let alone the validity of what sense the researcher makes of a given set of responses.

Barker and Petley (2001) have demonstrated that children will lie to researchers (in this case about videos which they could not have seen because they did not exist). Questions and discussions which depend on recall of violent material are suspect, to the extent that our ability to remember things is selective and fallible. Research can be seen as tendentious if, for example, it has pre-selected and predefined its material as being violent: 'Here are some violent videos, I want you to talk about them.'

Correlation studies

Depend on statistical analysis and observing 'significant' correlations between sets of data. The problem is that one cannot assume correlations to be causes and effects. They can be insignificant coincidences. Cumberbatch and Howitt (1989: 41ff.) provide a critique of this methodology in respect of the media and violence. Like content analysis, this is an example of quantitative research (as opposed to qualitative).

Longitudinal studies

Refer to studies carried out over a period of time. This approach might include methodologies such as focus group research or ethnographic research. The advantage would be for example that one could check on possible changes in attitudes or in the context of influence. The problems lie with the specific methodologies used. Ethnographic approaches can provide a good qualitative sense of some people's responses to media, but they are not necessarily representative of the audience as a whole.

5 Media effects models and their problems

Effects models are inherently problematic because they are hypothetical. Do they arise as a result of carrying out experiments (which we have just said will have their own drawbacks)? Or are they propositions prior to experimentation (in which case they are just a notion, but one which will influence how experimentation is carried out)?

Hypodermic models: short term and behavioural

These models are about short-term cause and effect, and would include so-called copycat killings. They are discredited, in spite of having a hold on the popular press and the popular imagination because it has never been demonstrated that media violence leads to violent behaviour. Even copycat killings are shown to exist in certain kinds of context – usually of the social environment around killer and victim – which renders them exceptional rather than usual. Examples have revealed false claims and blame on the media. For example, in September 2000, in a well-publicized court case, a 15-year-old Florida male blamed his abuse of his 8-year-old sister on ideas presented in an edition of the *Jerry Springer Show*. He lied: the show was blameless.

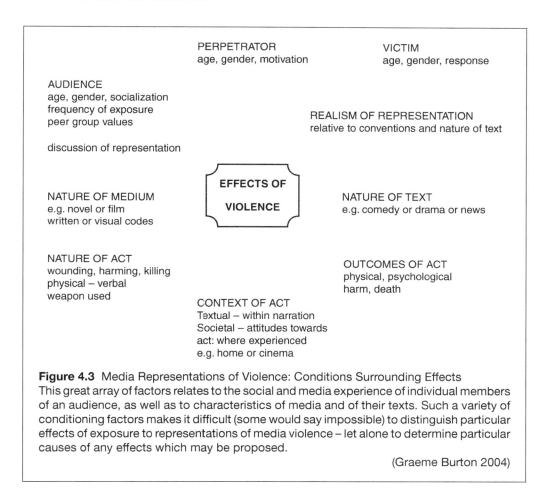

Figure 4.3 Media Representations of Violence: Conditions Surrounding Effects
This great array of factors relates to the social and media experience of individual members of an audience, as well as to characteristics of media and of their texts. Such a variety of conditioning factors makes it difficult (some would say impossible) to distinguish particular effects of exposure to representations of media violence – let alone to determine particular causes of any effects which may be proposed.

(Graeme Burton 2004)

Cultivation model: long term and attitudinal

The cultivation model of accumulated media effects leading to an internalized 'climate' of violence is also imperfect, though it is attractive in its willingness to look at long-term effects and at attitude change as much as at behaviours (see Gerbner et al. 1986). It suggests that heavy television viewing cultivates a negative view of the world as being a violent place. It has also been suggested that such effects vary between different social groups.

One problem is that it relies quite heavily on content analysis, of television in particular (see above). It also assumes that 'heavy' users of television are more likely to be influenced than are 'light' users. This does not necessarily follow, and ignores other factors which might in fact cause a light user to be influenced (first-hand experience of violence, for example). It assumes that television viewing is as much a passive as an active experience. It also begs the question of how one defines 'heavy' viewing.

Inoculation theory

This proposes that experience of media violence leads to desensitization and toleration of violent behaviour. This has been no more proven than Aristotle's theory of catharsis, which proposes the opposite – that experience of violence (through drama) purges violent thoughts and impulses in the audience. Feshback and Singer (1971) in particular have explored the idea that violence on TV can make some viewers less likely to commit violence in life.

Uses and gratifications theory

This proposes that we use media material to gratify certain internalized needs that drive our behaviours in general. Apart from the fact that this model has been little used to evaluate violent material and violent behaviours, persuasive as it is, it is predicated on the fact that such needs actually exist. Their existence as an internal mental structure is itself predicated on categorizing human behaviours. So far as violence may be related to this model, it would seem to fit in with a need for diversion and entertainment. But then there is nothing in the model that suggests, for instance, that reading crime thrillers with violent incidents in them has any influence on behaviour or on attitudes to violence. If anything, the effect may be to make the reader feel better for having been diverted.

▌6 Concluding remarks on influence and effects

One can prove that in some cases media exaggerate the nature and frequency of kinds of violence, as with other subjects of representation. One can be pretty clear about ways in which violence is treated, about the nature of its representation, and about the invocation of discourses about violence. What is less clear is the precise effect of representations on audiences, even if one may *feel* that the accumulative effects of some representations ought to be adverse. Equally, we should recognize that neither has it been proved that media have no effects at all.

> Undoubtedly, many viewers choose selectively to watch violent or stereotyped pro-grammes . . . However, it does not necessarily follow that there are no effects of viewing such programmes or that motivated viewers can successfully undermine any possible effects.
>
> (Livingstone 1996)

Effects are not necessarily clear and direct, or even those one might have expected. For example, it was reported that sales of child toddler reins went up after the notorious abduction and murder of a young child (James Bulger) by two older children in 1993. The increase in sales is a demonstrable effect. A related increase in parental anxiety levels is a probable effect, but still one that can only be inferred.

So there is no firm evidence that the media uniquely cause violent behaviour or engender violent attitudes. But it can be suggested that they are among a number of influences which can shape attitudes and responses towards violence and other subjects. These attitudes and responses relate to making sense of both media and real life experiences (violence or whatever). They may be part of a social and cultural context which predisposes some individuals towards approval of such attitudes and behaviours. The approval may or may not lead to certain behaviours by those individuals.

▌ 7 Discussion extract

In the Young People and New Media Report we used cluster analysis to identify four broad combinations of media among 6–17 year olds, arguing that, depending on access, children and young people generate their own styles of media use.

First, the *traditionalists* spend the bulk of their time with 'traditional' media, very little with computers and relatively little on computer games. They are a heterogeneous group with no strong affiliation to any particular medium but a readiness to enjoy television, books, magazines and music. They tend to lack a media-rich bedroom. The majority of traditionalists are aged 12–14, for after this young people have usually developed more specialist media tastes. Traditionalists are more likely to be girls, with no differentiation by social grade.

Secondly, *low media users* spend below average amounts of time with all media. Given the widespread interest in young people's media use, it is worth noting that one in five stands out for making relatively little use of media across the board, when compared with the majority. Low media users are particularly likely to be young: two thirds are under 12 years old and one third are between 15 and 17 years old, while in the middle age range (12–14 years) we found no such users. They are not especially associated with either gender or social grade groupings, though they do appear to have relatively more educated parents (though not higher income households). Predictably they have relatively fewer media in their bedrooms. Yet even for these children, television is important. Although they make rather little use of most media, television occupies a higher proportion of their 'media time' and they turn to it for both excitement and relaxation.

Thirdly, *screen entertainment fans* spend considerably more than average amounts of time watching television and videos and playing computer games and very little time with books. This style of media use is particularly popular among working class boys and is most common in the 12–14 age group. Sport is the main interest of screen entertainment fans – as an outdoor activity, a favourite computer game and television programme, and as a much valued skill when judging, for example, what 'makes you popular with people your own age'. This suggests that it is interest in content that is shaping their choice of media style, not an interest in the technologies per se. Interestingly, despite having comparatively media-rich bedrooms, this group are among the least likely to spend a great deal of time in their own rooms; thus it would be a mistake to regard this as a group of isolated children – their interests in sport, and in screen entertainment generally, are typically shared with both friends and family.

Fourthly, *specialists* spend more than average amounts of time with one particular medium. We identified three kinds of specialist: *book lovers, PC fans* and *music lovers.*

Livingtone, S. (2002) *Young People and New Media.*
London: Sage, pp. 91–2.

1   What kinds of variable affecting media use by young people are referred to in this passage? What is not mentioned; which might have been?

2   What inferences might be made about media influence on the young? What problems would there be in making such inferences?

3   How would you construct a piece of research into ways in which young people engage with the Net, allowing for what problems of methodology?

▌8 Further reading

Politics

Corner, J. and Pels, D. (eds) (2003) *Media and the Restyling of Politics*. London: Sage.
Davis, A. (2007) *The Mediation of Power: A Critical Introduction*. Abingdon: Routledge.
McNair, B. (2007) *An Introduction to Political Communication*, 4th edn. Abingdon: Routledge.
Negrine, R. and Stanyer, J. (eds) (2007) *The Political Communication Reader*. Abingdon: Routledge.
Stanyer, J. (2007) *Modern Political Communication*. Cambridge: Polity.
Street, J. (2001) *Mass Media, Politics and Democracy*. Basingstoke: Palgrave Macmillan.

Children

Buckingham, D. (2000) *After the Death of Childhood: Growing Up in the Age of Electronic Media.* Cambridge: Polity Press
Gunter, B., Oates, C. and Blades, M. (2005) *Advertising to Children on Television.* Mahwah, NJ: Lawrence Erlbaum.
Livingstone, S. (2002) *Young People and New Media.* London: Sage.
Macklin, M.C. and Carlson, L. (eds) (1999) *Advertising to Children: Concepts and Controversies.* London: Sage.
Osgerby, B. (2004) *Youth Media.* London: Routledge.

5

Popular music

Questioning the popular, questioning control,
questioning the global

*In cultural terms, popular music is of enormous importance in daily life, and for some is
central to their social identities. In economic terms the products of the music industry make
it a leading cultural industry, with income including not just the sales of recorded music,
but also copyright revenue, tour profits, merchandising, sales of the music press, musical
instruments, sound systems and sheet music.*

Shuker, R. (2008) *Understanding Popular Music Culture,* 3rd edn.
Abingdon: Routledge.

1 Introduction

Popular music excites emotions and inspires devotion in fans. It brings together large and
active audiences at festival events. It sidesteps the demands of written and spoken languages.
It has an appeal that crosses national and continental boundaries. It also crosses media,
rather like advertising, in that, for example, it can accompany adverts, can be heard on film
soundtracks, has its dedicated outlet on MTV, is read about in dedicated publications, is a
staple of much radio broadcasting, provides editorial in many magazines, and is reviewed
in newspapers.

So what exactly is 'popular', and with whom? Is music about lyrics or melodies or
rhythms or all of these? How can one – indeed should one – separate music from its context?
Vivaldi is popular with a certain audience – possibly as popular in terms of numbers listening
as are groups such as The Scissor Sisters. Andrew Lloyd Webber's music is popular with
another audience – some of whom experience it only as part of the spectacle of a theatrical
performance. Spectacle is an inseparable part of the experience of most popular music
performances.

Again, it hardly makes sense to talk about music without referring to the global multinationals that still dominate the volume of production of CDs which bring music to huge
audiences. But equally, music of the people (that is, grass-roots material) is actually about
small, independent production, small audiences, alternative sounds. This is popular, in another sense of the term. This could mean the politically conscious work of Billy Bragg,
or the musically eclectic work of the Welsh group, Super Furry Animals. And in terms of
audiences one has to take account of a huge range, from those on the dance scene from the
1980s onwards, to the newer consumers of Americana.

Bennett et al. (2006: 2ff.) refer to three broad and interlinked changes in popular music which they argue one should take account of when trying to understand its appeal, its cultural significance and its place among other media:

The first change is about 'fragmentation of markets, styles and constituencies':

- in which rock is no longer the dominant musical genre or form, but one among many such as house or hip hop
- in which cultural capital and taste is spread across a variety of styles of music.

The second is about globalization:

- in which its processes first helped rock become a 'hegemonic global style' in the twentieth century, but which then have helped a creative mixing of style from around the world.

The third is about economics:

- in which the dominant music producers have gone global and are, broadly, the same producers of other media
- in which those producers are now battling to retain control of copyright and distribution against the consumer power of file sharing through the Net, and by trying to commodify use of the Net (Napster and iTunes).

Critics and critiques of popular music come from different academic directions, all valid in their own way. For example, there is a strong sociological tradition of examining youth cultures and subcultures, for whom music may be a strong part of their expressive behaviour. There are musicologists who have commented on the construction and effects of sound. There is a literary tradition which has picked up on lyrics, their effects and meanings. There are film critics who have taken an interest in the visual encodings and meanings to be derived from music video and music in film. There are the culturalists who have examined the nature of consumption, the importance of performance, the sense of identity which may be built through consumption of and participation in music material and music events. And there are media critics who are interested in questions about the industrial and marketing base to popular music, about music genres and their reception, about the kinds of meaning that audiences may derive from whatever one can agree is the text.

Shuker (2001) identifies six critical 'points of entry' in the critical literature about popular music:

- A high cultural, conservative critique, in which by definition pop music is low culture, transitory and of little value. Where this approach would place the scored, orchestrated and complex music of someone like Duke Ellington is an interesting question.
- The mass culture critique of the Frankfurt School (e.g. Adorno), which criticizes popular music as a product of industrialization, leading to mass culture and to a loss of the true culture of 'the people'. In this case, one wonders what one is meant to make of the rich variety of Indie music and specialist vinyl pressings.
- The political economy perspective, which would examine features such as regulation of music and lyrics (e.g. So Solid Crew) which were deemed offensive by 'authority': or would look at cultural control and exploitation of cultural capital by large media corporations. This approach would now have to accommodate strategies of 'resistance'

by artists such as David Bowie, who are bypassing corporations to release and control their material via the web.

- The structuralist-oriented approach of musicologists and literary critics, which makes formal analysis of music or lyrics in order to explain the production of meaning and of effect on the audience. This approach may have the limitations of a textually biased approach to media, ignoring, for example, contexts in which music is experienced. Dance culture in Agia Napa experiences music in a very different way from audiences at a benefit gig for some political cause.

- Culturalist perspectives including subcultural analysis, in which the construction of cultural identities or resistance to dominant forms of culture may be discussed. This approach has to account for qualifying factors such as the complexity of multiple identities, the temporary nature of weekend clubbing fans, or the consumption of music by loose constituencies in the population (such as youth in general or older women in general).

- The postmodern perspective, in which popular music may be discussed as something which is appropriated and reused, or as being typically fragmented and only to be made sense of in terms of the engagement of particular consumers with particular examples of music at particular times. Critiques of postmodernism also apply here: it is not valid simply to abandon that part of critical work which considers ownership and control or the relationship between media and society. What fans experience at an event such as the Fleadh cannot simply be disassociated from the way Mean Fiddler acts as the controlling organization, or from considerations of performing rights.

In what follows, I am going to approach a set of questions, problems and critical observations in this brief chapter, with relation mainly to institution and audience. What you will not find are descriptions or analyses of musical styles, or of the lyrics and music of specific texts. But as always in this book I am trying to make you aware that subject or discipline boundaries can be unhelpful, and that indeed *cross-disciplinary* interrogation may be useful, even more exciting. In terms of media studies, one may be then interested in the production of meaning, in that whole process which co-relates industries, audiences and the musical experience as text. A holistic approach is echoed by Hesmondhalgh and Negus (2002): 'A distinctive feature of popular music studies has been the willingness of participants to address the relations between musical meaning, social power and cultural value.'

▌2 Major questions

1   How may one define the term 'popular music'?

2   How does context affect the way we experience popular music?

3   In terms of institution, in what respects may one see popular music as just another industrialized example of media?

4   What is the relationship between institutional production, and the exploitation of musical forms and their existence as a minority interest?

5 How does popular music fit with notions about globalization?

6 What is the relationship between music genres, music industries and audiences?

7 In what ways do the different kinds of consumption of popular music change our ideas about the nature of audience?

8 In what respects is music production, performance, distribution and consumption affected by technology?

9 In what ways may audience consumption relate to ideas about hegemony and resistance?

10 What do we understand about popular music and a gendered audience?

3 Defining popular music

There is a general understanding of the term in Western society which relates to industry-created charts of popularity and to what is easily available on the radio. There is a question of whether 'popular' should refer to that which is attractive to large numbers of audience/consumers, or whether it should refer to that music which is generated and consumed by 'the people'. The latter definition might have nothing to do with mass media and numbers. It might have everything to do with, for example, Klezmer music of the Jewish diaspora or the Marrabenta rhythms of Mozambique.

Either way, popular music is also something which is often experienced with others – in concert, in dance, with social ceremonies, as an adjunct to a whole range of social practices. In this respect one is talking culture as much as media. In the narrow space available, let me offer a few definitions of the term, which may productively open up questions about the object and methods of study.

- *Popular music is the sum of its genres:* Americana, soul, drum 'n' bass and so on all attract large audiences and generate large sales of CDs. Further discussion of genre will follow, but one might already see problems with debates about what is included or excluded, about just how large 'large' has to be to equal popular. Genres are to an extent industry-generated categories, used as marketing tools. There was a time when acid house was very popular with a certain section of the (mainly young) population. But until raves made it into the press, the music was relatively unknown, and was certainly not an industry genre.

- *Popular music is that which appears in the charts:* but then British chart sales in a given week or month are small compared with, say, the sales of country and western (C&W) over a year. And is chart music seen as popular simply because it is understood to be bought mainly by the young, whereas C&W has an older audience and does not have the kind of cool image that hip hop music does?

- *Popular music is the experience of the everyday:* this might itself be defined in terms of what is easily available on radio stations. But it could also include the music we hear in stores or other commercial venues. It might exclude a variety of music which is not so easily available.

- *Popular music is the music of youth:* this might include the material of TV coverage – MTV. But this clearly does not do the job because 'youth' is demographically a declining proportion of the population. And there is a huge older audience for a variety of genres, from classic rock to 'easy listening'. This sign of the times is in the burgeoning audiences for BBC Radio 2 – the 'oldies' – and the static audiences of BBC Radio 1 – the 'kids'.

- *Popular music is the stuff of commercial mass production:* certainly this addresses the idea of popularity defined by audience numbers. It also opens up the idea that the popular may be that which is attractive to mass audiences because it has been marketed with that effect. But such comments ignore the 'pull' of popularity which is genuinely inspired from the audience end of the equation. It also gets one into fruitless arguments about just how many sales/how big an audience it needs before one passes the popularity test – a numbers game.

- *Popular music is of the people, as opposed to commercial interests:* the difference between Grunge when it emerged on the West Coast, and the 'manufacture' of groups such as Take That or the Spice Girls. But this definition also falls apart in a number of ways. For example, singers who emerge from talent shows such as *Pop Idol* and top the charts are nevertheless, it may be argued, genuinely popular with the disc-buying public. Or, one may argue that classical music (especially the mainstream classical pushed by Classic FM radio) is more popular with more people than are versions of Jungle. And anyway, 'the people' might include 'folkies', US urban-street cultures and an ageing middle class which enjoys Frank Sinatra and Kenny Rogers.

One might observe that attempts to tie a definition to the use of technology also fall apart, given ways in which musicians of all kinds – even those who produce music which is not popular in the commercial sense – create music through technologies. Similarly, one cannot go along with definitions which try to invoke performance, given the central place that forms of recorded music now have in popular culture. The best one can say is that it is music that is commercially successful, generally attractive to large audiences, and includes a collection of generally recognizable formats.

One might also engage with the problem of how 'music' is to be defined. Early rock was seen as being not 'proper music' by its critics. Music is modified by technologies so that it is not just about instruments. Music as genre is continually changing, not least because of the capacity of global society to circulate and modify that music.

Toynbee (2000) argues that 'popular music differs from both folk and classical in that it developed historically in and through the mass media'. This attempt to define popular music in terms of what it is not, has a degree of validity. But then there is a more recent history to folk and classical music which is also tied in with mass media. These forms or genres now owe as much as any other to media marketing, to institutional production techniques, to mass distribution and to creative input which also depends on global media. Equally and oppositely, one needs to recognize that popular music also develops through grass-roots creative musicianship, through the sharing of music on a global scale, which has nothing to do with the efforts of the music majors. Indeed, it is Toynbee (2000) who discusses the 'cycles' theory of popular music development, in which it is creative independents (working apart from the majors) who set off new styles and genres which may well then be taken up by the majors in a commercial sense. This was equally true of punk in the 1970s and hip hop in the 1990s. As Negus (1999) says, 'industry produces culture and culture produces an industry'.

Longhurst (1995) discusses Adorno's critique of popular music, and a contrast set up between popular and serious music. Longhurst refers to the 'standardised and routinised responses' of Adorno's listener, to the 'superficial and false' pleasure derived from listening to the standardized product produced by an industrialized music system. The contrast is a rerun of the high culture–low culture debate. Longhurst's (1995: 9) chart of contrasting features is interesting in its attempts to invoke judgements based on complexity–simplicity: what Barthes would have called writerly-readerly texts. But, at the risk of sounding condescending, the nature, production and reception of music which is popular has so far changed since the time when Adorno was writing, that discussion in his terms has become at least partially irrelevant. This is not to say that his larger arguments about the nature and possible effects of a then new phenomenon called mass culture are not still relevant. What Adorno would have made of the music of Michael Nyman or Philip Glass, let alone their relation to the popular medium of film, is a matter for productive reflection.

Such examples show how broad the definitions of the popular have become, and the fact that we have left behind understandings based on a two-tier culture. They say something about the relative flattening of class and indeed national cultural boundaries. Popular music is something which, in its various forms, unifies audiences, often across boundaries of class or race or region.

4 Experiencing popular music

One can see discussion of how and where we experience popular music as a way of defining what it means to us in cultural terms, in terms of our everyday lives. This is as important as trying to define popular music by form: those kinds of songs which appear in the Pepsi Chart of the most popular CD singles and downloads. Popular music permeates both the public and the private spheres of our existence. It may be foregrounded or in the background. It becomes part of experience and helps give identity to moments, to relationships, to events. It is technology that makes that experience possible – the iPod on one's belt, the CD player in the car. To this extent a lot of popular music is sourced as a recording rather than as live performance. Live performances at a local level are still prevalent, yet the line between 'live' and 'recorded' is now blurred, with the use of prerecorded tracks in public performances.

- *Popular music is a major feature of radio broadcasting:* radio accompanies us everywhere – in the home, in the car and as background music at work or even when shopping. Here, it may be an individual or a shared experience, but in this case the media choose the music.

- *Popular music is a considerable feature of TV broadcasting:* this is not just about the music programmes or the music channels or about talent shows, but about the insistent use of popular music in a variety of contexts. Songs accompany adverts or form part of programme titles sequences. They are heard in the background as part of a scene in drama. They may set the mood or the time for some documentary.

- *Popular music may be a more personal, individually chosen experience,* via a music centre in the home or the personal player that one carries around, or the CD that is played while working at a computer, or material downloaded from the Internet.

- *Popular music is an ubiquitous part of the retail environment in the public sphere:* muzak and copy material in stores. But it also inhabits other parts of this public sphere – elevator music, mall music, bars, and even swimming pools. Indeed, it is so common that some English pubs actually advertise the fact that they do not play recorded music.

- *Popular music is experienced as a leisure activity in the public sphere:* perhaps shopping and browsing for material, but also as a live experience – part of clubbing, concert-going and festivals. Live music may be part of the pub repertoire. It is something that a lot of people make as well as listen to.

- *Popular music is an adjunct to any number of activities and experiences:* from the fitness centre to the telephone-hold music.

All this contributes to a meaning of popular music in the experience of most people. The meaning may be about the ambience of shopping, the pleasure of intense listening, the emotional charge of a meeting in a public place. In many respects, popular music has become a 'taken-for-granted' emotional colouring to the processes of everyday living, a part of social practices. It becomes noticeable when it is not there. Sometimes it is intended to affect our moods. It has changed the public soundscape since the 1950s. Many of these examples are about the music from the corporations. A definition of what is popular is manufactured through reinforcement of particular tracks and particular sounds. To this extent, selective purchase, selective listening at home, selective clubbing, is a kind of resistance to this dominance.

From the above, and especially in relation to audience reception studies, it will be understood that the context of the reception of music is crucial to ways in which it is understood, used and responded to by an audience.

- *Mall music* is designed as a mood enhancer and a device to make a large public space seem more personal and private. Its style is anodyne because it wishes to be all things to all people.

- *Music in a music store* is designed to arouse the emotional levels and the interest of the shopper. It acts as a showcase for the product. Stores will even set up their own in-house pseudo radio station, to engage with and reassure the shopper. It is, like mall music, part of a social practice and the exchange of commodities.

- *Music in a club* is part of dance and social interaction. It helps define taste and lifestyle. It forms part of a cultural practice, of social interactions, of identity formation.

- *Bedroom music*, by contrast, is not chosen by others and may be a solitary experience. It may be part of asserting space and territory, especially as practised by young people. If others are invited into the space, it may be a way of asserting group identity, as well as being a part of social interaction.

- *PC music* is a new phenomenon which not only adds to the resources available in private domestic space, but also creates a private sharing of public experience. Music in private has been revolutionized by the availability of the PC as a medium that also links the user to a more public world. The downloading, and the playing of music from digital sources, which is increasing steadily year by year, can be a private experience. But it can also be seen as part of a new public experience, in cyberspace. Users can choose to 'talk about' their music without leaving their homes.

In a given context, music may be more or less actively responded to, it will be one part of social activities and cultural experience, it will evoke an emotional response, it will likely place the listener somewhere in the cultural landscape in terms of norms or of resistance.

5 Institutions and change

In talking about the dominant institutions in the popular music industry, one is addressing central issues about how far they manufacture the nature of popular music and control its availability. Certainly the characteristics of the most publicly accessible and familiar kinds of popular music are to do with the talent spotting, production practices distribution systems and marketing strategies of the dominant multinational players – Sony Entertainment/BMG (Bertelsmann Music Group), Warner Music (Time Warner), EMI Ltd and the Universal Music Group (Vivendi Universal). This dominance comes about partly because of the huge capital costs involved in production and distribution of music, because of the costs of developing and using new technologies, as well as the risks involved in bringing on new talent. In 2001 these groups took 70 per cent of all revenues for music production (Hesmondhalgh 2002: 193). These groups are themselves a part of larger media conglomerates. The German conglomerate Bertelsmann, for instance, owns Random House book publishers, magazines and newspapers in Europe, various print and media services, direct marketing companies (books and CDs), as well as BMG itself. Shuker (2001) observes that the US media are dominated by six such corporations, and the global media economy by 12 multinationals. Implications of this kind of ownership are in terms of synergy between parts of these groups. Sony, for example (which also owns CBS Records), will be interested in promoting sound tracks from its films (it owns Columbia Pictures as well as Columbia records). In 2007 Vivendi Universal bought out Bertelsmann Music Publishing (not the music group allied to Sony) for $2.1 million. There are of course many other sizeable institutions that are part of the whole music 'business', not least of which is MTV, which in 2006 was reaching 300 million households worldwide.

Any notions of the music business in general should also include elements as diverse as Billboard and its music listings, music retailers, related merchandising, those who organize tours and concerts, the Musicians' Union, royalties and their management, producers of hardware technologies, the music press, music publishing, artists' managers, and a range of production houses.

With all this, one is addressing questions about how far 'the popular' has been defined in terms of the political economy, and has been taken out of the hands of 'the people'. Yet at the same time one is also looking at ways in which cultural production still exists at social grass-roots level, at the level of the Indies: at ways in which 'institution' does not simply refer to corporate monoliths.

How far are social meanings and the process of consumption of music defined by the corporations, and how far do audiences have the ability to determine their own patterns of consumption and production of meanings? Is popular music all about delivering audiences for digital channels such as The Hits, with all its connotations of marketing the industry? Or is at about the 2002 Rave on the beach at Brighton, in which an unexpectedly large audience of over 100,000 temporarily took over the centre of a city for music which was not out of the charts?

To an extent the history of, and changes in, popular music industries match those of the rest of the media – a process of takeovers and concentration of power, of global power and marketing, of the value of copyright and property. On the other hand, changes are also marked by situations peculiar to popular music. For example, at least some of the most popular musicians have a position not matched even by the box-office power of Hollywood stars. Madonna is a miniature industry in her own right. Artists as diverse as Barry Manilow and Bruce Springsteen have achieved iconic status and a fan base such that none of their concerts could conceivable fail. There is something distinctively emotional about the effect of music and about the relationship between the music makers and their fans, which is not matched by the press or television industries, for instance. Music is a form which is felt as much as perceived. In terms of lyrics or of notation, it is much harder to analyse and to understand in terms of textual features, compared with, say, a TV-news programme.

Popular music is often seen to be a distinctively creative cultural industry, depending on individuals or small groups for its inspiration and force. But to a degree this is the result of a cultural and marketing myth. We have a long tradition of believing in the individual author, though the facts of media production of all kinds go against this view. It is also convenient for marketing to promote the 'star', to personalize the product, even when its production is collective. As David Sanjek (1999: 49) points out, 'all artifacts are made by means of cooperative networks of affiliated individuals or groups, not isolated geniuses'.

Equally, it is true that music institutions have never been able to control or industrialize the production and reception of music to the degree that Hollywood has achieved for cinema. 'The media or music industry cannot simply "construct" a market, produce a type of consumer, nor determine an artist's meaning' (Negus 1999). There is not, as Toynbee (2000) says, 'a unified commodity form' for the music industry, comparable with the production and distribution of that text labelled 'a film'.

Having said this, and while acknowledging the trenchant criticism of the control exerted by music majors, it is also worth noting points made by Shank (2006: 227). He points out that it is the music industry that has produced popular music, not lone individuals. He argues that the majors are actually good (in some parts of the world at least) at making sure that royalties and copyright enforcement bring money back to producers and artists; popular music is backed by an industry and its labour, as much as being a spontaneous, individualist and creative art form.

5.1 Ownership and control of the popular

The recording industry establishes specific control strategies and dominant agendas while a considerable amount of musical production, distribution and consumption is beyond the immediate influence and understanding of the corporations.

(Negus 1999)

One is caught between political economy arguments about the power of the corporate strategies used by the entertainment conglomerates, and culturalist arguments about the influence and survival of music made and distributed beyond the reach of the corporations. There is the question of how far any musicians can be entirely beyond such 'reach'. In one sense, if the 'music pool' uses the technology of the business or listens to CDs produced by the majors, then they are touched by that power of ownership – even if they do not sign a recording contract. As with other media, it is almost impossible to remain truly independent in terms of musical innovation, production and distribution.

Given that content is of prime importance it is not surprising that the music industry favours promotion of celebrity talent, the exploitation of back catalogues, association with the film and TV majors who are part of their parent corporations anyway, and taking over new independents who have identified new markets for them.

To the extent that multinationals do control popular music, it is not so much in respect of the creative base as in respect of distribution. From a commercial point of view, popular music is about the numbers of units shifted. Institutionally, popular music is about that which sells, that which is on the CDs, that which can be categorized into markets, and that which is marketable. The nature of the creative core of popular music also means that for institutions there is a high cost and risk involved in signing musicians and producing material. It costs relatively little to run off the CDs, so volume is also important – the more one sells, the more profit rises in relation to production costs. This is another argument for hanging on to control of distribution. This is why Warners and others went to court to get the free file-sharing website Napster made illegal (and were happy that it was then relaunched by Bertelsmann as a paid-for downloading site). This is why CD piracy and illegal Net downloads cause high anxiety in music corporation boardrooms.

A track becomes a commodity which can be released in different ways through different media. This is very much like Hollywood and film release. So is the way in which merchandising accompanies the marketing of successful music groups.

In April 2001, worldwide music sales started to fall for the first time, and have continued to fall. In 2003 the International Federation of the Phonographic Industry (IFPI) reported an average 10.9 per cent fall in worldwide music sales for the first half of the year, twice as much in the USA (12 per cent) as in Britain. By 2007 it was reported that sales of CDs had fallen by 8 per cent in the first half of 2007 (*The Independent*, 11 July 2007). However, the same article also points out that if one takes into account legally downloaded music, the decline is not so bad. Nevertheless, high street sales are declining. In 2007 the retailer Fopp closed down its 81 stores in the UK. The value of these sales had dropped to $12.7 billion for the half year. The *Guardian* (15 March 2008) reported that although legal download stores such as iTunes or 7Digital had reduced piracy to an extent, research showed that 28 per cent of music fans were still sharing files illegally. It was also the case that the number of people regularly buying downloads actually fell slightly from 2006 to 2007 – 16 per cent to 14 per cent. A survey by public relations agency Edelman found that 24 per cent of respondents admitted to copying CDs, 18 per cent had shared files online and 9 per cent had used a hacking tool to get round rights-protection software (*Guardian* 21 April 2008).

Cheap CD production and the Internet work against a centralized industry and in favour of independence and/or piracy. Domestic computers can easily burn music CDs. The Internet cannot be controlled in the way that, for instance, broadcasting is. Whatever situation emerges from the present struggle to control Internet distribution, it will represent a profound change in respect of the availability and consumption of popular music. The Net is already integral to popular music experience, with fan sites jostling company sites, with online retailing as well as piracy, with Web radio stations and journals becoming as important as their traditional equivalents. Given that peer to peer (P2P) file sharing seems impossible to control (in spite of individual court cases) it is clear that the majors are seeking ways of making money through the Web; iTunes led the way in 2003. We7 has signed a deal with Sony BMG for free downloading, paid for by embedded audio ads. Qtrax has signed a deal with Universal Music for a similar service. It will also offer concert tickets and merchandising, as well as a facility for transferring downloaded tracks to iPods. There are other websites around the world starting to offer similar services in which music is legally downloaded for free or for a fee (*Guardian* 8 May 2008). For example, Last.fm (owned by CBS) offers three free downloads before you have to start paying for the tracks. Indeed, the editor of *Wired* magazine claims that 'we are entering an era when free will be seen as the norm' (*Guardian* 13 March 2008). It is not clear that this will happen – that advertising can generate enough income to compensate for free tracks. But it is fair to say that the new generation coming through is very impatient with conventional practices that involve buying an object on which their music is recorded. The evidence of surveys mentioned above is that consumers are very fed up with the majors in respect of music consumption; only 31 per cent in the Edelman survey said that they trusted the majors and their practices. Music groups are also part of new attitudes and new practices. Radiohead released their new album online in 2007, and allowed fans to pay what they thought was a fair price for it. Portishead put their new album online a week before it was sold in the shops. Clearly we are in new territory. This is not just about 'conventional' downloading. The mobile phone operator O2 (owned by the Spanish media corporation Telefonica) is reported to be doing a deal with Napster to download tracks to phones (*Guardian* 10 March 2008). There is another emerging change which may see the end of digital rights management (DRM) or electronic copyright protection, which stops legitimately downloaded tracks from then being copied. Apple's iTunes online music store has always used this. But in 2007 one of its major providers, EMI, abandoned the protection, and it was found that this had no effect on piracy. Ironically, it has been argued that Apple was so successful in protecting its material that it became the third largest retailer in the USA, and rivals could not produce equally successful DRM. Apple was the dominant market player, and others saw abandoning DRM as a way of challenging this dominance (*Guardian* 15 March 2008). There is a battle for control of the market between corporations, and between corporations and consumers. Some would see it as a battle between the suits and the creatives. Some would see it as a battle over benefits – for artists, producers, distributors, consumers. Would an (unlikely) collapse of music majors take away widely available popular music, or would it reinvigorate it on a regional and local level?

We now have a situation of tension in which the definition of what popular music is, and the availability of popular music in a reproduced form, is both within the control of commodity capitalism and yet also outside this, in the hands of individuals and small groups.

To an extent, this tension of scale, between mass and niche markets, between corporate control and individual inspiration, is paralleled in the availability of live music performances. Only certain high-profile organizations with access to serious capital can provide the venues, events and infrastructure to support a Rolling Stones' tour or a major music festival. In Britain, Mean Fiddler dominates the festival scene, now including a major stake in Glastonbury. There is no point in trying to play the Birmingham Centre unless you can guarantee an audience of thousands. On the other hand, there are thousands of musicians playing thousands of small venues every week. There are hundreds of groups who have never made the charts who are out there with boxes of CDs for sale.

Whatever the power of the music majors to foreground certain genres of music, to manufacture opportunities for certain groups, to make certain songs part of everyday experience, still they do not have the power to make the music popular. 'There is no point-to-point correlation between controlling the market-place economically and controlling the form, content and meaning of music' (Garofalo 1986).

This lack of control over something called 'creativity', and indeed 'popularity', may explain conflicting models of the music industry.

A *Post-Marxist model* might foreground centralized control and the role of the majors. In this case one might look at the comments on vertical integration made by Peterson and Berger (1990). It is also Simon Frith (1992) who, in assessing different perspectives, articulates a classic Marxist/commodity critique of the popular music industry:

> Pop is a classic case of what Marx called alienation: something human is taken from us and returned in the form of a commodity. Songs and singers are fetishised, made magical, and we can only reclaim them through possession, via cash transaction in the marketplace.
>
> (Frith 1992)

On the other hand, a *pluralist model* talking up consumer choice might foreground smaller institutions and the range of producers – a history of creativity which includes examples such as Stax Records, 2 Tone, Island and Rough Trade.

A *political economy model* might recognize both majors and Indies, and their interdependence, satisfying both mass and niche markets. Certainly Negus (1992) pointed out that majors would scout and eventually purchase from the innovative work of small companies. And those companies live interdependently with the majors (and major retailers), sometimes doing distribution deals with them, sometimes being taken over by them. It is a kind of symbiotic relationship which calls into question the degree and nature of independence. This situation and issue is analogous, for example, to the TV industry, where a nominally independent production company such as Hat Trick has a limited range of distributors or broadcasters to whom it can sell. It seems that Indies emerge from a genuinely popular and independent base – punk and Stiff Records, or grunge and SubPop – with new music which then needs the distribution power of the majors to get to an ever-widening fan base. Popularity then makes the style and the Indie outfit commercially attractive to the point where they are likely to be bought up by one of the majors.

Negus (1999) discusses ways in which the music industries try to control what is actually a very uncertain business (in terms of hits and profits) by trying to introduce order, predictability and accountability into the process of seeking, signing, nurturing, promoting and profiting from talent. He summarizes four corporate strategies (somewhat paraphrased) as follows:

- Throw enough mud at the wall and it sticks (i.e. put out enough material and some will succeed).
- Wait until an Indie finds the next big artist, group, sound and then jump on the bandwagon.
- What goes round comes round, so wait for the next profitable music cycle to turn up.
- Genius will out, so natural talent will emerge from your acquisitions.

What is clear is that music businesses, like Hollywood, work on the portfolio principle of spreading risks and assuming that only a few of the signings will generate big money. Negus (1999) also points out that control of distribution means that the companies get market information feedback about what is popular and is selling out there. This advantage is to an extent contradicted by a desire to shift big units and a failure to deal with small retailers and small numbers of units. Music corporations are good at selling what is already recognized, selling large numbers of CDs, and promoting successful bands and trends.

Note that all these comments place popular music as a commodity and measure its success in terms of profit. This says nothing about the value placed on it by musicians or audience in terms of emotional satisfaction or of its being part of forms of social resistance. We are talking here about creativity and musicianship and recordings as having a commercial value, a price placed on them. As with all media industries this is based on the notion of copyright, of ownership, of a price placed on use. There is a price paid for recording someone's music (mechanical rights); for using a recording or for using someone's music (performing rights). There are in Britain groups such as the Mechanical Copyright Protection Society set up to monitor use and to collect money for the record companies and artists. Most of the money goes back to the companies.

There is a struggle between two kinds of culture and ethos. On the one hand, commerce seeks to codify, control and materially benefit from the creative and social experience of music. This control is exerted through enforcement of copyright and through marketing power. On the other hand, musicians and social groups seek cultural ownership and sharing of their music. This is not a simple dichotomy between art and commerce. The companies get (recorded) music to those who would otherwise never hear it. They do lose a lot of money nurturing some talent that never hits the button. And musicians often aspire to the fame and cash that a deal can bring them: 'the music industry . . . is engaged in a constant struggle to control an uncertain market-place' (Shuker 2008: 13).

5.2 Globalization and technologies

There are also opposing positions that one may take, over the interaction of technology with popular music making and reception, and with processes of globalization. These two factors have both encouraged a kind of cultural imperialism in, for example, the global spread of rock music as a format, and yet have also opened up Western music to all sorts of traditions and influences. Born and Hesmondhalgh (2003) take a pessimistic view when speaking of corporate expansionism:

> The movement of musical styles and instruments across the world is nothing new, as the diasporic nature of African American music itself suggests. This mobility has intensified in the twentieth century, in part because of the activities of transnational corporations seeking markets for musical reproduction equipment and for recordings abroad. One result has been a spectacular inequality in the economic rewards and prestige accorded to western pop products outside the West when compared with how non-western recordings are viewed and rewarded in the West.

Yet they also acknowledge the creative possibilities in global music flows:

> Given music's suitability to mass, global commodification, and given the profitability of the music industry, the stakes in the exploitation of indigenous and marginalised groups' cultural properties are very high. At the same time, due to commodified music's boundless capacity to create and corral desire, the capacity of these other musics to generate new aesthetic forms of identification, new modes of the global imaginary, are also great.

> (Born and Hesmondhalgh 2003)

Western music industries have gone multinational and have global distribution power. They have had more than 50 years in which to establish their hegemony and their power over distribution. Yet the technology of CD production (for example) has brought what is loosely categorized as World Music to new audiences around the world. Major music groups which have come out of the pop industry put on hugely expensive world tours. But at the same time musicians from developing countries visit Britain to play local venues. Globalization has not brought economic or creative domination of popular music. It has indeed extended the influence and profits of the corporations and the mega groups. It has internationalized certain genres and styles of music; it has also given life to independents and it has brought two-way traffic around the world. This is what Shuker (2008: 223) calls 'new lines of influence and solidarity which are not bounded by geographically defined cultures'.

One also has to question *Determinist or Post-Marxist models* which assume the imposition of cultural artefacts on unwilling communities and audiences. Rock music has a global (not universal) audience. Without taking postmodern arguments about audience power to the other extreme, it is fair to say that youth in many countries such as Japan took to rock because it resonated in mood and attitude. They also took rock and did something with it, within their own musical sensibilities and needs for social resistance.

Negus (1996) argues that 'the productive powers of imperial corporations cannot directly determine consumption'. We cannot be talking about the simple imposition of commodities and predetermined meanings. He takes the view that 'the convergence of cultural practices and social activities is making it difficult to identify any power that might be directing such movements' (Negus 1996).

In terms of geographies and location, Negus (1996) also takes issue with the tendency to try to pinpoint place and 'ownership' of musical styles. Grunge was identified with Seattle in the 1980s, but is it really accurate to say that the entire style came out of one city? Clearly not. Negus (1996) is not trying to deny cultural geographies in locating music on a global scale – the souk, for example. But he is saying that the 'ownership' and location of music has always been complex. One could go on to say that it has been made all the more fuzzy through the interactions of global travel, global electronic exchange, global practices in broadcasting and global distribution systems.

There are senses in which technology is explicitly global. I have already referred to the Internet as a global distribution system. Electrified instruments have produced for example, distinctive guitar sounds in South Africa, new accordion sounds in Scandinavia. Cheap tape and CD duplication has spread the sound of indigenous music within national and regional borders. As in Britain, there is no evidence that the spread of recorded sound has killed off live performance. Fela Kuti and then his son Femi, in Nigeria, have used a mixture of Western and indigenous instruments, have maintained a tradition of dance performed with music, have maintained a tradition of protest songs, have borrowed from jazz and reggae, have generated the style of Afrobeat and moved on through hip hop.

Shank (2006: 175) makes a point about such hybrid and adaptive global changes when he says of diasporas and their music that their value is not to be judged in terms of some kind of authenticity. Roots music of all kinds is not 'better' simply because it is about older forms. Similarly it is a misconception to say that any kind of music made by a person who happens to be black, therefore has to be 'black music'. The identity and quality of music may have nothing to do with where you come from – hence the fact that an Irishman is one of the most respected exponents of the Cretan loutra.

'In technological terms anyway the world is becoming the local and the global: the national level no longer matters when every household has access to the global flow' (Frith 1993). Clearly technology has changed the sound of music performed and recorded, has made recorded sound commonplace, has made the experience of music a recorded rather than a live one for most audiences – but it has not simply made popular music the creature of corporations. Here, the technologically determinist argument has no credibility. Rather there is an interaction between people and machines. Drummers play to click tracks. Drum machines have facilities to make them sound less mechanistically regular than their originals. Toynbee (2000) argues that there is now a disappearing distinction between musicianship and 'technician-ship', that some groups do not contain musicians in the conventional sense. He talks about a shift from 'the documentation of a performed song to the construction of a song-sound' – clearly thinking of the reformed role of the disc-jockey (DJ), as well as of groups like the Chemical Brothers. Technology allows the borrowing, reworking and construction of sounds and beats which are a long way from the straight performance of three guitars and a drummer sound of the 1960s. Indeed it has affected all genres of music. Here one might think of the reworking of traditional folk music by artists like Jim Moray.

Toynbee (2002) also argues for 'global networks and forms of affiliation' which 'transcend the preceding organization of mainstream hegemony'. In this view, globalization is about nothing so simple as multinationals or the use made of technologies. He is talking about music and global audience responses, in three areas, or global formations.

- *World music:* a dialogical network which mixes traditional and Western sounds, and which uses technology as it pleases.

- *Rap and reggae:* another network in music of specific origins that has been borrowed and reworked across the globe. Toynbee (2002) also describes these forms as adaptable and attractive in their association with cultures of resistance.

- *Market blocs:* these have emerged in addition to Anglo-American – Mandarin and Cantonese pop; Spanish language in the Americas; pan-European music, especially a dance repertoire.

Andy Bennett (2001) talks about globalization in terms of interaction of musical styles and of commonalty in moods of resistance. He refers to ways in which punk in the 1970s and 1980s was colonized by other countries as a form of protest – by 'a globally situated youth culture whose music and stylistic shock tactics have become bound up with highly particularised local conditions and circumstances'. He talks in much the same way about rap and hip hop: 'Rap and hip hop are now re-worked in ways that reflect and engage with local issues in different cities and regions around the world.'

Chris Wood (*Times Higher Education Supplement* 16 August 2002) discusses music as a tool of political resistance. He quotes examples from Scotland to Tibet to East Timor: 'political song is alive and well and being used to express disapproval of bureaucratic incompetence as well as to foster nationalist movements'.

Negus (1999) remains more concerned about the local dimension being lost as the economic importance of a world market grows. He refers to an interview with the then president of Sony Music in 1996, who argued that the cost of signing, recording and promoting a new artist was even then so great ($1 million), that one had to sell in a world market to make a profit. But as Negus (1999) points out, this world market is not a given thing. The music industry is creating it. Cultural and technological factors such as the reach of satellite TV, the common format of the tape or CD and the spread of English as a common language, all help this manufacture of a global business for music trading in dominant genres – whose dominance is also partly a result of marketing practices. Also, this new world order in music is very selective in its markets. The multinationals actually prefer to develop markets where copyright is enforced and they have measures of control. So Japan is significant in their global music business, India less so.

In talking about the construction of a global music market, it should be said that I am making a clear distinction between the dominant balladic and western originated forms that do sell successfully around the world, and that loose genre of world music which is about traffic the other way – Damon Albarn's promotion of music from Mali.

Debates on the effects of this global market continue to split between pessimistic views of the effects on local music, musicianship and even music industries, and optimistic views of the creative exchange, with evidence that many local artists continue to succeed in spite of the multinationals.

5.3 Production

The production background to the popular music industry, like that of the other media industries, is tied up with an inclination to vertical integration and with a consequent desire to control distribution and what is sold in the retail outlets. 'The aim is to make intellectual property, package it and maximise revenues by selling it as many times as is feasible to the widest possible audience at the highest possible price' (Doyle 2002).

Production of recorded sound is also tied up with technology, format and costs. Live performance is also a kind of production. But – without ignoring the value of live broadcasting – recording is the device through which popular music is turned into a commodity. Most broadcast music originates in a recorded format. Even TV uses CD-ROM or tape formats. So it is hardly an exaggeration to say that recording created the music industries. Recording has developed through a number of formats, from the hard vinyl 78s, to the soft vinyl 78s, 45s and LPs of the late 1950s, to tape cassette format from the 1970s, and then the CD in the 1990s, followed by MP3 (not forgetting music video cassettes along the way). The drive has been to make the technology cheap, portable, available and with good sound quality. There has been a struggle between industry attempts to retain control of recording and copying, and audience attempts to use versions of technology to make their own copies for free (not forgetting the important question of mass pirating on an industrial scale). Technology has developed in ways that facilitate that struggle.

On the one hand, the music business has controlled the pressing plants and at least some of the expensive recording facilities. On the other hand (and ironically), other related industries have, for example, produced copying devices and relatively cheap multitracking devices which audiences and musicians have used to avoid paying for recordings and to make their own recordings cheaply. One could say that capitalism eats itself. Still, the control of mass production and of material property (CDs) is central to the music business.

Even where music majors do not control the production source, their control of distribution networks and of access to retailers means that they still retain economic power. And then there is the issue of who owns the copyright on the music contained on the CDs that they are distributing. And it is interesting to see that technology is continually changing the way that the industry thinks. For example, Apple is distributing a free music production program called *Garageband* on all its MACs. This is based on a successful professional program called *LogicPro*, and is available to millions of MAC users. It is proving very successful because it makes it possible for any local band to produce a high quality (64-track) recording that can be turned into demo CDs or into a net release. It has been used by established artists such as Courtney Love. Others (Erasure) have released music as *Garageband* files for the fans to play with (see *Guardian* 18 October 2007).

Production should be seen to start with the musicians. The people who play do indeed produce the music, sometimes in a live context, with immediate access to their audiences. But in the realities of media production, it is the companies who record, and indeed creatively rearrange, the sound of the music.

This last comment raises the point about creativity, origins and credit for production. A&R (artists and repertoire) people and the studio technicians play a significant part in producing the music that appeals to the consumer. We also have the phenomenon of the DJ as music producer. From Grandmaster Flash to Fatboy Slim, the DJ as mixer and controller of the sound coming from various sources has become a musician in front of the crowd and the producer of best-selling CDs. In terms of stardom and the marketing of popular music, these music makers have become as significant as those who actually sing or play musical instruments.

Historically, the production of popular music has moved on from an early-twentieth-century model in which musicians play live to 'the people', and in which the music may be shared with musicians (not least in the audience) via the selling of sheet music. It has moved through a mid-twentieth-century model in which the main experience of popular music was through recorded sound, but that sound was more or less what the musicians would produce at live events. Now we are in a current model in which popular music is the sound of recording studio construction, and in which live performance is also mediated and constructed through technologies. Even amateur groups now use monitor speakers, backing tracks, digital source material and sound-mixing desks as a matter of course.

Marketing

Points about the construction of a categorized marketplace and sets of audience through genres are made below. Another feature that is now taken for granted in media marketing is the promotion of the star or the cult of personality. Especially for youth audiences, the point of contact is as much the musician or DJ as it is the music or the song. This reinforces a point that music may be about a complex cultural experience, about practising social interactions, about identity formation. While it is true that popular music has always had a share of well-known and admired performers, the songs and the music have also been dominant, even in respect of the performer's public image. It is now true that the performer's image and the performance experience for the audience is sold as hard as the music. The business activity looks for personalities to promote. It has manufactured groups, from The Monkees to Milli Vanilli to Girls Aloud. The songs are written for 'the group as product to be sold'. Nobody is arguing that one can successfully market any old music. There are still many songs that become hits on the grounds of their own appeal. But now the music industry is selling more than lyrics and melodies.

6 Genres and styles

'Genre: the way in which musical categories and systems of classification shape the music that we might listen to, mediating both the experience of the music and its formal organisation by an entertainment industry' (Negus 1999). Music, like other media industries, is infused with genres, which offer the dual attractions of giving pleasure to the audience and providing profits for the industries. Genre categories become a kind of 'making sense of music' for both consumer and producer. They are not simply imposed on the audience. Musicians also define themselves in terms of their musical genre or style. Musical borrowing creates a great range of what might be called sub-genres. Rock spawned Heavy Metal, Thrash and the like. Garage gave rise to Speed Garage and interacted with other genres.

In terms of music making, Negus (1996) produces an interesting three-part definition of approaches to genre:

- *Genericists:* those who work entirely within the conventions of a particular style.

- *Pastichists:* those who imitate a style, but only as part of a more varied repertoire.

- *Synthesists:* those who mix and extend the conventions of a style to extend a genre, or even produce a new form.

However, lengthy discussions of the precise features of a particular genre and its variations can lead to unproductive quibbling. What is significant is how genre is associated with lifestyle, ideology and other kinds of media consumption. The significance is both commercial and cultural. Music genres in the media are about social practices and forms of consumption, not just about the style of music.

Negus (1992) talks about evidence from the marketing side of the industry, which is absolutely clear that dress codes are key to the visual identity of the music. They are what people think of when they are asked about a particular style of music: 'Record companies initially position acts sartorially in relation to other artists and genres of music, and signify the adoption of an implicit lifestyle and set of values denoted by these visual codes' (Negus 1992).

Shuker (2008: 121ff.) also comments on popular music genres as being about more than the music. He refers to

- historical roots, antecedents and performers
- musical/stylistic traits (as in kinds of instrumentation or dominant sounds)
- non-musical stylistic traits such as aspects of the personal image seen in dress, hair or make-up (as seen in the performers or on CD covers)
- the primary audience for particular styles
- the longevity and influence of the genre.

'The relationship between fans and their genre preferences is a form of transaction, mediated by forms of delivery, creating specific cultural forms with sets of expectations' (Shuker 2008).

One needs to recognize that popular music is integral to other genres and spin-offs in other media. There are 'rockumentaries' in film and on television, documenting the lives, tours and performances of stars and groups. Some explore the history of a given genre.

Others are bio-pics of a given star. There are TV showcase programmes which present current hits or aspiring groups. The MTV channel is available worldwide, with well over 100 million households subscribing. There are rock musicals in the theatre and in cinema. There are dramas constructed around song, the music industry and dance performance. There is the soundtrack from the film. There is the music video. These might all be regarded as genres in their own right. They all represent ways in which popular music is heard, promoted and familiarized, other than through radio, CD and the Net. They stand for the integration of media and the intertextuality of its genres. They represent a stage in the development and dissemination of popular music which is a long way from 100 or so years ago, when one might reasonably talk about popular music as being the stuff of the music hall and of folk culture, as being something that was performed.

The significant issue underlying genre-ness is how far categories of music are used as convenient labels within marketing strategies, and how far they stand for a category of musicality and experience which is validated by the audience. The labelling within music stores is, I suggest, a convenience but only a starting point, for both the industry and the audience. It is arguable that in musical terms the genres keep on changing because of experimentation, interaction, cultural influences and technology. 'What is really striking about the recent development of popular music is its progressive shift away from conventional tonality and structured conformity' (Goodwin 1992).

Toynbee (2000) argues that audiences are as much constructed as found, that they are constructed for commercial reasons, that they are exploited through a desire to achieve and express identities. 'Musical communities . . . provide the basis for genre markets' and 'the music industry has helped to construct musical communities by commercially exploiting the desire to find a common identity in music.' So he tries to extend a definition of genre from identifying style or product or audience preferences, to something described as 'genre cultures' in which identity, lifestyle and values give the genre life. This moves the weight of genre definition from institution to audience. Unfortunately it does not look so convincing in practice when he talks about categories such as 'race music' or 'cross-over'. It is more convincing when explored through a discussion of 'dance music'. It is more useful when discussed in terms of genres which seem specific to a time and a style, and those which appear to transcend time and place.

Negus (1999) also talks about genre cultures as 'an unstable intersection of music industry and media, fans and audience cultures, musician networks and broader social collectivities informed by distinct features of solidarity and social identity'. So he too is arguing that genre is about more than musical style – 'genres are more than musical labels: they are social categories'.

Brackett (2002) refers to the fluidity of genre characteristics and sees them as being more specific than transcendent. They 'exist as a group of stylistic tendencies, codes, conventions, and expectations that become meaningful in relation to one another at a particular moment in time'. He also elaborates the industry–audience relationship: 'genres may be understood as mediating the discursive web (spun between the media, consumers and industry personnel) in which musical meaning circulates'. But he argues that genre is about more than style – genres are defined by 'performance rituals, visual appearance, the types of social and ideological connotations associated with them, and their relationships to the material conditions of production'.

Toynbee (2000) discusses the idea of 'mainstream' both as a genre category and as something to which other genres stand in relation. He argues against mainstream as being the antithesis of subculture and as being ideologically normative. He talks in terms of affiliations. 'A mainstream is a formation that brings together large numbers of people from diverse social groups and across large geographical areas in common affiliation to a musical style.' His view is that the popular music mainstream is informed by three 'currents':

- hegemony, in which there is alliance and negotiation with subordinate groups
- a popular urge to find an aesthetic of the centre, or stylistic middle ground
- economics, the industry trying to 'map a market' on to audience tastes.

Further, Toynbee (2000) argues that there have been three recognizable mainstreams in popular music – TinPan Alley/Hollywood, rock and rap/reggae.

In the case of rap, Negus (1999) argues that the industry is still trying to contain the style and label in genre terms, whereas so far as the audience is concerned it crosses 'numerous borders of class, neighbourhood, gender, ethnic label and "national" belonging'.

Toynbee (2000) points out that genres are distinctive through their difference from other musical styles (as much as through a coherent body of characteristics). In marketing terms the industry has gone for either the mainstream (with high-volume production and rapidly increasing returns on start-up costs) or for segmented markets, in which categories may be marked by their difference from the mainstream (with lower volume but good audience targeting that produces good returns). Negus (1999) refers to the inflexibility of genre categories as used by the music industry to determine its finance and marketing strategies. In at least some cases, 'artists, audiences and industry personnel remain within genre boxes'. Certainly the music conglomerates base many of their divisions on genres and allocate resources accordingly.

So genre-ness may positively create bonds and affiliations between the music and the audience, but it may negatively confine creative interactions between musicians and limit opportunities for audiences to hear (or want to hear) different genre material.

These bonds depend on knowledge and enjoyment of the conventions which make a genre distinctive. In terms of understanding audiences and the meanings they may generate from the experience of music, Frith (1993) argues that one essential question is 'How do words and voices work differently for different types of pop and audience?' One cannot talk about text, audience, meaning in general terms. Genre makes a difference.

7 Audiences and consumption

Popular music may be a solitary experience – heard privately at home or within the personal technology of the iPod (even in public places). But generally speaking, popular music is something that is shared. That sharing may be part of a large cultural experience (festivals) or it may be more intense and confined to listening and discussion with friends at home.

The process of consumption can have many features, apart from listening and participating in public music events. For some it is about collecting and cataloguing, about the pleasures of searching and purchasing. For others it is about exploring one genre of music. For others it is about accruing group credibility and personal identity – in the ownership, in the discussion about what one owns. For others it is about the personalities and background of the singer or group. It may be about enhancing moods. It may be about diversion from other experiences. It may have the retrospective effect of becoming a key to unlock a life experience, a period of living. It may be about various combinations of these experiences. Clearly consumption is not just about a bare commodity transaction – cash for goods. It is about a cultural transaction in which the listener or purchaser may buy pleasure, status and a sense of place within the cultural flow.

A popular song, an album, is not something that is simply used up through consumption. For the listener, it is a reusable commodity. It runs through the memory. It unlocks emotions. Consumption may be an intentional act, but also an unintentional experience – the ubiquitous ambient music of public places. It is interesting how the music of artists such as Moby moves between this foreground and background in style and in use. Moby's tracks have been used for many adverts on television. The music, like much of that produced by Brian Eno, does not demand attention through lyrics or assert its location in one popular genre. The notion of consumption by stealth has even spawned a mini industry of mood music, pinned thematically on, for example, the Celtic harp, or the sounds of the sea. Compilations are sold on television as being 'cool music' or 'music to relax to' or 'romantic music'. The possibility of silence and solitude is being lost as we are sold music *for* silence and solitude. This kind of popular music may be seen as simply a backdrop – or perhaps as a distraction from the inner spaces of self.

7.1 Defining audiences

In media marketing terms, audiences are out there waiting to buy. In media critical terms, audiences are a concept waiting to happen, to be given life through the acts of buying, listening, going to musical events. For the media and the cultural analyst the important thing about the audiences is what they do with the music. The audience becomes defined by interacting with the music, but in all sorts of ways.

In saying this I am not arguing that the notion of audience as genre creature is entirely invalid. There are audiences for types of music. They do have very general characteristics of age, gender, lifestyle, dress. But those characteristics are to an extent the result of genre commodity selling: people are given an image to buy into, however much that image may once have originated 'on the street'.

The same people may be parts of the different audiences for different types of music. They may behave differently in response to the same type of music according to where and how they experience that music. In terms of a postmodern, cultural approach, it is possible to argue audiences out of existence – the collective audience vanishes as one approaches it, to the point where there is only an individual interacting with one piece of music at one time in one place. I suggest that it is not so hard to take on both a media analysis notion of audience as interacting with a text and having some collective features, and a rather more culturally oriented view that it is more important to make an account of the interaction than it is to conceptualize the audience.

7.2 Reception

I have already mentioned the context of reception and the uses to which music may be put by an audience. Middleton (1990) talks about values which both accrue to the music, but more importantly to its meaning and to its use for the audience.

- *Communicative values:* does the track say anything affective or relevant to the listener? This could be about how tonality links to emotional state or how lyrics relate to some life experience.

- *Ritual value:* does the music perform a 'culturally prescribed task'? This could be about emphasizing bonds with a social, group or about 'taking the mind off problems'.

- *Technical values:* within its own terms of reference, how skilfully made is the music? This could be about admiration for musical virtuosity or the mixing of some effect.

- *Erotic values:* does the music generate an emotional or physiological response? This could be about the pleasure of dancing or forms of arousal related to excitement and energy.

- *Political values:* does the track (and indeed associated visual elements) refer to interests and positions that the listener identifies with? This could be exemplified thorough reggae's reference to Rastafarianism.

So music may be valued for different things in different contexts by different people. At least it is clear that its reception is not a passive experience (pace Adorno). It is actively used and engaged with. Indeed that very activeness causes periodic moral panics and bouts of vilification in the mainstream media and politics – from the outrage around torn-up cinema seats and the film *Rock Around the Clock* in the 1950s, to the changing of the law to trap revellers on acid in rave culture of the 1990s.

Activity, then, is not just about cerebral appreciation or emotional charge for the individual (though it may be). It is as likely to be about participation in a multifaceted experience, in which the music itself is transformed by interaction, lighting and the technology of sound equipment in clubs. The idea of reception is not just about listening: it is more fluid than that. It is not just about the music. It is about the variety of places, situations and social relationships which may come to bear on reception. It is about the variety of media through which music is received. It is about the variety of cultural experiences and commodities with which music is associated.

Fandom

Another dimension of reception and a way of describing audience is recognized in the concept of *fandom*. We are talking about that kind of audience member who is obsessed with things like specific performers, certain genres. The obsession may be in terms of collecting information and relevant artefacts. It may also be seen in terms of getting locked into a certain kind of musical experience. Fans and fan clubs (core fans) operate as a cultural entity, celebrating repeatedly the object of their fandom. They also operate in a material sense (general fans) purchasing and promoting that which they admire. But one may also argue that the state of being a fan is not entirely admirable. An obsessive view of particular music and performers is by definition unlikely to be open to cross-overs, co-relations and global influences. It may be said that fans both support and confine musical forms and presentations. They represent a particular kind of listening and reception. It would be unfair to represent fandom as **deviancy**, but it is a kind of excess – of consumption.

Fans are about gut feelings, about partisan views, about communities, about stuff around the music, about identity and empowerment. Fans feel special in themselves, as well as feeling their musical style or 'their' performers are special. 'Pleasure and difference are central to fandom' (Shuker 2008: 183). Shuker also distinguishes between fans and aficionados, who he says are mainly into the music and operate at a more intellectual level.

Fandom is not just about singers, groups and genres. Nor is it just about youth – for example, popular media images of young females at concerts or gathering at an airport to see their favourite group arrive. It also has a media dimension. There are fans of film musicals. There are fans of radio DJs. The delivery of some daytime radio shows is clearly aimed at a less than youthful female audience. The material has facets of romance, domesticity, emotional experience, recollection of relationships. This is a kind of talk radio in which the music is at times just an excuse to conduct the conversations, the quizzes, the letter readings which are the devices designed to give life and meaning to the pseudo-relationship being set up between the DJ and the individual listener, and sometimes between the listeners themselves.

What we need to remind ourselves of here, is that reception and consumption is not merely passive. For instance, styles of dance music keep mutating rapidly, fuelled by the role of the DJ as producer, experimenting, mixing and responding to the audience in live situations. The companies have to work hard to keep up with what is happening out there, to be able to produce saleable compilations of new styles before they become out of date. This is why the DJs are wooed by the companies for the knowledge of what is happening at the point of reception, and for their skills in a new form of musical production.

7.3 Subcultures and identities – resistance

> the significance of subcultures for their participants is that they offer a solution, albeit at a 'magical' level, to structural dislocations through the establishment of an 'achieved identity'.
>
> (Shuker 2008: 193)

Popular music is much talked about in terms of youth culture and kinds of resistance. This is both valid and yet misleading. Not all subcultures are about youth – ethnic groups, gay groups, regional groups. And 'youth' itself is a notion that contains great diversity. It is a label that appeals to marketeers and sociologists, but still conceals a range of ages and of cultural behaviours. So consumers of Irish folk music or of Indian film music or of reggae may feel their identities are being reinforced, and may feel that they are asserting that identity against dominant cultural forms – but they are not necessarily young, and they are not resisting with a kind of loud public display which makes the tabloids. Brackett (2002) talks about the dangers of interpreting music only through youth culture and about a 'naïve, romanticised celebration of youth rebellion'. Demographic realities mean that youth audiences have grown old, yet have not simply abandoned the popular music of their younger days for some form of easy listening. Rock music is still part of the identity of a now middle-aged generation. Where they stand in relation to kinds of resistance and to counter culture, has not been adequately explored.

Of course it also valid to recognize the relationship of youth to forms such as punk or bhangra or drum 'n' bass. Punk has been analysed by Dick Hebdige (1979) and clearly shows kinds of anger about and resistance to the status quo of the 1970s. The pared-down energy was a reaction against the elaborate pomposities of some stadium rock music. There was anger about the effects of an economic downturn. There was contempt for a self-serving establishment, famously encapsulated in the furore over the Sex Pistols' ironic version of

God Save the Queen. It can be seen that punk as a style was colonized by other countries and cultures as an expression of protest. But it also needs to be recognized that punk was as much to do with a middle-class art college movement as it was about working-class protest. It had as much to do with film and theatre and display as to do with music. And people like Malcolm McLaren and Derek Jarman, while young, were not exactly teenagers.

Bennett et al. (2006: 96) would, however, dispute that musical subcultures are about class any more. Referring to club culture he says that being part of it is more about 'the possession of the required musical knowledge and stylistic sensibilities'.

In the same way, reggae, from which punk borrowed elements of its musical style, was about youth and ethnic experience, and yet was not; many of the performers were not kids, and it gained a solid following among white youth. Certainly it was about a new generation of African Caribbeans in Britain celebrating black identity, and not being prepared to be as accommodating as their parents. But it was also about a fair age range of Rude Boys and Rastas, about Black culture as much as age, about social conditions in Britain but also about social divisions back in Jamaica. So there is a danger in presenting popular music and even particular forms of this as simply belonging to the young, let alone as being a ritual form of resistance against the current status quo, or their parents' generation.

One may not argue with the kind of comment made by Lull (1992): 'historically, much subcultural music has come from oppressed groups'. But one may argue with the notion that all examples have come from youth and are for youth. Preferable are comments made by Toynbee (2000): 'popular music publics may . . . be articulated with social formations of class, race, gender and sexuality'. And (of Britain in the 1990s) – 'class subordination intersects with regional and ethnic identity to produce musical genre-cultures' – thinking for example of Manchester and the Oasis version of Britpop, or of South London and Jungle. Again, he refers to ethnicity and class as much as youth when commenting that 'music-making can represent social formations in struggle'. He invokes ideas from Bourdieu to justify a view of the active role of music and musicians in expressing and working through social relations (not merely reflecting them).

Hebdige (1979) expresses the idea that style (including music) becomes a form of resistance. He is still in effect arguing (vis-à-vis punks) that there are class elements. But style covers fashion and fashion objects, as well as social behaviours and physical locations. Resistance and subculture become synonymous. Longhurst (1995: 212–13) includes chronological diagrams which try to map subcultures, change, music, class and resistance to socio-economic circumstances. Certainly it would be hard not to see some media texts as products of their times, with something to say. What they may actually do about such conditions is another matter.

To an extent one might argue that the association of popular music with 'resistance' has to do with views of the musician in society. The musician is seen as a free and creative spirit, having little to do with working 9 to 5. In this view, music making is intrinsically resisting the system, and involves work temporally out of step with most of the population. Sara Cohen (1991) has explored this in a study of the Liverpool music scene. She found that music making was seen as both exotic and pragmatic – the youth labour market was sufficiently inadequate and the music scene sufficiently strong, that a 'career' in music did not seem unrealistic.

Goodwin (1992) argues that 'pop production and consumption should be interpreted as building resistance to corporate control and rationalisation'. One would not dispute that some examples of music, lyrics, and audience behaviour do challenge social norms and even political attitudes. But still there is a lot of popular music which is ideologically conformist.

Maxwell (2002) warns us against getting caught in 'the Birmingham oppositionality paradigm when talking about music and audience – "insider versus outsider; authentic versus mass market"' (referring to a tradition within the Birmingham Centre for Cultural Studies). It is indeed fair not to assume that all music from the streets is culturally, let alone politically oppositional. It is fair not to label youth movements (and musical developments) as working class and oppositional, simply because some of those involved happen to be working class. Because people belong to a certain class does not mean to say that their media consumption will be either oppositional or passive: popular music is an experience. It is woven into everyday routines. It is not necessarily a tool of resistance.

We also need to ask whether oppositionality and the consumption of music feeding resistant attitudes belongs only to youth. Somewhere in this debate one has to factor in examples like Bono of U2 touring Africa with a senior US politician in 2002, opposed to economic imperialism, and seeking material support for crisis situations in Africa. This is a long way from Johnny Rotten spitting on the audience in 1979, and from Rock Against Racism opposing neo-Nazi movements in the 1980s. One has to accommodate various takes on resistance – opposing or subverting dominant cultural forms of music, opposing dominant social attitudes and prejudices – possibly as political activism.

7.4 Gender

> Rock music in particular has been characterized by male-voiced lyrics that articulate gendered structures of power that tend to mirror social relationships in the real world.
>
> (Kruse 1999: 87)

Both in performance and in reception, the music media show various kinds of gender affiliations. These are, not surprisingly, most apparent in relation to young audiences, in their identity-forming years. So it is easy to point out the masculine and narcissistic posturings of what has been called 'cock rock'. Similarly, there is the idolization or idealization offered by young female audiences to certain groups, both as screaming live audiences (what used to be called 'teenyboppers') and as followers through articles in girls' magazines.

In terms of young fandom, one might reasonably talk about gender bonding. The male groups bond around the sometimes aggressive sounds, lyrics and stage postures of rock 'n' roll forms – the guitar as 'axe' as phallic symbol. Female groups bond around the look of performers, discussion of their lives, the lyrics of balladic forms. This fits with the suggestion that in terms of learning to perform there is a tendency for males to learn the music (and to improvise), whereas females learn the lyrics, from which the music follows (Kruse 1999: 94).

This argument about musical style and gender affiliations may be extended into other genres – the rhythmic and technical masculinities of drum 'n' bass, the balladic femininities of rhythm and blues (R 'n' B). It has been observed that female performers predominate or hold their own in forms such as folk and country music, in gospel and a capella singing. But on the whole DJ-ing is dominated by males. It is interesting that female audiences have allegiances to female as well as male stars. Whereas, considering hip hop for example, male audiences latch on to female performers only when they are marketed sexually and with their own kinds of explicit lyrics – Lil' Kim. The preferences and behaviour of females may have something to do with emotional priorities, as well as with social conditioning and economic pressures.

Of course all these observations are ultimately generalizations. Performers and audiences do not fit rigid moulds. Groups and purchasing patterns throw up ambivalent examples – Pulp, for instance. Middleton (1990) argues that one should attend to a 'variety of gender-specific subject positions constructed within musical discourse, and their relationship to other discourses, rather than insisting on music's representation of pre-existing social stereotypes'. This is fine, so long as not insisting also means not denying.

Negus (1996) in a useful section on gender, music and identity, also argues that there have been dangerous assumptions about gender difference in popular music. He points out that in terms of the youth subculture approach, part of the 'problem' has been that male youth has been much more visible in the public arena than female youth. He talks up cultural variety and change over a period of time. For example, he discusses a disjunction between gay culture and jazz music, as well as the support k.d. lang gained from female fans in respect of her lesbian orientation and after the problems she had in trying to break in to the country music scene.

Kruse (1999: 90) discusses aspects of vocalization and how men and women 'should' sound in popular music. She thinks that men are allowed more latitude in their performances. I would argue that gendered expectations are about the whole performance and image. One has to agree that there is a long tradition of the 'nice' female singer-songwriter, from Joni Mitchell, through Tori Amos, to Katie Melua. On the other hand, if the sound has a certain sweet polish, the lyrics are not necessarily so sweet. And then there are those female singers who don't simply 'sing sweet' – Kate Bush and Bjork come to mind. Courtney Love and Hole are not exactly a sweet sound. And equally there are plenty of examples of sweet sound male balladeers. I would also argue that such female performers have a wide range of images, adopted or manufactured, in which they are very capable of representing sexuality ironically. Male performers, not least those within the broad church of Rock, seem to take themselves rather too seriously.

Longhurst (1995) discusses writing on female fans and audiences. He points out that such evidence as there is suggests that they enjoy the bonding and the tie-in materials, as much as the music or the group. It appears that girls may make sense of male performers as pseudo-friends: where boys may seem the same performer as a kind of sexual hero. To this extent the audience appears to impose meanings on the music and the musician. The evidence also indicates that the emotional quality of the experience is important, as is the question of what is done for the individual's sense of self.

There are indeed a number of gender inflected strands to reflect on in popular music. There is the tradition of the female singer-songwriter and their female audiences – from Joni Mitchell to Alanis Morissette. There is music for, and appropriated by, gay subculture, including Dusty Springfield, Jimmy Somerville and the Pet Shop Boys, as well as Queen and Freddie Mercury. There is the placing of a line of 'rock chicks', from Suzi Quatro to Chrissie Hynde. One might evaluate the attraction of the male audience to the female singers such as Shania Twain. There are questions about the nature of the audience and audience attraction in relation to performers presenting ambivalent sexuality – Morrissey, Boy George, Brett Anderson. There is the successful marketing of a singer like KT Tunstall to both females and males. And as audiences grow older there is the question of how far the notion of gendered genres or gendered audiences really holds up. Country and western would be an example of this. The older audience for C&W has moved beyond a stage of same-sex bonding, and into stages and experiences of one-to-one relationships, loss and ageing.

In terms of creation and production (Whiteley et al. 2004: 153ff.), female artists who acquire a reputation as being critically significant are also song writers, such as P.J. Harvey. Interestingly this would seem to be about the status of authorship in Western culture – always ironic when one considers the intrinsically collaborative nature of media production. They refer to 'the patriarchal positioning of the producer as individual author'. The writers criticize ways in which women's contributions may be diminished – Courtney Love losing credit to Kurt Cobain or Billy Corgan. They refer to contradictory judgements made on women involved in production, where they may be accused of overreaching themselves, or undermining their 'real' talents as performers – even when there is no argument about the female artist's achievements, as when Kate Bush showed considerable technical skill in engineering *Hounds of Love*. The lack of female production involvement in popular music, and the dominance of male producers, is of a piece with our history of art as one in which male genius and creativity is reified. Similarly, the pre-eminent position in the UK of a DJ and broadcaster such as Jo Whiley is, perhaps for the same reason, the exception rather than the rule. And as with other media occupations – perhaps newspaper journalism – one is also talking about a history of a gendered culture.

Shuker (2001) raises acute questions about where our understanding of gender in popular music comes from:

> Dance pop is generally seen as 'a girls' genre', while hard rock and heavy metal are regarded as primarily male-oriented genres. Women performers predominate in a cappella and gospel music, and are prominent in folk and country, and among singer-songwriters. Male DJs are the norm in the contemporary dance music scene. How 'natural' are such associations, and what ways are they social constructs?
>
> (Shuker 2001)

He refers to the male-dominated music industry and to evidence that women are actively excluded from the band experience. Instruments are seen as masculine or feminine – and the guitar (and the music shops which sell guitars) is seen as male territory. He refers to Bayton's work in evidencing gender socialization as a major factor in producing a gender divide in popular music. The strength of this divide is evident when one tries to consider counter examples, and has to see them as exceptions to a 'rule' – Hazel O'Connor and Punk, or Riot Grrrl and Hardcore. Sarah Thornton (2006: 104) also points to social or cultural factors as separating females from males in the ways that they become involved with popular music: – 'women spend less time and money on music, the music press and going out, and more on clothes and cosmetics'.

It would be surprising if popular music was not a site of struggle, of alternatives, of norm affirmation, of challenge to norms – given that it is part of the cultures which embrace and express different and contradictory positions on gender, all at the same time. But there is a danger of missing the variety of those positions. And, apart from issues of gender, popular music is appropriated by culturally diverse groups both to celebrate their character and to be enjoyed for its own sake. As much as being associated with public disturbances and drug use, popular music is a unifying force across age groups and geographies.

8 Discussion extract

It may be that globally we are witnessing the creation and expansion of mediascapes made up of a variety of elements which are used in alternative ways in different places by particular groups of people. Furthermore, such mediascapes would not be the product of one group or controlling organization, but involve complex negotiations and struggles around the placing together of different elements. The mediascape is like a landscape, in that it can be seen in different ways from alternative perspectives and is relatively open to different uses. The idea suggests that configurations of media are very complex, and that whilst they are affected by the operations of power, they are not simply subject to the whims of decisions of the powerful – a motorway may be built through it for instance – but such decisions may be fought, or parts of the landscape may come under the control of smaller owners, and so on.

In this sort of approach the attempt is made to move away from more simplistic accounts resting on notions of the overpowering strength of a few capitalist corporations who can do more or less what they want. It suggests that more attention should be paid to the production (and consumption) of music in specific contexts, as part of a consideration of the interaction of the global and the local. However, it is important to recognize the leading role of large corporations and to study their aims and the potential effects they can have in a detailed fashion.

Three summary points can be made. First, these processes are dynamic and contradictory. As can be argued, globalization does not mean that everything is becoming the same . . .

Second, different aspects of globalization are connected. Thus, the consumption of a CD as part of the way of life of an individual will depend on the social interaction of those who made it, who may be globally separated, the political processes that facilitate trade and the economic patterns of production and organization that led to it being produced and marketed.

Third, the practices of globalization are contested. This may be the overt struggle that has led to violent and explicit confrontations around specific meetings of the global elite, the organization of pop/rock concerts, and so on. However, the practices of hybridization also involve modes of contestation as well as accommodation and the production of new forms through collaboration.

Longhurst, B. (2007) *Popular Music and Society*, 2nd edn. Cambridge: Polity.

1   In respect of a music mediascape, where can one see struggles going on, and where can one see examples of the control of smaller owners?

2   Where can one see processes which contradict models of global dominance for the production of popular music?

3   Where can one see examples of confrontation and hybridization which illustrate the point about practices of globalization being contested?

4   How far is popular music different from or similar to other media industries and forms in respect of the points behind the first three questions?

9 Further reading

Bennett, A. (2001) *Cultures of Popular Music*. Buckingham: Open University Press.

Bennett, A., Shank, B. and Toynbee, J. (eds) (2006) *The Popular Music Studies Reader.* Abingdon: Routledge.

Hesmondhalgh, D. and Negus, K. (eds) (2002) *Popular Music Studies*. London: Arnold.

Longhurst, B. (2007) *Popular Music and Society*, 2nd edn. Cambridge: Polity.

Negus, K. (1999) *Music Genres and Corporate Cultures*. London: Routledge.

Shuker, R. (2008) *Understanding Popular Music Culture.* Abingdon: Routledge.

Toynbee, J. (2000) *Making Popular Music*. London: Arnold.

|6

The media and new technology

Technologies changing the media and
changing consumption

different cultures and different political regimes will exploit nascent technologies in radically different ways

Jenkins, H. and Thorburn, D. (eds) (2003) *Democracy and New Media*.
Cambridge, MA: MIT Press.

1 Introduction

All media use a range of technologies to manufacture representations (see also Chapter 2). In whatever way media make a connection between their productions and their audiences, this connection is dependent on technology. All technologies are new in their time. There is an assumption behind this chapter that we are talking mainly about computer-based technologies from the 1980s onwards. But just as one wonders what comes after postmodernism, so also one wonders when new technology starts to seem old. Even hot-metal type was new to the printing industry something over a hundred years ago. Now it has gone. But in its time it made possible the mass production and mass circulation of daily newspapers from the late nineteenth century to the late twentieth century. The cassette tape video recorder has gone after about 25 years of being part of domestic culture.

1.1 When is technology new?

New technologies are not always that new, but depend on developments of earlier technologies and their applications. Truly new technologies are usually not the creation of the media themselves. It is often the technological pressure-cooker of military innovation which provides the opportunity for later civil applications, and for the media. Satellites were at first developed and launched in the 1960s for their military applications – surveillance and communications. The Internet was originally created for its military convenience – to find a robust form of communication that could not be knocked out by a couple of Russian intercontinental ballistic missiles (ICBMs).

Cornford and Robins (1999) talk about 'an accommodation between old and new' and point out that 'new media are often heavily reliant on repackaged older media content'. Even interactivity is not new in itself (radio phone-ins): rather it may be the speed and embeddedness of interactivity on the back of technology, which is new. And this interactivity is not all about benefit to the audience. 'New technologies . . . enable producers of new media products and services to monitor, segment and target audiences in new ways' (Cornford and Robbins 1999).

1.2 When is the future present?

There is also a run-in time to technologies, so that one may forget how long it takes for a technology to become really embedded in cultural usage. For instance, the public in the West was well aware of the media potential of satellites through early but laborious broadcast links. However, it was not until the 1980s that the launch and proliferation of communication satellites had become so common that the period of technological novelty had worn off, and audiences began to take for granted the idea that they should expect to see images from more or less anywhere on the planet. Vested interests in media businesses may be keen to tell their consumers that the future is here now. But experience tells us that the real, lived-in future takes a little longer to arrive. This is what Paschal Preston (2001) refers to as 'a long history of undelivered promises'.

One should also be cautious about making assumptions about what constitutes new media and new technology, and about how these are being taken up. For example, the clockwork Freeplay radio is a recent invention, using old technology, and with great benefits for Africans who can neither afford nor get access to electric technologies. By contrast, a city like Tallin in Estonia is one of the most wired-up communities in the world, in that it has jumped straight to the latest wireless technology that links every mobile in the city, and gives users access to other technologies. It is Preston (2001) again, taking a cautious and even sceptical view of the advance of technologies of new media, who identifies three kinds of error perpetrated by pundits and the industries:

- An overemphasis on technology which misses other factors which influence innovation and acceptance

- A tendency to talk about products (gizmos), related to a failure to attend to process innovation (how products will be used by the average consumer)

- An inclination to ignore political or economic brakes on matters of demand and consumption.

Lister et al. (2003) warn against overemphasis on technological features when trying to make sense of new media. They point out that, for example, virtuality and cyberspace are about senses of self and of identities as much as technological ingenuities. They also warn against assumptions as to how technology will be used, and as to what future media will look like. There is no inevitable line of development towards some predictable kind of media world, based on technological reductionism – 'when we get enough computing power'. What they do lay out is what they see as being six characteristics of what is happening with new media:

- The creation of new textual experiences
- The arrival of new ways of representing the world
- The development of new relationships between subject (both users and consumers) and media technologies
- The creation of new experiences of the relationship between embodiment, identity and community
- New conceptions of the biological body's relationship to technology and media
- The development of new patterns of organization and production.

Their work most usefully develops areas outside the remit of this chapter – realisms and the history of representation, virtual realities and the transformation of the sense of self through media technologies.

Andrew Brown (*Independent on Sunday* 19 September 1999) makes the interesting point that new technology will only really have arrived in the domestic sphere when one no longer recognizes its presence, nor where information comes from. Technology becomes invisible and unremarkable – like the television set.

Television and new technology

Curran (2002) takes a sceptical view of the supposed dominance of new media and new technologies, not least with relation to television. He points out that in 2000 for example, 89 per cent of British prime time TV was viewed across only four (largely broadcast) channels. He asserts that PSB is far from collapsing, that audiences have not fragmented, and that this is generally the case, being one of the myths of globalization. In particular he argues against the position of Elihu Katz (1996), which he summarizes as suggesting the following:

- Because audiences are being dispersed by consumption of new media, nations are no longer united by a shared experience of mass television viewing.

- People are less informed because of the decline of public service broadcasting, under 'the constraints of new media technology' and 'the seductions of multinational corporations'.

- Liberal democracy within the nation state is being weakened because new media and globalization have weakened a sense of national identity.

But Curran himself argues that:

- 'British television continues to be a national medium.'
- 'The life-support system supposedly supporting national democracy is not about to be switched off.'
- Because of regulation many broadcasters across Europe are in fact PSB broadcasters (like Channel 4).
- There is plenty of information material in prime time (whatever is happening in the USA).
- Even globally, while economics and technology may have brought about some changes, they have not torn apart the national channel.
- In Britain, at least, forecasts of the take-up of the new technologies of satellite and cable have proved to be manifestly and expensively wrong (for the companies concerned).

However, I would argue that while the nature and pace of technological change is often exaggerated by those who have a vested interest in it, still Curran's position is less tenable, even in 2010. Satellite and cable have now been taken up massively, not least through innovations such as Freeview. And audiences are steadily fragmenting – not just to other TV channels, but to other media activities. The viewing figures for prime time soap operas or news are about two-thirds of what they were in the late 1980s.

2 Major questions

1   Does technology shape the development of media?
2   Is the development of technology itself shaped by commercial forces and social pressures?
3   How has technology affected the work of media businesses, and their outputs?
4   How has technology affected the relationship between media and society?
5   Is the significance of technology as much about information as about entertainment?
6   How may one describe the nature of the change in media practices and media experience for the audience, brought about by new technology?
7   Has technology affected the 'balance of power' between media institutions and society (audiences)?
8   What is the place of the Net, in particular, within all these questions?
9   Has the arrival of new media, and changes to old media, produced any kinds of benefit for society?

3 Determinism or opportunism? Technology and media developments

The essence of the debate here is about how far one may see technology as determining the nature of media developments and output, and how far one sees the media or even media users as grabbing technological opportunities when they come along.

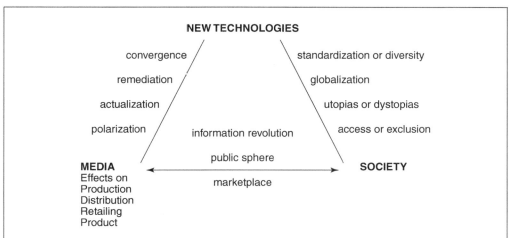

Figure 6.1 Media Technology: Terms and Debates
The co-relationship between technology, media and society is most obviously characterized by kinds of change to production and text/product, as well as by issues then raised concerning that relationship. What is ambiguous is how far technologies and media drive changes, and how far society and audiences induce them.

(Graeme Burton 2004)

The notion of **technological determinism** represents an argument that technology of itself shapes society and can be a cause of social change. However, I would argue that while any technology may have kinds of potential, it does not of itself have intentionality. It has to be used and developed, and media industries determine that development. It may simultaneously be true, that once a given technology has reached a certain level of development and availability, then the exact nature of its continuing use, especially by consumers, it is not so easy to control. Opportunities are not so easy to envisage. And whether technology works for social benefit or social damage is neither certain nor consistent when one looks at its effects.

The development and effects of technologies are unpredictable. Van Loon (2008: 13) opposes the idea of technological determinism, as well as the idea of 'linear evolutionism', seeing the latter as a projection of modernism. On the one hand, one might have seen television as a technology waiting to happen, because it was written about more than 30 years before it first became a reality. On the other hand, there is no linear logic in the ways that television has come to be used. Similarly, the development of the Web follows no particular logic stemming from its creators, its users, or the nature of its technologies.

Classic and largely opposing positions on technology and media appeared in the 1960s and 1970s in the writings of Marshall McLuhan (McLuhan 1994; McLuhan and Fiore 1967) and Raymond Williams (1974). McLuhan advanced ideas about the power of technology within a new electric culture – powers to create a new age of complex relationships. He had a facility for the arresting phrase: 'global village' is one of his. He spoke up for television at a time when it was receiving a lot of bad press, critically speaking. He saw television as a medium which engages the senses, and opposed it to the sensory alienation of what he describes as the Gutenberg culture of print media. He was interested in effects as much as in causes. He saw the media as extensions of the senses. He was interested in characteristics of media, and saw media as being more than mere carriers of content – the medium itself was the message, for McLuhan. For him, technology was a determining factor in media development and use, though he would also have seen new developments like the World Wide Web as providing opportunities for users.

Williams (1974) argued that media development is more about the economic and social structures that shape this (not the technologies). He is interested in things like cause, agency and context. He does not see the technology of any given media as determining its use. He would see opportunities as accruing to media institutions, driven by economic determinants. He would not have interpreted the Web within an optimistic framework.

As Bolter and Grusin (2000) say, 'The idea that new electronic technologies of communication will determine our social organization is clearly not threatening to corporations that produce and market those technologies.' The market does not see new media as being out of their control.

Van Loon (2008) would argue that you cannot separate media technology from what it does or what it carries, nor from its social dimensions. Technology cannot be defined as being the sum of its devices. Van Loon (2008: 9–14) refers to four factors which matter when trying to understand media technology:

- *Form:* so that how the technology may shape the content is as important as the content itself (e.g. a political speech delivered for television will be peppered with soundbites).

- *Historicity:* in that the immediate impact of any technology is different from its later impact when it has become familiar to the point of being invisible (the phone).

- *Cultural embedding:* in that social practices develop as to how technologies may be used (e.g. the Blackberry becomes an extension of its user's social and working lives – to the extent, it was reported, that the entertainer Madonna sleeps with hers under her pillow).

- *Embodiment and disembodiment:* in that technologies both extend the communication capacity of the human body, but also are detached from it when used remotely (e.g. videophone links).

The debates around the Napster case (2001–02) saw the coexistence of equally valid views about what technology should be used for. Shawn Fanning, who set up the Napster website, had taken an opportunity to use Internet technology to provide a community of music users and copiers – file sharing and downloading without paying. Music providers, both corporations and many groups, saw the technology as being used to deny their copyright and to deprive them of rightful income. They sued Fanning and Napster on this basis, and forced closure of the website.

The consequences or implications of the uses of technology are, in this sense, complex and fluid. Bertelsmann has bought a controlling interest in Napster, and is now making money out of the site through legitimized sales of music files. AppleMac is making millions out of iTunes' website because it has created the iPod, a very successful digital, portable MP3 music store/play device. It is paying for the rights to offer tracks for downloading (for a fee, of course). It is estimated that iTunes has 70 per cent of the online music market (*The Independent* 10 June 2004). One thing leads to another in unpredictable ways. Determining factors or conditions are malleable.

John Street (1999) refers to this, with a political rather than a commercial inflection:

> At one level, the technology is the embodiment of certain interests and possibilities, but at another it is the bearer of effects: it changes what we can imagine and what we can want, it alters our politics. Though we can identify the interests and choices around a technology, they do not automatically become the authors of that technology. The technology is not something [that] exists as a simple object for our use. It acts to structure our choices and preferences, but not in a wholly determinist way. The relationship is in constant flux: political processes shape technology; and then it shapes politics.
>
> (Street 1999)

Similarly, media cannot control audience use of technologies. Once technologies are in the public domain then they, and the ways that they are used, shape the media, just as the media once shaped the technologies. For example, concern has been expressed over the relationship between children and their mobile phones. In a *Guardian* article (10 May 2001), Michael Fitzpatrick refers to the concerns of sociologists (and of research in Japan) that a generation of young people may be developing in ways which

- make them unable to form and maintain relationships without the help of mobiles

- make them dependent on the act of contact via the mobile, rather than being able to conduct a sustained and face-to-face relationship.

Again, Bolter and Grusin (2000) emphasize the interaction between media, especially the reworking of old media by new and the appropriation of new technologies by old media. 'We cannot even recognize the representational power of a medium except with reference to other media.'

So it is that they discuss the *remediation* of medieval manuscripts by Gutenberg's printing technology, or the remediation of classic works of art by digital artists. Their view is that 'new' media successively mediate that which has already been mediated – hence the notion of remediation. Remediation is also about an inseparability between processes of mediation and constructions of reality (see section 6.4 on Actualization). In the case of current new technologies, this would be about that continuing cultural project which seeks to make the process of remediation (and representation) a transparent one, in which the medium apparently opens up access to that chimera, 'reality'.

Both the reworking of material through different media and the appropriation and manipulation of texts in digital form raise interesting questions as to what the text is, and who is the author of which text. Ownership (copyright) and authorship are deeply embedded values within a capitalist system. This is exemplified by a public row over the validity of information released by the British government in relation to the run-up to the US-led invasion of Iraq. Much had been made of the fact that one foundation for this information was an old PhD thesis which was not credited to its author (found by trawling the Internet): the issue was about plagiarism as much as about accuracy. And yet, every day, both undergraduates and advertisers are plagiarizing material to produce new texts. Technology has created ideological conflict. New media forms are generating cultural stress fractures.

Equally one can argue that new media give a new lease of life to old forms of communication. For all the downloading of TV programmes or the appearance videos on YouTube, the written word has not been diminished by a supposedly more visual culture. Andrew Brown (*Guardian* 27 September 2007) argues that text is a 'naturally interactive medium'. He points out that the Net is full of examples of this, not least blog sites. He argues that reading text compresses time and conveys meaning quickly, whereas visual media expand time because they 'take more time to convey less meaning'. Again we see that media technologies do not supplant one another, but rather they proliferate forms for communication.

Media production and distribution is not run by technologies; it is made possible by them. Technologies are developed which it is believed the media will want to take up. So one can just as well argue that it is the media that drive technologies. In any case, the applications of and success of technologically based change in the media is something which cannot be predicted with certainty. One can indeed argue that there is a kind of inertia, related to investment costs and costs to the consumer, which actually works against the introduction of new technologies.

It is understood that we 'should' be moving to high definition TV and to digital TV broadcasting in Britain. But the technology is not driving this change simply because it is there. Consumers are slowing down the change because they are not prepared to spend the money – and so government dates for switching off analogue transmitters have been put back progressively (though the first area of the UK, Cumbria, did go digital in 2007).

The huge investment in G3 mobile phone technology has not paid off. The operators tried to develop and sell the technology in order to make money – to determine progress. But the consumer has not been that interested in the cost of the technological opportunity. Small screens and shaky connections to the Net do not make sense when one can use a WiFi enabled laptop in many urban public spaces. Equally, the explosion of text messaging via mobiles was not determined by either producers or technology, in the sense of being intentionally targeted on the consumer, but was a facility of which the users took the opportunity. With hindsight one can see the attractions of this low cost function to the millions of young users, as well as the email-like advantages of not having to make voice contact in real time.

This example illustrates contradictory forces behind media technologies. On the one hand, their cost (of development and introduction) can be so great that only global media players can afford it. On the other hand, their cost (of production hardware) can be so reduced that, for instance, pressure groups such as People for the Ethical Treatment of Animals (PETA) can produce broadcastable video material. The concept of the citizen journalist is now with us.

4 The impact of technology on the media: production, distribution, exhibition, retailing, consumption

First, I want to clarify the fact that the applications and implications of technology for the media need to be understood within the functional areas of media business. Media technology is not just about the drama of, say, a live night-time videophone link with a correspondent in a war zone being shown on evening TV news.

Technology is embedded in every area of a business. So I make but passing reference to digitized research material, computer graphics in publicity divisions, spreadsheet predictions in accounts, email communication, client databases – all the applications of technologies that have changed the nature of work and of how businesses operate. They have transformed general company functions such as accounting, administration and public relations.

Outside the media, one may look at our everyday experiences of department stores and supermarkets. Technology enables these businesses to monitor stock purchase, sales and reordering very tightly. But what is going on here is not just about the purchasing experience for the customer – choice and availability. Indirectly, the technologies involved affect, for instance, farming practices or factory work, around the world.

Media studies have traditionally understood media organizations in terms of institutions which manufacture product, which get these products directly to audiences, or to outlets where audiences may purchase them. In this way consumption takes place. A magazine is composed and printed, distributed by road and rail, and is sold in shops. A television programme is also made, distributed via cable/broadcast/satellite, and shown on screen.

However, before commenting on the impact of technology within this framework, there needs to be a further caveat about describing the media landscape. The institutions and functions model works for general categories of media – radio or the press. But it does not properly recognize the huge number of specialist media industries, and their complex relations with categories of media in general. For example, Reuters provides material for the 'trade', not directly to audiences. It is fundamentally a distributor of news material (although it is possible to argue that it produces a kind of product and has news operations as its audiences). Music may well be manufactured in an independently owned studio, even if it is distributed by EMI. The entire advertising industry is integral to the distribution and promotion of media goods. But it is not one of the media in itself: it uses the media. Then there are the specialist businesses which supply services integral to the production of a film or of a newspaper, but which have nothing to do with processes such as writing or editing. There are the catering services which feed film and TV crews on location. There are the independent printers that produce magazine supplements for newspapers. New technologies affect the work of all these specialists. Indeed, often the basis of their specialist value is a particular expertise and investment in technology – such as the small digital editing businesses that use AvidPro programs.

The Web has helped corporations create a business model in which they use small companies on a global basis, rather as supermarkets use carriers and producers without having to take financial responsibility for these functions:

> networking has transformed many corporations into transnational, de-centralized, out-sourced, distributed firms that make use of new technologies in order to co-ordinate production and allocation.
>
> (Fuchs 2008: 343)

In this sense I am arguing for simultaneous kinds of understanding of the media – as fitting a vertically integrated general functions model at the macro level, but looking much more like a 'services to core business' model when one looks at them closely. I am arguing for both examination of general industries, and for recognition of interlocking and specific businesses. The BBC is a classic example of a move from in-house control to outsourcing and freelancing during the 1980s and 1990s. I am arguing for both a simple general model of media industry, which recognizes, for example, the cycle of news gathering, composition, production, distribution and retailing for a newspaper, yet also for a complex model, which recognizes the interlocking media businesses that make possible the detail of this cycle for the newspaper industry.

Returning to the general model, within limited space, it is important to identify key features about the impact of technology. The sections which follow – for example, on convergence of technologies – are also relevant, but will examine overarching implications, and the effects of technology on product in particular.

4.1 Production

- *Reduction of cost:* as in electronic animation used by Pixar and others, which is far cheaper than manually drawn cell-type animation production, used for classic Disney films; as in digicam production of TV material for reality TV shows in particular. However, this is partially offset by factors such as the cost of investment or buying in of technology. Also by factors such as, in the case of movies, the ever-increasing above the line costs of key personnel such as stars and directors.

  Digital production is slowly emerging as a huge cost saver. George Lucas has not shot on 35 mm film since 2001. Digital post-production is becoming commonplace in film. It is also becoming cheaper – the reason for its prevalence in advertising. And, of course, news and advertising photography is now entirely digital.

- *Reduction of labour:* this is a major component of any organization's wages bill. All media industries have seen a reduction in the numbers of people it takes to make their product (except possibly film), not only because of general 'efficiency' pressures, but also because, for example, promotional material can be made, edited and printed by one person. The move from mechanical to electronic technologies has greatly reduced the numbers of people needed to put together a newspaper.

- *Ease of use:* without denying a continued need for creative expertise in the use of technologies, it is the case that many examples have made the practicalities of production easier. Time-based editing machines transformed television and video in the 1970s and

1980s, meaning that one no longer needed costly, technically expert operatives. In music production, multichannel mixing, electronic sampling and sound production, digital editing, have made production in one sense less technically skilled though in other senses more creatively complex. But again, 'domestic' versions of industrial technologies have also brought easy-to-use music production literally into the home and sometimes out into the marketplace (for example, some DJ mixes of dance music).

- *Access to information:* as in the use of the Internet as a research source for the press. In 2003 a scandal involving a *New York Times* reporter, who wrote pieces on people and places that he had never met or been to, is a nice example of how access to data (and indeed to images) has been hugely enhanced by technologies.

- *Speed of production:* it is faster as well as easier to compose magazine copy electronically. It is possible to acquire news material for TV via satellite from the other side of the world and edit it, all within minutes.

- *Enhancement of production values:* most obviously to audiences, the material that they read, see and hear has qualities dependent on various applications of technology. One example is the arrival of colour images in newspapers since the 1980s, now sourced from digital cameras and printed on digital presses. Movie theatres have digital surround sound. Film action sequences may incorporate electronic effects to make the impossible appear plausible, using electronic matting and inserts. CD music is 'clean' and has a tonal range not generally heard in the home before 1985, when Dire Straits' *Brothers in Arms* album sold over 1 million copies.

In general, both new forms of media and new developments in old media have created, so far as the audience is concerned, a much more 'image-rich' media landscape, as well as a more completely 'real' set of media representations. In other words, we have more pictures in more places, from more sources, than our grandparents did. And within the bounds of representational conventions, technology has made film and television in particular seem more real.

4.2 Distribution

In economic terms technology has enhanced the wealth production of those who control the flow of product, as much as the rewards for those who make media product. Where the text can be converted to a digital form, then the distribution flow can take place electronically. This is the dominant practice in broadcasting and is central to debates about development of the Internet as a distributor of radio and video. The readership figures for regional newspapers are dropping steadily as they and their audiences go online, and as their all important classified ads also move onto the Net.

An electronic divide has opened up between those media which can be distributed in a material form and those which can be transformed into digitized electronic data. This divide in some cases has a further separation in terms of distribution for production, as opposed to distribution for consumption. So, television reaches its audiences via electronic carriers, but magazines remain as objects to be bought off the shelf.

The complication of this divide is that some media may distribute their texts in electronic form within the production industry. It will be interesting to see if the film industries can move to digital distribution successfully. In Britain, money is now being pumped into a project to create digital distribution to about a hundred specialist cinemas. The idea is to make minority film more accessible to audiences and at the same time to get round the huge costs of striking prints in conventional form (up to £1500 a time) and carrying them around the country. In Britain, the total cost of this was estimated as being £100 million in 2002, plus £30 million in freight charges (*Guardian* 20 March 2003). Films have long been distributed via satellite (HBO) and on DVD. It is significant that Viacom (essentially a telecommunications distributor, though it also owns the video retailer Blockbuster) bought Paramount – a producer. This is a move towards vertical integration.

In the music industry traditionally, like magazines, an object (a CD) has to be carried to a point of sale. But Internet downloading has moved from a pirate stage to one where the music majors have set up their own websites for selling their product direct into the home computer, which has itself become a dominant medium for playing music. It is significant that global companies like Sony and Bertelsmann have moved onto the Net in order to control distribution and to profit from the downloading of their music product (and to compete with new distributors like iTunes). These kinds of division of distribution reflect on the context of use (domestic–public), on the nature of use (individual–collective), on economics (high cost of shifting objects as opposed to data), on copyright (it is relatively easier to pirate media texts as objects).

A similar pattern is emerging for DVDs as a medium for renting or buying, and watching films. Downloading movies is slow and a minority practice at the moment. But some are predicting a great change as distribution technology improves, and as the Blu-ray format can be downloaded. Opinion is divided over this, but still it is interesting to see the patterns predicted in the illustration (p. 183), in which DVD purchases slide down over the four years from 2008, and the purchase of the new Blu-ray discs rises. Video download sites such as Blinkbox exist now, offering films for rental or purchase, and having 300,000 unique users a month (*Guardian* 30 June 2008). It is perhaps significant that Warners is now releasing films for download at the same time that they are being released on DVD.

Global reach is a consequence of the arrival of satellite communications and enhanced cable links, in the second half of the twentieth century. Distribution of media goods, as well as of the information which goes into the manufacture of those goods, is something which now happens worldwide. Television is the obvious example of a new era of distribution which offers multiple channels to transnational audiences. Newspapers and magazines are available in a global range of major cities, partly on the back of electronic distribution to regional printing, but mainly because of the explosion of global air travel.

Radio has been transformed by the arrival of VHF and the allocation of many channels, which has turned it most successfully into a regionalized and genre-specific medium. Technology has made it possible to run a radio station with very few staff – like Klassik Rock in Europe. There is much excitement about digital audio broadcasting (DAB); so far the cost of receivers and the output available has confined DAB to a small audience – but this is changing. In 2007 over 30 per cent of radio listening was through one digital medium or another. Half of these listeners used the Net or digital TV. What is just as interesting is distribution via the Internet. Barnard (2000) enthuses about this: it 'automatically redefines radio's notion of "territory" and, with it, changes the very concept of a listening community from the parochial and domestic into something more powerful and challenging'.

Elsewhere he is more realistic about what is actually available on the Internet, balancing the possibility of a local station having a worldwide audience against the fact that this has not actually happened. What is happening more is the availability of radio via satellite – all BBC networks for example.

Alternative channels are about new forms of media and their distribution. Examples are embedded in the paragraphs above. In the film industry, distribution can be about the transporting of DVDs to retailers, as much as about moving large cans of 35 mm film to movie theatres. It can be about PayTV and films accessed via cable, as much as via satellite movie channels. It is now possible to transmit movies directly from their production house to exhibition, via satellite. Different formats require different forms of distribution. And different forms of distribution may influence different kinds of production – micro movies on the Internet.

New forms of audience use of new technology appear frequently. But it is not possible to predict which will succeed. One service which has taken off is the BBC iPlayer which allows viewers to either stream their chosen shows immediately or download them to watch later. It was reported by the BBC in June 2008 that the catch-up service had received 100 million programme requests in six months. At the moment dominant use is by streaming via a PC, but the use of TV and recording for time-shifting (within the 30 days allowed) is expected to increase hugely. In any case iPlayer is adding to those all-important viewing figures, not least in respect of the minor digital channels such as BBC3 and BBC4. This free to user service increases in its take-up after 10.00 p.m. – that is outside prime time. Virgin Media offers another example of a subscription video on demand service, which is also proving successful.

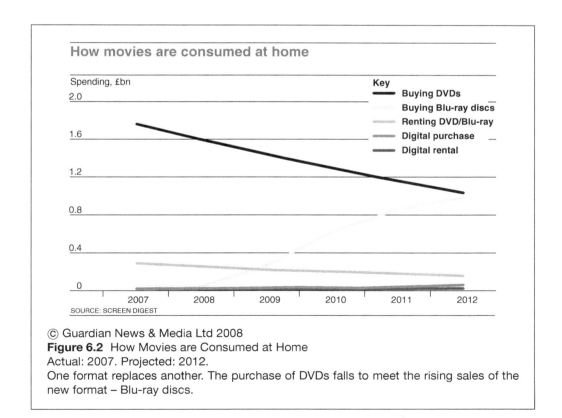

© Guardian News & Media Ltd 2008

Figure 6.2 How Movies are Consumed at Home
Actual: 2007. Projected: 2012.
One format replaces another. The purchase of DVDs falls to meet the rising sales of the new format – Blu-ray discs.

4.3 Exhibition and sales

Domestic consumption has increased as a result of technologies making possible new media formats and new kinds of distribution. Of course all this goes along with increases in disposable income and in leisure time. One is looking at a proliferation of examples since the late 1980s, from mini hi-fi systems to interactive TV, to the Internet, to digital image making, to domestic minicams, to multiple-function CD players.

What is noticeable here is the proliferation of technology in the home not merely for reproducing images and sound, but also for constructing materials (for example, editing home-produced music and burning it onto a CD). Domestic screens have increased greatly in number because not only are they dedicated to functions such as computer display, but also they serve multiple TV channels, teletext, email, electronic games, DVD viewing and so on.

> Home television is being redesigned to concentrate recreation and cultural consumption within the home, thus lodging within private space the means to manipulate public opinion and taste for a corporate sector with increasing need to sell images and information!
>
> (Johnson 1996)

Preston (2001) argues for caution in making claims, even for the private sphere and domestic consumption. He has produced tables of data drawn from a range of sources which demonstrate that old media like telephone systems are well embedded, and that the take-up of new media is not as great as many claim. He asserts that its (new media) rate of diffusion among households is much less than was the case for previous new technologies; that the Internet is relatively expensive and technically unreliable.

Similarly, there is a tension between the sides of a debate which on the one hand applaud the Internet as a convenient point of sale offering consumer choice, and those who point out that goods still have to be delivered reliably, and that security breaches on the Internet frighten away customers.

5 The information revolution

It has become fashionable to use this phrase as if it is clearly understood that such a revolution is taking place and is to the general public benefit. This is not so. Questions need to be asked about 'What information?', 'To whose benefit?'

Technology has for example made it easy to produce colour, image-rich junk mail and advertising which pours through the letterboxes of the data-identified, 'wealthy enough to spend money' citizens. Data on ourselves as citizen consumers is held electronically by credit agencies and market researchers (not to mention the police, banks and government agencies). Any telephone contact with an organization offering goods and services produces an identity check in which it is clear that one is being matched against a name and place of residence database. Exactly what kind of gain to the citizen there is in such examples of information storage or distribution is rather questionable.

What *is* clear is that 'the revolution' has benefited institutions of government and the media. The ability of media organizations to acquire, exchange and manipulate information has made it easier for them to function economically, to compete with each other and to target their consumers and users. There are industry-serving businesses such as DataMonitor whose work is the processing and provision of information. The revolution has given media access to information about us: the ability to target households on grounds of lifestyle. There is not much traffic the other way.

This does not denigrate the value of information sources on the World Wide Web. Genuinely, there is a speed, scope, volume and precision of information out there which is wholly dramatic compared with research facilities a generation ago. But it is patchy and specialized, and only as good as the search engine being used. Websites for media organizations tell us what they want to reveal, not always what we want to know. And those citizens who cannot afford computer access at home, those who cannot afford or cannot get (for technical reasons) broadband, are actually disenfranchised from the information revolution. We live in an era of contradiction: information wealth for some, information poverty for others. Television can inform us through simulations about the creation of the Earth. But only a minority of the Earth's population can afford the television. We can email a friend in China. But the friend in China does not have free access to all the information on the Web.

Preston (2001) is especially sceptical. He acknowledges the capacity of the Internet to bring together technologies in a new way, but also asserts that it 'falls far short of meeting the promise of a seamless, fully integrated and interconnecting communication system offering "instant access" to diverse forms of information'.

The UK government can spend millions cabling information highways alongside British motorways (apparently to facilitate display of information and use of cameras), but it does not spend similar amounts on the provision of Internet access at public information points such as libraries and advice centres. From a negative point of view this reinforces interpretations of the information revolution as supporting existing mechanisms of power and control. This invokes Foucault and ideas about state surveillance of its citizens. One is talking about benefits to media institutions and to capitalism in general – preserving the status quo of power.

In terms of naked power, one should also note that armed conflict has also been transformed by the information revolution. Psychological warfare can use blogging or email bombing. Techno warfare can swarm enemy sites and systems, or hack into and destroy their data bases. Smart bombs and missiles can use information from global positioning systems (GPS) to target the hardware of war on enemy territory. Similarly miniature aircraft can send back digital information about enemy locations. Communication may be by satphones and satcameras. War planning can use information and computer programs to model possible strategies.

Underlying issues here are about the effects of technology and new media, about the rate of their take-up, about social and cultural change. Underlying positions vary from the conservative to the enthusiastically proselytizing. There is a danger in overselling things like the Web 2.0 Wiki universe, in which the users participate in the construction of freely available information. Wikipedia information is only as good as its producers – and nobody is checking their level of expertise, let alone the accuracy of what is produced. Material is also by its nature accessible to modification by the powerful and self interested. It has been demonstrated that government departments and the BBC have altered entries about their functions and achievements to put a more favourable gloss on their work. As Tara Brabazon puts it (*Times Higher Education Supplement* 16 November 2007): 'global businesses and universities have used Wikipedia as another site of branding and marketing'. In terms of information revolutions, it is worth asking who has what access to what sources of information, as well as asking what power they may have to act on that information. It is worth remembering that so-called old media are still vital sources of information, especially television. All the evidence assembled and referred to in this chapter points to the fact that new media may be part of a process of transformation, but in fact they are not the dominant source of information for most people about the world, even in the USA. Finally, we need to remember that the very word 'information' is not just about data, nor even that questionable term, 'facts'. The information that comes via any technology is importantly also about how we understand social relations, how we form social practices, how we understand terms such as community and society.

6 The nature of change

6.1 *Interactivity*

This is much talked about with relation to new media and digital technology (see also section 7 on the Internet and the World Wide Web). Computer games are interactive, within terms of reference determined by the provider. Some would argue for the value of the choices and problems that games users have to make and to solve. Others would look more cynically at the value of the games market (over £800 million a year in the UK), and at the spin-off of clearly passive media texts such as TV programmes and magazines about games. Again,

Figure 6.3 Looking At Me, Looking At You
New technologies spread rapidly and invade cultural practices. Digital technologies converge. Mobiles and cell phones have also become cameras, as well as devices through which to access the Internet.

one could say that audiences can email newspaper editors and programme producers – and so they do, in their hundreds. But this is not real-time interaction and guarantees no response from the institutions.

In this regard, of course, one must acknowledge the real-time interaction that happens in Web chat rooms. However, in general, much interaction on the Web is about completing questionnaires, moving to shopping baskets and responding to menus.

There is much talk about power accruing to the user, consumer or audience. But generally speaking, this happens only within a commercial framework, and has been much hyped up. There is some interactivity in examples of video on demand (PayTV to watch the movie of your choice when you choose via your TV set). Shopping channels are obviously interactive. Famously, the UK docu-game-show programme, *Big Brother* (Channel 4), was available on the Internet in 2000. It picked up audiences of 750,000, and allowed these Internet viewers to choose camera views and to watch at will. Voting on game shows or grabbing links to programme-connected websites is becoming more common. But all this begs questions about what interactivity really means, or should mean. Not only do audiences have an experiential history of assuming passivity in viewing and listening, but also one has to consider what active role an audience could actually play, especially within a commercial framework.

6.2 Convergence

Technology has brought about a convergence in the electronic codes which carry the material of media texts. There has also been some convergence of the formats that carry this encoding. Predominantly, this is about our ability to encode all visuals, sound and print in binary digital terms, and about the CD or DVD. One can store, copy, edit and transmit media content in this binary code. The discs can carry print, movies, photos, music. All media functions which use computers at some stage are also using digital. British television is scheduled to become totally digital by 2018. Movie theatre screening is starting to move that way. Home entertainment – music, film, games – is largely digitized. Hard-disc formats for recording off-air TV are becoming ever more common. Digitized domestic photography is well established. Mobile phones can take and transmit digital pictures; they allow connection with the Internet. Digital compression means a greater use of bandwidth, whether broadcast or carried by cable. The Internet is the most complete example of such convergence. In principle, it is a means of distribution of all media content, but commercial providers have to find ways of making money from sending such content. Moving images, for example, require a degree of compression which has yet to be achieved in order for standard length movies to be transmitted in anything like an acceptable time. Castells (2002) observes that there is limited convergence between the Internet and multimedia because of a lack of bandwidth. This cannot cope easily with the demands of video, and is susceptible to excesses of local use and therefore overloading in any given area. In the UK we suffer from a huge lack of investment in fibre-optic cable needed for bandwidth – especially in more rural areas and towns. In other words, the technology is not here, now. What has happened in general is that previously separate industries of telecommunications, broadcasting and computing (information technology) are merging, both commercially and technologically. These mergers are therefore also about globalization, about larger corporations with a larger reach across the planet.

Who will benefit from this convergence is debatable. It is convenient for media producers if their material is in digital form because it can most easily be edited and manipulated.

For example, computer-based film rerecording studios can move and 'stretch' voices to achieve perfect synch and to change emphasis, rather than have to go for endless retakes. Digital distribution is cheaper than moving objects around.

What is not evident is a reduction in cost of the domestic technology which stores or records this digital text (at least, not after the initial and expensive period of establishing a new format). Benefits of cost and availability to the consumer seem to come only when the multinationals lose control of product and copyright – music on the Internet, pirate DVD copies, cheap copies of equipment from the developing world.

Practical examples of the trend towards kinds of convergence include the iPhone and Nokia Ovi mobile (2007), which can provide music, games and various Net services. Then there are games consoles which not only use the new generation of HD television sets as their screens but also can screen material from the Net or from disc. Broadband providers seek to sell converged packages of home-phone, mobile phone, television and Net access.

Convergence does not simply generate new media. It opens up new possibilities for 'old media'. Barnard (2000) neatly sums up the situation for radio, exemplifying these possibilities:

> Convergence offers the radio industry flexibility of operation, new means of delivery, raised production values and improved sound quality. The trade-off is the integration of radio into multimedia as a whole and the loss of control and distinctiveness that this implies, together with the opening up of radio to competition from new forms of broadcasting such as 'webcasting'.

This convergence and exchange between media is about more than the underpinning technologies of distribution and their codes, important as these are. Convergence affects corporate ownership, communications systems and their technologies, and cultural forms. It is visible to the consumer through the simultaneous release of books, computer games and music CDs with the high concept movie. Convergence is visible in what Bolter and Grusin (2000) refer to as 'the CNN look' in which the TV news screen has been reconfigured to include updates and inserts around the newscaster, so that it looks as much like a website or multimedia application as a 'traditional' news image. Convergence of screen aesthetics redefines what is 'normal', and what we expect to see. One kind of convergence may lead to another – so that convergence of technologies can lead to mergers of companies on the basis of economies of scale and convergence of interests.

6.3 Diversification and diversity

Technology has created some diversity of media formats and channels of communication. It appears to have generated more consumer choice – but it is a commonplace that 'more' is often about 'the same'. A diversity of cable and satellite channels conceals the fact that on the whole this just means more sport, more recycled movies, more of the same genres. Similarly, diversification into new formats such as DVD does not produce new movies (though it does offer supplementary material that would not otherwise be seen). What this diversification through new technologies does do for media companies is to produce new sets of profits through sales of new (or even recycled) products. One must also recognize the positive in respect of new work for new companies making more television for these new channels.

The Internet typifies these progressive and retrogressive forces. It is a new medium in which the user controls access, and has that access to services and information sources that were previously far less available. On the other hand, it does not give direct access to that many media leisure products. And media company websites are – not surprisingly – cast within a traditional model of enticement and publicity, but do not give anything away. The Internet is used socially for cultural exchange in chat rooms, but it is also used commercially for profit, for example, eBay. Amazon is probably the most successful online retailer. E-commerce has now passed 1 per cent of total sales in the USA. When one looks back to cross-media ownership, then the question of who benefits from diversification of technologies becomes rather sharp. Time Warner owns dozens of successful media companies, and has a turnover greater than the GDP of many developing nations. It has interests in television, publishing, film, cable, satellite, the Internet and music. It owns HBO, CNN, DC comics, New Line Cinema, Time Magazine, Warner Records, Netscape, Warner Picture, Warner Television, Turner Broadcasting – to pick a few of the better known names. What is clear is that the 'old' media are doing very nicely, and are exploiting new technology where it suits them.

Issues around diversification have to address apparent contradictions about a measurable increase in media channels, media products and media consumption – set against a lack of actual diversity. In a commercial sense one can talk about media companies diversifying into related businesses. One may talk about the media in general as offering product diversity, where diversity is defined as 'numbers of'. But one may not be able to talk about diversity in terms of choice. The argument here relates back to more general debates about the nature, and validity, of pluralistic interpretations of the media.

6.4 Actualization

Actualization refers to the use of technologies to enhance a sense of that which is visually immediate and present and 'real'. This actualization of representations has a history going back into the nineteenth century, at least. The camera gave the illusion of capturing an immediate scene and experience. Victorian painting went through a movement which tried to reproduce the texture and surface of reality, the actuality of experience, the immediacy of a scene or a portrait. It is, of course, all about the illusions of representations and the tricks that we play on our own sense of the real, because we accept and are seduced by conventions of the media. But actualization in various forms has continued to fascinate the media, even though there are also plenty of examples of media forms in which material actuality is deliberately ignored and challenged. So the placing of minicams in cricket stumps or birds' nests to capture the immediacy of the game or of the wildlife is, I would argue, part of this tradition in which we are complicit with the media. In various ways, new technologies contribute to a sense of 'being there', of the material experience.

Lister et al. (2003) make an excellent discussion of new media and visual culture in which they explore ideas about how technology is affecting:

- image making and images as texts

- an emphasis on effects and sensual experience above the manufacture of narrative and meaning

- new experiences of being immersed within images.

They would see actualization as being part of Western discourses of the truth and of the real – and opposed, for example, to Islamic ideas in which seeing is no guarantee of the truth or of reality. 'Different realisms are not mere aesthetic choices, but each correlates with a particular ideology of what constitutes the "real world" in the first place' (Lister et al. 2003). They would point out that technology has proliferated images in our culture well beyond a conventional media frame. Different kinds of judgement and visual literacy are required to make sense of, for example, CAT scans, computer games or holograms.

Lister et al. (2003) point out that a sense of actuality is not only about technology used to reproduce the world out there, but also about the manufacture of that which seems actual by virtue of being believable. This is true of cinema in particular, in relation to which they quote Michael Allen (1998): 'The intention of all technical systems developed since the beginning of the 1950s (in cinema), has been towards reducing the spectators' sense of their "real" world, and replacing it with a fully believable artificial one.'

6.5 Polarization

Technologies have enabled a polarization of audiences and markets by simultaneously reaching out to mass markets and focusing on very specific audiences. Set-top hard disc recording devices can read preference patterns into our viewing, and offer a selective recording of TV that is meant to represent our interests. Cable channels can serve very local audiences with very specific material that is of no interest on a national level. New technology enables relatively cheap yet quality production of texts such as specialist magazines for niche markets – something that Emap specializes in. The Internet can be used to search for specific books or CDs in an individualized way, that runs counter to the generalized global marketing areas and genres of the music business. Emap has its own web-based magazine (www.FHM.co.uk), which is typical in that it enables individuals to make specific purchases from specific features in the magazine (this makes more money than the advertising around the site). There is nothing so new in this stretch between large and small audiences. But technology is sharpening different kinds of media provision and use. This may be challenging the argument that mass media produce homogenization. Some media may indeed offer mass appeal products, or products of the 'lowest common denominator'. But there are small media producers out there. Individuals can become producers and distributors on a limited scale. There are the indies and the alternatives. In this sense, polarization may be nothing but a good thing if it is about genuine alternatives to 'mass'. It suggests that media critiques which focus only on major media players, popular products and mass audiences are missing some of the point. Political economy pessimism is not inconsistent with postmodern cultural optimism.

6.6 Confirmation

From one point of view, however, technology may appear to be about innovation but, actually, it is used to confirm our experience of and views of the world. In commercial terms it works to confirm the hegemony of certain genres. In industrial terms it confirms the existing powers of media ownership.

For example, technologies employed for television news gathering offer live on-the-spot reporting from around the world. They provide on-air interviews across continents. But – news values being as they are – what those technologies actually do is to confirm a world in which the footballer David Beckham gets more coverage than Aung San Suu Kyi, the elected but imprisoned prime minister of Burma; in which stories about rulers predominate over stories from the ruled; in which some parts of the planet merit many news stories and others apparently deserve none. In other words, it is what the technology is used for that is more interesting than the 'wonders' of the technology itself. It would be perfectly possible to use the same global reach of technology to provide stories from other news organizations – from another point of view. It would be possible to offer a digital choice of news stories within a news programme – stories at the press of a button. But what the technology is used for is to enhance the long-existing conventions of news genre, to enhance the predominance of certain kinds of stories, and to confirm our picture of how the world works.

In a similar way one can see technology used to produce more of the same entertainment genres. Cinema has always had special effects and action movies – a love of spectacle. Technology has enhanced the commercial possibilities of these, particularly since the late 1970s. The high concept series of Bond films or of *Star Wars* films has amalgamated post-production optical effects with on-screen graphics and such technology as robotics, to make the impossible appear possible, to make that which does not exist seem to exist. So technology confirms the power of given genres, but also constructs 'the real' – and in doing so confirms that cultural project which is to make our material and imaginative worlds equally real. And in the case of all media, the financial investment needed to deploy and develop technologies to produce all kinds of product is such that the market dominance of a diminishing range of companies is confirmed.

All this is not to deny the impact of new technologies on the operation of media institutions, on production processes, on what is produced, and so of course on the audiences. But it is to argue a view that technologies have in general not been revolutionary in their long-term effects, so much as evolutionary. There has been less of a big bang than a slow burn.

6.7 Naturalization

I am referring here to a naturalization of the consumption of technologies of the media. We are talking about an assimilation of the uses and effects of new technologies into the pattern of everyday life. This naturalization is not just about some quick decay of the impact of novelty in the minds of the audience. It is also to do with the uses of technology by the media. The BBC may have made publicity capital out of the effects used in their technologically ground-breaking series *Walking with Dinosaurs* (2001), but in fact the relatively low-budget combination of models and computer animation was used within a familiar wildlife documentary format. The voice-of-God narrator placed us on location. The editor constructed mini-dramas to hold our attentions. We were conscious of being educated, but pleasurably, within a familiar model (see previous comments about genres on pp. 27–42).

A central value of computer games has to do with the continued development of authenticity. Memory and programming, for genres such as car-race games in particular, is devoted to providing natural looking backgrounds and smooth movement, as much as interactive options. 'Realism' of representation contributes to the cultural naturalization of the experience of computer games playing (see section 6.4 on Actualization). We become used to certain kinds of media experience in which the use of technology becomes invisible. Even where the textual experience is changed – personal sound systems, or morphing in advertisements – the audience rapidly becomes used to that which is 'impossible' in an image, or to people wearing earphones in public places.

The cross-over and intertextuality between texts, especially in the medium of television, also contributes to this naturalization of what is in fact a technically adroit experience. In TV thrillers, the creation of false CCTV footage or the use of night vision cameras has a lot to do with their use on reality TV shows, just as the use of reconstructive drama sequences in *Crimewatch* owes a lot to fiction examples. That which is familiar becomes natural by virtue of its repetition within everyday experience.

7 The Internet and the World Wide Web

The Internet is a communication medium which allows, for the first time, the communication of many to many, in chosen time, on a global scale.
The Internet is, above all else, a cultural creation.

(Castells 2002)

7.1 Dominance and use

Here, you should cross-refer to previous comments on the Internet, especially as they relate to a debate about the potential for the Internet to remain 'a users' paradise', or to become colonized by the major media institutions. Again, one needs to preserve a sense of caution and realism when talking about the impact of new technology. Research by Point Topic, as reported in the *Guardian* (8 November 2007) shows that 10.6 million, or about 40 per cent of UK households still do not have access to broadband and the Net. This is confirmed by Ofcom research reported in the *Guardian* (22 May 2008) (see illustration on p. 194). The number of dialup users has been reduced to 'only' 2.1 million households. And a considerable number of the 13 million which do have broadband will not have high speed. Ironically, there is more Internet use in rural areas, which have more low-grade (hardwire) links to the Web than do urban areas. Probably this is because basic functions such as shopping, banking and general communication are harder to exercise in dispersed rural communities. This is far from any vision of a wired-up, interactive society, tapped into a global Web (www.ofcom.org.uk). The Internet is exceptional as a medium of distribution because it is not (and cannot be) owned by any commercial media conglomerate. It is not a business but a medium of exchange, a carrier. It is not set up as a broadcast medium – though it does carry radio broadcasts. It is not set up as a medium for selling 'hard' texts, but it is used to sell books, for example. Although there are examples of it being used in terms of a broadcast model – wireless streaming, podcasts, mass emailing – still much of its activity is driven by users and involves groups or one on one.

The issue becomes one of dominance rather than of outright control: dominance of content. It is the same issue which dogs cable providers. It is one thing having a means of distribution, but without attractive product there is no audience or consumer. Kevin Williams (2003) refers to the Time Warner merger with AOL in 2001 as an example of how 'in a market-driven system control of new technology will be dominated by large media conglomerates'.

Preston (2001) disagrees that a product or content-based revolution has happened or succeeded, except in the case of computer games (though I would say that these are generally very derivative of old media products). He would argue that distribution is everything, and argues that 'the mature media are the real masters of multimedia markets'. In the case of the Internet, dominance can be specifically about the portal providers or ISPs – the companies that give you access to the Net. It is not just a question of profit from this service; it is about the advertising on screen. It is about the other companies to which you are linked when you make some generic enquiry. They own the biggest doors to the Web, and direct users to sites of their choice. This control of access is technologically represented through objects such as the set-top boxes which Sky is offering at knock-down prices in order to get people to access its digital satellite TV in Britain. The boxes are being more or less given away, because once we have them, 'they' own our attention to their content and their promotional material. In 2007 the mobile phone operator Orange was giving away cheap laptops in order to persuade people to sign up to its broadband service. If the system becomes market driven, it may be argued that the Web becomes just another means of consumption, rather than (possibly) some kind of global forum for the free exchange of knowledge and ideas.

The argument that the Net is a new stamping ground for media corporations – and not simply a media paradise for users supported by users – is symbolized by the rise of Google. This company is not just an ISP. Among many other things it offers the most popular search engine in the world (28.6 million unique users in the UK as of September 2007), the dominant email service, online news, mapping, an online alternative to Microsoft Office. It is moving into social networking and the mobile phone industry. It is worth far more than General Motors, McDonald's or Coca-Cola. In November 2007 it was the fifth biggest company listed on the US stock market (*Guardian* 1 November 2007). It has gone into partnership with the ISP Yahoo! This has raised competition concerns, given that the two companies would account for 74 per cent of global Internet searches.

One should also understand that the user is complicit in this process of commercialized Internet use. It may be argued that we are well practised at being seduced, but one cannot throw the free-will position out of the window. It may be that Web users are choosing to become consumers, to use technology to buy goods, book tickets and so on. Taking the audience or consumer perspective may also invoke a pessimistic take on new technologies, in that one cannot assume that the way forward is a moral, interactive and politically aware high road. Users can choose their own cultural capital, whether this is represented by the Amnesty International site or by those purporting to offer webcam views of the goings-on in college dorms.

Present user patterns suggest that there will be at least as much taking from the Net as there is contributing and exchanging. People will be free to choose sites at which they are (as with much of the rest of media use) simply entertained. A popular choice is to join the world of online gaming – back to the Net as a corporate stamping ground. *The World of Warcraft* is the largest virtual gaming world on the Net, with over 9 million users. Its production company, Blizzard Entertainment, is owned by the global media corporation Vivendi. Vivendi has merged Blizzard with the US company Activision to create the largest computer games company in the world. It is predicted that the income from subscriptions to online gaming worlds in general will reach $1.5 billion by 2011. The related goods used to play these games are now worth £750 million a year (*Guardian* 3 December 2007). Such an example also illustrates the impossibility of separating media technologies and uses when one notes that the companies involved are also into the home games market. In May 2008 the release of the game *Grand Theft Auto 4* made more money than the most successful release of a Hollywood blockbuster.

The very accessibility of the Internet has raised interesting questions about freedom, consumption and regulation. If the Internet is about private use of a media resource, then who is to argue about users accessing sadomasochism (S&M) 'rooms', for example? However, British authorities have been prosecuting people for accessing paedophile websites set up in the USA and in the public domain. The US authorities moved to close down a website of an anti-abortion group which included a hit list of pro-abortion names, one of whom was murdered. There are a range of control programs available to parents which deny children access to certain sites.

Those who talk up the freedoms and the virtual communities created by the Net tend to forget the downsides – surveillance, for example. A company named Ewatch asserts that it can trace the identity of any name on a screen – for a fee of US$5000.

In terms of talking about Internet uses and users, these are tremendously dispersed and varied, not least by comparison with any other media. That word 'audience' is generally not appropriate, nor is the term 'consumption'. Online shopping may be a form of consumption, but many other uses look like cultural production – blogging, posting self-produced videos. Engagement with 'traditional' media presence on the Net is active to a degree not seen in the audience relationship with those media in other settings. The user decides whether or not to download a TV programme from the USA. The user chooses what news item to examine. The user opts to post feedback opinion about a given film. The computer user flicks between sites and operations. Although we know that some Net uses dominate – emailing or shopping – still it is hard to generalize about the users themselves. They are geographically and socially dispersed, even when they form user groups, when a number of them are online at the same time. Net users are like clumps or clusters that appear and disappear. They appear clustered around some popular YouTube video and then disappear, to pop up again on someone's Facebook site. Thousands may log on to Wikipedia, but to access different entries for different reasons. Use is functional (e.g. renewing car tax) as much as recreational.

> Users are hard to perceive as a social group that shares a common technological frame because of their dispersed state of existence, as well as their diverse cognitive and material resources, interests and ideologies.
>
> (Bakardjieva 2005: 13)

At the same time, and though users may be dispersed, Bakardjieva (2005: 167) suggests that Net use and Net groups may be popular precisely because communities have become dispersed in real life. People are using the Net to reconstruct social networks modelled on family or a village community because this socio-geographic closeness has been lost for many in the Western world. She is not suggesting that the Net is a straightforward replacement for real life. But she does see 'virtual togetherness' as being positive. She discusses a range of social Net-use examples, in which users are able to form relationships on various levels – informational and emotional – which they may not be able to in their real-life situations. One example refers to a woman's online friend, to whom she felt able to reveal her experience of an abusive husband and talk through a course of action.

Bakardjieva (2005) looks positively at social uses of the Net, and sees it as empowering. She does not argue for the medium to become a replacement for real-life encounters, but rather as, in different instances, a substitute, an enhancement, a new form of sociability.

> Two conceptual dichotomies powerfully shape the theoretical debate concerning social life on the Internet: virtual versus real and public versus private. The first polarity opposes 'virtual' to 'real' community. The second, compels us to choose between images of the Internet as a medium fostering the extreme privatization of society and the Internet as an automatic community-building technology enhancing public participation.
>
> (Bakardjieva 2005: 186)

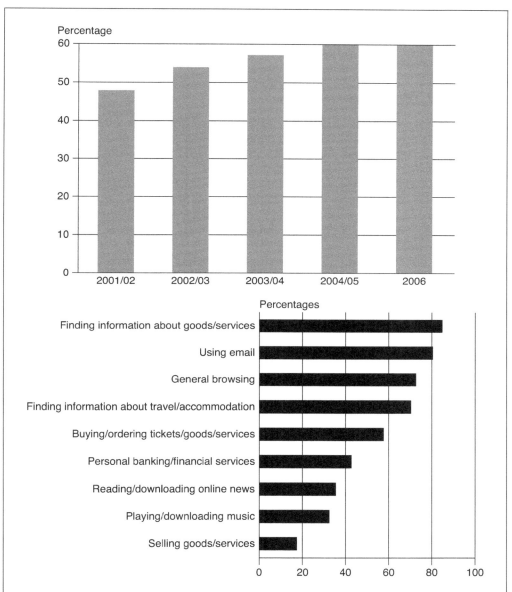

Source: Office for National Statistics
Figure 6.4 Use of the Internet
This shows the percentage of British adults aged 16 and over who had used the Internet in the three months previous to that year's survey – and selected online activities in the same period, by percentage of users. We see that six in ten of Internet users over the age of 16 went online most days in 2006. But Internet use is much more common among young people (84 per cent of 16–24 year olds) than among older people (15 per cent of 65+ year olds).

- What are the implications of this?

Bakardjieva questions the usefulness of buying into such entrenched views. She would say that it is not that simple, and that one should keep an open mind towards understanding social use of the Net in terms of 'humanistic and empowering variations of technological practice'.

7.2 Utopias and dystopias

Much critical comment on new media and on the Internet in particular tends to fall into either utopian camps which propose attractive visions such as new communities in cyberspace, or dystopian futures in which a pessimistic political economist's nightmare of a totally commodified world comes true.

Schiller (1996) would see technology as being driven by the economy and dominated by US capitalism. Stevenson (2002) interprets Schiller's position as seeing that: 'Economic forces are the main structures behind technological developments such as the super information highway and the Internet, and they also help determine the superficiality of mainstream mass culture.'

Of course, the optimist would argue that mass culture is being fragmented by these same technologies, which are putting more power in the hands of the consumer or audience. The pessimist would argue that technologies are extending the power of the market, giving it a new realm in cyberspace. Interactivity may be seen as working for greater market access – log on, sign up and pay up. Malls in cyberspace can be reached at the flick of a finger. The notion of the American imperium, currently materialized through its dominance as a world military power, extends to the economy, is backed by technological imperialism, and revivifies theories of cultural imperialism.

On the other hand, one can well argue that, in spite of increased consumption by and through technologies, our social realities are more diverse and less determined than pessimistic models suggest. People are still mobile, community action still happens on a grand scale, technology is used for political resistance and by alternative media, the media majors do not control everything, least of all the Internet. Castells (1997) has argued for positive outcomes from media and technology. He refers to various social movements and political groups as making use of technology and the media to get their views on to national and global agendas, to resist dominance. He gives the example of the Zapatista guerrilla movement in Mexico, in particular, using the Internet – email and online discussion – and video coverage. Castell's (1997) measured views on the coexistence of opposing trends and possibilities are summarized by Stevenson (2002): 'New media technologies therefore simultaneously reinforce relations of cultural capital, hierarchy and distinction while enabling social movements to publicise campaigns and connect with distant publics.' Castells (1997) rejects the idea that new media can be simply read in terms of domination or emancipation.

This dualistic view of the economy of the Net and how it is used is also voiced by Fuchs (2008: 209): 'The Internet economy is characterized by an antagonism between cooperation and competition, between the informational gift economy and informational commodity economy'. So on the one hand, one can search Wikipedia, which is provided and maintained by its users – no charge. On the other hand, one can Google for information, but there is an indirect charge on those who pay for the low key ads and links to their services. Even using Googlemail throws up a surrounding galaxy of suggested links to commercial sites.

Elsewhere, commentators refer to alternative practices and the opportunities afforded by new media of communication. Atton (2002) makes the point that 'alternative' does not always have to be radical or politically resistant. He cites the example of one Jody LaFerriere's website (www.bigdumptruck.com) in which the owner is by any definition an ordinary citizen doing her own thing – pretty alternative to mainstream practices. But the material on the site is framed within dominant ideology, is about personal enthusiasms, and for example endorses that very materialist enterprise, Amazon.com. Again the point is that technologies are malleable and can be used for a variety of purposes.

Terranova (2004) talks optimistically about Internet communities that are no longer enclosed by national boundaries, that encourage diversity and difference. But she also comments realistically that 'network politics able to traverse the global spaces of communication is not some kind of easy utopia'. Those same communities can encourage conflict and misunderstanding. I would take a similarly sceptical view of her optimistic comments about free labour and net work as it may support communities and use of the Net. People can give labour time to the Net only if they can afford the relevant hardware and software. They can give it only if they have that time free from paid labour – the privilege of leisure time in the Western economies.

7.3 New democracy, new marketplace

First, there is an issue as to whether the Internet offers us a new democracy or a new marketplace. Its uses, qualities and potential as a medium are only as good as its users, its websites, its search engines and portal providers. One could say that, seen as a technology, it is of itself value free – yet it certainly is not in respect of its operation. Sites supporting minorities or ecological causes coexist with sites offering pornography or with those encouraging a range of eccentric beliefs. It seems to offer a new democracy of a free exchange of ideas, but that democracy includes some pretty tacky ideas and no means of achieving political change. Fuchs (2008) would argue that the Net works politically only when it hosts activism or possibly direct decision making. Trying to use it for voting, for instance, would only endorse the present political process. The implication is that the present system of voting and representation does not work – not least if it is controlled by political parties and governments.

The Net does offer the chance to satirize and criticize the media themselves, but it also provides media institutions with a point of sale for their products and with an extension to their publicity machines. If the media provide the most attractive websites (and use new technologies to develop accessible streaming of moving images) then the Internet could become just an extension of the media. If governments baulk at the democratic free-for-all and introduce legal sanctions against those who set up sites they do not like (as they are now doing against pornography), then they can close down politically dissident sites. This happened with a Chinese political and spiritual movement named Falun Gong, whose leader was based in New York, and which had thousands of supporters on the Net. When it came to street protests these were severely suppressed in China, where the authorities also sought the means to close down access to the Internet. If the Internet becomes a propaganda tool for any position on given political issues, it becomes a tool of both the Right and the Left. It becomes more confusing as a source of information. It has in effect moved out of a radical phase. As technology makes it more accessible to more people with more materials, so it becomes a mainstream medium, albeit one with special qualities.

Van Loon (2008: 46) also argues that the political process in the context of new media is now more about affectivity and association than it is about argument and persuasion. In other words, emotional appeals, addressing social identity, invoking social context count for at least as much as a reasoned case. I would say that the political process in all media has moved this way. The Net is not a medium which inherently favours emotion above reason. I would say that it is rather an advertising culture in particular which has used all media to address consumers in terms which provoke emotional arousal, invoke short term responses where possible, and evade reflection and argument.

Accessibility and take-up are also issues at stake. Stephen Lax (2000) raises questions about just how much use is made of the Internet, just how many people are connected to it – in Britain, at least. He refers to the fact that where there are examples of community or area Web communities with social and political concerns, the evidence seems to be that involvement drops away after an initial surge of interest, and that core elites within the community come to dominate its agenda. Not much democracy there, then. Lax (2000) also refers to research which indicated that two out of three people neither had, nor intended to get, access to the Internet. Further, the profile of those least interested in these technologies is dominated by females in the C/D/E socio-economic classes. So politics and democracy may not be well served through new media, and women in particular may be 'disenfranchised'. Such evidence suggests that great caution is needed before proclaiming new technology as the bearer of new democracy.

7.4 A public sphere

> The current public sphere is not a sphere of mediation between state and civil society, but the site of a permanent conflict, informed by strategies of media warfare.
>
> (Terranova 2004: 134)

This is a pessimistic view, but not unrealistic, and it is consistent with Habermas's own view that publicity machines (including presumably those working for political parties) have corrupted reasonable debate (see also Chapter 8). But still, the idea that the Internet becomes a redefined public sphere is not impossible, if not a done deal. Its technology has potentially created a new public forum for social and political debate. The relationship of that debate to the political process is still in formation. For example, Oxfam campaigns on specific causes worldwide and invites lobbying action by its email recipients. But it is not a complete public sphere if sections of society do not possess and cannot afford the relevant technology to access it. Neither is it a *global* public sphere, for the same reason – access to the Internet is partial. And in some countries – China for example – governments are using various strategies to control access to the Internet, just as former East Germany tried to stop its citizens watching TV from the West.

Even within national boundaries, one is talking about technological inequalities. We may well be creating a new definition of 'underclass' – those without access to new technologies and their political and material opportunities. Globally, there is a similar division between developed and developing worlds. Kevin Williams (2003) quotes Thussu (2000) when he refers to the fact that only 12 per cent of Internet usage is in the global South where two-thirds of the world's population lives.

Similarly, Devereux (2003) refers to Cullen (2001) when stating that South-east Asia has 19 per cent of the world's population, but only 1 per cent of Internet connections.

Castells (2002) points out that in 2000, 266 million of 378 million global users were in North America and Europe. Even within designated areas of study there are huge

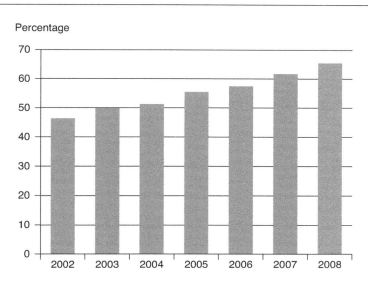

Source: Office for National Statistics
Figure 6.5 Internet Access: Percentage of Households with Access to the Internet, 2002–08
In 2008 56 per cent of all households had a broadband connection, and 65 per cent had access to the Internet (when one includes dialup). The fact that 35 per cent (or roughly one-third) of all households had no connections or access leaves other questions unasked.

● What kinds of questions?

differences of take-up. In Europe, for instance, Scandinavia has by far the greatest of national populations online. He talks about a digital divide in the USA, in which teenagers had twice as much access to the Internet as those over 50 years old; in which 50 per cent of white and Asian Americans had access, but only 29 per cent of African Americans and 23 per cent of Hispanic Americans.

Somewhat contradictorily, Castells (2002) also talks up the importance of the Internet to various social movements and protests such as those against the World Trade Organization meeting in Seattle in December 1999. Castells (2002) argues that the Internet is indispensable for the following reasons:

● It permits mobilization around values shared electronically.

● It replaces 'the shells' of vertically integrated organizations such as political parties, which, he argues, have become agencies of information dissemination, but are no longer about real, value-laden debates.

● It has a global reach which matches that of other power structures (multinationals), and bypasses the limitations of the nation state.

These points may be true, but I would draw attention to the fact that they are of advantage to fascism, as much as to democrats or environmentalists. And they give the advantage to those who are already technologically equipped and articulate – as opposed to those who are socially and financially disadvantaged. In any case, the point that may be missed here is that, like other examples, the Internet may be a generic description for a given medium built on the back of given technologies. But, in fact, all media are fragmented in their use. So the Internet is not so much one giant forum for political debate as it is a collection of discussion rooms. And this public sphere does not have to be an overtly politicized space, least of all one that especially benefits a democratic model. Its coexistent spaces are inhabited by paedophiles, Friends Reunited, dating rooms, memorial sites for the dead, sites for ethnic groups, religious groups, and so on. In fact, technology has allowed an Internet that is more like a cyber society which can be just as fragmented as the real-space society from which it emanates. 'The public', rather like 'the audience', becomes less cohesive and collective the more one interrogates its features. Indeed, in many ways this is but a notion that the media themselves have played a great part in manufacturing. News people and politicians are fond of referring to 'members of the public' as if the phrase meant something definable.

Who is *not* a member of the public? But being a 'member of the public' does not necessarily put one in a public sphere. Neither is the nature of the public sphere something to be taken for granted.

There is an issue of how far one has a genuine free flow and interchange of information and rational public debate. The media in general have already failed, we might say, as a forum for open public access and discussion. Certain media uses – especially the political lobbying around elections – point to a corruption of an ideal. Whether the Internet in particular opens up a genuine freedom, or itself is now polluted by power interests and hobbled by lack of whole public access, is part of an ongoing debate. The practice of free access to and free speech on the Internet means that extreme and minority opinions have as much of a place as mainstream comments, not least where blogging is concerned. A *Guardian* (19 May 2008) article on problems caused for the *Telegraph* website reveals the difficulties surrounding ideals of free speech. The online paper (like others) has to employ a team of people to moderate user content, because for example the paper and its bloggers are not exempt from the laws of libel and slander.

7.5 Cyber living

The Internet has permeated people's lives. It is an information resource, a place for play, a place where one can construct a new identity, a means of social interaction, and for some at least a place where they can live parallel lives. Without the use of webcams, the keyboard and text on screen become the only point of contact. This can transform social relationships in that users can conceal transgressive or marginalized identities. Net socializing provides a degree of detachment, of anonymity and de-individuation that may be helpful to the user – lack of mobility has no consequences on the Net. Or it may be unhelpful to other users: 'flaming' and 'swarming' are aggressive and abusive uses of the technology which the perpetrators could not get away with in real life.

Watt et al. (2002) also argue that assessing sociability on the Net, and making comparisons with real life, can lead to different and sometime contradictory conclusions about the quality of social interaction. One point they make is that the specific application (e.g. chat room or email) makes a considerable difference to assessment of this quality. They take a positive view of computer-mediated communication: 'the internet seems to be richly social, regulated by its own inhabitants and by group norms' (Watt et al. 2002: 77).

Cyberworlds offer places in which to live alternative lives. *Second Life*, with its own currency (Linden dollar) and real estate and 10.5 millions users, has become well known as a place for cyber living. In it, cyber estate has changed hands for real-life money: Ailin Graef became a millionaire developer. Cyber romances (and marriages) have broken up real-life relationships. This was documented by the BBC documentary *Wonderland: Virtual Love and Cyberspace* (2008), which showed an American wife obsessively retreating into an online 'adulterous' fantasy with a British man and in effect abandoning her family. A related story is told in a *Guardian* (4 September 2008) article relating to SexGen software designed to allow avatars (in *Second Life*) to touch and generally simulate any form of human contact. The founder of the company (Eros) which has created the software is also in an intimate online relationship. The fact that he and his cyber-partner are both married raises very interesting ethical issues about behaviour in cyberspace and in the real world. However, such cyber-living may not be an idealized alternative to the pain and corruption of real life. The sex industry has moved in, and even a paedophile fantasy location – Wonderland. The line between real life and cyberlife is very blurred. Online gambling in the USA was banned in 2006; some of it moved to *Second Life*, where the Linden dollar can be converted to the US dollar. Gambling is now banned in *Second Life*, but it is hard to see how this and other illegal or antisocial practices can be monitored in a cyberworld that is the size of a country.

Indeed, there are many such cyberworlds. *Runescape*, for example, has 9 million members worldwide, and involves multiple 'worlds' and the use of up to 23 'skills' when operating in these worlds. Players (or is it citizens?) can opt for one to one exchange with others, as well as operating in its public spaces. The *Guardian* (12 February 2008) reports on a Chinese project to create nine virtual universes in which billions of users can project their avatars and live a virtual life. The underlying rational for building these worlds and all the real-life infrastructure communication is that the designers conceive of avatars from around the planet inhabiting these worlds, consuming and buying just as they would in the real world.

Van Loon (2008: 105ff.) talks about such Net living as an extension of the human body, where one may occupy multiple locations simultaneously or switch identities, and enjoy simulated interactions. A key aspect of the debate about cyber worlds is to do with how far one sees any interactions as only simulated, and how far one sees them as another dimension of reality. Van Loon (2008) goes so far as to talk about the combination of the visual and the tactile (screen and keyboard) as being a 'totally embedded experience'. I would argue that this crosses a line from fact and objectifiable reality:

> the human should not be conceived as an integral entity, bound by the flesh of the body, but instead as an open system, a network, or even better, an 'assemblage', imbued with particular values, which has seemingly infinite capacity to adapt to changing conditions and uncertainty.
>
> (Van Loon 2008)

This is in Donna Haraway (1990) country, invoking the idea that the flesh and the machine can be as one (the cyborg), and that gendered limitations of the 'meat' body can be surmounted. The notion of reframing and suppressing gender has a particular edge for women when one considers how they are confined and diminished in the real world. Nobody need know much about you in cyberspace. Ironically, sexism may be rife in cyberspace as well, especially games. The *Guardian* (6 March 2008) reports research at Nottingham Trent University which shows that 70 per cent of female players opt to construct male game players, to protect themselves from online abuse.

Social networking sites have emerged as an important facet of cyber living. These are dominated by Facebook, Bebo (AOL) and MySpace (NewsCorp), with the video sharing website YouTube also very popular. The numbers of users involved is huge: Bebo has 40 million users, Facebook 116 million, with 2.5 million in London alone. MySpace has 118 million users, with revenues of $1 billion in 2007. Nielsen Online *(Guardian* 14 January 2008) reports that 17.5 million users in the UK were recorded in November 2007. They are especially popular with teenagers – in effect an extension of their experiments with socialization and group identities. To some extent one can see the logic and attraction of a technology which enables the unconfident person, the person without transport, the person living in a remote location or the person choosing to socialize in unsocial hours, the chance to 'meet' others, to present an idealized identity to the world, to feel part of something – especially something that parents cannot easily monitor. But there are downside arguments, from the Net grooming of young girls by secret predators, to the loss of the complexity and richness of face-to-face interaction. The *Guardian* (7 August 2008) reported that over 750,000 children in the UK between the ages of 8 and 12 were using social network websites, whatever their rules of use may say. And there may be other issues to this cyber-sociality, as a report from Entertainment Media Research suggests (*Guardian* 3 March 2008). This report indicates that nearly one-third of 15–19 year olds say they do less homework because of time spent on these networking sites. One-fifth of girls and one-tenth of boys also say that they spend less time watching TV for the same reason. The consequences of such changes in social behaviour have yet to work themselves through. But for a start there is that question about whether the Net is enriching the range of experiences in living for future generations, or is in some way diminishing them through a retreat from real-life experience. There are privacy and libel issues relating to the ease with which comments and photos can be posted – perhaps of those who do not wish to be put on public display by their friends, or abused on the walls of others. In 2007 a Canadian singer won a libel action against a former employee who posted details of her private life on Facebook. Such sites may not feel like one is sticking one's holiday snaps on the walls of the town square, but that is exactly what one is doing in this public cyberspace.

More positively, elderly people are becoming an example of growing niche markets for Net use. A new site for this social group – Finerday – was released in June 2008. Screen size, links, large screen buttons and a package including a large-screen cheap computer are all designed to be attractive and useful to this group. Advertising and links to suggested gifts for the extended family are intended to make the site commercially viable.

Users as 'stars' have emerged via these new media and in these cyberworlds. MySpace is well known for its use by Indie bands, and the launch of Brit band Arctic Monkeys via the Net has passed into legend. These new platforms have put success and celebrity power into the hands of the users rather than the corporations. Videoblogger Paperlilies from London has passed a million hits on her profile page. Tila Tequila created a cult following on MySpace as a glamour model, then a singer and now with a show on MTV. This example shows how the boundaries between new media are permeable. The *Guardian* (14 March 2008) reports on the career of Hayden Black, who is writing and starring in one-minute drama episodes about a teenage girl, released on his Webtv site. The podcasts registered 1.5 million hits in three months. He is his own one-person production outfit – as much as is an 80-year-old Leicestershire widower who is a minor celebrity with his autobiographical video postings.

Net-life and social life have become intertwined in many ways beyond the social use of specific sites. Uses of new technologies become taken for granted in everyday life with remarkable speed. World travellers take it for granted that they can stay in touch with family and friends via internet cafés and mobiles from around the planet. Social support groups for those suffering from specific illnesses, or as result of bereavement, or other causes of distress and isolation, have also flourished on the Net. They provide information and virtual connections which would be impossible in real life.

The younger generations use their mobiles and their camera functions as a social tool, not as an information medium. Such camera use is stronger in the UK than anywhere else in the world. The UK has 121 mobiles for every 100 people (Ofcom International Communications Market report, October 2008). UK net use is second only to that of the USA: Internet users spent 839 minutes a week online in 2008. Of course there is a question about just how strong are the social bonds created by postings on Bebo or by sending location pictures to contacts off a phone list.

An interesting and specific example of a social network is reported in the *Guardian* (4 October 2007). It reports on how internet cafés are being used in the West Bank city of Nablus, especially in the context of isolation created by the Israeli control of borders and mobility. People keep in touch with families whom they are no longer allowed to visit each other because of visa restrictions. People socialize over the Net when there is an Israeli curfew. Young men and women can 'chat' over the Messenger service, yet also preserve their cultural restrictions on contact between unmarried men and women.

An addition to social life via the Web and via mobiles is *Twitter*. This is a micro message service limited to 140 characters. It has been very successful as a gossip circuit through which people chat about the minutiae of their lives. It also has potential to act as a barometer of taste, as people chat about purchases and preferences. Like other networks, it may well act as an instant news brief service, when people find themselves in the middle of some breaking news situation. Twitter has become a social networking tool and a barometer of fame, defined by the number of Tweets received by a given user. Stephen Fry, actor and broadcaster, has become a famous user, even talking to his fans while trapped in a lift in 2009.

Another interesting development has been a cross-over between games and online networks. *Playfish* has accumulated a million users in a year. It operates on the back of sites such as *Facebook*, and offers a variety of games involving multiple users and players. One game is named *Pet Society*, and allows players to design and decorate their own homes, visit friends, and earn points by kissing them (*Guardian* 29 December 2008).

8 Discussion extract

while the contemporary vision of virtual space is usually presented as one of openness and exploration, one can also readily see that virtual space often, in practice, actually functions as a space of withdrawal into closed communities of the 'like-minded' – of those who subscribe to the same email list or bulletin board or chat room. We might also think of the personalised computer news services, about which there has been so much excitement in some quarters, as providing the same 'cocooning' effect. More broadly it has recently been argued that, in the face of the barrage of spam and computer viruses that trouble so many of its users, the Internet itself is now showing signs of 'Balkanisation' as defensive communities of trust are formed. In this 'new net' traffic is only accepted from known and accredited senders – with the prospect, according to one commentator, that eventually there may be two nets – a clean one, where security is part of the infrastructure and a 'dirty internet' for all those with old insecure technologies.

Just as Freud argued that it is only by paying due attention to the unconscious that we can ever hope to rescue ourselves from its overweening determinations, so Jeffery Alexander argues that 'only by understanding the omnipresent shaping of technological consciousness by discourse can we hope to gain control over technology in its material form. To do so, we must gain some distance from the visions of salvation and apocalypse in which technology is so deeply embedded. If improvements in the speed and reach of technologies of communication have often been mistaken for the advent of an Eldorado of greater understanding in human affairs, as Benjamin famously noted, 'it is only by remembrance that we can strip the future of its magic, to which all those succumb, who turn to soothsayers for enlightenment'.

Morley, D. (2007) *Media, Modernity and Technology*. Abingdon: Routledge.

1   Do you agree that the Internet encourages closed communities?

2   In terms of democracy or a public sphere, what would be the consequences of moving to a situation where there were 'two nets'?

3   How can discourse shape 'technological consciousness'?

4   What evidence could you provide to support each of the two sides of an argument about how we should view technologies, as outlined at the beginning of this passage?

▌9 Further reading

Atton, C. (2002) *Alternative Media*. London: Sage.

Bakardjieva, M. (2005) *Internet Society: The Internet in Everyday Life*. London: Sage.

Fuchs, C. (2008) *The Internet and Society*. Abingdon: Routledge.

Gauntlett, D. and Horsley, R. (eds) (2004) *Web Studies*, 2nd edn. London: Arnold.

Jenkins, H. and Thorburn, D. (eds) (2003) *Democracy and New Media*. Cambridge, MA: MIT Press.

Lister, M., Dovey, J., Giddings, S., Grant, I. and Kelly, K. (2003) *New Media: A Critical Introduction*. London: Routledge.

Preston, P. (2001) *Reshaping Communications*. London: Sage.

7

Advertising

Its relationship with media industries and with audiences

That consumers exercise limited choice in the market or see through advertising persuasive strategies does not imply that advertising's social communication is benign or inconsequential.

Leiss, W., Kline, S., Jhally, S. and Botteril, J. (2005) *Social Communication in Advertising*, 3rd edn. London: Routledge.

1 Introduction

The conduct of the advertising industries, and the materials that they produce, has sometimes given rise to fierce differences of opinion over the functions and effects of advertising in society. Some might see certain television adverts as little creative masterpieces. Others might damn advertising as condescending in its representation of social groups, trite in its view of human behaviour, and even as pernicious in being a creature of capitalism and its ideology.

In this chapter I want to examine advertising mainly in relation to key concepts and debates already outlined in this book, not least in relation to ideas about media influence. The intention is not to describe the functions and working of the advertising industry; that has been sufficiently covered by books such as *The Advertising Handbook* by Sean Brierley (1995), as well as being supported by resources such as the website for the Advertising Standards Authority. My purpose is, rather,

- to engage with critiques of advertising
- to relate advertising to key terms central to this book
- to comment on the relationship of advertising to the media in general.

The lead quotation above identifies a classic critique of advertising which nevertheless does not represent all perspectives, let alone all concerns about the role and effects of advertising. Schudson (1993), for example, argues that the process of influence through advertising media is not so much about the advertising as such, as it is about culture and social context.

2 Major questions

1 What is the nature and place of advertising in society, and in relation to media?
2 How may one relate advertising to critiques of the relationship between media and society, between institutions and consumers, between texts and audiences?

3   How do adverts relate to consumers, especially in terms of persuasion?

4   How does advertising relate to ideas about commodification?

5   In what ways does advertising promote mythologies through its representations and its invocation of discourses?

3 The nature of advertising

It needs to be clear that what follows is inextricably connected with marketing and promotion, as much as being about advertising alone – paid-for intentional persuasive communication. Publicity usually works alongside advertising, and is about activities which draw attention to, and create a favourable attitude towards, the product or service being sold. Publicity is not paid for, as in a TV slot or a magazine page. But it still costs – for example, to run a promotion party or to create a press pack.

Marketing and promotion are more suitable terms to describe persuasive activities which work across media, which use more than just media, which operate on national and even global scales, and which resonate off one another. By this last comment I mean, for instance, that a TV interview with a film star may in the first place be set up to market a given movie. But then it also promotes the star as a business, and the idea of stardom in general, and film as a medium, and the attractions of television. Marketing as an activity is utterly pervasive within the media, but also within our cultural and social experiences. 'Each promotional message refers us to a commodity which is itself the site of another promotion' (Wernick 1991).

Goods themselves become a kind of advertisement. Like an advert they are referential and intertextual. Advertising, marketing, promotion, publicity, commodities, are all stitched together. The so-called developed world and its cultures are a dominant part of this stitchwork. They are extending their reach globally. The advertising world is one of multinational corporations, regional markets such as South-east Asia, and trading blocs. It operates on the back of international money markets, internationalized labour practices and information technologies.

As Myers (1999) puts it:

> What is new after the 1980s is not the multinationals but a combination of deregulated capital markets, less unionized labour markets, and extended trading areas that gave these companies more power to move production and distribution for increased profits, and give them advantages over companies based in one nation.
>
> (Myers 1999)

Advertising in itself is such a vast economic activity and is so explicitly devoted to promoting partial views of products and services that it merits critical attention. This is true even if there are questions about the extent of its effectiveness, as well as about the nature of its 'collateral damage' in ideological terms.

In May 2001 Coca-Cola spent approximately $400 million worldwide on its brands. In the same year, it spent £30 million in the UK on promotion.

Jamieson and Campbell (2001) report that in the USA in 1990, 13,300 new products were introduced, 75 per cent of which were foodstuffs. In 1998, $200 billion was spent on advertising in the USA, an increase of 7.5 per cent on the previous year. It cost $2 million to place a 30-second ad around TV screenings of the Superbowl series.

Doyle (2002) refers to the level of global expenditure on advertising in 2000, estimated at $330 billion. The advertising industry operates like its hosts, the media, in respect of the global dominance of three agencies – Interpublic, Omnicom and WPP. Advertising expenditure is itself dominated by the media of the press and television. In Britain, 85 per cent of expenditure is on these two media, and twice as much is spent on the press as on television.

But again, one should not underestimate the huge sums of money which are also spent on other media. Outdoor advertising is an interesting case in point, covering all kinds of devices, from billboards to bus shelters to video screens to Evian sponsoring the refurbishment of a south London Lido in exchange for its brand name being visible in huge letters at the bottom of the pool. In the year to March 2007, Vodafone spent £20 million on outdoor media. The advertiser JCDecaux spent £25 million upgrading its airport advertising sites in relation to the opening of Heathrow's Terminal 5, including 300 digital sites in the terminal. Piccadilly Circus is a prime outdoor advertising site in London because over a million people pass through it each week. People are spending more time outside the home than ever before – 6.5 hours a day for the average British adult. Some outdoor ads have become icons in cultural history, from the huge posters for Wonderbra (Hello Boys) to the photo projection of a rear view of a naked Gail Porter onto the Houses of Parliament. Digital bus side displays can be programmed to switch to an ad for the Boots stores when the bus passes a store. Star Wars 3 was launched in 2005 with the voice of Darth Vader coded into certain bus shelters in London and Birmingham, UK (*Guardian* special on outdoor media, 25 June 2007).

The cutting edge of technology is raising some interesting issues around developments in advertising. For example it is now possible for machines (see neuro-science) to 'read' brain responses to external stimuli. In 2008 a campaign for Jack Daniels whiskey was adapted in response to research in this area (*Guardian* 3 April 2008). Another kind of issue has developed around the work of an Internet company, Phorm, which has deals with British Telecom, Virgin Media and TalkTalk, which mean that it tracks the Internet habits (including purchasing) of 10 million customers. Given that customers were not told about this tracking and cannot opt out of it, there are ethical questions raised about surveillance.

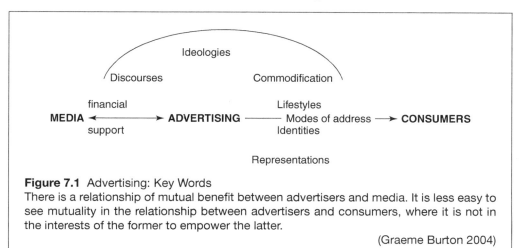

Figure 7.1 Advertising: Key Words
There is a relationship of mutual benefit between advertisers and media. It is less easy to see mutuality in the relationship between advertisers and consumers, where it is not in the interests of the former to empower the latter.

(Graeme Burton 2004)

At least some of this advertising has had the effect of creating new sales, increasing market shares, maintaining sales and generating profits on a gigantic scale. Some advertising does work some of the time. What is more interesting to the context of this book are its effects on social attitudes, social practices, cultural values, identities and people's understanding of the kind of world that they believe they live in.

We tend to take advertising for granted, as a cultural experience. It has been around for so long that we take it as a 'given' in everyday life. Kline (1993) refers to the fact that by 1900 the pages of some daily newspapers were literally half full of adverts. Even 50 years earlier, laws were passed to stop the proliferation of advertising carts choking up city streets. But it does not have to exist in the form that it does. Indeed, Falk (1996) points out that an interesting shift took place roughly from the early nineteenth to the early twentieth centuries, to produce the kind of promotional environment that now seems normal to us. There was a shift from product-centred adverts to those that were about a product–user relationship, about the experiential aspect of the product concerned. There was a shift from adverts whose copy provided arguments about and for the product, to those that represented satisfaction from using the product. There was a general shift from adverts dominated by verbal and literary modes, to those dominated by visual modes of communication. This has led to a kind of advertising in which the advert is detached from the product as such. It has led to a situation in which the consumption of experience and the experience of consumption are interlinked.

Advertising came to fill that space that opened up between production and consumption, when people no longer lived next to, or were themselves the source of production. Broadly, this is also about the shift from rural economies to predominantly urban populations in the West (by 1920, 52 per cent of Americans lived in towns and cities: Fowle 1996). Mass production, with all its advantages of economies of scale, also meant that a throughput of goods needed to be maintained in order to justify investment and to keep those production lines in business. Advertising to maintain consumption helped keep that throughput going. 'Advertising offered itself as a way of efficiently creating consumers and as a way of homogeneously controlling the consumption of a product' (Ewen 1977).

Kline (1993) refers to Ewen's (1977) work when he says that a crucial point was reached in the development of advertising when industrial producers recognized 'that all goods were cultural artefacts and that selling them was mostly a matter of communication'.

Fowles (1996) provides some interesting ideas about oppositions and tensions which are part of the nature of adverts and of the advertising process. These ideas question that surface of inevitability that ads present to us. They suggest that the production of such texts and their meanings is problematic. They are now set out, with some paraphrasing and interpretation.

- *The needs of the client v. the needs of the agency:* that conflict between the needs of the agency to be creative and to gain the approval of their peers within the industry, and the direct need of the client for promotion through whatever works.

- *Research information v. creative execution:* the disjunction between what researchers may tell the agency and what their creative instincts may tell them about the market and promotional methods – e.g. the famous, surrealist run of Benson & Hedges cigarette ads would never have seen the light of day if the agency had listened to what research was saying.

- *Product v. appeal:* devices to appeal must not lose sight of the product. This is a conflict between actuality and the ideal – that problem where people remember the ad but not the product.

- *Words v. images:* negotiating the symbolic order of spoken and written language, as opposed to the direct iconic impact of images.

- *The frame as container v. bursting the frame:* alternative strategies in which the ad is either contained and ordered, or those in which images and text may appear to be bursting out of frame, or bled to the margins of the sheet.

- *Text v. text:* that sense of intertextual strain where, in their subconscious, consumers are setting one product against another. Ads, their genres, their categories of product cannot live in a conceptual vacuum – the problem is to make the comparisons favourable without seeming to recognize the opposition.

- *Advert v. consumer:* the problem that advertisers have, especially nowadays, to combat consumer resistance and scepticism towards a communication process which is seen to be manipulative.

- *The one v. the many:* negotiating that stretch within the ad and the campaign in which the appeal has to address the individual and yet also reach a mass market.

4 Advertising and media: a relationship

Marketing and promotion are integral to the workings of a capitalist economy, in which goods (including their cultural dimensions) have to be sold to consumers within a marketplace (whether literal or virtual). The media are integral to the workings of advertising. Advertising is integral to the finances of the media. In Britain, as globally (with the exception of the BBC and its licence fee income), virtually all media depend on selling advertising to stay in business. There is also income from devices such as sponsorship and product placement to be taken into account (see also Chapter 2).

Without advertising support, based on a profitable audience, media can and do go to the wall. The magazine *Ms* went bust in the 1990s although it had 3 million readers, because the advertisers did not like its feminist stance. On the other hand the specialist style magazine *Wallpaper* was bought by TimeInc in 2003 for $1.63 million because its 150,000 readers had money to spend (Leiss et al. 2005: 360).

This relationship has predictably produced opposing critiques which talk up the dependency of the one element upon the other, and vice versa. Those who defend the marketplace economy would argue that advertising provides a kind of subsidy to the economy (and possibly the media), whereby its activity boosts and maintains sales (and in so doing also covers the cost of advertising). The other view is that advertising inevitably pressures the media that depend upon it into assuming certain ideological positions, which of course are favourable to the work of advertising. This view would also draw attention to the dominance of the few in all markets, and to the consequent lack of real consumer choice.

It is clear that both media and advertisers are interested in reaching audiences. There is a view that media 'locate' audiences for advertisers and therefore operate in the interests of advertisers as much as those of media audiences. One may also argue that the way media have developed has quite a lot to do with the history of their relationship with advertising.

Broadcasting could have been more of a regional or local medium early on. But in the USA, and in Britain from the 1950s, the mass market characteristics of television may be at least partly to do with commercial interest in its ability to reach into millions of homes at one time. It offered the kind of visuality and immediacy which the press did not have. Indeed its popularity as an advertising medium is now near to becoming a problem when one notes that in the USA in 1999 there was an average of 16.43 minutes of advertising per prime time hour (Leiss et al. 2005: 353). Equally, the development of magazines into niche markets and their characteristic of running features which in effect promote their subject (computers or cars or fashion) may also be said to be a result of the interests of advertisers – whose interests are in turn those of their paymasters, the companies who commission them.

Andersen (1995) provides many examples of self-interest at work. He comments on the 'banned list' which many US companies have, with relation to TV programmes with which they will not be associated. For example, Mars will not advertise M&Ms in or around a list of 50 programmes. Andersen (1995) refers to that practice of agencies and their clients which routinely provides 'complimentary copy' for inclusion in magazines. He refers to Gloria Steinem writing about her own experience in the magazine industry when he says that ' "advertisers" control over the editorial content of women's magazines had become "so institutionalized that it is written into insertion orders or dictated to ad salespeople as official policy" '.

'Advertorials' have been a major element of such magazines since the 1990s, using devices such as the celebrity interview, and involving, for example, tie-ins with a travel company. In many magazines the page quietly headed 'advertising feature' is hardly to be distinguished from the general features. What is not said may also be about the power of the advertiser in their relationship with the media. The magazines *Cosmopolitan*, *Nova* and *Marie-Claire* refused in 2001 to run an RSPCA ad against the use of animals in testing for cosmetic products. The proposed ad showed a rabbit having its eyes sprayed. Such magazines do, of course, obtain a significant income from ads about cosmetic products. There are also instore shopping magazines which further erase the distinction between editorial and advertising.

Promotional activities may extend to apparently neutral and factual TV programmes, which one might think fall outside even the practice of product placement. Andersen (1995) refers to 'the escalating unity of entertainment, news and advertising on television'. He describes how in 1990 three successive nightly editions of NBC news featured an item drawing attention to a new machine for detecting breast cancer. He points out that this item did not appear on other networks; that the machine was made by General Electric, which owns RCA, which owns NBC.

Branding and product placement have become commonplace in the media of film and television. The Bond film *Casino Royale* (2006) included a Ford Mondeo at one point, and a Ford Ka appeared in the next Bond movie *Quantum of Solace* (2008). It was also the Ford name that featured prominently in shots of the stadia hosting the European Football Champion's League in 2008. The line between manufacturing companies and media companies becomes even more blurred when one considers that the Orange mobile phone company not only sponsors the Cannes film festival but also has set up a movie production arm. Audi cars has its own digital TV channel (also online) (*Independent on Sunday* 6 April 2008). There seems to be no end to the 'reach' of advertising, in its various forms, into the everyday lives of consumer citizens.

Of course, one has to recognize the moderating influence of political regulation of the advertising industry, when arguing for the debilitating effects of advertising on the media. These effects are to do with the dependency of media on advertising and the shaping of media development by advertising. But again, the effectiveness of regulation within individual nation states is very much open to question.

In Britain, media industries are largely self-regulated. The Advertising Standards Authority covers magazines, the press and cinema. It was set up by the Advertising Association. The Broadcast Advertising Clearance Centre was set up by broadcasters. Until December 2003 this worked closely with the Independent Television Commission and the Radio Authority. Now this relationship is with the new broadcast regulator, Ofcom, a quasi-independent body set up by government, but given autonomy in that it is not run by any government department. But clearly the hand of government is upon it, just as government may also affect advertising indirectly through the legal system. For example, the Obscene Publications Act 1959 would ensure that nothing too extreme could be 'published' by advertisers. Yet it may not be straightforward obscenity that needs regulating. In 2002 an advert for Opium perfume caused public protests. The objections were not so much about the apparent nudity of a reclining female model, with orgasmic signification, but concerned the renewal of the objectification of women in a public display.

There are practices and possible effects wider even than those where advertisers interfere with the free choice of content in media texts. For instance, intertextuality is an established commercial strategy, most obviously in cases where personalities and stars lend their persona to a product. Angela Lansbury (of the much rerun series *Murder, She Wrote*) has been used to promote aspirin on US TV. Music tracks and old film clips are frequently used in adverts. One might argue that such devices falsely attach values to products which have nothing legitimate to do with such referents. It might be said that such intertextual appropriation is a form of cultural terrorism.

In terms of the relationship between the media and advertising, it is assumed that the debate is mainly with relation to television. But more cash is spent on press advertising. It is true that TV remains the only really mass medium. But still, its income from adverts is diminishing. The audience share of the US networks is down to around 40 per cent (Doyle 2002). The ITV share in Britain is less than 25 per cent of the audience, with the BBC having nearer to a 30 per cent share. In 2002, ITV advertising revenues were down by 17 per cent from the 2000 figure, when it grossed £2 billion. This slide has continued. In August 2008 ITV's advertising revenues were reported as having dropped by 20 per cent from the previous month. The company was said to be £1.54 billion in the red (*Guardian* 7 August 2008). By the end of September 2008 its nine month ad revenues were just a little over £1 billion (*Guardian* 6 November 2008). Interestingly, its online revenues are growing steadily, though nowhere near enough to help the company out of its difficulties.

Satellite and cable is competing for its share of advertising. So is the Internet, where advertising is actually more expensive than on TV, on the grounds that this medium offers a better match with individual audience targets. Generally speaking, the Net is now biting into newspaper revenues, and is holding up better than conventional media in the face of an economic downturn. For the newspaper group Trinity Mirror, advertising revenues fell by 12.6 per cent in June and July 2008. Similarly, a major regional newspaper group, Johnston Press, saw its year-on-year advertising revenue fall by 21 per cent (August 2008). Classified ads are moving online. More and younger people are reading news online. As newspaper sales in general continue to decline, so their advertising revenues must also fall back. Advertising on the Net, which was predicted to rise by over 20 per cent in 2008–09, is also overtaking that on radio.

All the same, when one looks at all commercial television in the UK (including digital), it is still the case that viewers watch an average of 40 commercials a day (BARB/Thinkbox 2007). In the 16–34 age group – much sought after by advertisers – BARB analysis also confirms an average of 3.33 hours of TV viewing per day. Thinkbox confirms that TV viewing by the young must also be seen as an activity happening at the same time as other things, and alongside digital networking and the use of many other media devices.

5 Advertising and society: critiques

Critical positions on advertising in relation to society reflect a range of views.

- *Pluralist positions* argue for the benefits of consumption and choice for the consumer and for the economy.
- *Neo-Marxist positions* argue against the debilitating effects of monopoly markets and the corrupting effects of representations in advertisements.
- *Cultural critiques* would emphasize the insidious effects of commodification.

Sinclair (1987) sees the critiques in terms of an opposition between optimistic and pessimistic views, between those who see advertising as a tool whose function is to make the economy work, and those who see the working of the economy as destructive of social and cultural values. 'For the functionalists, advertising in society operates towards the utilitarian end of creating "the greatest happiness for the greatest number", while for the Marxists, advertising maintains the illusions by which an exploitative and irrational system is perpetuated' (Sinclair 1987). Pluralists might object to a conflation of functionalism and pluralism, but in Sinclair's terms there is little distinction to be made between the two.

However one understands the functions and effects of advertising, what is clear is that it is bound up with a complex relationship between society and economy and culture and politics. Critiques of advertising are a paradigm for critiques of those media that provide advertising with a means of approaching audiences. Transparent views of advertising see it being synonymous with democracy and consumption and choice of goods. Opaque views would draw attention to what advertising conceals. 'Advertisements obscure and avoid the real issues of society', 'they create systems of social differentiation', 'basic issues . . . are sublimated into "meanings", "images", "lifestyles", to be bought with products, not money' (Williamson 1978).

Differentiation, it might be said, has to do with advertising constructing us as audiences, creating social categories, generating what become naturalized truths. These differences are as false as differences between commodities, which advertising also constructs. Commodities may appear to be different from one another, defined by their patents if nothing else. But it may be said that such differences are insignificant until advertising makes them appear so. Differences are validated in terms of the discourse of individualism. To be different or individual in these terms is a 'good thing'. The illusion is fostered that one becomes different by choosing a brand. But of course this is nonsense. The inherent contradiction is that thousands of others are also buying your brand of jeans or car. This is guaranteeing sameness at the point at which you are being told that you have guaranteed individuality. You are what you buy or consume. But you are not who you think you are.

One may also contrast critical views in terms of those which are more holistic and those which are more selective. Post-Marxist views are concerned with the 'big picture', the part played by advertising in the overall relationship between media and society. In this view, advertising flatters to deceive. It subverts use value into exchange value. Its representations incorporate the meanings of the dominant ideology. Its naturalized place in social experience would place it at the heart of hegemony. It helps engineer acceptance of difference and of inequality. All adverts, in varying degrees, are trying to sell capitalism.

A cultural approach, on the other hand, would tend to concentrate on texts and audiences, just as a political economy perspective would tend to emphasize institution, production and regulation. The former would look at the part played by advertising and advertisements in respect of meaning and consumption. The latter would look at the influence of advertising on the workings of media institutions, and at the influence of regulators on both producers and the text.

Leiss et al. (2005: 15) comment that 'advertising mediates between commodity production and cultural production' – and again – 'situated between producers and consumers in the expanding marketplace, advertising became a key site of negotiation between the economic and cultural spheres'.

Nava et al. (1996) is unsympathetic towards what she describes as totalizing, Fordist views. She argues that the advertising industry itself is unsure or sceptical about the effects of its own work. She suggests that investigation of the industry's own analysis of advertising (and not its confident pronouncements to its clients) demonstrates 'demoralization, fragmentation and suspension of belief'. In this view, holistic models which include unqualified assumptions about persuasive effects and especially assertions of a Marxist nature about mass media and mass culture, simply do not work.

By way of contrast, Robert Goldman (1992) works out of an essentially Althusseran Marxist position when he sees advertising as 'a key social and economic institution in producing and reproducing the material and ideological supremacy of commodity relations'. In this case, one is looking at ways in which a system of production reproduces itself. This reproduction of a system and of ideology has a lot to do with advertising, and how deeply it is embedded within our social and cultural lives. It is seen rather as a force of nature, than as a tool of corporations. Advertising helps manifest those imaginary relations of the individual to the real relations in which they live: the imaginary conceals the real.

Capitalist pluralism sees advertising as benign, and tends to regard it optimistically, as an information provider, drawing attention to the merits of goods and services. This was much more true in the Victorian period. Though this is a position still argued for by many in the industry, it really has not been valid for decades. Ever since Pears soap began to construct mythologies around cleanliness and childhood, advertisements have become increasingly about culture, not raw goods; about values, not facts; about mythic worlds, not social reality. Sinclair (1987) takes a political economy perspective when he describes the idea that advertising is merely a source of information as disingenuous – 'truth in advertising is what the law says it is'.

Both a political economy and a market perspective on advertising would see media funding as an important part of the place of advertising in society. The latter would see advertising as a kind of engine of the market, maintaining the circulation of goods and wealth and providing employment.

A political economist, on the other hand, would regard advertising (and its income) as underwriting the power of media institutions. This economic power is checked only by the regulatory power of political institutions, acting through law. And advertising does not just underwrite media businesses financially, by providing much of their income. It also underwrites them culturally by constructing a view of the world which legitimizes what they produce, how they produce it, and the very operation of advertising itself.

Advertising has become a naturalized component of the media economy. Naturalization legitimizes its work, its products, its effects. It is a product of ideological positions on freedom of speech and the idea of a free market. But in another social context one might argue that these freedoms are relative, and tend to benefit those with the power to exercise such freedoms. The freedoms in turn become a source of power. From this follows an argument that there should be no advertising, or that it should be heavily regulated.

Doyle (2002) points out that there is a strong correlation between advertising expenditure and economic wealth in any given country, however that wealth is measured. But even if one agrees that advertising contributes to economic growth, this does not mean that it contributes to social well-being. Indeed, by helping a few corporations become globally successful, it actually helps create a situation of commercial oligopoly in which the few dominate the many. Again, it is Doyle (2002) who points out that 'advertising is a feature of oligopoly market structures'. In this sense one needs to deconstruct not only advertisements, but also the very process of advertising. For example the notion of 'the market' is itself a construction which is convenient to the promotion industries. 'Contrary to marketing ideology, markets do not already exist "out there" in social reality but are "constructed"' (Sinclair 1987).

This links with a wider point about media audiences – they are not ready formed, out there, waiting for their programme to come along. They come into being for the programme, and only for as long as the life of the programme. Similarly, a consumer market exists only while consumption takes place. The consumer and the market are only ideas that are waiting to happen – to be given life through purchase and use.

Cronin (2000) also develops ideas about the imagined world that advertisers manufacture. She argues that audiences and their relationships are indeed imagined, not discovered. The very work of marketers – through focus groups for instance – is a way of confirming as real what is in fact only imagined. It is a way of validating the work of agencies to their industry clients. Imagined markets are incorporated within the textual address of an advertisement – their existence is assumed. As readers and consumers we are invited to share that assumption.

While acknowledging that there are cultural consequences to the way advertising operates, still a political economy perspective would emphasize the economic significance of advertising and promotion. Within a Marxist framework, examining how dominant classes deploy cultural power, this position would be interested in the economic sources of that power. It may be said that positions drawn out of Marx are interested in the production of consumption, while more postmodern and culturalist critiques of advertising would concentrate on modes of consumption.

Matterlart (1991) is critical of advertising in terms of how it dominates 'public space': 'It forms a social network which enervates media economies, cultures, political and civil society, international relations.' It takes over public space, especially that created through media, for its own ends, and pushes aside genuine public interaction. It privileges form and image above content and the interchange of ideas – 'the new public space will be more and more driven by "images"'.

Kenway and Bullen (2001) make a similar point about public spaces being dominated by advertising and by practices of consumption. Jameson (1991) or Baudrillard (1988) might, on the other hand, critique advertising and a market culture in a more postmodern way. This approach would draw attention to a world of simulation, to a kind of hyper-reality. Advertising is full of simulated experiences. Even shopping in the vast new mall complexes becomes a kind of alternative reality, even an 'out of body' experience. There is a lack of distinction between the real and the imaginary. Identities become fluid, as people become detached from a real social world by advertising and by its capacity to cause us to continually redefine ourselves. We live in a world of commodity experiences, manifested through advertising.

▎6 Advertising and audiences

The demographic approach to explaining 'audiences' places them in objectifiable categories such as age, gender, occupation, place of domicile (see BARB in the UK or Nielsen in the USA; see also Chapters 3 and 4). Audiences are constructed, through marketing, for advertisers, by those in the business of promotion, out of social groups that may or may not interact in everyday life, that may or may not share cultural experiences. As audiences fragment and niche markets expand, signs of group membership, often supplied via advertising, become more and more embedded in our everyday lives. As Leiss et al. (2005: 245) say: 'we appear to be compelled to fashion our social interactions through goods'. The notion of 'consumer' has so far become naturalized: we are so far accustomed to the idea that adverts speak to bodies of people called 'housewives' or 'car drivers' that it is difficult for people to detach themselves from the unreality of such identities. Words such as 'consumer' stand for a certain state of cultural and political affairs – like 'the public' or 'the viewer'. Their coinage, and the kind of reality they stand for, works in the interests of institutions rather than of any social group. We talk about the 'advertiser' but not the 'advertisee' because the process of marketing does not involve an equal relationship. The 'consumer' has a subordinated function, just as the 'audience' is supposed to have a passive function. In both cases, there are arguments that the consumer or audience may be more active and constructive than appears to be the case. But one can hardly argue that advertising actually intends to empower the consumer with choice, with unbiased information, with the tools of resistance.

Appadurai (2007: 225) also talks about the lack of real consumer power: 'the consumer is consistently helped to believe that he or she is an actor, where in fact he or she is at best a chooser'.

The urge of the advertiser to objectify and classify is exemplified by the approach of the company, Experion, and their marketing tool, Financial Mosaic. This produces ten general classifications of consumer, based on postcodes and information about debts, loans, investments etc. Categories range from 'discerning investors' to 'burdened borrowers'. The audience is defined in the material terms of a commodity culture, which have nothing to do with social values (*Independent on Sunday* 5 September 1999).

Equally, one should balance such an instrumental example with reference to the use of ethnographic research by advertisers. In this case, the researchers may be out on the high street, or in clubs, talking to people, and observing shifts in fashion or in patterns of consumption. The ethnographer gets into life as it is lived, and completes a feedback loop to the producers. The chip-maker Intel commissioned ethnographic research into children's social behaviours and preferences, as part of the development of computer games consoles (*Independent on Sunday* 15 July 2001).

The arrival of 'viral marketing' in 2002 was also interesting in that it engaged the audience directly through an elaborate 'word-of-mouth' principle. For example, Dulux Paints emailed 10,000 women, inviting them to play a 'belly fluff' game on a specially created website. Some 13,000 women responded. Respondents get interested. Some make purchases; more tell their friends. Other devices in this area might include the use of street flyers, lamppost labels, backed up by regular posters and websites. Mobile phones have been stencilled on pavements. The Cerne Abbas Giant (a huge primitive fertility figure cut into the hill chalk of Dorset) has been 'dressed' in a pair of jeans. On the Internet, a Japanese electrical goods firm in Australia pledged to plant a tree if its display 'leaf' received 100 messages a day.

Source: Walker Werbeagentur AG
Figure 7.2 Amnesty International Street Poster: 'It doesn't happen here, but now!'
This clever optical illusion is created by a street poster for Amnesty International in Switzerland. Amnesty is not selling commodities, but is promoting the interests of its organization – to identify and support victims of political injustice around the planet.

There are multiple audiences for advertising. Many are part of 'the public', but some are trade audiences. These audiences are sought for a variety of reasons, not just to persuade consumers to buy. Other reasons for advertising are to

- hold on to one's share of a given market in the face of competition
- get a bigger share of the market
- create awareness of a given product or service
- reassure existing customers that what they have been buying is still good
- reassure the trade and one's sales force that the product is good and that advertising is working.

In the context of advertising, the audience itself becomes a product, another commodity. The circulation and marketing managers of any magazine will talk about being able to deliver a certain kind of reader with a certain kind of profile to the advertiser – the one who really pays the bills. As Andersen (1995) puts it, the audience has 'market value' and television seeks to package its viewers 'into more desirable commodities'. Jhally (1990) picks up the same theme when talking about how goods acquire value through their exchange. Advertisers use the media to sell goods to consumers. In this process of exchange, goods might acquire value of social status or of sexuality; one is never just buying a sweatshirt or a lipstick. The consumer gives cash as their part of the exchange. But, Jhally (1990) says, businesses and media organizations are also engaged in a process of exchange – audiences as a commodity in exchange for cash or some other kind of reward.

Advertising plays on ideas about individualism, it invokes this discourse. It often appears to address the individual consumer. Of course, the contradiction is that it does not, and cannot. The market is committed to packaging and delivering consumers in the plural. It is equally committed to packaging the goods that it sells to consumers. Volume production and economies of scale would be impossible otherwise. So the market sees the audience in one way, but the advertisements produced by the market pretend to see the audience in another way. 'Consumer ads usually invite viewers into fantasies of individualism, though the promise of individuality is likely to be premised on conformity of consumption preferences' (Goldman and Papson 1998).

Lifestyles

It has become a commonplace that audiences are conceived of in terms of their lifestyles. Once more, it would be ingenuous to argue that as members of society we simply have lifestyles which the market identifies and slots into. The market (as all our cultural assumptions about consumption) has been around for so long that we are born into lifestyles which it has already shaped. We grow up into a set of assumptions about what living is, what shopping is, and the market continues to work on the idea of lifestyle through an apparently everlasting succession of campaigns. It is constructing and reconstructing lifestyles all the time. The main thing that lifestyle is about is the consumers' conception of their place in society, their social relations, their persona – it is nothing to do with material needs as such. The possession of SUVs (sport utility vehicles) or 4×4 vehicles is about how the owners wish to be seen by others. Few of these owners could support an argument that the vehicle was necessary to their work or the well-being of their family.

Lifestyle advertising involves what is called psychographic research, in which the intention is to profile work and leisure time, interests, attitudes and opinions. People are categorized by sets of characteristics and defined in such terms as 'those who are achievement oriented', or 'those who are driven by the need to belong'. Gough-Yates (2003) refers to a significant change in the way that the advertisement addressed the consumer from the 1970s onwards. These new forms of research attempted to stay 'close' to the customer, to address the individual. Contemporary families are reflected in for example the BT ads of 2007–08, where Kris Marshall is the boyfriend of a single mother with two children.

What these lifestyles all have in common is consumption. Audiences already believe in consumption as a way of life. Advertising seeks to fit the nature of the consumption to the particular lifestyle preferences of the consumer group. 'Consumption is now recognized as a defining characteristic of the life-style of the Western world' (Kenway and Bullen 2001). But, in line with the alternatives of the passive–active audience debate, Kenway and Bullen (2001) also recognize that consumers do things with goods. So, in terms of a kind of passivity and arguments about what the media do to people, they assert that: 'It is through advertising and marketing that commodities acquire certain cultural meanings or "sign value" and it is thus that advertising participates in the social construction of our needs.'

We are taught to need things. We learn to be an audience for ads. But then they also argue that people may use ads in unexpected ways – 'people use consumption to create identities, social bonds or distinctions'. Ruddock (2001) refers to the 'communicative function' of goods which are 'purchased not only for their function, but for what they say about the user'.

Kenway and Bullen (2001) go on to suggest that ads are changing and that the ad–audience relationship is also shifting. They say that there is a 'broader cultural shift to a concentration on style, form and image and away from use-value, substance or direct address'. Some may argue that the outcomes of focus group research, complaints to the regulators and the widespread use of remote control channel and ad zapping shows that consumers are not a pushover for the advertisers. Leiss et al. (2005: 451) assert that research has showed that audiences responded to advertisers 'who matched contemporary values in relation to women and ethnicity'. But I would suggest that the question of who dominates the ad–audience relationship is still a matter for debate.

7 Advertising and persuasion

Advertising is a bit like a gun in the hands of a drunkard on a firing range – sometimes it hits the target, sometimes it does not – as in the famous case of the 1985 Coke fiasco, when market research misled Coca-Cola into marketing a new-tasting Coke, and then had to write off millions of dollars when it all went wrong, and the consumers made it clear they were not going to buy the taste. Equally, although arguments about oppositional reading and the power of readers to appropriate cultural goods and use them in their own interests (for example, Fiske 1989), have some validity, this does not contradict the presence and effects of persuasive devices within advertising. The form of words and images is constructed to resonate with the psychology of the consumer. Promotion locks into our attitudes and values. Advertising, above all textual forms, does have preferred readings. 'Advertising's first-order function as promotion leads it to engage with values, norms, goals and dreams of those to whom it is addressed' (Wernick 1991). And of course those values and norms have an ideological dimension because ideology is already in our heads, as much as in advertisements. We may be the more easily persuaded if, as it were, we are ready to be persuaded. We already believe in the 'rightness' of possessing things, of taking pleasure in leisure time, of doing things 'for love', of cleanliness and personal hygiene. It may be that, historically, advertising has been one of the sources of such beliefs. It may be that presently, advertising and the media reinforce those beliefs.

Up to a point one may argue that the point of origin of an ideological position is not as important as the fact of its existence. So adverts for slimming products (always for women) may be linked to myths and ideologies about body shape, which themselves may have some historical location in Victorian advertisements for corsets. There may also be a classic ideological contradiction at the heart of both products in both eras. That is to say, beliefs in health are also invoked, but corsets and the over-use of slimming products (and diets) are in fact injurious to health. They are certainly injurious to clear thinking about one's identity as a woman. The quality of the person has nothing to do with a wasp waist, body weight or body shape. We only think it does. And because the consumer thinks it does, so the conditions for persuasion by the advert have already been set up. Adverts are persuasive because they are based in premises which we are disinclined to question.

Devices of persuasion always have beliefs and values at their heart. Classically, ads are about rewards or punishments – it is good to purchase; it is bad not to purchase – based on core values about love of family, the importance of self-image, and so on. It is common to see adverts invoking needs or anxieties which can only be assuaged by purchase. Reading the advert creates an internal dissonance between what one believes and what one is not doing (consuming). So the anxiety or **cognitive dissonance** is relieved by purchase of, say, the baby goods or the medicine, which makes one a good mother or a caring wife.

Jamieson and Campbell (2001) suggest that most adverts are based on principles of identification, differentiation and association. That is, what person or lifestyle do we identify with? What makes us feel different from others? What do we associate favourably with the world of the advert? Jamieson and Campbell (2001) point out that salient life experiences such as birth, marriage and death are often invoked. They too comment on how adverts trade on values, and they refer to environmentalism, status, nationalism and love as examples. They also recognize the punishment model, and discuss adverts which invoke guilt. They identify the device of participation in which the consumer is made a kind of accomplice within the world of the advert, through **mode of address**. They talk about how admired models and even mythic characters are used. In the case of the former, the use of endorsement by sports stars is a common example. They refer to ways in which 'good names' are exploited – President Abraham Lincoln would be a classic example, not least in the case of the Lincoln car.

There are common devices of cause and effect, where the consumer has, for instance, the pseudo-medical causes of pain explained graphically, and is then promised the effect of pain relief after using the medication in question. There is the common device of juxtaposition, often practised graphically: placing a 4×4 vehicle in some beautiful country background juxtaposes two visual elements, but more importantly juxtaposes ideas about leisure and the splendour of nature with possession of the vehicle. They refer to the device of the 'unspecified other'. In this case, one needs to think of adverts which use the comparative argument – that the product or service is 'better than' that of someone else – but that 'someone' is not specified (unless one is thinking of particular and unusual examples of 'knocking copy', where the competitor is actually named in some price comparison).

One thing Jamieson and Campbell (2001) do refer to is the use of children in adverts in some persuasive capacity. Of course, children are the specified audience of a certain range of adverts – toys and snack foods, for example. But they point out that children are also targeted in respect of goods for apparently adult consumers because it has been recognized since the late 1980s that children have become increasingly important in influencing adult decisions about certain kinds of sales – most obviously domestic goods bought in the supermarket run.

Tellis (2004) makes an exhaustive analysis of research when evaluating how effective advertising may be. He suggests that the 'various appeals [of advertising] can be classified under four heads: argument, endorsement, emotions, passive processing' (Tellis 2004: 131). But when it comes to demonstrating that these appeals work (or how they may work) then his evidence is inconsistent. For example, at one point (p. 14) he argues that humour can trivialize an advert, and that it is a myth that it works. Yet at another point (p. 24) he is arguing that it does work because it attracts attention, relaxes the consumer, and so on. Similarly, the device of repetition shows up inconclusively through various studies. Some show that it works after a period of time, some that it does not work because it is irritating, and some that it does work because ads can acquire an iconic familiarity. As he says himself: 'the effectiveness of repetition depends on many factors that change substantially from advertisement to advertisement' (Tellis 2004: 131). He also comments on a familiar problem with 'proving' media effects or influence – advertising is only one among many reasons why consumers may purchase. He also points to other problems with demonstrating the persuasive power of advertising:

- Different consumer segments may respond in different ways to an ad.
- Successive ads can have overlapping effects.
- Ads operate across different media with different characteristics.
- There may be other long-term and short-term effects.
- The effectiveness of ads may vary over the life of a campaign.

Schudson (1993) constructs an argument against the persuasive power of advertising: 'Advertising is propaganda and everyone knows it.' As part of arguing this case, he suggests that market domination by a few companies means that people are deprived of alternative sources of information about products, so it is not surprising that advertising appears to work. He argues that received beliefs about the extent of the power of advertising are not borne out by the facts. He suggests that there are few instances where one may identify advertising as the dominant factor in decisions made about purchases. He addresses a range of conditioning factors. So, there is clear evidence that factors such as distribution and packaging are as important as advertising to sales. He points out that retailers prefer to stock well-advertised goods, so it is no surprise that those goods sell well. He refers to the effect of big marketing budgets on the morale of sales staff, suggesting that it is they who actually make the sales happen. Big public advertising campaigns create a high profile for any company, as well as for their goods. So that company sees itself and is seen as a success. He points to the illogicality of setting next year's advertising budget as a percentage of last year's sales – a fairly common practice. He cites an example of a period in the 1980s when coffee consumption fell at the same time as expenditure on advertising coffee was going up. It seems that people had decided that they just did not want to drink as much coffee as before. He draws attention to the fact that advertising is often a defensive strategy in the marketplace, trying to hold on to the market share rather than actually to boost sales. The

Hershey company in the USA used no media advertising until 1970, when it finally decided it had to use ads to fight off rivals such as Mars. Concerning the limitations of advertising and misplaced claims for its persuasive effects, as he sees them, Schudson (1993) states that 'the capacity of advertising to persuade is contingent on the social and informational location of the consumer'.

John Philip Jones (2004) also takes a sceptical view of so-called 'truths' about advertising and its effectiveness. For example he says that it is demonstrated that in a given year less than 28 per cent of brands increase their sales significantly. His view is that 'most people are habitual users of brands and one of the main functions of ads is to persuade them to maintain the habit' (Jones 2004: 16). As with other critics of the claims made for advertising, he says that there are too many variables for one to be sure that an increase in sales really is the result of a campaign. He points out that one group of professionals in the business once counted 36 different stimuli that could affect sales. Jones (2004: 95) refers to fieldwork carried out in 1991–92 by the Nielsen company which showed that:

- Television advertising produced a sales 'jolt' in only 30 per cent of cases; in 10 per cent of cases it appeared to maintain large brand sales; but in 60 per cent of cases it had only a weak or negative effect.

- Only a single exposure to advertising produced nearly all the effects measured (this of course would be an argument against the use of repetition and frequency in campaigns).

Jones does argue that if anything, differentiation (between products) is what helps sales. But again he argues that advertisers are not necessarily mainly concerned with consumers and sales: 'marketing companies are more concerned with their competitors than they are with the people who actually buy their brands' (Jones 2004: 6).

One should, however, be cautious about completely buying into arguments leading to a view that advertising has no effect on any person at any time. For example, Jones (2004) repeats the well-demonstrated fact that the public has a poor recollection of advertisements. However, an inability to identify or describe an ad does not prove that meanings have not been generated by the consumer, and that the idea of effects can be simply dismissed.

Leiss et al. (2005: 506) take a more nuanced view of reasons why ads may not work, especially with specific social groups. They refer to contemporary adults – the so-called Generation X which has come of age – and identify three factors (kinds of resistance) which explain why this 'media-savvy' group is hard to sell to.

- *Ideological resistance:* e.g. they have grown up with feminism and all that signifies for how gender may be viewed in its representation within ads.

- *Resistance to modes of address:* e.g. they may have affective and aesthetic objections to the way they are being 'talked at' through ads. So, for instance, ads which try too hard to be 'cool' will feel just condescending; or ads which employ some voice of authority will be felt to be impertinently parental to a generation which is not as deferential to authority as its parents were.

- *Lifestyle resistance:* e.g. the message and content of the ad is simply out of touch with what the audience is really doing and really values.

Clearly there are many reasons and strong arguments as to why advertising may not be able to persuade consumers to change their attitudes or behaviours. It is also in the interests of the marketers to argue that the billions of dollars spent each year on their activities are indeed justified. I would suggest that the old saw about some of advertising having an effect but no one knows exactly what part, is nearer the truth. I would also argue that we should be less concerned about the identifiable persuasive objectives of advertising, than we should be worried about the subversive and unintentional effects. In one case it may be pretty clear that we are being persuaded to take out some form of insurance. What is much less obvious is that as a culture our views and understanding of the concept of 'risk' are also being shaped by the accumulation of insurance marketing.

8 Commodification

I do not want to rehearse previous explanations of the essential ideas behind commodification and the fetishization of goods, but it is worth underlining various points, such as the fact that advertising refers to cultural as well as material commodities. It refers to the turning of material goods into cultural commodities. As Kenway and Bullen (2001) put it, advertisements 're-make the meaning of goods in order to sell them'.

There is indeed a wonderful contradiction behind commodification and the capitalist enterprise of marketing. That is, implicitly commodification needs leisure time in which goods can be consumed, but it also needs work time to produce the cash to pay for the goods (as well as to produce the goods themselves). The use of technology and the exploitation of cheap labour from the developing world makes perfect sense if it minimizes earning time and maximizes consumption or purchase time in the West. But where this leaves that labourer is another matter.

Jhally (1990) talks of different kinds of value generated through advertising. In Marxist terms he is talking about the transformation of the practical, material value of goods into something else: 'In market societies, the exchange-value of commodities dominates their use-value.' But he also points out that the notion of objects having a symbolic value beyond their usefulness has been around in societies for a very long time – certainly before advertising was developed. Societies which are not obviously materialistic nevertheless have fetish objects that are valued in terms beyond what they are made of, or what one can do with them. In our market societies it is advertising which has given such a range of goods their symbolic dimensions. Leiss et al. (2005: 258) would say that 'a market society is a masked ball' in which the real nature and value of goods is concealed.

Jhally (1990) sees advertising as having a social role. He argues that it creates connections between person and object; use and symbol; symbolism and power; communication and satisfaction. 'Through advertising, goods are knitted into the fabric of social life and cultural significance.'

Similarly, Kline (1993) suggests that: 'goods also locate daily acts of consumption within the continuities of personal and family history, group and national styles, the cross-cutting tensions of work and leisure.' Goods are 'social symbols that can articulate social aspirations'. I would say that it is advertising which encourages that 'location', which generates the symbolism.

Of course, advertising does not just promote material goods. It is about services, corporate images and many more subjects. Nor are 'commodities' just about objects. Lee (1993), for example, identifies 'experiential commodities' which are exemplified by sport as a spectacle, or by theme parks. These are, of course, promoted through advertising. They are also very much part of lived-in experience.

Commodification becomes as one with living. It is difficult to separate one part of experience from another. However, I would argue that not only can one spot the joins, but also one is entitled, for example, to criticize the commodification of sport without denying the pleasure of the experience.

Ewen (1977) is cutting in his contempt for what commodification has done in terms of misappropriating values and subverting ideals: 'The linking of the market-place to utopian ideals, to political and social freedom, to material well-being, and to the realization of fantasy, represents the spectacle of liberation emerging from the bowels of domination and denial.'

9 Discourse, ideology, myths and representations

It is a truism to say that adverts are about discourses. As vehicles for ideologies, they must be. They often invoke dominant discourses of gender and age. Their representations are constructed through the language of these discourses. Car adverts talk through discourses of technology, sexuality, fashion, urban and rural environments and individualism, among many others. The language of advertising depends on the language of discourses because it depends on invocation of and identification with the value meanings generated through the discourses.

And just as there is an interrelationship between discourse, ideology and representation, so also one must place mythologies within this model. One may see myths as false ideas of the false consciousness of ideology. One may see them as the meanings generated by the language of any discourse. One may see them as embodied by the representations which also depend on discourses. The myth of everlasting youth is embodied within visual representations of 'active' and 'beautiful' young men and women – especially in those ads for age-defying beauty products. The language of such ads actually talks out of its discourses about youthfulness and 'not age' when it uses words like 'rejuvenating'. The myth becomes ideological when it intimates that the young are empowered, socially and culturally, and by implication the old are disempowered. The release of the movie *Terminator 3* (2003), starring the now ageing Arnold Schwarzenegger, condemned to be ever superman, young and fit (with the help of technology), encapsulates such myth-making. Leiss et al. (2005: 368) refer to an obsession with a constructed idea of youth when they say that youth is more than an age category, it has become 'a fetish signifying all that is creative, fun, innovative, and exciting'.

What is not said in texts is as important as what is said. Fowles (1996) remarks of adverts that 'missing is most of human life work, duty, routines, small kindnesses as well as unpleasantness'. Reality is reconstructed. There is a disjunction between the world of adverts and the lives we live. The work of advertising is to conceal this difference, to construct representations which so permeate our consciousness that they affect our perception of what is really going on. Schudson (1993) refers to research that he carried out, looking into images of couples depicted within magazine ads. He identified a frequency of behaviour shown in which these couples were 'invariably attentive to each other'. As Schudson (1993) points out dryly, this level of attention and mutuality is simply not sustained by real-life couples.

Of course, many adverts do not pretend to be about life, to be real, to act as a social document. But what they all aspire to do is to get inside our heads, to frame our consciousness

ITV/Rex Features
Figure 7.3 Celebrities and Reality TV: *I'm a Celebrity ... Get Me Out of Here!*
The media inevitably transform the 'real' people who may become the subjects of their texts. They repackage the real person in order to sell them (the programme) to the audience. Celebrities have already been packaged and promoted before they appear in a TV programme – which continues that process. So celebrity reality programmes not only are part of marketing, but also raise questions about the nature of 'the real'.

- What is it that is being sold to us through such programmes?
- Why might we believe that we are seeing the real person behind the celebrity persona in such programmes?

in a way that is favourable to their clients. As Ewen (1977) says when surveying the development of advertising in the USA: 'In the broader context of a burgeoning commercial culture, the foremost political imperative was what to dream.' So, we are faced with a further argument – that advertising and the development of the market, with its representations and discourses, has also been a political and social project. The political vision is that what is good for the market is good for the people, and is good for a happy and stable society. The political problem is that this correlation manifestly does not hold good.

In terms of the reconstruction of social experience and the construction of representations, Kline (1993) draws attention to the way in which media, especially television, 'privilege fiction as a cultural form and the fantasy mode of consciousness and expression'. He is referring to texts for children in particular. But what he says could easily be applied to entertainment for older consumers. All modes of realism involve construction and representation. Fiction and fantasy have a particular licence. The success of the *Lord of the Rings*

(2001–03) trilogy in cinema, or the creation of docusoaps on television, both exemplify this inclination.

Fantasy may not be just about, say, cartoon forms, in advertising and other texts. It is also about idealization and myth-making. Cartoon promotions for a cereal (such as Rice Krispies), involving invented characters, are a kind of fantasy. But then so was the Gold Blend series of coffee adverts on TV, in the early 1990s – this was fantasy romance. Family life in the television programme *The Fresh Prince of Bel Air* is another kind of fantasy and myth-making. I am not saying that there is no difference between adverts and other kinds of texts. But I am trying to draw attention to their similarities, their connections, and to a critical line of continuity which links them.

One might ask if there is any real difference between the self-absorption of women in, say, the Gaultier perfume adverts of 2000 (witty as these are, showing, for example, the woman as goddess worshipped by young animal men), or the qualities and fantasies manifested in the character of *Ally McBeal* on TV (who experiences her dream moments played out as life).

Myth-making in contemporary media involves all sorts of cross-overs and fusions. The Armani underwear ad featuring David Beckham in 2008 treads a line between fashion photography and pornography. The footballer has joined a celebrity category which includes pop stars and TV stars. The image fuses the sport and the fashion industries. To this extent it also signifies how sport as an activity has become a cultural industry in its own right.

O'Barr (1994) examines the representation and discourse of race in US advertising, both through historical and contemporary examples. He examines how notions of tourism (as opposed to travel) emerged and were appropriated by advertising. He provides many examples of photographic colonialism and of the representation of racial groups not only as stereotypes, but also as 'others'. Such implicit oppositionality is common in discourses. O'Barr (1994) also notes, for example, that where non-Western groups are shown (in airline adverts for instance), there are subtle oppositions set up between a West which has a history and other cultures which have (only) traditions. The essential opposition is between power or lack of power, as he notes in an examination of adverts using African Americans: 'at the core of this discourse are lessons about dominance and hierarchy, subordination and inequality' (O'Barr 1994).

Goldman and Papson (1998) discuss examples of female representation in the context of Nike adverts. In general terms they argue that, while female representations (in sport in particular) may have largely got away from sexist bodies and the male gaze, still the ads invite self-absorption as much as self-celebration. Even when they cite Nike campaigns such as 'If You Let Me Play', as addressing gender discrimination in childhood with regard to sport, still they are uneasy about the corporate self-interest residing behind the series. There are interesting questions here about the validity of adverts that refer to the empowerment of women, while belonging to an industry which in many manifestations celebrates the disempowerment of women.

In any case, I would suggest that the objectifying and mythologizing of women in adverts has by no means been left behind in the twenty-first century. Substantial critiques offered by Williamson (1978) and Goldman (1992) still apply.

Mistry Reena (n.d.) discusses the 'use' of gender ambivalence in adverts on the basis that 'advertising has become a central socialising agent for cultural values connected with gender'. But she is clear that both images of 'new woman' and ambivalent representations are nothing but a front to confirm the validity of heterosexual differentiation. '"New" images of men and women merely update bi-polar definitions of gender.' Even where there are apparently transgressive images used in chic advertising, we are not, Mistry argues, looking at a genuinely political challenge. We are actually meant to experience heterosexual transgressive pleasures which, apart from the frisson, merely confirm the heterosexual position from which the gaze is meant to come (www.theory.org.uk/mistry).

'Research into the portrayal and use of the sexes in advertising has revealed widespread stereotyping in terms of gender roles and gender traits', asserts Gunter (1995b). 'Stereotyping in television advertising is typified by the way the sexes appear to be allocated disproportionately to different types of product and in the degree of authority attached to each sex in commercials.' From the late 1980s onwards,

> more advertising emerged featuring women in central, independent roles . . . As yet this new pattern in gender role portrayal has been visible in advertisements aimed at adults, while recent research has indicated that adverts aimed at children have remained as gender-stereotyped as ever.

However, Gunter (1995b) points out that there is no evidence of television's part in constructing children's attitudes towards gender roles. Indeed he says that one has to look at other and social sources of attitude formation.

Johnson and Young (2002) nevertheless argue that gendered representation in advertising is especially important when children are the target audience: 'One main type of image based influence targets gender identity, and uses it to link products to their consumers.' They argue that one can see gendered characters, gendered behaviours and gendered language used in commercials. Toy names may be used as examples: 'Big Time Action Hero' or 'California Roller Girl'. They refer to the gender of voiceovers, to the kinds of voice, to the choice of action verbs and to the invocation of discourses, not least that of power. They argue that gender differentiation enhances market targeting: 'From a marketing perspective, it is also more profitable for producers of children's toys to create separate toys for boys and girls as a way of placing more items in the market-place' (Johnson and Young 2002).

10 Discussion extract

> Brand advertising had succeeded (in the 1970s), more than any economic process or sociopolitical movement, in promoting and ensconcing a global community, albeit an imaginary one. By proposing marketplace solutions to virtually all social problems, branding has emerged as a form of persuasive ideology in itself. Perhaps, as some social activists warn, we do indeed live in a world conjured up by lifestyle ads and TV commercials. Yet it is far too easy to blame rampant consumerism for all our ills. We must not forget that human-made systems may, in the end, be reflexes of innate human tendencies. One of these is the so-called 'pleasure principle', as philosopher John Locke (1632–1704) called it – namely, instinctual drive to seek maximum pleasure or gratification and minimum pain. According to Freudian psychology, the principle originates in the libido and is the force that governs the id. Without necessarily embracing a Freudian perspective outright, there is little doubt that the pleasure principle is what probably directs a large percentage of human behavior and shapes human needs. It is, as

Stewart Ewen aptly puts it, a tendency 'that is closely interwoven with modern patterns of survival and desire' (1988: 20).

The images that suffuse life in the Global Village are, in actual fact, geared towards the achievement of pleasure through the acquisition of products. But therein lies the paradox of modern life – pleasures and desires can never be truly satisfied by means of consumption. The warnings come not only from religious communities, but also from the social scientific research domain, although the question remains: to what extent are such warnings objectively justifiable? Is advertising to blame for virtually everything that ails modern cultures, from a spiraling growth of obesity to street violence? Are media moguls the shapers of behavior that so many would claim they are today? Has advertising spawned the contemporary form of ennui? Are common folk today 'victims' of media messages, as Key (1989: 13) suggests, who 'scream and shout hysterically at rock concerts and later in life at religious revival meetings'? Media representations, like all kinds of representations, do indeed play a role in shaping behavior and groupthink. But, even though we might mindlessly absorb the messages promulgated constantly by the image-makers of the Global Village, and although these may have some subliminal effects on our behavior, we accept media images, by and large, only if they suit our already established preferences. As Freedman (2002) has recently argued, after assessing the relevant scientific literature on the effects of media on human behavior, we will never be able to say what these effects really are.

Danesi, M. (2006) *Brands*. Abingdon: Routledge.

1   What supports the writer's assertion that brand advertising has created an imaginary global community?

2   In what ways may ads appeal to our sense of pleasure?

3   What are the arguments which support the view that advertising has created a 'contemporary form of ennui'?

4   What do you think the writer means when he talks about us 'accepting' media images?

5   Give reasons for agreeing (or not) with the proposition that we can say nothing about the effects of advertising on human behaviour.

▌11 Further reading

Brierley, S. (2002) *The Advertising Handbook*, 2nd edn. London: Routledge.
Danesi, M. (2006) *Brands*. Abingdon: Routledge.
Goldman, R. (1992) *Reading Ads Socially*. London: Routledge.
Jamieson, K. and Campbell, K. (2001) *The Interplay of Influence: News, Advertising, Politics and the Mass Media*, 5th edn. Belmont, CA: Wadsworth/Thompson Learning.
Jones, J.P. (2004) *Fables, Fashions and Facts about Advertising*. London: Sage.
Leiss, W., Kline, S., Jhally, S. and Botteril, J. (2005) *Social Communication in Advertising*, 3rd edn. London: Routledge.

8

News
Different kinds of news: constructing the world

The news media of a particular society ... tend to construct accounts of events which are structured and framed by the dominant values and interests of that society, and to marginalise (if not necessarily exclude) alternative accounts.

McNair, B. (2003) *News and Journalism in the UK*, 4th edn. London: Routledge.

1 Introduction

In this chapter I want to attend to the unusual position which news has achieved within media output. This will involve revisiting key concepts and laying out critical positions on news, not least as it is meant to represent an interface between the public and ideas about 'the truth out there'. News has its own versions of what 'information' and 'truth' mean. 'News is characteristically about events rather than processes, and effects rather than causes' (McNair 2003: 64). In this sense news is much less complete than it purports to be, as a 'snapshot' of the world, day by day. The unusual position of news rests on its mass of contradictions and its special place in social and political consciousness. There are contradictions between the following:

- News as it appears to be an open conduit to a world of events, and news as it actually is – controlled and constructed through a 'closed' factory system of production.

- News as an apparently agreed general truth about what matters and what must be told, and the fact that across a range of newspapers and channels, across nations, there is actually no agreement about what is important out there in the world. There is certainly no agreement about how events are to be interpreted.

- News as it is at least loosely understood to be about important matters of the day and important people, and news as it actually is – about providing entertainment, about providing gossip, as much as politics.

- News as an apparently objectified account of source events, and news as it in fact is – an ideologically inflected selection and account of such events.

- News as an apparently neutral and expert report, and yet also being a global business enterprise – with all the partiality that must follow from that.

So what follows is something of a critique of the pretence of news. We should not be surprised that news is like it is, given the circumstances of its production. It is not surprising that in various ways it reflects the interests of commercial cultures, of the market, of national preferences, of cultural values. One might suggest that audiences collude in news being like it is, as much as news operations making it like it is. There is an extent to which people hear what they want to hear, and get the news operations that they deserve. One could say that news matters because we *believe* it matters: that we should not be so naïve as to respect it. Yet, given the unique position of news media in providing us with information about all aspects of our lives, and about a world that we do not experience directly – and in shaping that information – it is not enough to give a critical shrug of resignation. That would be to collude in an imperfect process. In many ways news is at the political cutting edge of the making and maintenance of societies. So news-making should be understood, deconstructed and at least implicitly be offered an agenda for reform.

One also needs to consider the position of news media in the context of the fact that broadcast audiences are fragmenting as channels multiply, and that newspaper circulation in general is declining. British national daily newspaper circulation is down 25 per cent from what it was in the 1960s. In 2007 BARB reported a fall in yearly total news viewing per individual from 108.5 hours in 1994 to 90.8 hours in 2006 – about 10 per cent drop. Meanwhile, there is an increase in the accessing of Net sources for news among young males from socio-economic groups A to C.

Harrison (2006: 83) refers to a US study, *The State of News Media 2004*, which identifies the following trends:

- Shrinking audiences – bringing problems with falling profits and with raising resources.

- The gathering of news via wire services, rather than putting staff in the field.

- An expansion of 24-hour news, which creates pressures on the pace of production, and the use of some inadequately considered footage.

- The same news organizations packaging material for different audiences through different platforms, which leads to varying standards.

- Those news organizations that are losing audiences (and not diversifying) are cutting costs and dividends, with consequences for quality.

- Digital convergence is helpful to news provision in that it offers audience choice and take-up of new media.

- This produces a counter-problem in that Internet platforms may not produce much profit.

- Increasing costs for news providers when competing for stories from high-profile sources – i.e. the dangers of rising costs in a free market.

Fragmentation of audience share on UK television is illustrated through a BARB/TNS survey in October 2006, which puts the BBC1 share of the news viewing audience at 50.6 per cent and the ITV1 share at 26.8 per cent. Among the rest it is interesting to see that the shares for BBC2, Channel 4 and Sky are all roughly the same – 4.6 per cent, 4.5 per cent and 4.9 per cent respectively.

2 Major questions

1   What may one understand about the constructed nature of news and about the consequences of this?

2   How does news represent the world?

3   What values and practices inform news-work, and with what effects?

4   What is the significance of the fact that one may critique news as entertainment, as genre, and as being defined and manufactured in different ways for different audiences?

5   How meaningful are the concepts of objectivity and impartiality when one looks at how news is made?

6   How do concepts such as discourse, representation and ideology help one understand news institutions, news texts and news audiences?

7   What is the nature of global news?

8   In what ways do commercial practices and technologies affect the nature of news?

9   Does news material and news presentation contribute to a viable and active public sphere?

▌3 Defining news

There may be an assumption that the term 'news', as it refers to certain media material, is generally understood and agreed. If something is 'in the news', it is assumed to be the subject matter of main daily papers and broadcast news programmes. But in spite of the dominance of TV news as a source of 'news', there is no universal pattern of news material or of news consumption by audiences. If 1 million people read the *Daily Mail* every day, that leaves a lot who do not. Even if 7 million on average watch the *BBC News at Ten*, still there are millions of others who do not; and not all of these people are consistent readers and watchers. So even though I will argue that there is a dominant news agenda of news, still this does not mean that all people have the same news experience. It is not hard to demonstrate that across the eight leading daily newspapers in the UK there is variation in definitions of what news is, especially if one looks beyond the lead articles and the first few pages. Even lead stories will vary, depending on what big events are or are not out there. Common news values may predominate, but there is still, for example, a hard news and soft news divide. Television (and radio) is not allowed to editorialize in the partial way that newspapers may. Yet even here there are variations in what is shown and heard. Radio 1 news bulletins are headlining, populist and tabloid, where Radio 4 and the *Today* programme in particular are much more mainstream hard news – political events and social issues. Channel 5 TV news is populist in its selection of news items, and relaxed in its presentation and linguistic style, where Channel 4 is much more formal and indeed investigative. Both channels are commercial ones. One can – and this chapter will – identify common news practices and common ideological positions behind these. Yet there are also variations in news content and treatment which are just as interesting in what they tell us about marketized news, about audiences, and about the mythologies surrounding a news view of the world.

Deregulation of broadcasting has brought in a multiplicity of channels, brought to life a variety of audiences and so manufactured a variety of 'news'. 'The news' is not a coherent object of attention. Neither is it as varied as it could (and perhaps should) be. If we believe that we do have an understanding of a coherent thing called news, then that is a false notion. On the one hand, people may well assume that what they read and view and understand as individuals is 'the news'. But that cannot be so because there is this variation: there is more than one 'news', in terms of both content and treatment. Our understanding of what news is, what it should be and how it should be presented, assumes a view of politics, an ideological inflection. On the other hand, just because there is a variety of news content and news styles, this does not mean that news is truly plural. Versions of news can be different and yet at the same time similar in some respects. There are consistent discourses and ideological threads that run through different versions of news. For instance, deaths as a consequence of acts of terrorism are usually magnified in news reports – certainly by comparison with the greater number of people who are killed on the roads every year. Terrorism, which threatens the state, is higher up the ideological agenda.

Deregulation has also brought a kind of contradiction in broadcasting policies, given that it is a process designed to liberate the commercial instincts of media providers, as well as to encourage what may be described as 'healthy' competition. Harrison (2006: 126) refers to current European policy on audiovisual media, which 'seeks to promote both the social value of the media and the virtues of a de-regulated media environment'. As far as news is concerned, the social value of news must attach itself to social benefits, to public broadcasting, to ideals of representing the world to the citizen as truthfully as possible. But a deregulated commercial environment shows no evidence of aspiring to such ideals. Competition comes to be about the commercial value of news and news audiences. It seeks to reduce costs. The consequences of this are described below, in section 5 in particular.

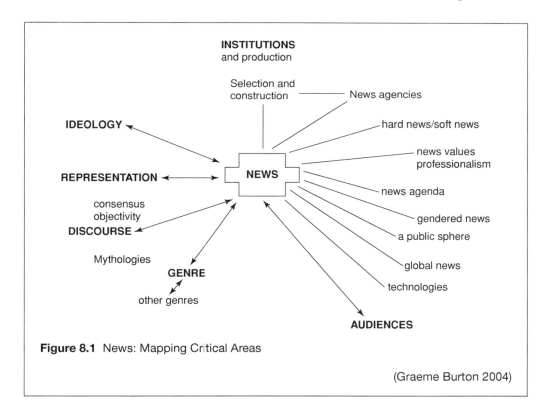

Figure 8.1 News: Mapping Critical Areas

(Graeme Burton 2004)

The substance of news has been characterized in various ways by commentators. One example is that which describes news values – the well-known catalogue that is offered by

Galtung and Ruge (1970), for example. In this case it would be said that news is defined as being about events and people, characterized by factors such as the following:

- consonance with audience beliefs
- continuity with what is already in the news
- cultural proximity
- elites

- negativity
- personification of what has happened
- size of the event
- unexpectedness

Or there is the work of Herbert Gans (1980), in which he identifies news as being defined in its composition by

- 'actors' who are likely to be known already
- predictable 'activities' such as crime, protests and government decisions
- either divisions or examples of unity in the nation and society
- domestic themes which relate to foreign news (the relationship between the USA and Israel would be relevant here).

News is a constructed version of its source material. It is a kind of narrative. It is a media representation. It is a selective version of original events, utterances and behaviours. 'News, like all public documents, is a constructed reality possessing it own internal validity' (Tuchman 1976). It constructs a world in which the militant is pitted against the moderate, the normal against the deviant, and in which problems are defined for us.

If news is a 'constructed reality', it may be argued that it is also bound up with that slippery notion of 'social reality' – that which seems real and true for a society which itself shares a certain set of views. Stuart Allan (1997) says that 'news is a form of social knowledge'. One might say that it is shared information and shared understandings about how the world is. But again, one problem is that knowledge which is shared and so included, must presume information which is excluded – other knowledge. And knowledge is not a matter of fact or even of truth, so much as a matter of 'understandings', which comprise ways in which that knowledge is valued and used within social practices. News about football presumes understanding of the place of football within our society. But knowledge of football, or understanding of that place, may not be shared by other societies. The very notion of 'football' may be different for different societies, as in, say, England, Brazil or the USA.

We also need to understand that 'news' is something which we gather from a range of sources, not least within the media. Any given newspaper includes elements such as reports, features, interviews and editorials. Any given news topic within any newspaper is likely to be supported (in the mind of the reader) by material on the same topic acquired from other sources. Documentary programmes such as *Horizon* on BBC1 expand on news topics and debates. There are kinds of spin-off programmes and reality shows – e.g. *Crimestoppers* on ITV – which cause the news genre to bleed into other programming. But then a street conversation may also contribute to that same topic. Commonplace phrases such as 'on/in the news' promote illusions not only about the coherence of some notion of 'core news', but also about the dominance of the national press or of 'flagship' broadcast news programmes.

Such dominance of certain news providers in the public consciousness, combined with the undoubted control exerted by specific news (and media) producers, conspires to deny a substantial place for 'other kinds of news'. Yet these exist. There are local and regional newspapers. Globally, there are regional news agencies. There are various alternative news providers, from the British Undercurrents organization, putting out news videos with ideologically challenging items, to a variety of Web-based providers, including bloggers. Manning (2001) is critical of the lack of profile of and lack of access to such sources: 'The obstacles faced by subordinate news sources in the struggle to supply a wider range of sharper (critical) tools are rather more perplexing than is good for the health of democracy.' He also points out that the circulation of news, indeed the nature of news, is affected by the reliance of news sources on advertising revenue. It advantages 'certain kinds of newspaper and particular broadcasting formats to the disadvantage of others'.

It may be argued that the nature of news makes it inherently ideological. McNair (1998) asserts this both on the larger principle that it is a work of human agency and that, 'as an authored narrative, [it] is at the same time an ideological force, communicating not just "the facts" but also a way of understanding and making sense of the facts'.

McNair (1998) goes on to invoke notions of hegemony and the public sphere when he says, 'journalism is thus an arena between competing ways of sense-making'. It is difficult to argue that news may be defined as anything other than ideological work. It patently brings us version(s) of the world; it brings certain kinds of understanding of the world, and indeed of what we refer to as the truth and as reality. Its material is in part explicitly about politics and the state, and in part implicitly about social politics, about power relations between social groups.

In the same vein, the Goldsmiths Media Group (1999), taking a political economy approach, argue that the news media, 'although a site of social conflict, relays the "dominant ideas" of the ruling classes'. Their view is that economic concerns prevail, given that: news production is expensive, business is the main financier of news and news is a commodity.

Davies (2008) argues that cuts to news services and news staffing, especially in respect of news gathering, have followed from corporate ownership and commercial practices. He talks of

> the behaviour of the new corporate owners of the media, who have cut editorial staffing while increasing editorial output; slashed the old supply lines which used to feed raw information up from the ground; and, with the advent of news websites, added the new imperative of speed.
>
> (Davies 2008: 73)

4 Hard news, soft news: tabloidization and dumbing down

I have already referred to the fact that often 'proper' news is assumed to be about weighty political and social matters – hard news. It is also assumed that gossip, celebrity news, even the human interest angle on disasters, is just soft news. But from its broadsheet beginning in the seventeenth century, news has always covered this range – from the times of tides to accounts of murder. Soft news sells – as popular newspapers like *The National Enquirer* have found out – even if it includes a degree of dramatic licence, or downright invention. As broadcasting proliferates channels, so news for niche markets appears. This is often soft news, concerned with domestic events, with celebrity-dom, with tales of the unexpected. It gets ratings. Even the mainstream providers of evening hard-news programmes soften the news for breakfast and lunchtime viewers. One might say that in these respects news is simply going further down the road of entertainment. It has always sought to amuse its audience, notwithstanding perceptions of hard news as defining the genre. Victorian newspapers, like those of today, were full of crime stories and lurid engravings. Stories about pop stars, dramatic news footage, celebrity newscasters – these are all about an ongoing tendency in news to want to entertain, to dramatize, to attract readers and audiences.

This is what Ross and Nightingale (2003: 97) mean when they talk about 'the news industry, where stories of (apparent) interest *to* the public have largely replaced stories which are *in* the public interest'.

The supposed shift towards an emphasis on entertainment values (tabloidization) has indeed been deplored, even by newsmakers. The *British Journalism Review* (1989) talks of a downward spiral in standards of journalism: 'the trivialisation of material, vulgarisation, invasion of privacy, squalid behaviour by certain groups of publishers and journalists' (quoted in Bromley and O'Malley 1997).

But news may also be accused of being 'dumbed down' because of its presentation, as much as because of the items selected. The short-lived *Live TV* of the late 1990s was notorious for having a miming 'news bunny' behind the newsreader. The former *Big Breakfast Show* on Channel 4 treated news in a chat show format. It was actually quite a good way of introducing news topics and issues to a younger audience, who generally do not watch news programmes. An Ofcom report of 2007 says that 16 to 24 year olds watch an average of 40 hours of TV news in a year, half that of the general population. Two-thirds of this younger age group say that they find most news irrelevant to them. Of course all this raises questions about what news should be. Some might say that selecting items simply to fit the audience's sphere of experience, or presenting them in some colloquial, simplified manner, is demeaning to the audience and untruthful to offering a complete picture of the world out there. Others might argue that selection and presentation are a fact of news life, and that there is no one true picture of the world.

But one should also acknowledge that any debate about the 'dumbing down' of journalism should not be confused with a discussion of the nature and 'validity' of soft news. Human interest stories do not have to be expressed in simplistic terms, nor are they unworthy in themselves.

It is true that the debate about a coarsening of press journalistic standards in particular, and what is assumed to be a deplorable softening of news in general, does go on. In terms of standards, there are in Britain periodic calls for legal regulation of the press with respect to invasion of privacy. Doorstepping of victims of tragedy, chequebook journalism to induce sources to talk about intimate details of the lives of the famous – both are pretty difficult to defend. But again, here the danger is that criticism confuses arguments about the morality of the way that news is gathered with those about the worth of the subject of news.

Critics such as Langer (1998) are robust in defending the validity of soft news. He points out that 'populist, emotional journalism is well established'. He argues that so-called trivial news may in fact be very political. One might argue that paparazzi journalism is a kind of challenge to the false status and privileges of celebrity, a questioning of the nature of celebrity. The problem here is that the very inclusion of any person – but especially established public figures – in the news, serves to confirm the idea that they are newsworthy

Figure 8.2 Soft News Headlines
Soft news stories also fit news values. They represent a social world, and the wider media world inhabited by celebrities.

- Does this make such stories less valid than those which are about national and international events and politics?
- Is the disparaging of news which emphasizes social and emotional experience another expression of gender politics?

(Graeme Burton 2009)

and therefore do have a kind of status. This is how news values are confirmed in the ideological consciousness of the audience.

With broadcasting especially, it may be the newscasters and reporters who themselves become celebrities. The BBC's Rageh Omaar opted to go freelance in 2003 after himself becoming the object of media (and female audience) attention while reporting news from Iraq. He was cashing in on his celebrity status. Macdonald (2003) points out that there has been a shift in news reporting. This shift is about the reporter emphasizing his or her experience of an event and a location, perhaps on an emotional level, to make the piece feel more immediate for the audience. But this then draws attention to the reporter. It creates the danger that the reporter becomes the news rather than what they are reporting on.

Even broadcast news is expanding the soft end of its spectrum – and not only populist channels such as Channel 5 (which changed its news provider from ITV News to Sky News in 2004). In 2001 ITV1 made a conscious decision to run with more human interest and sports stories, losing its traditional reference to ITN and then rebadging as ITV News. Langer (1998) points out that our notion of 'news' is itself an ideological construct. He says that most critiques of news assume a liberal democratic approach in which 'proper news' provides a reliable source of information for the good citizen. Populist TV news is commonly damned for being a commodity enterprise, for becoming mere entertainment, for providing gratuitous spectacle, for offering too much image and too little information, for indulging triviality and emotionalism, for descending into exploitation of its subjects. But, Langer (1998) would argue, soft news secures hegemonic consent as much as does hard news. Disaster stories are designed to restore faith in the idea of a harmonious world, with emphasis on reassertion of control, on rescue, on coming to terms with disaster. He argues that the 'other news' on television is about five main story types:

- the especially remarkable
- victims
- communities at risk
- ritual
- tradition and the past.

Contradictions are played out, for example between a world in which the state is supposed to be in control of crime, and yet assaults do take place. We 'learn' to react resignedly to events 'beyond our control'. Soft news endorses the idea of elites. So, one may argue that soft news is no more or less valid as news than is hard news. It performs kinds of social and mythic functions in providing topics of social exchange. It does the same ideological work as hard news. It may be said that the reporting of domestic and private matters concerning the prime minister or a star footballer, is equally about celebrity-dom and an endorsement of masculine power.

It is indeed a problem to know where one draws the line between hard news and soft news (if indeed this matters); where one draws the line between prurient poking around in people's lives and genuine investigative journalism. It has been commonplace to talk about the *tabloidization* of news. Mainstream broadcast news will carry items about ephemera involving pop stars or the world of fashion. Current affairs programmes will also report on celebrity subjects such as the 'racial slur' row involving the late Jade Goody and Shilpa Shetty on Channel 4's *Celebrity Big Brother* in 2007 and – it is asserted – spend less time on investigative reporting. The media will carry any number of articles about the private lives of the royal family – a journalistic soap opera of celebrity-dom. And yet it could also be argued that this news-work has in fact exposed, to the benefit of society, the various failings of people who hold a unique position of cultural status and privilege. Similarly, although other investigations have involved human interest stories which looked at details of private life – MPs' expenses, their spouses' expenditure, and their employment of family members (2007–09) – it may fairly be said that these were to the public benefit. This kind of news can be about both hard politics and soft gossip stories. This kind of news fits the argument that feminization (or tabloidization?) has blurred the boundaries between public and private domains. Politicians no longer fit in the frame of hard news, of stories about the exercise (male) political power. David Cameron as leader of the conservative party may be seen on a webcam in his kitchen at home making breakfast for the kids. The public figure is located in a private domain. There is a collapse (postmodernity?) of traditional distinctions between categories of news.

If news has been reframed, not least in its presentation, to make it more accessible to a female audience, then this raises an interesting debate about motives and effects. Is the motive behind 'softened' news a selfish economic one, driven by market interests – soft news sells. Or is it driven by a genuine urge to democratize news reporting? One might say, to take it outside a masculinized, politicized ghetto? And if it achieves that end of greater accessibility, then do the motives matter?

It is argued that soft news is gendered news: human interest stories appeal to a female audience. It is also said that such news is gendered in production because its stories – about celebrities, motherhood, caring – are assigned to female journalists. This is less true than it was in the 1950s. But again, successful war reporters such as Kate Adie have given accounts of having problems in being taken seriously, not least by male colleagues. She has commented on her success being put down by others to use of her sexuality (Skidmore 1998).

However, if there is an increase in soft news, a softening of hard news – a change in news which feminizes it, in terms of reporters, reporting, presentation, audiences – then this will work to the benefit of women working within news. Van Zoonen (1998) asserts that '"human interest" has become an integral part of the news'. She argues that a shift towards soft news is market driven. This kind of journalism is, she says, dominated by audience needs, emotional investment and sensationalism, as well as by human interest. And it is this kind of journalism which, it appears to be assumed by journalists, women are especially good at producing. Economic arguments support the expansion of soft news and the validation of female news-workers.

5 News traduced

I have just argued that if there has been a change since the 1980s in the nature of news, this is not necessarily a bad thing. But some commentators are very pessimistic about the provision and quality of news:

> Entertainment has superseded the provision of information; human interest has supplanted the public interest; measured judgment has succumbed to sensationalism; the trivial has triumphed over the weighty; the intimate relationships of celebrities from soap operas, the world of sport or the royal family are judged more 'newsworthy' than the reporting of significant issues of international consequence.
>
> (Franklin 2008: 13)

Franklin (2008) accepts that in terms of news provision entertainment and the needs of a democracy have always rubbed up against one another. But he goes on to argue that

- The decline of genuinely informational serious news has become extreme.
- There is a decline in the provision of foreign and investigative news in particular.
- These changes are happening across all news media.

We have seen the convergence of newspapers in Britain since the late 1980s, in terms of presentation and content. That is to say, the differences between the broadsheets (largely no longer broadsheet) and the red tops have become much less obvious. The so-called quality press has acquired more photos, the banner headlines and puns of the popular papers, and has less raw text. With that there has been a rise in the use of columnists and opinion driven material; talk is cheap but journalistic research costs time and money. The quality press has acquired more tabloid type material: soft news, gossip items, celebrity news, 'you-wouldn't-believe-it' items, problem pages. Indeed some might argue that many newspapers are as much like magazines as they are papers defined by new and nationally or globally significant content. You could look at any newspaper and ask of many items, does it really matter which day of the week this article is printed?

The drive to reduce costs, to compete, to be profitable, is behind these changes. The blind imperatives of the market, and of the corporations which own the press (no longer just in the newspaper business) are behind this drive. The same problems afflict broadcasting. The competition for ratings, the 1980s managerialist revamp of the BBC, the effects of the Broadcasting Act 1990 forcing ITN to become 'profitable', are all behind these changes. Presenters have become celebrities. The availability of pictures determines more than ever the presence of items on screen. Franklin (2008: 20) refers to analysis which shows a doubling of show-business and entertainment type news on screen, between 1989 and 1995. In the same period there was a 65 per cent decline in the screening of international news. Local broadcasting is now largely run on shoestrings, with few staff, low budgets, soft news, largely syndicated sources, and a shaky representation of local identity. It may be noted that the same is true for the local press, largely owned by national and global corporations. It is rare to see any challenging of local political decisions or of the operation of local government. There is no money to do the kind of investigative reporting needed. Local news operations do not have a firm independent base. The public relations departments of local government and other institutions control the flow of news.

As an example of this, in the *Guardian* (12 May 2008) reporter Nigel Green asserts that the Northumbrian Police Force 'has repeatedly obstructed press enquiries about serious and violent crimes for "operational reasons"'. In the article he points out that the press office for that police force costs £700,000 a year, and that it promotes stories about how crime rates are falling. But he also compiled a list of 150 incidents over recent years (including stabbings and armed robberies) that were not released at all or were released very late by the police press office. On one weekend no crimes were put on the police press line, but Green later discovered that in fact there had been 5083 incidents, of which 45 were serious. As an example of institutional control of news flow, this speaks for itself.

If this seems to be a pessimistic and critical view of news provision in the UK, then the work of Davies (2008) provides an even bleaker picture. His central thesis, backed by research from Cardiff University, as well as his own years as a journalist, is that news as we knew it around 1980 has all but disappeared. He provides compelling evidence of a news world in which sources are not checked, pressures to meet deadlines have supplanted beliefs in accuracy and the truth, and news material is effectively dominated by that which is supplied through Reuters and Associated Press (AP). Reuters itself became Thompson Reuters in 2008, and as usual with such take-overs, job cuts were promised. This further supports Davies' (2008) analysis of what is happening. The number of reporters in the field has already been slashed. Davies (2008: 74) refers to the Cardiff researchers who found when examining the content of five leading UK newspapers that

- 30 per cent were a direct rewrite of Press Association material (or some from smaller agencies)
- 19 per cent were largely rewrites
- 21 per cent were partial rewrites.

As one journalist put it, they are told to 'take it off the wires and knock it into shape'.

This is not just another debate about the definitions and merits of soft news and hard news. It is an evidenced assertion that much of news of any kind is badly researched and carelessly presented. It is a picture of an industry which is out of control, and traduced by market forces. The consequences are that it is difficult to see how one can either believe much of what is presented, or at least to see it as anything like an accurate account of our world, whether that world is about politics or celebrities. Such observations are severe. But one cannot reject the substance of Davies' (2008) criticism unless one believes that much of his evidence and that of supposedly reputable researchers is an elaborate invention – which simply is not credible.

Part of his thesis is that the public relations business (marketing) has come to fill the gap in news material left by emasculated legitimate news services:

> What emerges from all this is a national news factory which is unable to fill its pages with its own high-quality product, because it lacks the staff and front-line workers on the ground, and which then relies on a wire agency which is itself severely limited. And yet the pressure to carry on producing more and more copy is relentless. Starved of time, desperate for material, a system which should be protecting itself with rigorous checks instead starts to suck in anything which looks like a story. This is where the PR industry comes in.
>
> (Davies 2008: 84)

It is a reflection of Habermas's concerns about the distorting influence of the public relations industry on the idea of a public sphere (see pp. 265–7) when Davies (2008: 204) comments on the effects of 'interference' by public relations firms: 'all kinds of public debates which should be being settled on the basis of evidence and logic are instead being settled by the power of competing agencies to push their line'.

An interview article with the former newscaster Anna Ford (*Guardian* 27 August 2007) confirms the above on a case study basis. She criticizes time pressures:

> people are now producing, for one news programme, three or four items, which means getting in at the crack of dawn, commissioning each item, ringing the interviewee, getting film crews round, writing the script and getting it on air. They are stressed beyond belief, and on very short-term contracts. They're afraid and they are bullied.

Ford reflects critically on her last job experience presenting the *BBC News at One* (until 2006):

> And so often the concentration was on a paedophile, a dead girl or two, some sort of traumatic, overdeveloped event about a child – whether it be a lost child or some sort of molestation – which is of course news, but I think we spent far too much time on these things. I think the crunch came when Bruce Forsyth's wife's dog was missing at a time when a lot of other things were going on.

▌6 News values

News material is selected from sources and constructed into a text. Sources are dominated by news agencies such as Reuters. Wealthy news operations carry their own teams of reporters and can dispatch these people to events if they do not already have a correspondent geographically near. But many news operations rely on agency sources. All news makers can use stringers, or local sources who are paid by the item. Press releases and news conferences are also a major source of information. But of course, as with agencies, the material has already been selected and processed. Institutions such as government departments or local councils, which have information that news makers want, do therefore exercise indirect control and power over the production of news.

But for all this variety of sources, news remains a made thing. So one may ask the questions:

- Why are certain events selected in and others left out?
- Why are news items treated in the ways that they are?
- Why is it that, within the qualification of remarks made above, news makers may select identical stories on a given day, and often treat the subject matter in a similar manner?

One concludes that certain values inform selection and construction. That which is valued is included. Certain ways of telling stories are valued. Such values may be peculiar to news operations, to the news discourse. They may also be part of more general social values and ideological positions that are shared by other institutions or indeed by society at large. This 'sharing' of values makes it difficult to determine where they are located, where the impetus for news practices really comes from. Because, generally speaking, the public shares a sense of news values with news producers. News agencies are producers as much as, say, CNN, and institutions (and their public relations departments) will also understand those values. News values would select in a story about a multiple pile-up on a motorway. But then is this an imposition on the audience? Do they get their sense of values from newspapers? Or should one argue that readers have an interest in such disasters anyway? Is it in a sense audience pressure which induces the papers to put the story in? And certainly the emergency services would expect to have to release information to the press because, sharing the same area of values, they would see this pile-up as an important event in their working lives, and something which needed to be told.

What one is saying is that news makers, like the media in general, are both of society and yet different in certain ways. One is renewing those earlier questions about the relationship between media and society, about how concepts such as hegemony may explain that relationship, about where power really lies, about how far our understanding of the world is a shared construction or an imposition. Certainly it is hard to think outside the ideological framework. But at least understanding what these values are, how they are expressed, where they may come from, enables one to see that there is a framework. Seeing the framework denaturalizes the apparent truths of news and exposes its constructedness.

News values are selective and cultural and ideological when they led to reporting of deaths in Iraq (in 2003) as

- the result of terrorist attacks, assuming that the word 'terrorist' accurately describes the motives and social location of those who are prepared to kill themselves in order to kill others

- resulting in the deaths of X numbers of American troops, or embassy staff, or UN officials, assuming that it is normal not to report the numbers of Iraqis killed (or indeed anything about them).

Allan (1999) argues that, while news values are not set in concrete, from time to time or from provider to provider, still they are significantly consistent.

> While news values are always changing over time and are inflected differently from one news organisation to the next, it is still possible to point to these and related news values as being relatively consistent criteria informing these assignments of significance.
>
> (Allan 1999)

Von Ginneken (1998) offers an interesting five-part categorization of core values in news which is not so much about types of story as thinking about the world within broad areas:

- *Economic:* free enterprise and the free market.
- *Social:* individualism and social mobility.
- *Political:* pragmatism and moderation.
- *Lifestyle:* materialism and autonomy.
- *Ideological:* we have no ideology.

In other words, events will be chosen that allow a story to be constructed around these sets of beliefs, the last of which links with the news myth of objectivity. The news story comes out of these beliefs and values, and feeds back into them, reinforcing their apparent validity.

6.1 Professionalism as a value

The illusion of being non-ideological is something which, like other journalistic values, is bound up with the production of news and with notions of professionalism. 'The journalist is a professional communicator whose work is structured and shaped by a variety of practices, conventions and ethical norms' (McNair 1998).

The invocation of the term 'professionalism' conjures up a discourse in which ideas about expertise, codified behaviour, status and reliability are also invoked. These are reasons why people like to call themselves professionals. News produced by 'professionals' is therefore truthful and reliable. Journalists share a culture in which they operate out of standard practices. 'A journalistic culture is produced by and produces a set of consistent formulas, practices, normative judgments and explicit values' (Harrison 2000).

Langer (1998) says something similar, but is more explicit about the ideological work of news:

> Through processes of selection, classification and repetition, the practices of journalism produced sense, meanings and interpretations of events which naturalised ways of looking at the world that were implicated in validating and reproducing the existing authoritative and distributive order.
>
> (Langer 1998)

Allan (1997) also refers to the development of journalistic practices and to a certain kind of journalistic language that came out of the beginnings of Associated Press in 1848. In this case, 'dry language' and 'routinised newswork practices' helped 'secure the codification of objectivity as a normative standard'. Soloski (1997) sees professionalism as an instrument of control used by those behind the journalists: 'Professionalism is an efficient and economical method by which news organisations control the behaviour of reporters and editors.' In effect it incorporates values and working practices which are in the interests of news owners and which are assimilated by news workers. This assimilation is itself helped by an industry-controlled training system and by the press card system, through which journalists ratify the right of others to practise journalism.

This is not to argue that any codified training or invocation of professional values is entirely suspect. But it does constitute a kind of regulation which leads to values and practices that are not easily challenged. Other factors in news work contribute to this. For example, the British Lobby system, by which the Whips of political parties accredit certain journalists, and give them (and not others) access to information, is clearly undesirable. It echoes the British class system in respect of turning selected political correspondents into a club. Its very informality as a social practice makes it difficult to challenge. Similarly, the habit of journalists of covering stories in groups and feeding off one another, is clearly not conducive to critical, independent journalism. But, given that news organizations encourage competition, then pack journalism becomes a way of keeping an eye on the competitor. It is also the case that other working conditions encourage this group behaviour and group-think. Journalists are in a group at press conferences and briefings. The military corral journalists into given locations when they are covering wars – and can keep 'undesirable' journalists out of the privileged pack if they wish.

Of course, one should not imagine that professionalism is uniform, or that formal and informal strategies for regulating news always work in the interests of the powerful. In 1999, the British government could not prevent the names of 117 MI6 agents being published on the Internet.

7 The news agenda

in general, news outlets of all kinds often tell the same stories, from the same perspectives, using much the same material.

(Ofcom 2008)

The idea of the news agenda is that news operations tend to consistently prioritize certain categories of news material. Here, there is natural progression from discussion of news values, since the construction of a certain kind of agenda itself implies a value system. It is a commonplace that news values and prioritizes stories that have pictures. The notion of categorization also links agendas to genres. It is difficult to separate matters of content and treatment, when talking about agenda setting. So it may be argued that stories about crime are consistently on the news agenda, especially negative ones. The public is induced to see the idea of crime and issues around crime (for example, the use of guns in crime) as being important. This might be contrasted for example with a lack of a firm place on the agenda for stories about social inclusion – that is positive news about ways in which social minorities (such as migrant workers) are brought into a more equal relationship with the mainstream of society. The presence or absence of such stories implies value-laden decisions. So does the positive or negative treatment of the subject. Indeed negativity as a news value (see Galtung and Ruge 1970) infuses the handling of the content of the news agenda, as much as the content of that agenda commonly includes stories about powerful politicians, for example. And in a sense politicians (and others) are defined as being powerful simply by being the stuff of news. The 'not powerful' are defined by their absence.

The negative agenda is ideological for the following reasons:

- It defines what is meant to be unacceptable behaviour.
- It defines which are to be seen as unacceptable (or deviant, unimportant and not valuable) social groups.
- It defines beliefs that are unacceptable to the dominant ideology.

Asylum seekers are described as being 'on the run' when they leave holding centres without permission: a phrase associated with criminal escapees. But these people are not known to have committed a crime.

In terms of categories of news, Hartley (1982) summarized the news agenda as being about politics, the economy, foreign affairs, domestic stories, one-off items and sport. This

Figure 8.3 Newspaper Front Pages
Different headlines on the same day remind us that there are different versions of what we call 'news'.

- Do these differences add up to enough for one to argue that we have a real pluralism of news texts, and therefore real diversity and choice?

is still a fair account, but the agenda also has particular features. For instance, one will get particular stories at particular times, or in particular eras. So, the reunification of East and West Germany (and related problems) often resurfaces on the news agenda in relation to stories about the German economy or about German politics. The Israeli–Palestinian conflict remains on the agenda at this point in history, not least because it continually generates newsworthy events involving global politics and loss of life.

The idea of the news agenda is important because it helps manifest a structure of thinking about the world. It suggests to news consumers ways in which the world should be understood. News values and the news agenda give form and direction to practices of news gathering and news making. In a sense they legitimize their illegitimate normative power. It feels acceptable to see certain kinds of story because that is what one expects to see. It denies alternative views, and in that sense denies real pluralism.

Chomsky (1989) argues that this agenda is dominated by the interests of the state. And one needs to remember that the state not only exerts degrees of regulatory power over news, but also is an essential source of news material. The debate over the relationship between news media and state (as between news media and advertisers) is one in which it is possible to argue in both directions, that one is the client of the other, that one is subordinate to the other. 'The mainstream media not only allow the mainstream agendas of news to be bent in accordance with state demands and criteria of utility, they also accept the presuppositions of the state without question' (Chomsky 1989).

In the setting of the agenda there is a co-relationship between news media and news agencies. The media set the agency agenda in the sense that items they ask for and then choose will tend to be ones that agencies prioritize. Equally the agencies set the media agenda through their choice of topics. Behind all this is the influence of technology – what it enables the news producers to obtain – how investment in it puts pressure on news makers to justify such costs by using the technology.

8 News as genre

News is the most well-established and recognizable factual genre.

(Hill 2007: 4)

News clearly has repetitive elements of content and treatment which the producers may trade on and the audience may expect. What is in the news in any given week is therefore to an extent predictable – contradicting the idea of news as new. Repetitions range from the 'stand up to camera reporter piece' to the editorial or opinion section of any newspaper. As with other genres, production routines can operate, predicated on these expectations. Sources are regularly trawled. TV news has a daily schedule of meetings and news exchanges with other providers around the world. News conferences and story exchanges involving Eurovision and Asiavision happen six times a day, as the broadcast news organizations buy from and sell to one another. Indeed, significant analogies may be drawn with fiction genres. The production base for TV news is little different in principle from that of a soap opera, with a continuous production of familiar storylines to satisfy the anticipation of an established audience. News broadcasts have their long-running mythologized heroes and villains (David Beckham or Osama bin Laden) like any fiction genre. They have stock characters like the 'expert' or the dedicated correspondent. They have repetitive storylines:

'police have recovered drugs worth X on the street', 'plucky mother of four averts disaster when she raises the alarm'. The fact that a news article may be referred to as a news *story* alludes to the blurring of lines between fact and fiction. Although, in terms of trying to preserve the integrity and distinctiveness of the news genre, we should recognize that reputable journalists do base their stories on verifiable facts.

One example of news operations working to routines – the repetitive character of genres – is given by Tuchman (1995). In this case, she is talking about a 'news net' and assumptions made about the interests of the audience. This net works through notions of geography, organization and topic, and is about the rationale behind the assigning of reporters. Geographically, the world is divided into areas that may be systematically trawled for news events. Organizationally, one is talking about the systematic assigning of reporters to those organizations that are known to provide news (e.g. local government). In terms of topic, one is talking about specialization, news departments, the categorization of news.

Genres evolve, and one may recognize this in news, not least broadcast news. Even the heavyweight, flagship evening television news programmes have moved in the direction of entertainment. Compared with the late 1980s, they offer a greater range of human interest stories and personalization of news content and news presentation. One has star presenters who have become celebrities (e.g. Sir Trevor McDonald). Many stories are about celebrities. Presentation is faster. Studio sets are 'warmer'. More dramatic content is offered, not least as it is shown on camera. Stories are often shorter, so that there are more of them within the programme. The programmes look for happy endings. These tendencies are more marked when one looks at newer channels and the provision of something more like soft news in broadcasting.

The fact that news may be seen as a genre matters only in the context of what news purports to be. It pretends to be different from other print and broadcast material, not least because it *is* different in respect of its ability to bring us information about the world in all its forms – political, social, economic, geographical, cultural. It assumes a truthfulness and an authority – especially mainstream broadcast news – which is actually dissipated if one realizes that it is just another genre. This diminishing of its status will be endorsed by critical points made in other sections, not least that which questions the objectivity of news.

Consideration of the institutional side of news as genre may alter the perspective taken on the value attached to news within media operations. News also has to pull in audiences and has to pay. It is a commodity with a market value. Routines help keep down production costs. It may be seen as a standardized product with a standard set of values. It has to meet competition in the marketplace. So one can hardly talk about getting at the truth at all costs. News can hardly be all about 'breaking events' and what is 'up-to-date' if it is predictable, and if it depends on factors such as a news editor deciding to allocate resources to a story before there is much of a story. Many events stories are put together after the event, i.e. the news people were not actually there when something happened. Much of a so-called live news broadcast is in fact prepared before it happens.

Gitlin (1980) and others refer to the idea of 'frames' which structure the understanding of journalists and their news material. In some respects one may say that these frames refer back to news values, to the idea of what is newsworthy: 'Frames enable journalists to process large amounts of information quickly and routinely.'

It is production routines allied to routine ways of thinking about news which link to genre, which produces versions of the news that are characterized by similarities, under the appearance of difference. These frames are inclusive, and do ideological work in the sense that they may incorporate some views that dissent from the dominant ideology. Under the guise of objectivity, they manage to contain contradictory views. An example of a frame specific to Britain is that which contains inconsistent views about the National Health Service. Views are inconsistent in respect of simultaneously talking about the need for private and selective funding for health services, and yet also talking about a public and comprehensive service. The frame contains contradictions within a spurious assertion that everyone believes in this service, that indeed Britain actually has a genuinely national health service (however imperfect).

It should be understood that these and other criticisms of news in this chapter should not lead to conclusions that newspapers and news broadcasts have no importance. To recognize news as a genre is to put it into a context. To describe news as partial if it employs degrees of dramatization like other genres, should be to generate reservations about what we are being told, not necessarily to lead to straightforward rejection of it as a useful source of information.

9 Global news

It may be believed that global news is with us and is happening now (see also Chapter 9). It is true that technologies allow a worldwide reach of information exchange. There are at least some relatively international 'global newspapers' – the *International Herald Tribune*, the *Guardian*, the *China Daily*. There are 24-hour satellite-based news services, dominated by CNN, but including BBC World, NBC, Asia Business News, EuroNews, Fox 24 and others. News stories about different places, events and personalities around the planet can appear on national news, just as CNN has its *World Report*, with contributions from national journalists around the world. Yet it is also true that one may argue that a global news service exists only in part and serves only sections of the world's population. One has to ask questions about who is able to view *World Report*, and about what kind of world it speaks of anyway.

One needs to make a distinction between the one definition of global news as that which is generated by a global producer for a global audience, and that which is actually news about 'the world', but for a national audience. Most global news is actually the latter – at best for a regional audience. There is no global social or cultural coherence which would make possible global news, in the full meaning of the term. This point has, of course, consequences for the idea of a global public sphere.

Globalization as a notion is nothing new: news has been brought back from far places for hundreds of years. It just took a lot longer to arrive, and might not have been so accurate. Anyway, globalization is a problematic concept: it is not about some inevitable line of development or process of **homogenization**. Globalization has a lot to do with global financial networks. In this case, it is no accident that from the beginning of modern news services, one thing that (commercial) organizations were prepared to pay for was news about trade and about finance.

> 'News' represented the re-formulation of 'information' as a commodity gathered and distributed for the three purposes of political communication, trade and pleasure and was directed in its generic form by technology . . . scientism . . . and the development of mass media markets.
>
> (Boyd-Barrett and Rantanen 1998)

Reuters became a global news agency on the back of its ability to control and distribute such information. Globalization also has a lot to do with what we call 'the West', and not so much to do with the rest of the planet. The dominant global news agencies, like most of the dominant global money markets, are located in the West. Reuters is based in London (but owned by the Thomson group in Canada); AP is in the USA; AFP is in France. Reuters has 'commercial understandings' with Murdoch's NewsCorp in particular. Reuters has over 260 client broadcasters in 85 countries. TV material is dominated by Visnews (part of Reuters) and WTN. WTN has commercial links with AP, ABC and CNN. ABC network is owned by the Disney Corporation. CNN (ex Turner Broadcasting) is part of Time Warner. The global web of ownership and alliances is as powerful in respect of news as it is for the rest of the media.

The greatest volume of news flow is in and about the West. News is about what is happening in London, Paris, Brussels and Washington. A disproportionate number of correspondents are based in the USA and in Europe. And only the biggest news organizations can afford them anyway – hence the power of the agencies. So one has to dispute the idea that news flow and access to news material is global in the proper meaning of the term. 'The perspectives of the great mass of the world population are under-represented in global news, while those of relatively small elites are over-represented' (Von Ginneken 1998).

Davies (2008: 100) points out that anyway, global news operations are severely under-resourced. He talks about a 'vacuum of information', which has to be filled with something, but that is not necessarily well-researched news. He describes the limited nature of cover by the dominant news providers, AP and Reuters, where, for example, neither organization has a TV bureau in either Canada or New Zealand.

The Western dominance of news operations also once more raises questions about imperialism and power, about the hegemony of the West. The answers are not cut and dried. Paterson (1998) asserts that 'the cultural product of the international television news agencies serves to perpetuate a western hegemony hostile to developing nations'. But globalization, such as it is, has been accompanied by counter-forces of regionalism and resurgences of national and intra-national identities. So too, the creation of global news agencies and news makers, alongside other transnational media institutions, has been accompanied by the appearance of regional news centres and specialist agencies which feed into the multinationals.

One example that has risen to prominence in recent years is the Arab station/agency, Al-Jazeera, based in the Gulf state of Qatar. Its very status is of interest. Certainly it broadcasts news: 'Approximately seventy percent of Arabs who own a satellite dish rely primarily on Al-Jazeera for news, documentaries and political information' (El-Nawawy and Iskandar 2002).

But it is also in a sense a news source, because of the material which it creates and supplies to other broadcasters, most famously video recordings sent to the station by the Western-styled terrorist leader, Osama bin Laden. It has a huge influence in its region of the Middle East. As a news source it rivals the global provider, CNN. It has a liberal editorial policy, one that has caused waves among Arab nations, not least when, for instance, it has broadcast a range of views on Muslim polygamy. It is diplomatic in avoiding criticism of its host state, whose ruler is its protector. As a successful and influential regional station it runs counter to notions of globalization of news.

Al-Jazeera has revolutionised the Arabic Middle East, challenging censorship imposed by the government-controlled media, addressing any relevant issue, including weak democratic institutions, fundamentalism, state corruption, political inequality, and human rights violations.

(El-Nawawy and Iskandar 2002)

The authors' most telling remarks are those about global news being part of global information wars. They see news institutions as being used in these wars, which dispute views of how the world should be, and compete for the acceptance and beliefs of audiences round the planet. This would be a nice example in action of Gramsci's notion of the struggle for the hegemony of ideas. Certainly this is how Boyd-Barrett and Rantanen (1998) see it: 'a process of dialectic, not least between the local, national, regional and global, a process of conflict and struggle both among the agencies of globalisation and the alleged subjects of globalisation'.

If news is *perceived* as being generally truthful (whether or not it is), then it is attractive for governments (and other interests) with positions to promote in global politics, to get on the news agenda, to get their positions heard. News has always been a target of propaganda. Propaganda has been part of state news services in various places at various times. News programmes have been simulated in propaganda wars. Von Ginneken (1998) points out, drawing from a *New York Times* article of 27 December 1977, that 'the CIA has at various times owned or subsidised more than 50 newspapers, news services, radio stations, periodicals'. And that was written in the mid-1970s. Again it is Davies (2008) who brings us up to date with a chapter (6) in which he details US propaganda and misinformation regarding the Middle East and Iraq in particular. He details ways in which the USA has infiltrated and manipulated the news agenda.

In terms of propaganda and influence on public opinion, Flournoy and Stewart (1997) suggest that world news providers have become unavoidably involved in the conduct of diplomacy. Technology can bring events, comments and diplomatic statements into the home as things happen. News is driven by valuation of immediacy, of the 'scoop', of drama, of bringing us an unfolding narrative in which it might be said, things have to happen. But diplomacy needs time for negotiation and reflection, for things not to happen immediately.

McGregor (1997) exemplifies the start of this time, and scoop-obsessed, technologically supported revolution in global news through the early reporting of CNN. On 28 June 1986 the fledgling world news channel took unique video footage of the shuttle *Challenger* explosion, as much by luck as judgement. In 15 minutes pictures were on ITV News in Britain.

In terms of the partiality and ideology of Western news businesses, one may argue that news about the rest of the world is very selective. Some places, events and personalities appear on the news briefly and then disappear again. 'The viewer gets a dispersed mosaic of events' (Horvat 2001). He points out cultural bias in terms of production and reception. For example, a British newspaper might well favour a story about a train crash in Pakistan, given the historical links between the two countries. Equally, viewers in the USA or in Britain, viewing images of a demonstration in a given eastern country, may be missing cultural nuances. They may read the demonstrators as a strangely dressed rabble, even assume a position of superiority to the scene and its people.

In other respects, where there is more continuity of attention, it may still be largely negative. One could argue that chunks of the south and east of the planet (relative to the West, of course!) are seen mainly in terms of crises. Disasters often make a 'good' news story for the West. But so-called 'natural' disasters may be nothing of the kind when, for example, deforestation is the major cause of flooding off hillsides. It is not fair to say that no newspapers have investigated causes of such stories, including perhaps the responsibility of Western business interests for the cutting down of forests. But the popular tabloids and much of TV are interested in picture impact and scale. They do not give time or space to background, especially if it is uncomfortable in political terms.

10 News and new technologies

The development of global news, like other facets of globalization, depends on technology. Newspapers have their online versions; so do some radio channels, also offering podcasts. The potential audiences are huge. Star satellite in Asia has 220 million viewers in 12 countries.

News on the Web is important for its diversity and alternative character (for an account of various world websites offering alternative accounts of events, see Pavlik 2001). CNN.com will post information on the Web from CNN broadcasts that certain governments will not allow on air. Text services offering to keep one updated on news stories are offered, whether streamed to one's computer or mobile. Website design tries to be mobile and interesting, offering video clips and user voting on issues. Digital also offers devices such as onscreen rolling banners updating news even while it is being delivered on channels such as Sky.

Davies (2008: 107), however, points out how much of web news is recycled: research shows that an average of 50 per cent of news material on major media websites is reproduced from wire. He says of iGoogle, a dominant provider: 'Google does not even pretend to be checking its stories or exercising any kind of journalistic judgement. Google simply presents what everybody else is saying.'

So-called Net news sites are not necessarily what one would recognize as news based at all. *The Drudge Report* garners a lot of interest and a few scoops. It is entertaining, but largely its postings are a matter of gossip and opinion, backed by no serious news reporting as such.

The arrival of kinds of digital technology affects national as much as international news reporting. Pavlik (2001) refers, for instance, to the advantages of digitized newsrooms:

- increased efficiency
- greater productivity
- enhanced creativity
- greater accuracy and range of cover
- fully searchable digital archives and news libraries.

On the other hand, Burton (2002) points to the deleterious effects of bringing in computer-controlled broadcast news studios – fewer staff, more reliance on syndicated news, less reflection and analysis because this requires time and labour. This can be particularly evident at a local level, where material is brought in from standardized providers. 'There is now a fundamental lack of real diversity in news provided by broadcasters at the local level' (Harrison 2006: 84).

At the same time, new technical resources and facilities place greater pressures on news-workers, in terms of requiring greater speed of response to events, of meeting ever shorter deadlines, of coping with ever sharper competition. Television news is 'a competitive, technologically intensive industry where great value is placed on being one step ahead of the competition' (McGregor 1997).

There was a furore in 2003 over the BBC's reporting by Andrew Gilligan of what an expert adviser is supposed to have said about the reliability of intelligence information, leading to a decision to go to war in Iraq. This episode owed a lot to news technologies, to the importance to government of news as political communication, and to competitive practices, all putting pressure on government and reporter to 'talk up' the news. Behind all this were news production pressures, which led to a slip of the tongue at 6 o'clock in the morning – an error of wording which was later corrected – and even later vindicated when it became clear that there was indeed a political decision at some level to enhance intelligence reports with the effect of moving public opinion in favour of the decision to go to war.

Pavlik (2001) refers to this 'talking up', and to other issues around changes in news ownership and provision, when he says that there are 'enormous threats to privacy, increasing concentration of ownership, a shrinking diversity of voices, an ever-escalating race to report the news more rapidly, an inequitable access to information technology and digital journalism'.

Pavlik (2001) argues that technology is changing the nature of journalism, on global and other levels: 'There is emerging a new form of journalism whose distinguishing qualities include ubiquitous news, global information access, instantaneous reporting, interactivity, multimedia content, and extreme content customisation.'

Certainly immediacy through technology was a characteristic of the war in Kosovo in 1999. Evening news would show video taken from attacking aircraft of missile strikes made that day. Burton (2002) points out that not only has one's sense of immediacy and reality been changed, 'but also the very definition of war and news of war has shifted', bringing us

- war from the front – now
- war as spectacle (the computer game syndrome)
- war as techno-combat
- clean war
- war as refugees.

All this raises questions:

- How far is news technology used for its own sake, because of a love of gadgetry, because it connotes professionalism, because of the millions invested in it?
- Or is it used because of the professional imperatives of news, the value of immediacy, of getting the news first?
- Or is technology, as elsewhere in the media, used because it is part of an ongoing reality trip in which the illusion of reality is constructed in the cause of creating actuality?

And of course news operations value the notion of 'being there' because that contributes to the sense of the truth of news.

11 News discourse, news mythologies

One needs to understand that inevitably news texts draw upon and recirculate discourses. They use discourses to make sense, within an ideological framework, of that about which they speak. Some discourses, such as those of gender, are dominant; they are frequently inscribed in news material and the assumptions that this makes about how the world is. To use a discourse is to use codes in such a way that certain meanings about the discourse subject are privileged. So news will talk in certain ways, through the language of pictures, through the language of the newscaster or reporter, about any of its subjects – from Parliament to poverty, from a given nation to a given social group. It may be said that news, as with all forms of communication and especially the media, talks about and visualizes the world in ways which privilege and make dominant some cultures and some ways of understanding that world. For example, there is much talk in news about 'democracy'. It is represented in approving ways as if one inevitably agrees with the concept. Even a definition of democracy is assumed. But, for instance, if just one way of understanding democracy involves the practice of 'one person, one vote' then how does democracy really shape up when, as in some elections, more people do not vote than those who do? And why should the West assume that any model of democracy (as endorsed through news) is beneficial to a nation torn apart by tribal disagreements (and there are many such examples in the world)? News discourse becomes a prism through which certain meanings are refracted. Other meanings may never escape the prism.

News also has its own discourse or way of speaking about itself. It speaks of its own authority and credibility. It speaks of these things through its presentation. Studio sets, newscasters' body language and actuality footage are all part of the language of this news discourse. As discourses do, it also speaks through a pattern of oppositions, talking up that which is approved, and diminishing or simply ignoring that which is disapproved of. In terms of the previous point about democracy, news always speaks in favour of **consensus**. In political or industrial disputes we hear that 'no agreement has yet been reached', as if it is inevitable that it must. Indeed, it speaks about disputes in terms of opposing views, as if there is some middle ground to be found along an axis which joins two sides. It hardly ever talks about three or more differing views, let alone about how the notion of 'middle ground' is going to be realized in such a case.

As an Ofcom (2008: 1.70) report puts it, 'views that do not fit easily within a conventional two-sided debate can struggle to be heard'.

The mythologies, or false understandings, which news promotes, may be understood in the same way as discourses are. Indeed, it is perfectly arguable that the subjects of a given discourse and the meanings which they generate are one and the same as these mythologies. The same core meanings are approached through different critical terms, and methods of analysis. Von Ginneken (1998) comments that 'news discourse refers to the common-place views of certain issues, shared by (most members of) a society or culture'. One instance might be the (Western) idea that having rapid population growth stunts economic growth. This has not been the case in China or India or Brazil. Bird and Dardenne (1997) say much the same thing when they argue that one has to look at the totality of news stories in order to see the large framework within which news stories exist.

Through doing this one understands that news is a myth-making process in which people are told about themselves, about others, and about the world. An example, they say, would be stories about social behaviour and the way in which deviant behaviour is defined and boundaries are set. So, for instance, there is an emphasis on murder in news reporting, but not on the far more frequent occurrence of car theft.

Consensus

One could also take the example of 'consensus', which I have described as being part of news discourse and its meanings. One could just as well say that the idea of consensus is a myth promoted through news language. It is part of a way of understanding the world and of talking about news events which helps simplify explanations of news. It is simultaneously very ideological and convenient to the hegemony of a dominant ideology. What I mean by this is that consensus invokes the ideas of agreement and compromise. Its discourse also defines it as a 'reasonable position'. Therefore any person or group who is not for consensus is against compromise and against reason. This is very convenient if the consensual position on an issue either actually works in favour of the powerful or in practice undercuts the views and actions of those lacking power. Therein lies the myth that consensus is always the reasonable solution to any problem. Consensus is indeed an ideological notion.

To take an example of one news story in 2003, Diego Garcian islanders went to court in order to try to get back to their homes on an Indian Ocean island from which they were evicted in 1971 by the British government, so that the USA could build a base there. The story is not to be explained in terms of a consensus to be sought between the needs of the islanders and the needs of the USA, or even of some world security policy. The nub of the story is that either the islanders get back to their homes or they do not; they won their case in 2008, but still have not been allowed back to their island. Consensus is a mythology that becomes a cloak to conceal the naked exercise of power.

Reese (1997) asserts baldly that 'the news media play an essential role in maintaining the authority of the political system'. He also points out that consensus starts with how news is gathered, and is linked with its hegemony because agreement about what should be gathered is itself naturalized. It is defined as being normal. So is the notion of consensus when it is about making sense of news stories themselves. 'The consensual nature of news gathering supports the notion of a guiding news paradigm' and 'the self-policing nature of the news paradigm is essential for its hegemonic effectiveness' (Reese 1997).

Objectivity

Similarly, one may argue that other ways in which news makers operate and make sense of news are also mythologies, are also part of news discourse, as well as possibly being seen as subordinate discourses in themselves. For example, 'objectivity' is a notion integral to news. It is an abstract, even an idealized notion. It is an aspiration. But to say that news is or ever can become truly objective is nonsense; it is a myth. Larsen (1997) calls it 'the myth ritual of objectivity' when arguing that it is bound up with the concept of professionalism in journalism. This means that it is also bound up with the training and induction of journalists. One has to ask how far journalists are genuinely autonomous within their workplaces (and of course they aren't). One can raise questions about the allegiances of at least some journalists to particular political or social groups (and of course they will have some such allegiances). 'The myth of objectivity . . . also allows them (media managers) to pretend that they have a special claim on the truth' (Davies 2008: 112).

Davies (2008) is also blunt in his debunking of the possibility of real objectivity: 'The great blockbuster myth of modern journalism is objectivity, the idea that a good newspaper or broadcaster simply collects and reproduces the objective truth' – 'It has never happened and never will happen because it cannot happen' – 'All stories have to view reality from some particular point of view' (Davies 2008: 111).

A version of the classic industry position is expressed in Herbert (2000): 'Although absolute objectivity is impossible, the quest for factual accuracy, balance and fairness remains the goal of every professional reporter.' The desire is to create an aura around news, to attach meanings of 'authority' and 'truth' to news productions. The idea is to validate news-work, to create a certain kind of relationship with the news audience: 'the claim of journalistic objectivity is essentially an appeal for trust' (McNair 1998).

News values are patently cultural and partial; they are subjective. News stories are plainly constructed with an angle – often the 'human interest' angle. The whole selection and decision-making process of news is one in which degrees of subjectivity must appear. Omissions will occur. Normative judgements will be made. This does not mean that news is a pack of lies. Neither does it mean that one cannot argue for degrees of objectivity and subjectivity. One may still talk of at least some facts behind a news story. In any case, a collection of facts do not express the truth of an event. But then hardly any stories are simply a recital of bare facts. Any act of communication carries some inflection and interpretation, coming from the experience and world view of the communicator. So one may say at least that the way the news aspires to and asserts objectivity is part of its own mythologizing about itself.

Von Ginneken (1998) points out that objectivity can be seen as merely a set of rhetorical devices which do not necessarily express 'the truth'. Anonymity – of source, of newspaper journalist, of TV camera operator – is one such device that contributes to the illusion of objectivity.

Exnomination

Anonymity may be identified with Fiske's concept of exnomination (Fiske 1987). In this case he argues that sources such as companies and government departments which are spoken of as institutions rather than represented through specific names or faces, acquire a certain authority. There is respect implied in the distancing, respect for the status and truthfulness of the source. It was interesting to see the dissolution of this authority in reporting of the Hutton Inquiry (2003–04) in Britain. This inquiry examined the death of a weapons adviser and conflicting statements made by the British government and by a BBC reporter, in relation to the lead-in to the US/UK war on Iraq. In this case there was a reversal of a common news process, which emphasized the personal involvement of one named journalist (Andrew Gilligan), and even of a member of the secret services (John Scarlett). This naming – continued through the personal involvement of the prime minister (Tony Blair) and his director of communications (Alastair Campbell) – served in reverse to show how the anonymity of the exnominating process does blow out a kind of smokescreen of false objectivity. The bitterness of this dispute between government and the BBC news machine hinged precisely on a challenge to the accuracy and objectivity of news reporting.

Impartiality

Much the same may be said of notions like balance, impartiality and (lack of) bias. Balance implies a mid-point between two views – criticized above. Impartiality suggests a capacity to be objective – just criticized. And lack of bias suggests a capacity to avoid being subjective – also criticized.

These key words invoked by news makers and news regulators to manage and defend the status of news operations, do not stand up in an absolute sense. To be fair, the BBC code of practice, referring to impartiality, says that it 'does not imply absolute neutrality, nor detachment from basic moral and constitutional beliefs'. But then guidelines do invoke that discourse of objectivity, with all its associations and implications, through words such as 'fairness' and 'dispassionate'. They are creating a cradle which supports news conventions, news values and journalistic practices. A BBC Trust (2007) report says that impartiality 'involves a mixture of accuracy, balance, context, distance, evenhandedness, fairness, objectivity, open-mindedness, rigour, self-awareness, transparency and truth'.

At this point one should recognize a distinction between broadcast news and press news. Broadcasting is obliged to attempt some kind of objectivity because of the terms of the Acts of Parliament which allow it. The press is not so obliged. British newspapers, which have been known to campaign against BBC 'bias', do not even pretend to aspire to such ideals when they support the policies of particular political parties. Nor is one much encouraged by the kinds of journalistic practice which saw editors of the *News of the World* imprisoned in 2007 for using phone-tapping technology to obtain information from mobiles used by members of the royal family. Even the fact that the paper did not report on transgressions by its own staff is a kind of bias or lack impartiality. Talking of another Murdoch-owned operation – Fox News – Paul Krugman (*Guardian* 2 July 2007) comments:

> they usually convey misinformation through innuendo. During the early months of the Iraq War, for example, Fox gave breathless coverage to each report of possible WMDs, with little or no coverage of the subsequent discovery that it was a false alarm. No wonder, then, that many Fox viewers got the impression that WMDs had been found.

Some Americans still believe this.

12 News representations

If one understands that news – in any medium – is a text, then it will by its nature be full of representations. Texts must be representations of the world, of groups, of institutions – and so of ideas that are the dominant views of the society which produces those texts. Understanding of representations also needs to take account of the nature of the news institutions that construct them, as well as of the audiences that assimilate and interpret them.

It may be said that the representation within the text is carried out through the operation of discourses. The way the subject is talked about is how it is represented. For instance, news tends to talk about certain social groups as problems. Young people are 'making trouble on the street'. They are 'truanting from school'. We hear about young (male) footballers who are 'getting out of control' and involved with sexual escapades (not old or female footballers!). This is an updated version of the ongoing representation of 'youth as trouble'. I am not suggesting that the news reports are based on complete fabrication; indeed, in 2008 one young footballer, Joe Barton, was sentenced for violent behaviour in the street. But I am saying that the nature of how the subject (the young) is being spoken of does tend to generalization and to exaggeration, in the popular press in particular. The proportion of the young or of footballers who 'transgress' is very small. News representations give disproportionate space to illegal acts or to those who are perceived as illegitimate in a cultural sense.

The very fact of news makers operating as a kind of pack also tends to make this distortion worse. News makers compete for headlines, check each other for stories being broken, and so one ends up at one time with the same stories being told through many news outlets, as the agenda principle cuts in. This collation of the same stories, and indeed similar approaches, tends to profile the subject, to emphasize the kind of representation.

The 'other' and 'difference' in news

One may also revisit the notion of 'othering' through news. Just as certain kinds of social behaviour are branded as 'deviant', so certain groups are implicitly represented as 'other' from 'the rest of us', not least on grounds of ethnicity. To label someone as an 'asylum seeker' is to define them as being distinct from the rest who are not asylum seekers. To identify them as Somali is to imply that they are therefore 'not British' – and to imply that this matters. The same emphasis on 'difference' and on Western values as a benchmark by which a news story is assumed to be properly judged was seen in 1997. An American schoolboy was caned by a Singaporean court for an act of vandalism. For all their usual tendency to talk tough on crime, the Western press was in this case rather more vocal about these 'others' who dared to commit a kind of violence on one of 'our' children.

The 'othering' principle in news representations is of a piece with the oppositions within discourses. In the case of asylum seekers at least some newspapers take ideological positions on immigration – that it is not a good thing, and that 'we' do not really want all these people here. Consider other possible kinds of representation and treatment that would be reasonable, but are never seen in the following terms.

> Among the latest group of asylum seekers to enter Britain are three qualified doctors. The Chief Medical Officer welcomed them into a conversion course which will enable them to work in and support our National Health Service.

> Interviews with refugees who flew into Britain four days ago (i.e. who were not put in a holding centre for many weeks) have established evidence of torture in X country. The Foreign Office is making strong representations to X regarding this evidence.

Macdonald (2003) discusses the 'othering' of Islam and of Arab peoples. She refers to a range of media strategies in which the words and images contained within a discourse produce this effect. Emphasis on the wearing of the burkha by women, as news photos select this dress to make an iconic image, is an example of this process (not to mention the mingling of discourses).

> The 'difference' of Islam has been repeatedly emphasised, serving both to alienate Islamic practices from modernity and from civilisation, and to shore up the West's own sense of self-worth, and its liberal and fair-minded credentials. Signifiers of difference can be apparently modest, but insistent in their reiteration. British radio news items making reference to Islam almost without exception feature the 'sound effect' of the Muslim call to prayer.
>
> (Macdonald 2003)

Of course, the ideological 'othering' of groups is something which news does not invent of itself. It is about cultural attitudes and positions taken by various sections of society, including politicians. But then to say that divisive ideological positions emerging from news representations are also embedded in parts of society does not mean that one should excuse news (or the media in general) when they offer such negative representations.

Almost at random I can pluck out a headline in the *Daily Express* (22 August 2008): '1650 New Migrants Invade UK Every Day'. Page 5 has a large picture of a woman wearing the burkha and pushing a pram in a street. Its subheads include 'Asylum Bids Soar'. News makers are aware of the power of their position and of the choices that they are making in representing the world. Some have, for example, castigated politicians for ways in which they deal with refugees (see Robert Fisk in *The Independent*). Yet in general, news services support the status quo and naturalization of dominant ideas, rather than challenging these. They will support the interests of a political and economically powerful social establishment. It has to be repeated that this is likely to happen not least because of contextual pressures from proprietors, shareholders, advertisers and powerful news sources.

It was interesting to see how in September 2003 news reports came out that were critical of the British army and the notorious Bloody Sunday shooting incident in 1979 (following a long delayed public inquiry). One paratrooper was reported as admitting shooting and killing unarmed demonstrators. But at the time of the original events, almost all news reports represented the incident in ways supportive of the institutions of the army and of the state.

Some might argue that, as with the notion that gendered representations in news stories reflect gender inequalities in news management, so also the 'othering' of ethnic groups in particular relates to a lack of journalists from a range of ethnic backgrounds, especially in senior positions. Joseph Harker writes about this in the *Guardian* (3 March 2008). He points out that most of the main desks on the nationals are run by white teams. Harker discusses the issue of recruitment and of needing to 'fit in'. He refers to a survey which revealed the white, middle-class, public school inflection of senior management. He talks of a need for news staff to reflect the society that they address, not least where one is talking about those columnists and critics who are influential opinion formers: 'What surely we all want is for all sections of society to feel they are properly represented in the range, variety and balance of stories written about them.'

12.1 Misrepresentation and moral panics

News media have a well-established tendency to represent certain events in such a selective and emphatic way that they both engender and represent what have been called moral panics (see Cohen 1973; Cohen and Young 1973). Their seminal studies of the representation of youth gangs, or those by Hall et al. (1978) of 'black muggers', recognized a pattern of news reporting in which public anxiety and moral issues were hyped up. This hyping often takes place over a certain period of time and is tied to one or two emblematic incidents. Moral panics may be revived if a suitable incident of sufficient impact occurs. In 1996 the so-called Dunblane massacre in Scotland of a school teacher and 16 children by a deranged person provoked a media debate about gun crime. It contributed indirectly to the legal ban on handguns, made law later in the year. The killing of a little girl in 2003 in what appeared to be a gang hit led to a revival of the debate about gun control. The arrest of an individual for converting to use and selling replica weapons revived the debate in 2008. In the period 2006–08 there was an ongoing moral panic about teenage knife crime. The deaths of young people were indeed tragic and reprehensible. But they did not prove that the teenage male section of the entire UK population was out of control, or carrying or using knives. Kinds of criminality are often the subject of the exaggerated and selective reporting that characterizes a moral panic. Misrepresentation by the popular press in particular is common in such periods of panic.

12.2 Gendered news

One may consider issues around gendered news as relating to representation. As an aside it might be said that one could also, therefore, validate particular studies of, say, 'age-ized news' or 'ethnicized news'. In the case of gender, and within a brief space, it has to be understood that one needs to take account of the gendering of news operations as much as of news texts.

So it is that Van Zoonen (1994, 1998) describes how women are culturalized into the news business, into an occupation in which the majority of senior positions are still taken by males. Skidmore (1998) describes research by Dougary (1994) in which she established that across 12 tabloid newspapers, top editorial jobs were held by 64 men and 11 women. The ratio was worse in the case of the broadsheets.

Jamieson and Campbell (2001) report an analysis conducted by the *New York Times* in 1993 which found that 82 per cent of senior newspaper editors were men (and that women were the subject of only 13 per cent of all newspaper stories).

In Britain Rebekah Brooks (née Wade) was editor of the *Sun* newspaper from 2003 to September 2009, when she became Chief Executive of News International (publishing the *Sun*, *The Times* and *News of the World*). Veronica Wadley was editor of the *London Evening Standard* from 2002 to February 2009 (and is no longer working in the news industry). But this is exceptional rather than normal, and of course their genders and positions make no reflection on the content of their newspapers (see comments on the culture of newsrooms below). The National Union of Journalists (reported by Peter Wilby in the *Guardian* 12 May 2008) says that female journalists earn on average 11 per cent less than men.

Van Zoonen (1998) reports on research into news media in which it was found that in 1995, for the USA, 34 per cent of press employees were women and 25 per cent of TV journalists were women. For Britain, the figures were 23 per cent and 25 per cent respectively. Although there is a majority of females in journalism training, they do not end up in the mainstream press, but rather in associated areas such as public relations and magazines. (It is interesting that the circulation of magazines is rising as that of newspapers falls steadily.) There is evidence that it is nearly impossible for women to combine a mainstream journalistic career with bringing up a family. It is tough to attempt investigative journalism with its unsocial hours if you have a family to care about, and easier to take on the more flexibly timed news called 'features', which abounds in magazines. As Peter Wilby says:

> As profit margins become tighter and the industry more competitive, managements want to squeeze every last ounce from their staff. They are suspicious of people who work a 40 hour week, never mind anyone who wants to work 20 or 30 hours (as part timers). They prefer journalists who never go off duty, and can be rung at home day or night, weekends or weekdays.
>
> (*Guardian* 12 May 2008)

'Most newsrooms appear to be characterised by a gendered division between "hard" news (such as economics, politics, government and crime) reporters, who tend to be men, and "features" reporters, who are most likely, at least in relative terms, to be women' (Allan 1999). The culturalization of females into news-work raises interesting questions about gendered work and gendered discourses. Is news-work in fact just about masculine work patterns, which keep women out? Are the news values which drive news working really gender specific? And if there is a feminine discourse which links for example to the human interest story, is this in fact just a construct of the masculine discourse, rather than a genuinely female discourse in its own right?

There is a gender imbalance in terms of who produces news. There is a gender bias in terms of who gets to cover what kind of story. How this relates to representations of gender within any news text may be more complicated than assertions about men grabbing big factual stories about power, and women being given (and producing) softer stories about emotion and relationships.

At any rate, the gender bias of women's representation in the news media is unquestionable. Women are described and judged through news stories, in terms of their appearance in a way that hardly happens for men. News photographs often reproduce 'difference', showing for example women as fashion objects with articles on health and diet, and men as politicians or scientists influencing world affairs. Women are often talked about in relation to a man – their husband or boyfriend. Women, more than men, are identified as being a wife, a mistress or a girlfriend. The tabloids, far more than the broadsheets, sexualize women,

Figure 8.4 Women Represented Through the Popular Press
Newspapers are gendered texts, in which the effects of representation are reinforced through generic repetition of images and verbal features, as illustrated above.

- Describe kinds of reporting or image construction which might challenge this kind of representation in the popular press – in terms of achievements by women, the appearance of women, and the social roles of women.

(In other words, try creating an alternative news, bearing in mind what is *not* said about women at the present time.)

(Graeme Burton 2009)

whether it is through pin-up poses or through stories which talk about women dominantly in terms of their behaviour and their looks (e.g. stories about sex and footballers). Again at random, the *Daily Express* (22 August 2008) which has a page 36 article headlined 'Now Girls Say They Love Wolf Whistles'. Apparently a survey claims that more than one-third of women admit to being flattered by attention from workmen. What the rest of the survey – the vast majority – thought, we can only guess, because the article does not tell us.

Holland (1998) talks about the 'reassertion of the female body as spectacle' and points out the political implications of stories which obsess about women and sex (not to mention those which assume that stories about women should 'naturally' relate to domestic or caring contexts). Sexualization closes off democratic discourse. To represent women as sex objects, or even only as mothers and wives, is a way of trivializing them at worst, and at best of denying them access to equal exercise of power in the political and economic spheres. One might also say that all this is symptomatic of a Gramscian ideological struggle for hegemony, in which conservative forces are trying to put women back in a box, as women do indeed slowly achieve commercial and political power.

Where politics is the subject of news reporting, the way it is 'told' also represents a gender and class divide, according to Macdonald (2003). She describes the talk in the House of Commons as 'a public school, masculinised tradition of confrontational rhetoric', and as 'potentially alien to the majority of non-white, female and working-class citizens'. The implication is that hard news reporting which reproduces this talk is itself gendered.

Brookes and Holbrook (1998) provide a case-study example of gendered representation through discussion of the news and the BSE crisis of 1996 in which links were being established between brain disease in cattle and in humans. They describe how public concern was often depicted as female hysteria. Authoritative male actors in the news version told us how there was nothing to worry about. But the Shadow Health Secretary at the time (Harriet Harman) was represented as panicking and causing panic. The *Daily Star* misrepresented a male Tory MP as calling Ms Harman a 'mad cow' (though his original wording was also abusive). Women who were 'approved of' were represented as housewives and mothers who only wanted to feed their men good British beef. The difference between the treatment of women in public and private roles is interesting – something of a subtext of 'know your place'!

13 News audiences

> A market-driven news environment consider the audience as consumers who need to be entertained.
>
> (Harrison 2006: 161)

Like media audiences in general, the audiences for news output have, in varying degrees, polarized and fragmented. Polarization is seen through the increasing division of the British press, from the mid-twentieth century onwards, between populist, soft-news tabloids and the hard-news broadsheets. The takeover of the *Sun* in 1967 by what is now NewsCorp, and its transformation from a short-lived attempt at a soft left-of-political-centre broadsheet into a right-of-centre tabloid, with the first bared female chests, is symptomatic of this division of readers. The middle ground between two kinds of news has been slipping away. The *Daily Mail* has attempted to hold on to this, in tabloid format, with some success. But the

Daily Express has not so succeeded. It has, significantly, vacillated between inclinations to the right and the left in recent years. There are signs that this phenomenon of polarization is being repeated through broadcasting, as channels multiply. The nature of regulation limits extremes of polarization. All the same, the audiences for BBC2 television news, now targeting the over-35s, are different from those for Channel 5, targeting a younger age group. Younger audiences do not watch so much news anyway: 16–24 year olds watch less than 40 hours of TV news per year, compared to the figure of 90 hours per year for the population in general (Ofcom 2008). The kind of news and kind of audience for a big commercial radio station like Capital Radio is very different from the news presentation and audience for an upmarket kind of channel like BBC Radio 3.

Such an example would also serve as an instance of fragmentation, and of the niche markets that have emerged from competition in the newspaper industry, and from the deregulation of broadcasting. Equally, this change does need to be kept in perspective. The audiences for the flagship evening BBC and ITV news programmes are still very big, and run into several millions a night. (In May 2008, BBC1 main news achieved viewing figures of about 6 million, but ITV1 only about half that.) Their market share has been eroded since the 1980s by the arrival of Sky News, of two more terrestrial channels and by a variety of cable and satellite providers. Broadcasting is moving towards the situation of the press, in which different audiences may get differing understandings of what news is, of what is going on in the world. These differences may not particularly undermine a dominant ideology or a dominant news discourse. But it does represent some kind of change.

Another kind of change in audiences that needs to be recognized is in respect of the steady decline of newspaper readership, and the increase in online consumption. Since the mid-1980s a popular tabloid, the *Mirror*, has lost one-third of its readers – 3.15 million in 1987 to 1.56 million in 2007. In the same period the *Sun*'s circulation dropped from 3.94 million to 3.13 million. A former Sunday giant, the *News of the World*, has lost about half its readership. On the other hand, ABC research shows that Sun Online grew 40 per cent in the year to January 2008, to over 13 million users. The most used website is that of Mail Online (18.7 million users), closely followed by the *Telegraph* and the *Guardian* online websites, both with over 18 million users (*Guardian* 23 June 2008). What is more interesting is that 72 per cent of Mail Online's users came from outside the UK. The editors of these online editions are as interested in the global competition (BBC or Google News) as they are in their UK competitors. Also, these competitors have accused Mail Online of using celebrity stories and dramatic video clips as 'linkbait' to attract users and connections with gossip sites such as Drudge and Diggit. The items on such quasi-news sites are also driven by the users' postings and preferences, not by anything recognizable to a serious news provider. The idea of 'news to suit me' is also seen on sites such as Google News (linked to recognized news providers), where the user can select news preferences, such as having world news come up on the home page. News via the Net is, according to Jeff Jarvis (*Guardian* 30 June 2008), about a clash between an older content driven economy and a new online economy in which it is the links which are valuable. Online, one copy of an article with attractive links is all that is needed – printing presses are not required! But as he says this makes the headlines and intros all the more important because they 'advertise' the article.

A generation ago one could talk about a broad model, in which there was some consensus about major news content, in which that news was handed to the audience, in which there were dominantly mass audiences. That model is now crumbling.

But again, talk about the audience for news needs to be qualified. In terms of the news-workers, there is evidence from Burns (1977) onwards that journalists are less conscious of the audience out there than they are of their peers and of their editor as audience. Journalistic induction practices mean that this is likely to be so. Audiences impact on journalists only via circulation or viewing figures, and possibly via direct correspondence with the editor. In this sense, the conceptualization of audience is as much a critical and sociological undertaking, as it is much to do with the news media industries.

One audience that effectively does not exist for news is that of the child viewer. The only television news programme that now exists is *Newsround*, on BBC1. There was for a while *NickNews* on the Nickelodeon digital channel. It even won awards. But it has been pulled because of the low ratings. Conversely, children's programming is stuffed with drama and animation. This small but interesting corner of the media landscape may be connected with

- *Commodification and market forces:* ratings count for more than educational desirability.

- *Advertising:* advertisers pay the piper, and swing commitments to programme expenditure and production.

- *Regulation:* clearly the only force that could counteract this kind of behaviour would be that of the broadcast regulator, Ofcom.

- *Violence and media:* those who include news material in their concerns about the effect of violent material on children, ought to be concerned that there is no alternative interpretation (to main news) of the world, for children. This might be especially relevant in the case of news stories about violence committed on children.

- *Socialization and media influence:* children are not (unsurprisingly) great readers of newspapers or watchers of TV news. Notwithstanding critiques of how news represents the world, one may ask where else will children acquire any factual understanding of the world into which they are growing? The balance of children's programming (with the ads within it), tells them pretty clearly to consume and have fun that is what living is about!

There is of course a large *global audience* for news, which has some connection with the arrival of global news makers such as CNN. This also relates to questions about how far one may recognize something called 'global news' or a 'global public sphere'. But in fact this audience is pretty selective in its characteristics. For a start, much of it, as within national boundaries, is based in cities – and the nature of news reflects this. This also relates to the wealth of audiences – again, the highest per capita incomes are concentrated in urban areas. So these are where the greatest range of newspapers appears. These are the audiences to which news stories must appeal, because these are the people who have the money to spend on whatever it is that the newspaper advertisers (and TV channels) are promoting. As Von Ginneken (1998) puts it, 'most global media organisations are primarily geared to the interests and views of audiences in the G7, the largest Western nations'.

McGregor (1997) comments on the competition for audiences: 'In order to reach the largest possible audiences, news has become consensual.' This is the argument about pleasing the greatest number, about taking mainstream ideological positions. It is about endorsing a generality of news values and about approving established ways of telling news. It is one side of the debate about a stretch between mass and niche audiences, and about which direction globalization is moving in.

Jensen (1998) is interested in how news audiences around the world may be affected by news material. He is sceptical about simplistic assumptions regarding the influence of news. He refers to a Unesco report (Sreberny-Mohammadi et al. 1985) which among other things concludes that national news coverage is tied into its region rather than the world as such; that the nature of news is affected by the fact that most journalists around the world are socialized into western practices. So what audiences get is inflected by all sorts of assumptions and background factors. Jensen (1998) challenges ideas about audience power. What he does conclude, from a study of TV news, carried out across the world in a given week in 1993, using a mixture of content analysis and interviews, is the following:

- People have through news a sense of how they are located in relation to the status of the nation and to world affairs.
- News items often relate to a sense of security or of threat to that security, for the viewer.
- People acquire a sense of where power and authority lies, mainly as this relates to their place in a social hierarchy and to the power of the state.
- Within a time frame, people get a sense of what news items signify for where the country is going.
- People get a sense of their identity in relation to others, whether this is others abroad or within the nation state.

These conclusions are distilled out of research in a range of countries, from Mexico to Italy to India, and they suggest that people gain a sense of the world from the news, but they do not see themselves as world citizens.

So far as one may talk about *the effects of news consumption* on the audience, effects are more about ways of thinking than about behavioural changes. News reporting of an election does not so much affect people's voting decisions, as it affects the nature of informational material from which such decisions may be made. As János Horvát (2001) puts it: 'US journalists inform a domestic public that elects public officials who influence world affairs.'

News promotes agendas in the head. It creates internal visions of geographical and social worlds. Manning (2001) talks about mental maps: 'It is more useful to explore the ways in which intellectual frameworks for thinking issues through are constructed, and the contribution which the news media might make in the development of such "mental maps" among audiences.'

Allan (1999) is very clear that one should not exaggerate either the effects of news material on audiences, or the participation of news-workers in the cause of some ideological enterprise:

> Just as the claim that journalists are participants, knowingly or not, in some sort of wilful conspiracy to encodify the dictates of a 'dominant ideology' in the newsroom may be safely dismissed, so may the corresponding assertion that news viewers, listeners and readers be regarded as passive, alienated dupes indoctrinated into a state of 'false consciousness'.

Further, Allan (1999) points out audiences are perfectly able to distinguish between different representations of news and to accommodate these. He refers to a study which indicates that the audience may take TV news seriously as a source of information about the world, but acknowledges that tabloid news is just fun.

He points out that the reception of news by audiences has contexts which make glib assertions about influence untenable. For instance, there is the weaving of news consumption into the experience of everyday life. News reading or listening may be a ritual over breakfast. News viewing may be spasmodic and ongoing, as bulletins are picked up during the evening. The repetition of news, its way of interpreting and containing the world may generate 'a comforting sense of familiarity and predictability'. He refers to Silverstone (1994) when talking of 'the creation and maintenance of the viewer's sense of well-being and trustful attachment to the world beyond the television screen'. And, Allan (1999) argues, one has to recognize the capacity of different sections of the news audience to interpret news in different ways, not least in the context of their own experiences. Such experience might make some news items more salient than others. He talks of: 'the openings for different audience groups or "interpretive communities" to potentially recast the terms by which "truth" is defined in relation to their lived experiences of injustice and inequalities'.

This reminds us that the process of selective attention in news viewing and reading means that not only will some information be either lost or foregrounded, but also the sense and validity of that information will be understood differently by different sets of people. This is not an argument against news having effects on its audience. But it is to say that the audience is part of the making of any effects. And it is to say that one cannot assume a coherence of effects, even while arguing for a generality of influence.

One needs to remember that news makers are not entirely in control of their environment or their sources. The danger of depending on ritualized operations and of using powerful sources in industry and government has already been pointed out. News media are under continual pressures to influence them. For example, Jamieson and Campbell (2001) report on how the Federal Trade Commission launched a successful anti-trust investigation against the Santa Clara County Motor Dealers Association, who pulled out advertising worth $1 million because a reporter on the *San Jose Mercury News* produced an article telling readers how to get a better deal when purchasing a car.

TV news editors are now used to receiving unsolicited video material from many sources, including the environmental lobby (for example, Greenpeace). These videos, like expert press releases, are neatly produced, often to broadcast quality, offering convenient and free footage that fits in with news interests and values. Of course the newsroom retains editorial control. But there is a considerable pressure in some cases to put the story on the news agenda because it fits.

Online blogging also shapes news reporting in surprising ways – some might argue that it is a new kind of news reporting. Sites such as *The Huffington Post* have become a home to bloggers and are well read. Some talk about the new age of the citizen journalist (*Independent on Sunday* 8 June 2008). A German newspaper, *Bild*, has been actively encouraging its readers to send in pictures. It is now offering them a cheap digital camera deal, so that they become its citizen photojournalists. When the terrorist attacks happened in Mumbai, November 2008, there were many eyewitness accounts posted via Twitter and blogs. Where is the line to be drawn between this and professional journalism? Ordinary people with cheap equipment can and do catch out the politicians when they lie, or they can post recordings of uncontrolled comments. All this raises questions about the nature of journalism and about what is a journalist, as well as about the future of objectivity in journalism.

So there are attempts to influence the news from a range of commercial, political and interest group sources. News is produced within a nexus of forces, and in no sense is it something which is simply mined, smelted, cast and the ingots dropped into the laps of the audience.

> The news media are influenced by highly paid news managers and their clients, and by other individuals and groups. The media are also influenced by commercial pressures for ratings and revenues, and by the protests of those offended by news coverage. Finally, they respond to pressure from those in positions of political power.
>
> (Jamieson and Campbell 2001)

Trust and audiences

The points just made may be linked to issues around how far audiences can or should trust their news providers. Certainly news has a history of being trusted as a source of information – 'a contract of trust is co-produced by programme makers and viewers' (Hill 2007: 137).

But there are those who fear that this contract is being eroded and even abused by newsmakers. False reporting has been an ongoing problem, perhaps made worse by financial pressures and competition. Mark Lawson writes about the long-running Madeleine McCann case in the *Guardian* (20 March 2008). He refers to an apology extracted (front page) and to damages awarded (£550,000) against the *Daily Express* for making false accusations against the parents of that abducted child. His concern is that newspapers may see such fines as a small price to pay for vastly enhanced circulation figures. Press campaigns against public figures could also turn out to be destructive of public trust if they are as loud, as partisan and as personalized as they have been at times. Peter Wilby in the *Guardian* (19 November 2007) discusses what he describes as a witch hunt against the then Metropolitan police commissioner, Sir Ian Blair. Some newspapers had been furious when Blair accused them of a kind of institutional racism, concentrating on events such as the murders of white children, but ignoring black victims. Certainly he deserved the censure he did receive, with relation to his responsibilities and the shooting of an innocent man by some of his officers. The question remains as to whether such a partisan campaign constitutes legitimate news at all, and as to what its real motives were. Do we trust only those newspapers whose ideological positions we happen to agree with?

And then there are the issues of trust raised more directly by the behaviour of the press in particular. Davies (2008) discusses the evidence that journalists use dubious or even illegal practices through which to obtain news. He refers to the case of a listening device placed in a telephone exchange box to listen in to the phone calls of a minor celebrity – Angus Deayton. He refers to the activities of a character known as Benjy the Binman, who sifted the garbage of famous people to search out newsworthy material. Both these practices are illegal. But Davies (2008) points out that as with many other cases in which illegal acts were procured and paid for in order to obtain information, the journalists involved were never brought to court. Indeed few of those involved in many cases seem to have been punished. An exception was the case in 2006 of the royal editor of the *News of the World*, Clive Goodman, and a private investigator, Glenn Mulcaire, who were both sentenced to months in jail for illegally intercepting voice mail messages of a royal prince and an MP, among others. The editor of the paper resigned.

One might say that the sum of such instances is to raise doubts as to whether newspapers can be trusted in the manner of their newsgathering, let alone their editorializing and presentation. In this context it is interesting to see what was said in a report commissioned by the BBC on trust in the media (Globescan 2006, at www.globescan.com): 'television news is the most important source of information about the world' – but still, only 47 per cent of respondents said that they trusted the media.

14 News and the public sphere

One needs to recognize that the very notion of a public sphere is itself ideological because it is bound up with a liberal democratic ideal. It may be linked with social responsibility theories of the press. Without wishing to simply repeat previous points about the media offering some version of Habermas's vision of a public sphere, it is important to remind ourselves of the centrality of news to that vision. If within the term 'news' one includes that material which is about current affairs, or which provides a documentary type back-up to a given news topic, then news media become central to any discussion of this notion.

One has to recognize that news makers are not just information providers and producers of public knowledge. They express opinions and help form opinions. They can set the terms for debates. It is common for news broadcasters to summarize what they perceive to be various positions on a matter of public concern, such as a parliamentary debate in May 2008 about abortion terms and embryo research.

To this extent, the news agenda becomes an agenda for telling the public what they should be debating, and the treatment of those agenda topics can become the terms of the debate. Discussion in media programmes or within the pages of newspapers about current issues – perhaps involving the representatives of different positions – also becomes a kind of public debate, even if it does not involve the public at large. It is not a debate in which every citizen is free to join. Its terms of reference are defined by media makers. But one might say it is the best we have got. If there is anywhere that social and political events and issues appear to society in general, it is through news and current affairs. If there is any location in which problems and views are made apparent it is within news. If there is anywhere from which citizens may obtain information and at least witness debate – before exercising their rights to vote – it is from news. Once more it becomes apparent how important news media are within the range of media texts. It underlines the importance of subjecting news operations to criticism, to regulation and to continuing adjustment in the public interest. One might say, to re-mint a familiar statement: news is too important to be left solely in the hands of journalists or indeed their media masters. News has the capacity to be an enabling political and social force in an active public sphere. Or it may become a controlling force, one which closes down open debate through a range of views, one which manufactures a sham of a public sphere.

Some commentators seem to conflate the existence of a public sphere with the existence and survival of public service broadcasting. Granted, if an active public sphere, to which news contributes, is to be more than merely a public domain, then that sphere has to be preserved by regulators, yet supported financially. But in Britain at least, given regulation, one cannot say that issues raised by the (commercial) Channel 4 news are any the less sharp than those raised through the (PSB) channel, BBC1. What one must acknowledge is that, whatever the quality of debate, it is essentially controlled and packaged by the news makers. Harrison (2000) says: 'For Habermas the public sphere is a space which mediates between civil society and the state, and in which individuals and groups discuss and argue about public matters.'

But neither broadcast or press news, nor most of broadcasting in general, offers public access. Even in the most charitable interpretation, debates are conducted by the select few for the majority who do not participate. And then there are questions to ask. Are the terms of reference of the debate adequate in informing the citizen and voter? Is there a plurality and diversity of debates and views? Even the UK regulator Ofcom is doubtful about this: 'the traditional interpretation of plurality – based on a limited number of TV channels – may not at present be delivering a really diverse range of views' (Ofcom 2008: 1.33).

Another question is, how does one accommodate the fact of soft news – all that material which is subjective and felt, and not about discussion of social and political issues? In this sense, should we not plump for a model of alternative public spheres – one of which is, for example, where the public hears about and discusses the transgressions of soap stars?

Manning (2001) is highly critical of what he sees as a failure of news and of journalism to create a proper public sphere in which meaningful political debate takes place. 'The interface between private experience and public power is structured through the public sphere' but 'contemporary political news media offer the potential to involve and engage audiences in political debate at a deeper level than ever before, and yet this potential is rarely realised'. He also quotes Protess (1991) in saying 'news journalism has both reflected and encouraged a political apathy among citizens and a retreat from the public to the private domain'.

Through such views it is argued that news media promise much but deliver little, in terms of giving life to a public sphere in which genuine debate takes place. On the one hand, one may say that the press provides some kind of forum for discussion about subjects such as the introduction of genetically modified crops or the ethics of stem-cell research. On the other hand, there is the matter of the terms of reference for the debate in a given newspaper, the range of views allowed, and, of course, how far audiences choose to buy certain kinds of newspaper in which certain approaches to such issues are allowed or disallowed.

There is also a notion of the 'public interest', which news makers and politicians invoke, and which one would expect to underpin this public sphere. Regulators work on the principle that such a thing exists. The phrase appears for example in the 1994 White Paper on the future of the BBC (Department of National Heritage 1994). But if there is no coherent audience for a coherent news provision – nor a coherent and working public sphere – then what does public interest actually mean? One might say that it is a rhetorical and ideological device that news makers may invoke to challenge politicians and to extract information, and which politicians may use to resist assaults on their power and control of that information. This would model a public sphere as a battleground between competing ideas and institutions (ideology wars).

Paterson (1998) asserts that 'the globalisation of television news is producing an international public sphere, but one dominated by mainstream Anglo-Saxon ideologies'. But one might dispute the extent of that public sphere, and how it is conceptualized by news consumers, if at all. The Arab viewers of Al-Jazeera might be acquiring an expanded view of a kind of public sphere, not least in cultural and ethical terms. But this does not mean that they share that sphere with viewers in Indonesia.

Jensen (1998) says that 'the general information which is available from media is a decisive resource for the political and cultural action of publics around the world'. This does not mean that these publics are thinking or talking within the same public sphere. It may be that news has given audiences a larger global dimension as to how they think about the world, but this is not the same as a global public sphere shared by all citizens.

What seems more plausible is that news contributes to a public sphere for an elite – a commercial and political elite, by and large – which works and travels around the world, and therefore thinks in global terms. But given the technological limitations of TV news (let alone the ideological ones) it is simply not possible for citizens to debate or to share knowledge, on a global basis. It may be that supranational agendas are developing – the protestors at the 2003 World Trade Organization (WTO) summit were clearly thinking global. But then one has to consider their backgrounds, where they came from, and consider the fact that the WTO members themselves could not agree on a global strategy, so leading to the collapse of the conference.

Volkmer (1999) also enthuses about a 'global public sphere, consisting of a worldwide available audiovisual, satellite-transmitted "communication platform", *a global civil society*'. But she does not demonstrate that it actually exists. She talks about the importance of new satellite footprints, as opposed to old political boundaries. But then there is some contradiction in the statement that 'the global distribution of programmes such as those of CNN and MTV has shaped new regional markets which fragment and diversify'.

I am not arguing that the technological reach of news and other aspects of something called globalization have not had some effect on our conception of something called a public sphere (or spheres). But I am suggesting that the world of global TV news is geographically and ideologically selective, as well as limited, in its realization of 'global'. I am suggesting that there is no coherent global public sphere, even if some citizens of some nations are able to access more information about the world than in previous eras.

15 Discussion extract

Critics contend that processes of 'tabloidisation', to the extent that they erode 'serious', 'principled' journalistic criteria of newsworthiness, threaten to undermine the integrity of the 'quality' end of news reporting spectrum. In addition to the conflation of 'hard' and 'soft' news agendas, and with it the privileging of scandal, gossip, celebrity and sports over and above politics and economics, 'information' is said to be merging with 'entertainment' into an 'infotainment' muddle. Much is made therefore of how editorial commentary (features and opinion columns) appears to be flourishing at the expense of 'proper' reporting. These critics observe that it is evidently much more 'cost effective' to hire someone to sit at their desk and wax philosophical about the pressing issues of the day, as opposed to employing journalists to actually investigate what is happening. Quality reporting requires sufficient financial investment, but also time, effort and specialised knowledge, amongst other human resources. Comment may not be free, but facts are without doubt much more expensive – to re-inflect C.P. Scott's well-known declaration. Simon Hoggart (2003), who writes for Scott's *Guardian* today, is scathing in his criticism. 'The point about the tabs', he argues, 'is that they don't regard facts as having their own integrity. Instead they are treated like grains of wheat, puffed full of air, coated with sugar, and served up for breakfast in a brightly coloured box.' Moreover, in his view, the 'tabloids' have, deep down, a serious contempt for their readers, who are seen as simple souls, ready to believe what they are told.

Hoggart is one of many critics from within journalistic circles who take strong exception with this tendency to embrace a tabloid-driven ethos – one where truth, he adds, tends to be reduced to 'what you can get away with' (see also Hoggart 1995). Interestingly, however, when academic critics adopt a similar position, even using a language of 'moral panic' to describe the dangers of tabloidisation, others are more inclined to be circumspect. Tabloidisation, as Gripsrud (2000) points out, is something of a tabloid term itself, being more akin to a journalistic buzzword than a scholarly concept (2000: 285). In calling for a more nuanced understanding of the forms and processes in question, he argues that a 'degree of tabloidisation' is not always a bad thing. It takes, if not all sorts, then at least 'many sorts of journalism to make a democratic media system work as it should' (2000: 299). Arguing in a similar vein is Langer (1998), who affirms the general line of criticism outlined above while, at the same time, making a case for the 'other news' (tabloid journalism's so-called 'trivialities') to be given careful scrutiny on their own terms.

Allan, S. (2004) *News Culture*, 2nd edn. Maidenhead: Open University Press.

1   What do you understand by the term 'infotainment' as applied to the media in general?

2   What characteristics are there of some broadcast news or of some newspapers, which lead to the term 'tabloidization' being used?

3   What reasons are there for being concerned – or not – about any increase in this tabloidization?

16 Further reading

Allan, S. (2004) *News Culture*, 2nd edn. Maidenhead: Open University Press.
Davies, N. (2008) *Flat Earth News.* London: Chatto & Windus.
Harrison, J. (2006) *News.* Abingdon: Routledge.
Keeble, R. (2001) *The Newspapers Handbook,* 3rd edn. London: Routledge.
McNair, B. (2003) *News and Journalism in the UK,* 4th edn. London: Routledge.

9

Sport and representation

Media defining sport; sport as business; sport
and meaning

*Global TV networks . . . now virtually dictate both the form and the content of sport according
to the wishes of multinational sponsors and advertisers.*

Miller, T., Lawrence, G., McKay, J. and Rowe, D. (2001) *Globalization and Sport*.
London: Sage.

1 Introduction

This chapter deals with ways in which the media frame our understanding of the term 'sport',
as well as with the ways in which gender and ethnicity are inflected through their handling in
media sports material. Sporting events are dealt with dominantly through broadcast media
and the press. But sport, as a cultural phenomenon and as media material, is understood
through more than events. It is an essential component of the news genre across the media.
It may be the subject of texts as varied as television chat shows, novels and movies. Sport
is also a major economic factor in media institutions' finances. It is a staple attraction in
newspapers. It fills a lot of air time, sometimes quite cheaply, though not in the case of
major national and international events. As Jarvie (2006: 133) puts it: 'large parts of society
are immersed in media sport and virtually no aspect of life is untouched by it'.

Sport has an especially close relationship with television, based on the visual entertainment appeal of contest, the reach of the medium and the consequent income that it
can provide. Television has acquired the aura of live-ness and immediacy through its news
and sport coverage, in spite of its penchant for replays and recordings. Sport is often quite
a malleable material, in that in most cases the length of its performances is known and
can be fitted into pre-advertised slots, and in that it can be padded out with discussions
and action replays. It can be recycled and repackaged to provide yet more material for the
acres of air time to be filled. Sport is a popular activity, made the more popular by television through a process of mutual promotion. Sport provides attractive narratives, stories of
success and failure, victory and defeat, on national or global levels. Television brings us
such straightforward, rule-clear stories that appeal to a wide audience.

Sport and media now have a symbiotic relationship in which sport is a staple of media
content (and income), and the media are essential to the finances and promotion of sports:
'sport is increasingly shaped by the media, spectacularized by commerce, employed to
deliver audiences to sponsors, and intimately linked to the technological opportunities
afforded by various media delivery forms' (Miller et al. 2001: 24).

Sport is often represented in terms of individual conflict – going back to examples such
as the track race between Mary Decker and Zola Budd in 1985, watched by 11 million

TV viewers – or in terms of team conflict, framed in relation to regional or national identities (the Olympics). Sport and sporting figures are the stuff of myth – myths about national achievement, individual endeavour, heroic masculinity, myths which too often preclude heroic femininity. (Some might dispute the entirety of this position, perhaps citing the coverage of Ellen MacArthur racing her yacht around the world, linked to that world through webcam and email.) But in any case these myths circulate between the texts and the audiences, through representations, confirming a certain view of the world. 'Prominent sporting figures are both reflexive of the character of their public, yet at the same time larger than life. They embody the hopes of their followers' (A. Tomlinson 1999).

But sport can be framed in negative terms: 'a divisive version of society – one that reflects white above black, male above female, physical prowess above alternative qualities, certain body types above others' (Kay and Jeanes 2008: 130).

2 Major questions

1   How have notions of sport changed with the intervention of the media and the market?

2   In what respects is sport bound up with the conceptualization of national identity?

3   In what respects has media representation of sporting events and sports people conserved ideas about masculinity and restrained positive understandings of female gender?

4   How have media representations of sport affected conceptions of 'race'?

3 The representation of sport

> Does the media presentation of sport mirror reality or is it a representation and construction reflecting the media's objectives and the influences and practices of the professionals working in it?
>
> (Stead 2008)

We have acquired a web of ideas about sport, predominantly via the media, though partly through other agencies such as education. Some of these are elaborated on below. In any case, sport is more than just a social activity or a cultural practice. It has been colonized by the media. Its meaning is defined through metaphor and discourse (the use of language), through symbols (its stars, for example). The following are dominant ways in which ideas about sport, the definition of 'sport-ness', are represented through the media.

- *As a symbol of national identity:* through international competitions, particularly the Olympics.

- *As a world of personalities, stars and myths:* through gossip stories about the lifestyles of successful sportspeople.

- *As style:* through endorsements of style products made by sports stars, or through the adoption of sports-style clothing by millions of people worldwide spending billions of pounds in the process (in 1995 £2280 million was spent in Britain on sportswear and sports equipment: see Maguire 1999).

- *As a cultural activity with status:* through the space given to sports people and sports activities, as well as through approving coverage.

- *As a healthy social activity:* through items invoking the discourse of fitness and health, from *GQ* magazine to medical dramas.

- *As war:* through frequent uses of war metaphor in press coverage of sports events, the discussion of 'tactics' and so on.

- *As scandal:* through a range of magazine and news items which have covered everything from marital infidelities, to bad behaviour at nightclubs, to sexual preferences.

- *As commodity:* through news coverage of transfer fees, contract fees, media coverage rights and so on.

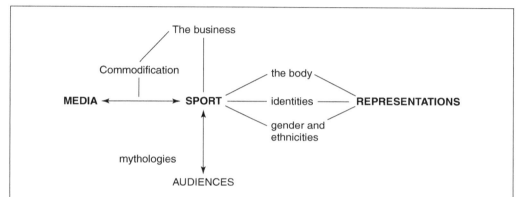

Figure 9.1 Sport and Representation: Terms for Reference
The business of sport and sporting celebrities are represented through the media in ways which tend to conceal the commodified nature of the relationship between sport, sports people and the media. Sporting celebrities are the subjects of myths about nationality, gender and ethnicity. Audiences for sport collude in this myth-making, as it fits in with representations (meanings) in areas apart from sport.

(Graeme Burton 2004)

- *As a spiritual event:* through the ritual associated with big national sporting occasions such as the singing involved with Welsh rugby events at the Cardiff Millennium Stadium.

Historically, sport has moved from competitive activities rooted in folk culture to global businesses rooted in commodity capitalism. Sport has moved from being about regulated play, games, to being about work and profit. Some sports like cricket and rugby league had a history of being rooted in class and class difference. The media have assimilated them all into popular culture and the market. At one time, sport was very much about a mixture of patriotism, masculinity and elements such as class and Christianity – the ethos of the 'healthy mind in the healthy body'. Here is the practice for teamwork, leadership and discipline. Sport has been changed by the rise of spectatorship (and the ability to charge for this). It has been transformed by the nurturing of its entertainment value. Only vestiges of the British imperial ethos remain in, for example, the continuing value of the hard and muscular body. Beynon (2002) comments on this, on bodybuilding, on the notion of empowerment (for the man) through the fit body which continues to be a dimension of sport.

Football became a popular leisure activity in the later part of the nineteenth century, when, along with other sports, it became defined as such, in the modern sense, through the imposition of rules – like the Queensbury rules that created boxing out of bare-knuckle fighting. This regulation of sport sprang out of middle-class impulses, as inspired within the education sphere and gave form to an ethos of 'playing the game'. Rules control performance and outcomes. They provide a shared understanding between players and spectators. They give a form to sports that makes them attractive to spectators, viable as entertainment and amenable to media coverage. At the same time (in the earlier twentieth century) literacy and the expansion of a popular press gave newspapers a new and more working-class audience – for football in particular. Cinema lacked the immediacy and domestic sphere of radio and then television, in the mid-twentieth century, though its newsreels did indeed report on sporting events. But still the genre of sport in news was well established through newspapers, and it is no accident that an early outside broadcast made on British television in 1937 was of the Derby horse race.

The representation and definition of sport has been stretched and redefined through the media, and through the influence of their cash and their technologies. The intensity and sudden death nature of one-day cricket was created to make a more exciting version of the game for TV. The medium has sanctified (and in some cases created) quasi-sports such as wrestling or those competitive action programmes typified by *Gladiators*. These quasi-sports cross the line into being explicitly entertainment vehicles. WWF (World Wrestling Foundation) wrestling is a fiction in which the outcome has been determined (the narrative closure). It is the getting to it that is fun. The extravagant grunts and throws, the illegal moves and the interventions from outside the ring are all part of a ritual and a spectacle. Brookes (2002) provides a useful commentary on WWF wrestling as a soap opera. He points out that most reports on sport define such wrestling as 'not sport' by not reporting it, and do this because it is perceived as parodying sport.

Part of the point of the wrestling bouts is, for example, that they break rules rather than enforcing them. They encourage undisciplined behaviour. But given the ritual surrounding all major sports (not to mention the occasional revelations of outcomes having been fixed), the line between pseudo sports and real ones can be pretty thin. In terms of achieving narrative closure – a kind of reassurance in a world of ambiguities – then, as Ellis (1999) says, 'sport promises that the events it shows will yield a definite ending'. Its representation provides a reassuring version of reality, compared with, say, the often indeterminate outcomes of political stories and events. He also points out the attractions and satisfactions of ways in which the replays and reflections on sporting events allow for a kind of 'working through' of what is going on, for the television audience.

Television's presentation of sport has become more and more dramatic, with commentators hyping elements of nationalism and competition, and with trails building audiences' anticipation of dramatic action (not to mention the now familiar action replay plus views of excited spectators).

The images of sport in the media are often about moments of emotional climax, about success, about implicit domination of an 'other', of the achievement of cultural status. They are of course also about competitiveness, about winning – and about others losing. They are, to a fair extent, about individualism within ideology – even team sports frequently report on the goal scorers, the victorious strikers, the man of the match. These images are about moments of victory, of celebration, of humiliation. 'Images of domination and subordination are central to the reading of the media sports text' (Rowe 1999).

In ideological terms, these image moments yield readings about sporting myths such as heroism, patriotism and the team. These myths are nurtured in school sports, but have their origins in that older version of sport which is about the gentleman and amateur. They come from a time when there was a closer correlation between sports and class, between the ethos of sport and the ethos of social behaviour. It is no accident that Kipling and others referred to the practice of international politics (and of spying) in the late nineteenth century as 'the great game'. In terms of the school analogy, it seems again significant that one will hear managers or captains of teams reflecting on games in terms of, '*the boys*' are doing a great job.

It is also ideological (and nostalgic) that a number of films about sport seek to emphasize notions of 'fair play', of (past) 'greatness'. They promote a mythical, even mystical idea of sport nurturing (masculine) virtues and cultural health. One thinks of films like *Chariots of Fire* (1981) or *Field of Dreams* (1989).

Stead (2008: 338–41) argues that sport 'talks up' qualities of power, aggression and competition. He proposes that the media represent sport in terms of nationalism, patriarchy, spectacle, and through dramatization and personalization – all of which stand for a very fair list of the qualities of media coverage of the 2008 Olympics.

3.1 Sport and media, globalization and commodification: the political economy

A large media sports audience is a very precious commodity indeed.

(Rowe 2000)

The media have transformed sport into a global mega-business in which the values of screen time, print space, sports stars, sports teams and their audiences are interrelated and have a serious cash dimension. In 2004 three-quarters of British adults watched or listened to live sport (Mintel 2005, cited in Houlihan 2008: 312). Brookes (2002) refers to one estimate which says that the global sports industry accounts for 3 per cent of world trade. Rowe (2004: 79) refers to ways in which sport has become a global business and underpins the finances of media when he says: 'the power of sports television to create and connect nations fragmented by space and time and social difference is shown to be its crowning economic advantage'.

The timing and conduct of sports events and contests has been adapted to suit the needs of television in particular. This is not least because television puts millions of pounds into sport by paying for rights to coverage. In 2000 BBC Sport cost an average of £102,000 per hour to produce, with an annual output of 1450 hours (Jarvie 2006: 44). 'The media transform sports consumption practices and also peoples' sense of geographical space' (Jarvie 2006: 42). 'Media sports culture is profoundly influenced by economic imperatives' (Rowe 2004: 66). The 'real' audience is the audience out there, not the audience in the stadium, and that audience can be enormous: FIFA (International Federation of Association Football) claimed to have attracted 28.8 billion viewers over 25 days for the 2002 Football World Cup.

The real paymasters are the advertisers and sponsors who buy the slots, buy space on the side of the indie car, supply the kit with their name on, place the advertising in the stadium – predominantly for the camera gaze of television. As Rowe (2004: 69) says, the media sports text became 'a commodity that could be produced, sold, exchanged and distributed'. Formula One racing sponsors pay their team up to $60 million a year (Robinson 2008). The value of UK sport sponsorship in 2005 was estimated as being $695 million (Mintel). Sponsorship is ubiquitous in that events, individuals, teams, competitions and locations can all be its subjects.

In 2001 the US sports economy was estimated to be worth $194 billion, mostly in terms of sales of sports product (mainly manufactured in the developing world) in the US and European markets (Horne 2006: 23). In 2002, the sports sponsorship market was valued at £450 million in Britain. In 2003, Vodafone spent approximately £7.45 million to sponsor the football club, Manchester United. In the same year the club had an income of £170 million, the same as the New York Yankees (*Independent on Sunday* 7 March 2004). Horne (2006) discusses details of the sponsorship of this football club at some length, pointing out that it received £9 million a year from its shirt sponsor. And lest one should be under any illusions about the real function of sponsorship, he also points out that the Inland Revenue taxes this activity as if it were advertising.

Boyle and Haynes (2000) identify other breathtaking figures for sponsorship deals when they refer to Nike's $200 million ten-year deal with the Brazilian national team in 1995, to the 45 companies that paid £300 million to be part of the 1998 Football World Cup in France and to Texaco paying £1 million a year to sponsor ITV coverage of Formula One motor racing. It was Nike again who paid out $90 million in 2006 for an exclusive contract with an 18-year-old basket ball player named Lebron James, gambling on his long-term success and use as a vehicle through which to promote their products (Jarvie 2006: 167).

> Television, more comprehensively than any other medium, has turned sport into an essential component of its organisational infrastructure and textual product, and has succeeded in transforming major sports events (and the remote viewers that they attract) into a pivotal commodity whose value can be realised and exploited in myriad ways.
>
> (Rowe 2000)

Television networks rely on sport not just for income, but also for credibility, to add value to their other 'properties'. Rowe (2004: 78) quotes Singer (1998) when he says: 'any viable network must have sport to help raise the profile of its other properties'. Where sport used to be a form of organized play, now it is a form of disciplined entertainment, a business, and something which is bought and sold in the marketplace. 'The formation of modern sport could be seen as an attempt both to *discipline* and *commodify* adult play' (Brookes 2002).

This commodification has gathered pace through developments in technology and through deregulation of ownership in Europe in particular, towards the end of the twentieth century. It could be argued that in Britain, for example, until the 1980s the duopoly of the BBC and the unofficial cartel of the ITV commercial companies meant that while they had an influence on the shape of sport, they also kept something of a lid on market value and costs. The situation in the USA was comparable, until the arrival of Fox TV as a fourth and aggressively competitive network, and then with the growth of specialist channels such as ESPN. Now, the proliferation of satellite and cable channels alongside new technologies has increased competition and the attraction of sport as a reliable and marketable product. In Britain, Sky satellite broadcasting (NewsCorp) has notoriously sought to top the bidding for rights to show major sports. Murdoch's company has also taken a direct stake in some of the teams on global display. In 2002 he had stakes in the British football teams Manchester United, Leeds United and Chelsea, as well as owning the Los Angeles Dodgers American football team. He owns 40 per cent of the New York Nicks and 40 per cent of Canadian TV SportNet channel. His own Fox SportsNet channel gets into 62 million US households via his ownership or control of 20 US regional TV cable channels (Miller et al. 2001). In terms of an economic model, this is close to vertical integration, where NewsCorp owns at least some of the sources of raw material, it owns the means of production, it owns the system of distribution. In 2004 Fox TV (NewsCorp) did a deal with the US National Football League for screening rights, for which it paid $712 million for the year (Robinson 2008: 308).

The dangers of this expensive relationship between new providers and sports bodies are, however, typified by the collapse of ITV Digital in 2002. The company paid too much for sports rights, mainly to football. The football clubs were asking for more than the market would bear. They operated on the basis of this projected income – not least in terms of buying and selling players. Now they have less money than they thought they would have, and one club (Leicester City) filed for bankruptcy. It was in the same year that the BBC refused to pay the fee demanded for World Cup screening rights, and Kirsch Media in Germany went bankrupt because it could not sell on the rights they had bought at a sufficient amount to recoup their costs. We are looking at a classic supply and demand model here. It was also in 2002 that Rowe (2004) refers to a $3 billion write-down in the value of US sports rights. Nevertheless networks will still pay out loss-leading sums for TV rights on sports because this raises their profile in public consciousness, and because the cultural capital this gives them enables them to raise advertising rates all round. 'Television coverage . . . has become the prime unit of currency in the cultural economy of sport' (Miller et al. 2001: 68).

In some ways English Premier League Football clubs are like Hollywood products. They have to carry the high cost of stars who form a collateral industry in their own right. They operate on the basis of pre-selling rights. In 1999 they each received about £8 million a season from broadcasting rights (compared with £0.5 million for the clubs in the championship: Horne 2006: 33). The game as core business is sold in different forms (news accounts, replays etc.). They incorporate product placement – the ball, boots etc. They have spin-offs – club magazines or replica kit or video clips for sale. Manchester United has its own branded toothpaste, as well as its own broadcast channel – MUTV Broadcasting. It is symptomatic of market thinking that the club appointed a former Disney executive as its commercial director in 2004 (*Guardian* 23 March 2003). British Premier League football clubs are businesses dealing in cultural as well as material commodities. Successful footballers can also become cultural commodities with a market value. David Beckham is probably the most famous example, where one could argue that he has almost transcended the game that gave him fame, as a world icon. His image sells many products, and is even plagiarized by look-alikes selling other goods, in a kind of postmodern ironic homage. In 2003 he earned £90,000 a week, and about £11 million in sponsorship deals. In 2008 Tiger Woods made $24 million from golf tour money, but an additional $110 million from sponsorship deals. In 2006 the tennis player Maria Sharapova earned around $20 million through her marketing activities.

This intensity of the commodification of sport operates in the context of globalization: 'transnational capital is commodifying and corporatizing sport' (Miller et al. 2001: 30). There are global agencies, such as IMG, that represent and promote stars across sports and across the world. There are global sports bodies managing and dealing on behalf of sports on a worldwide basis. These bodies are themselves big business. Brookes (2002) reports that FIFA (the governing body of world soccer) was estimated in 1998 to be worth $250 billion a year. The rights to the 2006 Football World Cup were sold by FIFA in 1996 for $1.2 billion (Real 1998: 18). In 2005 Adidas did a deal with FIFA for rights to all their football events between 2007 and 2014 – for $351 million – and that is just one company (L. Robinson 2008). In 2003, a 30-second slot in the nine-game baseball World Series cost approximately $325,000. This may be compared with the £250,000 per 30 seconds which ITV got in 1998 for the Football World Cup games in France (though it got only £150,000 per 30 seconds in the 2002 World Cup). In 2000, games played by the US National Basketball Association were seen on television in 206 countries via 128 networks, and in 28 languages (Miller et al. 2001: 64). Transnational companies negotiate with such bodies for major events that have a worldwide audience – most obviously examples like the Superbowl, the Olympics and Wimbledon. The US TV rights to the 2008 Olympics in Beijing were sold to NBC for $894 million; the Canadian rights cost $45 million; and the European Broadcasting Union paid $443 million (Horne 2006: 52). NBC has also bought the rights to the 2010/2012 Olympics for $2.2 billion. In such ways is sport not only globalized but also traduced in its presentation. It is difficult to keep sight of the Olympic ideals or sporting principles when so much money is at stake, and when competition is so pervasive. That is, competition for media rights, competition between clubs, competition between nations. 'Economic globalization is seen in arrangements for the production, exchange, distribution and consumption of sport' (Jarvie 2006: 97). We are talking about elements such as endorsements, trading of players, and prize money.

One example is Wimbledon, where the brand is sold for millions. Evian supplies the official bottled water. In 2007 350,000 pairs of branded Wimbledon sports shoes were sold in Japan. Slazenger supplies the Wimbledon balls. There is a deal with Blossom Hill for the wines. HSBC pays to be the official banker. There are licensing deals with 26 companies globally. Wimbledon Lawn Tennis Club has 34 shops in 14 cities in China. In 2008 there was a new Wimbledon superstore at the club (plus 14 other merchandising outlets at the site) where one could buy a range of branded goods, including a £200 Ralph Lauren sweater (*Guardian* 23 June 2008).

The rights to put logos on sportswear are sold; even sponsorship of the Olympics and the right to use the famous logo is sold. Miller et al. (2001: 4) take a gloomy view of the effects of the global commercialization of sport when they say 'the move towards a global sports complex is as much about commodification and alienation as it is to do with utopian internationalism'. This alienation is to do with the separation of global sport from national and local roots and culture. It is about the smothering of local-ness and amateurism: 'local sport has progressively given way to regulated professional competitions organized on national and international lines' (Miller et al. 2001: 60). They exemplify the global nature of sports economy by giving the example of some Canadian hockey gear – financed in Canada, designed in Sweden, made in Denmark, the USA and Japan, distributed across North America and Northern Europe. Global companies such as Kodak, Panasonic, Coca-Cola and Visa have dominated Olympic sponsorship since the late 1980s. Real (1998: 21) takes an acerbic view when he says that 'the post-modern Olympics have become a virtual circus of commodity values and fetishes'. Dunning (2002: 232) is also pessimistic about the globalization of sport when he says it has led to 'a diminishing of contrasts between countries as the personnel involved in the "media-sport production complex" have successfully marketed virtually identical sport forms, products and images around the world'.

This should remind us that what we understand sport to be is not contained just within the screening of sports events or within the sports pages of newspapers (though commodity elements are indeed clearly to be seen there). The social status of sport is represented when we see news pictures of sports stars invited to share space with senior politicians. Indeed, one might argue that it is, rather, the status of the politicians that is enhanced by images of such encounters. The cultural value of 'sporting-ness' is endorsed when we walk past stores devoted to these products. The window displays also represent sport. However, when talking of sporting goods, one might also remember that underbelly of the global economic scene, referred to by Horne (2006: 24): 'sports participants in the richer countries rely on the manufacturing, distribution and circulation of goods from a global sports industry whose key characteristics are sweatshops, high profit margins and exploitation of vulnerable groups of workers'.

The economic value of sport is represented when transfer fees or prize moneys are reported. The economic power of this material value was recognized when in 1998 the Monopolies and Mergers Commission blocked the agreed takeover of leading Premier League football club Manchester United by Sky Television. It would have been a logical outcome of mutual self-interest. The Commission also sought to protect the citizen from a monopoly of the presentation of sports events by one company. In this case the Commission was thinking of Sky Broadcasting and its bid to continue to control the screening of Premiership football as well as to dominate the showing of other sports such as rugby and cricket. The Commission created an A list of 'fully protected' sports, plus a B list, limiting the appearance of a monopoly market. As Alan Tomlinson (2001) says, 'Sport embodies the successful expansion and penetration of the universal market.'

It is pertinent to ask those political economy questions when making a critique of sport and its global commodification:

- How is sport organized and controlled, and to whose benefit?

- How does sport produce wealth and to whom does this wealth accrue?

- How is sport regulated, by who, and to whose benefit?

Global changes have transformed our concept of sport as a cultural form, as an activity, as spectatorship. Digital broadcasting has brought 'new' (minority) sports to new audiences, across national boundaries. The fan in the armchair outnumbers the fans at the grounds. Children overseas support clubs that play at grounds they are nowhere near and may never see. Houlihan (2008: 559) refers to a globalized sporting world that has become bigger than nations and nationality. Funding and regulation transcends national boundaries. There is intense international competition, and sport has become multinationalized. This means that when England were not playing in the European cup in 2008, still British fans were supporting European clubs, and following the progress of the competition with great fervour.

Westerbeek and Smith (2003) identify a number of key factors which explain the growth of sport in a global economy, now summarized with my gloss on their significance:

- The growth of leisure time and of affluence (i.e. more consumer spending power).

- The arrival of technologies (i.e. those which affect the practice of sport, such as carbon fibre rackets, or those which affect the media presentation of sport).

- Deregulation of media industries (which has stimulated a hunt for media content).

- The growth of global competition (which has stimulated bidding for screen rights, as well as the profile of sport in general).

- The growth of outsourcing to cheap manufacturing economies (which has provided cheap sporting goods and stimulated branding).

On the surface, sport is still represented as healthy competition, as a struggle between individuals or teams for sporting success and for being recognized as the best in the field. On the surface, it is about rankings and places. On the surface, it is about winning prizes.

Often these are visualized as symbolic – the cup or the plate – while the actual cash prize is not seen and is played down. On the surface, sport is about fair play, and a great fuss is made about the use of drugs as cheating. Much is made of the idea that in the arena and on the field, everyone is equal. In these respects the representation of sport and of sporting activity accords to a conservative and moralistic set of values, harking back to the nineteenth century. But in fact the financial and cultural pressures to win, to profit and to be famous are so great that these boundaries are breached. Football teams succeed in some proportion to their ability to purchase good players. Teams push the envelope of rules as far as they can – ice hockey, football, rugby – in terms of nobbling opponents and avoiding the gaze of the referee. Drugs are used in weight lifting, cycling, athletics and so on, and no one believes that the only users are the ones who are found out.

Economics, competitiveness and national identities all mean that the global sporting world is not an entirely equal one. It is expensive to seek out and nurture talent. The G8 countries gained 42 per cent of all medals at the Athens Olympics in 2004 (Houlihan 2008: 557). The league tables at the end of the Beijing Olympics in 2008 told a similar story of powerful nations exerting the most sporting clout.

The representation of sport as an economic activity and as a marketplace commodity is barely concealed. Cultural capital and financial capital come together in the sports company logo which is seen on the Olympic podium, and which is purchased from the shopping mall in order to be seen. Miller et al. (2001: 14) write about 'cultural industrialisation' in which sports, especially American sports such as basketball, baseball and American football, have been consciously developed as exports and money spinners. Even in 1990 6 million viewers in the UK watched the US Superbowl. In the cricket mad Indian subcontinent a similar phenomenon of cultural industrialization has led to a billion dollar cricket league. Twenty20 cricket has been a huge success in the Indian Premier League, with 250 million watching it on TV in 2008. The winners gained £1 million in prize money. The accompanying music and dance displays make the US Superbowl look a bit tame.

4 The sporting body

> bodies are socially constructed through a variety of discourses, such as medical, scientific and sports-related.
>
> (S. Thompson 2002: 119)

In one sense sport is represented by the body – that body which is so exercised and tested as to excel in a particular activity. It is usually a body in which musculature and other signs connote an exceptional body which is unlike that of the sport spectators and audience. And so the body sets the sportsperson apart.

Some sports such as swimming draw attention to the barely clothed body. We may see a collision of discourses in the case of female competitors in particular – fitness with sexuality. In all sports the specialized nature of clothing enhances signs of fitness. Lack of fitness undermines the legitimacy of the sport in the case of darts. It may also undermine the legitimacy of the sports person. One might think of the abuse suffered by the golfer, Colin Montgomery, in the year 2000, from course fans who commented insultingly on his being overweight.

Different bodies may be valued in different ways for different sports – and indeed by different audiences. One must be careful about too much generalization, including about the female athlete. Think of the high-achieving wheelchair-bound body of Paralympic athlete Dame Tanni Grey-Thompson or the Paralympic gold medals in 2008 for swimmer Ellie Simmonds. There is the concealed and high endurance body of the champion yachtswoman, Ellen MacArthur. There is the equally strong but necessarily more revealed body of the world class runner, Paula Radcliffe.

Maguire (1999) has defined various types of sporting body that are represented, and which provide a complex understanding of what sport is about. I offer these, with some interpretation of my own:

- There is the *biomedical body* of the world of the trainers, of weightlifters, of cartilage operations on footballers' knees, of calculations of leverage for pole-vaulters.
- There is the *disciplined body* of the athlete undergoing dietary and training regimes.
- There is the *commodified body* of the major league football player, that is sold for endorsements and sold between teams for vast sums.
- There is the *symbolic body* of Venus Williams, that has come to stand for women's tennis, for the success of black women, and which has iconic qualities in the braids and the beads.

These bodies coexist in the media environment and in the minds of audiences. The body has indeed become a controlled and competitive tool in a business called sport, compared with the more casual and amateurish body of the sportsman (usually) of the nineteenth and early twentieth centuries. Professionalism means that this body has an insurance value, a market value, a profit element. The idea of the controlled and managed body can also be seen to cross over into the leisure cultural sphere, perhaps because of those ubiquitous representations of fit sporting bodies. Running counter to current concerns about obesity in the population is that fact that gym membership and sports participation is higher than it has ever been. The managed body is in our cultural consciousness.

As Kay and Jeanes (2008: 149) say: 'masculinising and feminising practices associated with the body lie at the heart of the social construction of masculinity and femininity'.

The body is also a sexual and cultural commodity, displayed in media images – discussed further in terms of gender in the sections following. Examples such as Flo Joyner, Sharron Davies or Denise Lewis have been imaged both in the context of sporting competition and as female forms out of context, camera angled and cropped to attend to their sexuality. These female sports stars have also crossed over into the promotion of goods or have become TV celebrities, where once more their sexuality becomes a meaning of their images, as much as their sporting achievements. In 1999 the image of the American footballer, Brandi Chastain, was famously syndicated around the world when she stripped to her Nike sports bra in a shirt-removing victory gesture. In such cases it is, I suggest, important to use analytic tools such as semiotic analysis to be able to demonstrate that it is the text which inflects meaning towards the sexualized body. Alternatively, one has to consider how the spectator's gaze may impose sexual meaning on a sporting image. One may recognize that the still photograph of the sporting body allows it to be examined at leisure, that itself allows for a choice of sexual connotations.

Television has also taken to attracting female audiences through the sexualization of sportsmen. Their bodies have become the subject of magazine articles. Footballers such as

David Ginola have advertised coffee, via a film-star glamour pose. As Rowe (1999) says: 'Commodity logic and cultural politics have interacted.'

The exercised and toned sporting body becomes exotic and erotic, moving in the disciplined and ritualistic patterns relevant to a given sport.

5 Sport and national identity

> Sport, especially in the media, becomes deeply incorporated into people's sense of who they are and what other people are like.
>
> (Blain and Boyle 1998)

Sports events and sports people have come to represent national identities. These identities are understood in terms of certain sports, certain individuals. Baseball is seen as being quintessentially American, cricket as being very British. Muhammad Ali has been an icon of boxing and of the USA. Kenyans are 'known for' being good long-distance runners. National sports teams are constructed to represent the nation. Their success or failure, their 'uniforms', their use of national flags, their behaviours (see the New Zealand All Blacks pre-rugby match Maori war dance) come to stand for something called national identity. Indeed, it may be said that national identities have been to an extent invented through sport and its symbols. 'The nation constituted around its sporting representatives and communicated internally and externally by means of the media apparatus is the key cultural symbol linking media and sport at deep levels of human emotion' (Rowe 2000). Sport can be a unifying force and can create a sense of national identity in societies that have historical divisions; what football has done for Cameroon is a case in point.

There is a sense in which sport is invoked to construct an identity which represents 'the best of' a nation – a display of virtues and a denial of vices which helps the nation feel good about itself. This is what Alan Tomlinson (2001) means when he talks about 'sport as a moral site for the making of a national and sometimes regional identity'.

It could be argued that in so far as the images and the identity include black faces and female faces (see below), it also represents inclusiveness and a moral political correctness. The imaging of this kind of national identity may conflict with the absence of black and female faces in other spheres.

Sport as virtuous behaviour becomes acceptable as a means of competing, of dominating or subordinating. It is not war, even if it is reported in the metaphors and the discourse of war. But then, in the process of competition and seeking pre-eminence, identity coalesces around ideas of difference. The problem then arises that so often 'different' becomes an excuse for the assertion of 'better'. Fans fight on the football terraces because the assertion of club or team identity has become conflated with the need to assert superiority through any means. The outrageously chauvinistic reporting of the 1996 Football World Cup encounter between England and Germany in British tabloids drew on the language of the First and Second World Wars ('We have decided to teach the Hun a lesson' – quoted in Ferguson 1998). It implicitly proposed that a sporting contest was actually a physical conflict. It proposed that identity formation required humiliation of the other.

Beynon (2002) talks about 'Imperial man' as being invoked through international football contests in particular, and as a peculiarly British inheritance from the past which assumes superiority over others: 'It is in sport that the strongest echo of Imperial man survives. His sense of racial superiority and destiny has no place in multicultural, multi-ethnic, postcolonial Britain.'

Ferguson (1998) refers to the ideological work of this kind of representation of national identity. He refers to the notion that something called 'racial purity' is being invoked as part of this identity. This too is a strand drawn from Britain's imperial past – the construction of identity for Victorian England – an assumption of superiority and difference.

Brookes (2002) sees this invocation of the past as being not about superiority but about a malaise, ennui, a sense of loss and failure. This kind of narration by commentators expects the English cricket team to be beaten by former colonies: 'The decline of "our" sports teams mirrors the decline of a world order in which Britain was a major imperial power.'

National identity may become a kind of commodity, it can be argued, in that for example, one is selling US identity on the back of the distribution and promotion of games of basketball, baseball and American football, on a worldwide basis. This is the cultural imperialism thesis raising itself again. Sport becomes more than a matter of identity formation. It becomes identity marketing. It may be about promotion of ideology as much as the image of a sport or of a nation. For example, ideas about the symbolic importance of physical contact in sport, or of winning at all costs, are exported along with the TV rights and screenings.

The idea that sports stars or star teams come to represent 'the nation' is one which is now undermined by sporting practices. Ideological contradictions are exposed. Ironically, it is the process of commodification which has produced a situation in which star players may move from team to team on a global scale, selling their skills. These are not citizens moved to compete in promotion of a positive national identity, so much as players and entertainers seeking to maximize their worth in the global marketplace. Supported by a network of agents and marketers, the best sports people move where the money is (having regard for rules about national birth identity). Commercialization and professionalization of sport means that 'players' are sought out to stand for teams, cities, countries, as much as for individual excellence, achievement and even the good of the sport itself.

Yet the marketplace seeks to promote national identities in the cause of manufacturing loyal audiences. Where sport is conducted on a global scale, where the viewing audience is more important economically than the stadium audience, then the market wants there to be an imagined community of the nation 'out there'. National governments are also well aware of the cultural power of sport to bind a nation's identity, as well as of the economic power of sport – especially major sporting events – to generate wealth and employment. Miller et al. (2001: 25) report that the Australians spent AUD\$28 million on 'hospitality' for International Olympic Committee delegates in their efforts to secure the country as the location for the 2000 Summer Games.

Globalization has also produced some contradictions in audiences, however. Just as players may shift allegiances across national boundaries, so too at least some sections of national audiences may cross these boundaries. For example, in the 2002 Football World Cup played in Japan, there was substantial and active Japanese support for the British team.

National identity is partly an account and even a celebration of what the nation is meant to be. It is also an account of what it is not – again, of how it is different from other nations. There is a deal of stereotyping in here as well – that is the staple fare of representations. So sporting commentaries will refer to the methodical organization of the Germans and the passion of the Latin nationalities. Such national characteristics are historical inventions of our cultures – like the English bulldog. But they have always served the interests of groups that wish to move nations in certain directions – such as politicians at times of election, generals in times of war, and media organizations at times of sporting events. Brookes (2002) asserts that 'hegemonic representations define national identities in ways which reproduce dominant class, ethnic, regional, religious or gender interests'.

In this respect one may see the representation of national identity both drawing from and contributing to other representations and senses of identity. Brookes (2002) also sees sport as building some sort of bridge between everyday life as it is lived, and something more abstract – this sense of identity. Sport in the media helps make 'a psychological connection between the everyday life of the individual and the wider abstract category of the nation'.

Figure 9.2 Kevin Pietersen
The status of this gifted cricketer raises interesting questions about identity in a global sporting economy. He is South African by origin, but this was forgotten when he was promoted as a star England player. He has been an England hero and team captain, but got a rough ride from the press when the team didn't win matches and when he fell out with the cricketing establishment.

- How is it that some sports players have iconic status constructed for them by the media?
- Is the connection between sports players and national identity just an illusion in a global sports economy?

6 The representation of gender

> Sport remains one of the most problematically gender-defined and gender divided aspects of social life.
>
> (Shona Thompson 2002)

I have already questioned the extent to which it is textual producers or textual readers who impose gendered meanings on media texts, and on images in particular. On the other hand, one cannot dispute that sports representation of gender are skewed in various ways. Brookes (2002) refers to the fact that only 36 per cent of the athletes at the 1996 Atlanta Olympics were women. Only 11 of 51 NBC reporters were assigned to cover women's events, and most of the reporters were men anyway. He also comments that 'in general, coverage of women's sports routinely amounts to less than ten percent of the total available'. Kane and Greendorfer (1994) comment that 'women continue to be severely under-represented in the highly prestigious world of sport'. They also comment on research which showed that in 1991 only 5 per cent of US TV air time in sport was given to women's sports. Commentaries and media coverage tend to emphasize appearance and sportswomen's personal lives in a way that does not happen for the men.

The sexualization of sportswomen is perhaps not surprising given this kind of stereo-typical representation in our culture at large. Alan Tomlinson (2001) refers to the ways in which participation in sport in public places by women 'renders the body vulnerable to the gaze of others'. If visual representations of women have a long cultural history of assuming the male gaze, then it would not be surprising if at least some sports images are also constructed for that gaze. The reconstruction of sportswear as a fashion commodity by the clothing industries also invites the male gaze and sexually constructed images into the sphere of sport, because these two elements are staples of fashion photography. Beach volleyball is a particular example, where sexualization is reinforced by an official require-ment that female participants should wear briefs with sides no longer than 6 inches (Kay and Jeanes 2008: 142).

Rowe (1999) refers to various analyses of images of sports people which demonstrate that women are represented in more passive poses than men (60 per cent of one sample). He comments on an analysis of an Australian quasi-sporting magazine in which, when the theme was 'naked sports bodies', suddenly two-thirds of the pictures were of women! Again, this fits the dominant model of visual representation of females in other spheres. But Rowe (1999) also raises the question of whether it would be equally wrong to represent the sportswoman as rigorously athletic and simply to deny her sexuality. The line between representing a sexual dimension and soft pornographic representations is a difficult one to draw. What he does conclude is that 'sports photographs . . . are neither the innocent nor the "natural" products of value-free sport and sports culture'. Thompson (2002: 117) remarks that 'mediated sport has become a site where sexual differences are powerfully portrayed and guarded'.

The sportswoman is so often defined by contrast with the man. Margaret Ann Hall (1996) refers to work on representations within the America's Cup when she talks about images that 'naturalise the technological and sporting superiority of the man while at the same time marginalising, containing and incorporating visions of women'.

Too often, in commentaries and interviews, sportswomen are addressed in terms of appearance, or family relations, or their children or their partners, or even their relationship with their male coach. This is rarely the case for men. There is an assumed contradiction between feminine identity and being a serious athlete, which is not the case for men. Hall (1996) discusses the contradictions faced by female bodybuilders when they try to appear muscular and feminine at the same time. She points to examples where to be judged successful women would have to, for example, adopt feminine costumes. One could refer to the notorious example of Flo Joyner in the USA, who won three Olympic golds, but was reported and photographed more for her nails, hair and running clothes. When Jarvie (2006) comments on the popularity of surfing as a leisure activity for women he might have reflected on the reasons for this – one perhaps being that it does not involve putting the body on display; the body is concealed by wetsuit and water.

It would be unfair not to acknowledge that sportswomen and a female audience have been recognized and valued by the media in some respects. There is an increasing and sympathetic coverage given to sportswomen and female teams. There are more female reporters and writers than ever before in the media industries. One may see a newsreader such as Mishal Husain handing over to a sports presenter such as Mary Rhodes on BBC television news.

And yet the weight of resources, the amount of coverage, the nature of media images still works against women. The very language of sports coverage may be from the discourses of competition, violence and conflict, and favour a masculine, not a female, understanding of what sport is about. 'Sport expounds values that are conventionally prescribed in the rhetoric of war, industry, nationalism and ultimately masculinity' (Sabo and Runfola 1980). Women may be marked as different in taking on what are assumed to be men's sports. No one talks about 'men's cricket', 'men's football' or 'men's basketball'.

Brookes (2002) refers to features of this differentiation:

- *Sexualization:* for example the marketing of the Russian tennis player, Anna Kournikova.

- *Infantilization:* the use of the term 'girls' in discussion and commentary.

- *Trivialization:* the undervaluing of women's sporting achievements, or their representation as individual (and therefore rather exceptional) efforts: in this case one might think of Tim Henman's notorious endorsement of the inferior rewards for women in the Wimbledon Championships.

- *Familialization:* the invocation of sportswomen's private lives as a legitimate part of their representation: the assumption that one has a right to enter a more emotional sphere, as opposed to men.

Brookes (2002) comments on a tendency for women's sports to be valued for displays of grace or sexuality, on their selective coverage in the media. He refers to the 'ideological role of sport in maintaining unequal power relations between men and women'. Male sport encourages values of competitiveness, individualism, mate-ship, aggression and violence. Women are not valued, by men at least, for these qualities. As McKinnon (2003: 113) puts it: 'Not only does sport seem to marginalize women in the interests of men, it promotes a particular version of masculinity that is practically identical with the hegemonic'.

Women who appear to display real physical power make the commentators uneasy. Coverage of female shot putters – especially if they are from Eastern Europe – has made reference to their bulk and their masculine attributes. Coverage of female tennis players has sometimes seized on lesbianism as a way of explaining their 'unfeminine' strength, as a way of 'othering' them. Amelie Mauresmo, the French tennis player, received this treatment in 1999. Attitudes implied in the reporting of Venus and Serena Williams, dominant in women's world tennis, also allude to the exceptionality of their strength and stamina – as if this is unwomanly. Reporting of them has also revealed another gender framework, which is to talk about women's tennis rather more as if it is a soap opera. They are talked about in terms of conflict between them, or their relationship with their supposedly domineering father. Parents, boyfriends, coaches and emotional episodes (the vulnerable woman) are all the stuff of the reporting of women's tennis – but not of men's tennis.

And 'when it comes to sport playing a role in the construction of the nation it is almost always male sports teams that are seen as most important' (Brookes 2002). 'Men dominate and control sports structures, and sporting ideologies carry messages that connect masculinity, power and superiority' (S. Thompson 2002: 115).

Active masculine images and hard masculine bodies dominate the pages of newspapers. Games such as cricket, rugby and soccer are seen as 'naturally' masculine. The women's teams get little coverage. There is that underlying cliché that women form groups for social purposes, but men form groups to compete and to get things done. The coverage of sport on television reinforces a masculine bias and the dominance of male team sport activities. Men keep up with sport and the ongoing narration of how 'their' teams are doing. Indeed, one could argue that sports viewing is part of the 'life narrative' for many males. Gauntlett and Hill (1999) provide much evidence that sports viewing is seen as a male activity, and rejected by many women. So the act of viewing becomes an act of masculinity, just as the images and the style of coverage speaks of masculinity.

Sport with a masculine inflection permeates the press. It appears in lads' magazines such as *GQ* and *Loaded*. It is commonplace on television, not least in panel games such as *They Think It's All Over* and in quiz shows such as *A Question of Sport*. Such shows are dominated by males competing in the factual knowledge stakes, or fooling around.

Male representations in sport are still dominated by the ideal of the body as an 'athletic instrument'. It is a notion that promotes physical achievement and demotes a sexual function. It explains why the image reader is meant to take on those frequent pictures of sportsmen hugging each other in victory or goal scoring, without seeing it as contradicting male social behaviour out of the sports sphere. Indeed, that sphere is like a spiritual bubble that protects the male from criticism. In many ways the male has become a desexualized child. Footballers roll over on the ground when they have scored a goal, like gleeful children. They swagger and posture and square up to one another like competitive lads in rival gangs. Elsewhere, when the sporting male has become eroticized, the meaning is usually ring-fenced by the context – the adverts, the photospread, the pin-up in the magazine for females. It is interesting to read Rowe's (1999) account of the issues surrounding a successful libel case brought by Andrew Ettingshausen, an Australian rugby player. *HQ* magazine published a photograph of him naked in the sports showers in 1993, without his permission. This exposed the penis as a sign of sexuality and it was out of the arena of the sports event. There was no context protecting the concept of sporting masculinity. The body and male-ness was represented as that of a real person carrying out a conventional social activity. The person was not in athletic mode within the sphere of sporting activity.

Brookes (2002) discusses the hegemonic nature of masculinity (as opposed to femininity). He argues that there are various kinds of masculinity within society, and that sport defines only one of these, as well as interacting with the others. He quotes Connell (1995):

Because gender is a way of structuring social practice in general, not a special type of practice, it is unavoidably involved with other social structures. It is now common to say that gender 'intersects' – better, interacts – with race and class. We might add that it constantly interacts with nationality or position in the world order . . . to understand gender, then, we must constantly go beyond gender. The same applies in reverse. We cannot understand class, race or global inequality without constantly moving towards gender.

7 The representation of race

On the face of it, the media construct positive representations in terms of sport and race. Carl Lewis, Michael Jordan and Tiger Woods are rich men whose faces have been all over product endorsements as well as the sports pages. In Britain, black footballers are on the TV every week helping clubs in the top flight to win matches, including in Europe. Ian Wright had his own chat show on TV for a couple of series (1999–2001). And yet – where are the black sports commentators? Where are the black football managers? Where are the black coaches? (Though it must be acknowledged that Paul Ince was appointed manager of Blackburn Rovers in June 2008.) One does not wish to denigrate the achievements of individuals such as Lennox Lewis in the field of boxing. But – as well as the lack of Asian and oriental faces in Western sports media – there is a relative prevalence of black faces in at least some high-profile sports such as football, and a distinct lack of them in the media as a whole. In other words, the representation of ethnic minorities in sports media neither endorses their status in the sports industries, nor does it add up to a general media stand on social equality. 'There are clear dangers that the media's projection of attractive images of black athletes and concentration on their financial success imply a generalisable solution to the "race problem"' (Rowe 2000).

Some might argue that the very presence of black sportspersons in certain sports – especially in, say, football or basketball – is itself symptomatic of unresolved racism, not least where males are concerned. Critics such as Majors (2001) have commented on the notion that sport is a legitimate outlet for young black males, when other outlets for demonstrating masculinity and achievement are denied: 'contemporary black males often utilize sports as one means of masculine self-expression within an otherwise limited structure of opportunity' (Majors 2001: 209). He talks about the 'cool' factor where sport is concerned, even to the extent of its achievement being at the expense of education. Media representations reinforce the validity of this opportunity, and of the 'cool' factor.

Rowe (1999) has also pointed out that the use of black athletes to sell, for example, Nike commodities does not deal with the broader issues of social inequality and racial difference: it is 'the commodification and expropriation of their difference and resistance'.

Brookes (2002) is direct in his criticism: 'sport has played a fundamental role in the reproduction of unequal power relations . . . in reinforcing regressive stereotypes, particularly through conservative ideologies around "natural" difference'. He sees a contradiction between legal and cultural moves against sexism and racism in society, and the ways in which black people and women are actually represented in sports media and targeted as consumers. He is not proposing that all representations are equally negative, or indeed always negative. But he does point out the contrast between the positive representation of someone like Tiger Woods in the field of golf and the negative depiction of Mike Tyson in

Source: Richard Baker/Alamy
Figure 9.3 Sport and Ethnic Representations: Lewis Hamilton
In one sense, images of achievement in a public space provide positive role models for a black identity. In another sense – and in the context of general news reporting, where images of ethnic groups are far less common in respect of politics or business – images of the black sportsperson may place them in a 'sports ghetto'.

• Is ethnicity as a factor in reporting and representation only discussed with relation to some sports and not to others – Lewis Hamilton (above) and Formula One racing?

boxing. One is a role model (not flawed by scandal (December 2009) when Brookes made this argument), the other is a racial 'other'. But both conspire to conceal real poverty and racism underneath, as it affects black people and communities in the USA.

One might also point to the interesting contrast between the two sports in terms of image. Golf has the image of a 'civilized' middle-class sport in which one whacks a ball, not someone else's head. It is a competition played outdoors, by the affluent and captains of industry. Some golf clubs have a reputation for social exclusiveness. Boxing, on the other hand, is a high-contact working-class sport. It is a sport of physicality, half-naked bodies, of spectacle, of immediacy and the intense emotional involvement of spectators. It is more masculinized than golf, for all the existence of female boxers (as part of an exotic contest).

In spite of efforts to brand it as 'the noble art', it is a sport with high-profile cases of serious injury and death, and with publicized connections between some managers and criminal activity. In spite of the veneer of rules and the scoring of points, its clear objective is to cause some degree of physical harm to the opponent. I suggest that the representation of sport has as much to do with the nature of the competition and its status, as it has to do with competitors.

Some commentators have observed kinds of ambivalence towards black athletes and expressions of national identity. Jim Pines (2001) comments on the fact that black American athletes will wave and wear the American flag almost as a matter of course. But the same is not always true for British athletes and the Union flag, with its uncomfortable connotations of empire. More explicit are the occasions when black football players endure abusive barracking from the terraces. Pines (2001) refers to the 1998 Football World Cup when saying that: 'The overall emphasis in terms of media representation – or, if you like, in terms of public relations – stressed the recognition and acceptance of (ethnic) diversity and inclusiveness within the broader framework of national teams.' But then, as he goes on to say, apparently positive images of 'black English-ness' in sport remain 'an awkward construction' because they attempt to 'play down or elide unresolved discourses of British race relations and multiculturalism'. Nor should one regard this as simply a British problem. In 2008 the British Formula One racing driver Lewis Hamilton endured racist taunts from a Spanish crowd, apparently fuelled by his differences with his former McLaren Spanish team-mate Fernando Alonso, who also happens to be white. Here one can see that issues surrounding ethnic identities and national identity remain intertwined. Ferguson (1998), among many others, gives space to the notorious *Daily Mirror* coverage of the 1996 European football championship, in which anti-German sentiments were crude and rampant. As he says, whatever the backlash against the paper, the damage had been done. This is the power of negative representations.

Residual prejudices are confirmed. Racist representations in sport co-relate with racism elsewhere in the media. Images are intertextual. Meanings are mutually reinforced. 'All Germans had been confirmed, discursively, as sharing entirely negative characteristics, and the discursive reserve, carried in the memories of computers, editorials, readers and other members of the public, had been suitably replenished' (Ferguson 1998).

It seems that too often representations of sport and sports people do confirm negative characteristics, though one should also recognize more positive media celebrations of the success of such people as Paula Radcliffe, the British world class long-distance runner.

Again, in the 2008 world cricket series in Australia we have had a curious (and postcolonial?) episode where an Indian team was threatening to withdraw from play because of an accusation by a white umpire against one of their players of racial abuse against a black Australian player.

Clearly sport and its representations is an area where identities collide – national, ethnic, gendered; where discourses interact – the body standing for sexual distinction or sporting distinction; where cultural histories are renewed and revalued – past achievements by teams and individuals. Sport is not just the sum of its participants, but it is very much understood through them and how they are constructed by the media. It is relevant to a broader understanding of ideology and media that sports people are also, for instance, 'competitors'. They may stand for a degree of tension between the value placed on individualism and that placed on group commitment – a tension which we may read more widely into social institutions and social behaviours.

8 Discussion extract

Television has, indeed, become a principal leisure activity and source of information. Through it we gather our knowledge not only of our immediate world, but also of the complex global village in which we now live. It acts as a key socialisation agent and is integral to framing, determining and influencing our picture of reality. Our experience of sport is becoming increasingly constructed and ordered through television output.

Sport has become 'big business'. It is now a well-established global industry with international organising bodies, like the International Olympic Committee (IOC), eager to promote and structure further development. Sport, but not necessarily in all its forms, has something to sell. It has events, leagues, clubs, elite performers. Sport can make money but the costs involved, not least the large rewards paid to top performers in some sports and the capital and revenue expenses of increasingly spectacular sports stadiums, have left it with an insatiable appetite for more and more funding. The world of sport is a competitive one, in terms of not just which team tops the league or who wins the gold medal, but also which sports are able to attract the greatest financial resources. The relationship with media is central to the political economy of sport. Traditionally, it was the medium through which key information like schedules of events/matches, venues and times were transmitted to the public. Today, the media, primarily television, offer sport added attractions in terms of finance from broadcasting fees and exposure to advertisers, sponsors and a wider audience. Hence there is the all apparent readiness of sports organisations to get involved with the media. However, alongside the obvious benefits come possible costs to sport. To link with the media has meant sport losing a degree of control over its own activities and destiny. The promise of media attention and the wide-ranging spin-offs (in terms of increased profile, status and finance, greater numbers of participants and spectators and enhanced attractiveness to sponsors and advertisers) make such a loss of control something sport organisations appear willing to accept (Goldlust 1987). The ability to appreciate and deal with the full extent of the consequences of its partnership with the media is a major challenge confronting sport in the twenty-first century.

Stead, D. (2008) Sport and the Media, in B. Houlihan (ed.) *Sport and Society.* London: Sage.

1 What ideas about 'sport' does television represent to its audiences through various programmes such as news, documentaries and outside broadcast coverage of specific sports?

2 In what ways can one say that sport has lost some control over 'its activities and its destiny'?

3 What part do other media such as the Internet and the press play in the political economy of sport?

9 Further reading

Brookes, R. (2002) *Representing Sport.* London: Arnold.
Horne, J. (2006) *Sport in Consumer Culture.* Basingstoke: Palgrave Macmillan.

Houlihan, B. (ed.) (2008) *Sport and Society*. London: Sage.
Jarvie, G. (2006) *Sport, Culture and Society*. London: Routledge.
Maguire, J. (1999) *Global Sport: Identities, Societies, Civilisations*. Cambridge: Polity.
Maguire, J. and Young, K. (eds) (2002) *Theory, Sport and Society*. Oxford: Elsevier.
Miller, T., Lawrence, G., McKay, J. and Rowe, D. (2001) *Globalization and Sport*. London: Sage.
Rowe, D. (2004) *Sport, Culture and the Media*, 2nd edn. Buckingham: Open University Press.
Westerbeek, H. and Smith, A. (2003) *Sport Business in the Global Marketplace*. Basingstoke: Palgrave Macmillan.

10

Globalization and the media
Questions of power and of cultural exchange

Globalisation is restructuring the ways in which we live.

Giddens, A. (1999) *Runaway World*. London: Profile Books.

1 Introduction

Globalization is a contested concept which tries to make sense of a range of factors:

- the effects of technologies
- the extension of corporate power
- different kinds of cultural export and exchange
- the arrival of new media and the creation of new kinds of media texts for both local and transnational audiences.

The contestation produces utopian and dystopian models for understanding what is happening. For example, there are pessimistic views such as those of Schiller (2000) and cautiously optimistic views such as those of Giddens (1990). There is a contrast between a view of a media world dominated by the products of transnational businesses, and a view of media which facilitate information exchange and the creative interaction of cultures. 'The globalisation of capital also serves as a battering ram that relentlessly attacks working people's living standards' (Schiller 2000). Whereas Giddens (1990) says that 'globalisation . . . introduces new forms of world interdependence'. Giddens even argues that globalization is, in a positive sense, a sign of the declining grip of the West over the rest of the world, exemplified by phenomena such as the spread of the ubiquitous curry meal to the stream of immigration into the West.

Held (2000) discusses the contentious question of the condition of the nation state in the face of global forces. Some would suggest that the power of the nation state is being sidetracked by the global reach of capitalist commercial institutions (car manufacturers shifting production to their financial advantage). Others point to attempts to bolster state power (closing off access to dissident Internet sites). National identities are strengthened by global cultural events such as the Olympic Games. Nation states employ adaptive strategies in a global world – the use of European commissioners to act collectively for nations in a world trade situation. Held (2000) identifies three critical positions which describe views of what is happening with the nation state in a global world:

- globalism
- traditionalism
- transformationalism.

I would describe them through the examples given above, and as being about the superior power of globalization, or about the power of resistance by the state, or about adaptation and change.

This chapter will maintain a general focus on institution, text and audience. But you should note links with issues to do with the understanding of identity and cultural consumption. Media texts are produced and exchanged on a global scale. They continue to be cultural products. They continue to link with cultural practices. Media audiences are, as ever, simultaneously consumers of other cultural artefacts. In a social sense, they are practitioners, experimenters, generators of meaning and creators of culture. In this respect, globalization is not just about international politics or about kinds of media imperialism; it is about social practices, social institutions and about people's lives. This view would say that it is as much about the package holiday and the in-flight movie as it is about deals done with the global oil economy through OPEC. It is not just about money markets trading 24/7 or about global trade interdependency (the USA and China); it is about our food and drink (McDonald's and Coca-Cola), about patterns of migration, about global consumption of satellite TV, about the ubiquitous use of the cell phone, about the recognition of global icons (Nelson Mandela).

Moran (1998) suggests that 'social life is shaped by world wide mechanisms'. This is certainly true for a number of countries. But how social life is being shaped and with what consequences is not so clear. Moran (1998) also talks about national cultures, economies and borders as disappearing. I would dispute this. Certainly one can see some examples of ways in which diasporic communities are linked worldwide via global technologies and regardless of national boundaries. But equally, national regulation of the media persists as a way of marking borders. I would propose a dynamic model in which the relationship between the global, the regional, the national and the specifically local is in a creative state of flux – in terms of production, consumption and textual features.

Although examples of media communication such as the Internet and satellites have contributed to the much talked about contraction of time and space on a global scale, I would suggest that globalization is about much more than this. It is also something of an illusion. Swathes of the planet do not have television. Many countries have very limited access to telephones. Reporters going in to remote areas with videolinks and satellite phones do not make for a truly contracted global space. Instant global communication is the privilege of the wealthy. I would argue that globalization is an idea, a way of conceiving the world, as much as being a material phenomenon. There are, indeed, those people, cultures and businesses that think global. But they comprise those whose material practices and cultural histories have encouraged them to think this way – what is loosely called 'the developed world'. There are still many peoples who do not think in this way.

Another point of debate recognizes that globalization may not be an intentional process. The global extension of capitalist practices, is not something that has been explicitly plotted in the business boardroom. It is, rather, an unsurprising consequence of the following:

- The ideology of expansionism
- The need to attract more investment to pay for that expansion
- The continual feeding search for new markets
- The belief in meeting and eliminating economic competition
- The need to satisfy the unsatisfiable profit urge of shareholders.

The regional or global market is just an extension of the original local or national market. McQuail (2000) refers to 'the economic dynamics of global media markets that work blindly to shape the flows of media commodities' – dynamics which 'favour the free market model and in general promote capitalism'.

The American publisher Viking was not plotting to invade English culture when it took over Penguin books. It was seeking economic strength through acquisition. Amazon could not plan to be the pre-eminent online bookstore, in the sense that the technology that makes its business possible was not planned for commercial or social use in the first place. I am not saying that media businesses become globally powerful entirely by accident. But their intentions are not overtly political, social or cultural, even if these are some of the consequences of their existence. We are talking about opportunism and commercial impulses.

Of course, such comments place globalization within a dominantly economic context. And in this sense one would also comment on the selectiveness of economic globalization – the selection of certain audiences for certain media within certain countries or regions because they will make money. Latin America is attractive because 85 per cent of households have a television, and because many of the middle classes speak English.

One also has to recognize that there is something unintentional about other features of globalization. Holiday companies did not intend to create a global problem with the transmission of diseases from one part of the world to another. No one planned for media and their news operations to become information gatherers and million dollar fund raisers for disasters around the world – disasters which even 50 years ago ordinary people in the West would have hardly been aware of.

These last points remind us that, however one interprets globalization exactly, it operates at both a macro and micro level. It is not just some abstraction for economists or cultural critics. It is 'a transformation in the ways that we experience our everyday local lives as they are increasingly penetrated by distant global forces' (J. Tomlinson 1997).

2 Major questions

1   In what ways are the media part of globalization, especially with relation to technologies?

2   What are key features of globalization, especially as they relate to media of communication?

3   What is the substance of debates about imperialism, global flows and hybridization?

4   How may we understand the relationship between notions of the global and of the local, with relation to texts, media use and identities?

5   How meaningful are concepts of global ownership, global audiences and global culture?

3 Globalization as history

One needs to be aware that globalization, as we may now understand it, is not simply a product of late-twentieth-century technology and of modernity. The notion of exploration for new markets and of global trafficking in goods goes back to the endeavours of such institutions as the East India Company in the seventeenth century. Nowadays, the West brings back cheap DVD players, not spices. Politicking and shifting alliances between nation states in the eighteenth and nineteenth centuries, and the creation of empires, is a paradigm of shifting alliances and mergers between media corporations in the twentieth century. Again, the point is that these behaviours create ways of thinking global, of extending geography. Ideological bastions have fallen. The Berlin Wall fell. Chinese isolationism is melting. Consumerism is embraced. One way of looking at the history of globalization is to model it on the exploration of markets, the search for more consumers, the search for economies of production.

Our understanding of something called 'Japan' is one model for the historical dimensions of our understanding of this thing called 'globalization'. Japan has a geographical location because of exploration and maps of the nineteenth century. It has a political location because it was conquered by the USA in 1945, as part of Western alliances. It has a cultural location and identity because its cultural goods were brought back to the West – see the stir cause by Hokusai's woodcut *The Great Wave* (c. 1832) or by Kurosawa's film *Rashomon* (1950). It has an economic location because it embraced production-line Fordism, and in the 1960s began making the West its own market for motorcycles and cars.

The history of globalization is something that is still being made, so our understanding of it is shifting. Hamish McRae, in an article in the *Independent on Sunday* (27 April 2003), refers in economic terms to 'old' and 'new' globalization. He describes 'old globalization' as being about exporting goods and services (perhaps an old imperialism?). 'New globalization' is about local production based on foreign investment. This foreign investment happens within the developed world: it is not simply something which is done to the developing world. Either way, this kind of cross-border investment requires adjustment to local cultures and their values. Hamish McRae argues that this requires face-to-face contact – a global flow of people, as much as flows of trade and finance.

Giddens (1999) takes a bullish view of globalization when he talks about it challenging what he calls traditionalism. He takes a negative view of traditionalism when he says that fundamentalism is just an extreme manifestation of this. Indeed he argues that traditions are inventions (perhaps exemplified by the Victorian version of Christmas). Ironically, in a postmodern global world, there is more than an echo of twentieth-century modernist optimism for 'progress' in Giddens' views. The cultural power of local and regional traditions (the long lunch break in Mediterranean countries) is not to be trifled with, even by economic global forces.

4 Global flows: imposition or exchange, global and local

Debates about the nature and development of globalization tend to centre around alternative views. One is about the imposition of (media) cultures by the West on the rest of the world – as opposed to a model of free cultural exchange and mutual benefits. The other is about the inevitable rise of global powers and formations, to the detriment of local cultures and differences (the spread of English, for instance).

Accounts of the global flow of information and entertainment texts tend to emphasize the apparent breaching of national boundaries by examples such as 24-hour stock markets or Hollywood high-concept movies. But one needs to remember that there are many examples of texts that do not travel culturally; the British satirical chat-show performer Ali G was met by incomprehension in the USA in 2002. It is also the case that nation states continue to regulate media and protect their cultures by invoking all sorts of controls. All European countries operate some sort of protectionism. For example, France demands a 60 per cent 'local' quota for its television programming.

Moran (1998) raises some interesting points in a discussion of television formats and copyright. Formats are copyrighted and licensed to different countries – although the evidence of legal cases is that this copyright is not global (cases asserting global copyright have been lost). But he suggests that television 'owners' go along with the notion of global copyright because it is a convenience – 'a format is a cultural technology which governs the flow of program ideas across time and space'. It helps 'to organise and regulate the exchange of program ideas between media producers'. By the same token, TV ratings do not really tell one anything about audiences, but serve usefully as a 'mechanism of exchange between broadcasters and advertisers'.

the global	v	regional and local
one-way flow	v	exchange
cultural imperialism	v	hybridization
imposition	v	resistance
technology/domination	v	technical appropriation
global audiences	v	local audiences and identities
loss of identity	v	extension of the diaspora
copyright	v	piracy
genre standardization	v	local innovation

Figure 10.1 Globalization as a Set of Oppositions
In critical terms, one might also see an opposition between a pessimistic political economy analysis and an optimistic pluralist view of what is happening globally, in respect of media ownership, media products, media audiences, and the preservation of cultures.
(Graeme Burton 2004)

So one may say that a game show like *Wheel of Fortune* does represent a kind of media globalization; it turns up in various forms across many countries. But precisely because it is only the format that is licensed, because it is dubbed or adapted, then as a text it actually becomes 'nationalized'. So soaps or game shows may 'flow' around the planet to the benefit of media producers. But kinds of adaptation to local conditions represent a kind of cultural accommodation, rather than unalloyed cultural imperialism.

However, it should be recognized that some take a more pessimistic view of what is happening to national and local markets. For example, Frith (2000) comments on 'the increasing impossibility of a national (music) market the size of Britain sustaining the investment now needed to promote an act'. Steemers (2004: 4) points out that in spite of optimistic views of regional markets, 'the US still accounts for three quarters of the global trade in television by value'.

Much the same might be said about the British film industry. However, it has to be pointed out that Britain historically has an unusually close cultural and economic relationship with the USA, which renders it especially susceptible to kinds of US dominance. It also depends on how one chooses to define a given media industry and its audience. In the case of music, it is true that if one looks to a model in which acts are nurtured expensively and groomed for performance and profit on the international stage, then it takes the resources of a Sony Corporation to sustain investment. But if one chooses to look at British popular music at a local level, then clubs, pubs and even national venues are bursting with performance. There is independent production, and companies such as World Music Network are producing, distributing and bringing performers to Britain who had hardly been heard of in the late 1980s.

All this suggests that globalization produces simultaneous, different and even contradictory effects. There is global control of the production and flow of some kind of music – even homogenization. And yet alternative music cultures develop locally, and even tap into a global flow. 'Globalisation does not mean imposing homogenous solutions in a pluralistic world' (Das 2000). 'Globalisation and global cultural flows should not necessarily be understood in terms of a set of neat, linear determinations, but instead viewed as a series of overlapping, over-determined, complex and "chaotic" conditions' (Barker 1999).

Steemers (2004: 189) is not so optimistic with relation to television and the preservation of local cultural distinctiveness: 'As in America, the key to success seems to lie in suppressing the look and feel of programming that expresses national origins'.

Appadurai (2007: 225) proposes that homogeneity (sameness) and difference coexist in the pressure cooker of globalization: 'the central feature of global culture today is the politics of the mutual effect of sameness and difference to cannibalize one another and thus to proclaim their successful hijacking of the twin Enlightenment ideas of the triumphantly universal and the resiliently particular'.

There is an argument that market forces make global companies recognize and adapt to local media. Indeed Curran (2002) refers to the argument that, as global pressures erode national media, they actually promote something more local. There are those media which speak to, and for, a specifically Scottish or Basque identity and culture. It may also be said that global technologies enable local cultures to cross over, to create hybrid forms, to access new markets. The 1990s saw a surge of interest in Cuban music. In the same decade certain Australian soap operas took a firm hold on the British TV audience. From one point of view, we are back to a familiar argument about the media – determinism or pluralism? Do global media companies impose their production practices and products on local audiences – a one-way flow? Or are we seeing pluralistic globalization with cultural diversity, as practices, materials and ideas flow in many directions at once?

Sreberny (2000) would certainly think so, and rejects 'simplistic' imperialist models, without being happy either with the optimism of pluralists who see variety, diversity and choice in the global media landscape. She identifies four areas which she examines: media forms, media firms, media flows and media effects.

- *Media forms* are discussed in terms of wide-ranging technical developments but with the critical comment that global does not mean universal with regard to technical 'reach' across the planet.

- *Media firms* are discussed in terms of US company dominance, but with qualifications about the rapidly changing global scene, and about the true nature and extent of that dominance.

- *Media flows* are discussed in terms of examples like the extraordinary penetration of audio and video recording to remote places, but also in terms of the complex and varied picture at a local level; also in terms of corporations' relative lack of interest in the developing world, not least because of the problems with piracy. This is significant because it draws attention to control of product and of copyright as underpinning much of capitalism and media businesses in particular. Piracy is, even unintentionally, a form of resistance. Media do not want their products to flow into areas where there is no return – but they may be appropriated anyway.

- *Media effects* are discussed in terms of their ambiguity and unevenness, especially with relation to the developing world. There is evidence that global media affect leisure patterns and social lives, for instance, but not that they change beliefs. There are huge variations in consumption and assimilation because of factors such as illiteracy or the differences between urban and rural populations.

Sreberny (2000) discusses kinds of 'cultural bricolage', in which local audiences make selective and unexpected use of media and other cultural goods, rather than, for example, watching and making sense of television programmes in the way that a Western audience would. She argues that the exercise of global power, and the consumption of media goods and the effects of these, is complex. This is not to be understood in terms of comprehensive macro models of media imperialism or of audience resistance.

5 Facets of globalization

> The notion of globalisation is the assertion that a world-wide system of economic, cultural and political interdependence has come into being or is in the process of formation.
>
> (Moran 1998)

Here, I am concerned with various ways in which globalization is described and understood. Its dimensions, so far as they are agreed, go beyond the flow of media texts or the global influence of multinational corporations. Spybey (1996) talks about definitions in terms of 'polity, economy, communication and world order'. So the media context is one in which the following occur:

- Power is brokered on a global scale.
- The economies of nation states no longer stand alone.
- Information and indirect social contact is available instantly between technologically developed societies across the planet.
- The interdependence of economies and societies is conceived of and discussed on a global scale.

Whether this adds up to anything like an identifiable global society or global cultures is another matter.

Moran (1998) is very sceptical about this and points out that in terms of the accessibility of media texts (TV in particular) and uses of media technology, one is talking about only about one-third of the population of the planet, with a considerable bias towards the 'developed world'. In his view, the notion that there is some kind of internationalized economy does not add up to a global society, nor necessarily breaks down the nation state. What he does identify as both a feature of, and a context to, globalization is useful (my glosses in parentheses):

- New trading blocs (in which, for example, South-east Asia and South America become both important markets for and (to some extent) producers of goods – Globo TV in Brazil).

- Labour changes (in which, for example, production is outsourced to less developed countries – telephone call centres relocated to India).

- Mobility and tourism (in which the mobility of people around the world may be linked with cultural interactions and the mobility of media goods).

- Unemployment in the West (see outsourcing, the contraction of manufacturing, the growth of service industries and the growth of leisure industries, including media).

- New technologies (especially satellites, optic fibre cable and the Internet, which have enabled media convergence, digital systems and the global exchange of media texts).

Waters (1995) argues for broadly similar areas characterizing globalization as other commentators – economy, polity and culture. Behind these areas he posits kinds of exchange which work on different scales of geography. To summarize (with my glosses):

- Material exchanges localize (the exchange of material goods has to be about production on a local level, even if their distribution is global – labour is material).

- Political exchanges internationalize (the exchange of political views (diplomacy) constructs a web of international relations and geographies among nation states).

- Symbolic exchanges globalize (the exchange of symbols – whether this is a piece of written text or the Nike tick – works on a global level. It is not confined by political borders or by material constraints – media texts or financial dealings are symbolic goods).

Waters (1995) also defines globalization in social and geographical terms: 'a social process in which the constraints of geography and cultural arrangements recede and in which people become increasingly aware that they are receding'.

Here there is more than a touch of Marshall McLuhan's global village, and what one might call a populist view that globalization is all about the compression of time and space. This may be exemplified by the technologies of transport and electronic communication, which make it possible to reach the other side of the world in a day and to make contact with others in no time at all. However, you will see that throughout this chapter notions of what globalization is, let alone its causes and consequences, are more complex and questionable than the time/space model. Waters (1995) is as sceptical as others about the emergence of a genuine world society which threatens the nation state.

More interesting is his argument for four conditions that make globalization possible: individualization, internationalization, societalization and humanization. These conditions would seem to be very much about Western attitudes and development, and to some extent about modernity and materialism (again, my glosses):

- *Individualization* may be related to a belief in individual achievement and consumption (see the cult of celebrity in the media).

- *Internationalization* may be related to a politicized concept of the world as a network of alliances (see the view of the world expressed through news).

- *Societalization* may be related to the notion of something called 'society', which has global as much as national dimensions (see the directives of the European Union applying to a collection of member states; or see the assumptions behind international appeals for aid to the developing world).

- *Humanization* may be related to beliefs in human potential, in the individual, in achievement, in human morality and goodness, but apart from religion (see not only the content of media texts but also the very expansionism which is behind commercial and media global empires).

We are talking here about ways of modelling the world, of conceiving society, of constructing physical and cultural geographies, which make globalization possible, which influence how it has happened. One has to add in factors such as the notion of a market for goods, the assumptions with the kinds of rationalization that inform science and economics. Notions of science and economics are not shared by all cultures, though it may be true that they are being taken on board in some form. The example of younger generation Japanese is a good one in this case. They are embracing individualism and materialism (and even egalitarianism), whereas their grandparents thought more dominantly in terms of collectivism and kinds of spirituality.

Schirato and Webb (2003) argue that it is one thing to recognize global changes, another to be sure about what they mean. They point out that different views of globalization may see it as a source of problems of a solution to them. They are critical of what they see as general assertions offered by Beynon and Dunkerley (2000), saying that globalization may be understood in terms of the following:

- compression of time and space
- the spread of human rights
- democracy and intercultural understanding
- a new phase of Western capitalism
- US imperialism
- electronic imperialism
- disparities regarding control of and access to information
- the concentration of media production and distribution.

In a material sense, globalization is about the traffic of people and goods around the planet. It is about worldwide commercial alliances. It is about the interchange of information which enables global financial arrangements. One could be talking about media businesses and the distribution of media texts. In an immaterial sense, globalization is about that sense of the world which is generated through representations in people's heads. The words and images may be shared by different people in different countries. But, inevitably, a sense of what the world is will not be shared identically. So one can argue that globalization means different things to different audiences. Our sense of the world may seem real enough, supplied as it is by television in particular. News and documentaries seem to bring us in touch with a global dimension of places, peoples, political events and so on. But as Morley (1996b) comments: 'Television takes over from the real as the place where "real" things happen only if they are screened.' Here one might get into an argument which says that to some extent what we conceive of as globalization is just another media representation.

Appadurai (1993) posits a much quoted model of five connected and overlapping 'scapes' which describe global relations and processes. These are the mediascape, the financescape, the infoscape, the technoscape and the ethnoscape. Clearly these conceptions reinforce a general thinking about globalization in which technical innovations, information flow, finance, identities and media co-relate around the planet, albeit selectively, and with unpredictable consequences.

Held (2004) maps globalization in terms of economics, politics, the condition of the nation state and the slow internationalization of law. He points out that 'the richest 20% of the world population has 82.7% of the world's income, whereas the poorest 20% has 1.4% of that income'. He refers to the fact that 'the new economic order is increasingly integrated across space, real or virtual'. He observes that 'political events in one part of the world can rapidly acquire worldwide ramifications'. He asserts that 'the locus of effective political power is no longer simply that of national governments' (Held 2004: 35, 21, 73 and 89).

▌ 6 Globalization and technologies

> Among the deep drivers of globalization are changes in the global communications industries linked to the revolution in information technology.
>
> (Held 2004)

In talking about technology one needs to recognize the important role and effect of communicative media, and not be stuck in old mass-media models that emphasize entertainment and transmission. Indeed, the most significant technologies that underpin global exchange are to do with distribution, not content. It is cable and satellite that carries the material of telephone and the Web around the planet. One also needs to distinguish between those examples that are accessible to general populations, and those which are actually controlled by political, military or media elites. So you can access GPS positioning information to find out where you are on the planet, but you cannot use military channels to look into back gardens in Iran. You can pick up a telephone to talk around the world, but you are unlikely to have a satellite phone unless you are, for example, part of a TV news team.

It is also the case that talking about technology (or indeed anything) takes place through the prism of discourses. It is not just about facts, it is about how we understand what we think are facts. Technological change and development may well be interpreted through discourses of 'progress' or of 'freedom', for example. As a student, you need to be alert to the subversive effects of employing discourses. In some quarters global changes are linked to discourses of freedom and democracy, possibly underpinned by access to communications technologies. But one needs to examine what exactly democracy means, as well as perhaps to view critically the possible cultural disruption caused by the arrival of new technologies.

Control of the technology and understanding of globalization tends to be dominated by economic interpretations. One good example of this in Britain is the telephone. The core landline system was set up for national coverage as a public utility, though only those who could afford line rental would have had a phone. All the same, Britain achieved saturation coverage, and the phone became a medium of social exchange and family bonding, as much as a commercial tool. But the mobile phone is entirely controlled by commercial interests. It is not available to everyone; there are still many rural places where signals do not reach. It is a cultural commodity as much as a social tool. Certain models are coveted as are certain makes of trainers. It is being re-engineered as a kind of portable games machine, as a link with commercial providers of information. This is also an example of convergence – in commercial interests. Globalization of this technology is defined by economic forces.

An interesting starting point for considering the characteristics of global technologies is a model provided by Waters (1995), which is now summarized with my own examples:

- *Miniaturization:* the iPod portable music centre.
- *Personalization:* the handheld phone with picture messaging.
- *Integration:* the CD/DVD as a source for any example of audiovisual material, from films to 'encyclopedias'.
- *Diffusion:* satellite links or wireless to computer links.
- *Autonomization:* home recording studios or domestic computer editing programs for music and images.

I have somewhat skewed the examples towards a domestic sphere, to make the point that global innovations in technology are not all about linking cultures, privileging global flow from West to the rest, or perhaps helping manufacture something called 'global society'. Technology may spread globally but it can be used locally. Camcorders can be used to preserve and even promote local forms of dance or music. Regionalized television can carry advertising images, or it can carry images which reaffirm religious practices and convictions. Indeed some might argue that technology is not a determining factor in global change, but is generally part of greater social and cultural forces which ultimately determine how it is used.

There is a danger that one may become so 'excited' by the possibilities of technology, by visions of a harmonious world order, that one ignores the selectivity and limitations of such media technologies. Even in the West, domestic access to and familiar use of the Internet is by no means universal. The technology itself is not as reliable and user-friendly as commercial promoters would have us believe. So there are cultural divisions between elites that can afford the technology and its servicing, and those who cannot. Such divisions may be compounded by the nature of work. For some people it is in the interests of employers to supply technology and training; they may actually have access to global communication. Others never touch a keyboard, or need to talk to people in other countries. These divisions are magnified if one considers the world as a whole.

This technological elitism applies to other media – generally on grounds of cost, though there are also examples of regimes that control technology as a means of maintaining power (for example in Burma). There are still many households across the planet which do not own a telephone or a television (or running water for that matter). Technology has to be paid for, as well as make a profit for commercial enterprises, whether through purchase, installation or use. So in technological terms, the global map is selective, limited and drawn by political and commercial considerations. Indeed Curran (2002) comments that 'global regulation is heavily insulated from public influence'; in other words, it is pretty undemocratic.

At the same time, however selectively, one cannot deny that technology has made possible a huge expansion of media and communication markets. Deregulation and digitization in the West has caused an explosion in access to television in particular. The profits from new forms of distribution and new technological devices are huge. To make but one point – in 1989 there were fewer than 50 TV channels available in Europe, in 2004 there were over 1500 (Steemers 2004).

7 Institutions and global ownership

For media institutions, globalization means a global reach in terms of range of distribution, range of outlets, scope of the financial base, various audiences or consumers, range of products or texts, range of media owned, and the spread of the ownership or management base. To an extent, this global reach does mean more of the same, but on an international rather than a national scale. It does mean similar operations are spread out on a larger stage, and that cash flow works on a larger scale. Bigger sharks swim in larger oceans. The larger base and larger profits can mean more security in the face of competition.

The facts of global media ownership are indisputable. The significance of these facts is another matter. Clearly it raises issues of power – the power to manufacture and distribute representations on a global scale. There is the power to control certain views and understandings of the world through control of a few news agencies and news producers. There is the commodification of media goods. There is the categorization of media products. There is the setting up of global models for production and distribution that influence which films are made and how. And yet there is evidence against, as much as for, the homogenization of media texts. There are plenty of regional and local producers surviving. Audiences clearly prefer their own local cultural goods. And there is no evidence of a global and absolute control of meanings.

On the other hand, Held (2004) refers to a world of 'overlapping communities of fate', and to 'an expansion of global markets which has altered the political terrain', 'putting new questions about the regulation of national economies'. He clearly sees economics and the global market as a location of power and change, affecting societies and governments.

It is important to recognize that media institutions are merely some among others, on the global scale. In themselves they are often a part of corporations that have a complexity of material interests. They also coexist with, for instance, global mining corporations or car manufacturers. In particular, one needs to recognize the importance of global financial systems which make possible the conduct of any kind of global business. So, for example, General Electric owns Primestar satellite and various cable companies. Three of the largest publishers in the world are owned by Bertelsmann (Germany), Viacom (USA) and Time Warner (USA).

The multinational giant Time Warner is a model for economic determinants at work, which in turn raise questions about political influence and the effectiveness of regulation of media. The conglomerate has been driven by a need for profit and need to secure its position across media in the face of competition. It controls a range of products – books, comics, TV, films, music, video games, toys, TV news – and a range of distribution, through TV stations, Net portals, satellite channels (CNN), Home Box Office and Cinemax movie channels, the Cartoon Network, and other retail/exhibition networks, as well as the associated range of promotional companies that help secure it in the marketplace.

The expansion of global ownership was encouraged by widespread deregulation by Western governments in the 1990s. For example, the US Telecommunications Act 1996 removed even the existing power of the Federal Communications Commission (FCC) to regulate radio ownership. There is now no limit on the number of national stations that can be owned by one company. The guaranteed span of the licence period was extended for both radio and television. As Sterling (2000) reports, a maelstrom of mergers followed this Act, mostly involving the large telecommunications companies and radio stations. AT&T bought the largest cable operator, TCI. Viacom bought CBS and with it a major US TV and radio network, as well as a music label and advertising sites (it already owned Paramount Pictures, MTV, Blockbuster video and major cable and telecommunications interests). There was a notion to enhance public access to the so-called information highway. The price has been greater concentration of power in fewer hands. McChesney (2003: 29) describes how nine transnational majors emerged within the space of 15 years – General Electric (NBC), Liberty Media, Disney, Time Warner (formerly with AOL), Sony, NewsCorp, Viacom, Vivendi, Bertelsmann. Collectively they own the US film majors, the US TV networks, 80 per cent of the global music market, most global satellite broadcasting, much of cable broadcasting, chunks of European terrestrial television and a significant percentage of book and magazine publishing. McChesney (2003) points out that three-quarters of the global expenditure on advertising was taken by just 20 companies. German television, which is the second largest TV market in the world, is controlled by two companies – Kirch and Bertelsmann. The 'second tier' of 100 global media companies, also huge, is dominated by the USA and Europe. We have a 'neo-liberal global capitalist economy' (McChesney 2003: 31).

If there is some kind of *hegemony* of corporations and of their culture of consumption, it is on the back of concentration of control. But there is as much evidence of enriching cultural exchange as there is of cultural impoverishment. Small companies (e.g. Wrasse Records) survive to distribute world music on the back of new communications systems, in a way that was impossible even in the late 1980s. The BBC sells its 'classic dramas' across the world, and no one talks disparagingly about cultural imperialism in this case.

If there is an area of media in which one should be concerned about the predominance of one view of the world over another, it is in respect of news. It is worrying that a few news agencies – Reuters and Associated Press, for example – have come to determine what news is gathered from where, how it is structured, how it is available and at what price. Their only competitors are the big broadcasting networks. Military interventions, refugee aid, trading practices and so on, are all looked at from a Western perspective – put crudely, that what 'we' do and how 'we' do it is right.

The counter-argument is that technology allows cultural diffusion as much as cultural imperialism. John Tomlinson (1999) in *The Media Reader* argues against exaggeration of the cultural power of the West and refers to 'the myths of Western identity'. He concludes that 'the global future is much more radically open than the discourses of homogenisation and Westernisation suggest'.

Balance of income on intellectual property: royalties and licence fees, $ billion (1999)

US, UK, Sweden, Ireland, Russia, France, China, Italy, Australia, Netherlands, Germany, Spain, Japan, South Korea

Figure 10.2 The United States Dominates the Creative Industry
Culture translates into cash, as this chart shows. US royalty and licence income is disproportionately huge on a global scale.

(*The Independent* 2000)

8 Media (cultural) imperialism

Although this has been a dominant model for understanding the reach of global media institutions and their products from the 1970s onwards, it no longer constitutes an adequate single explanation for what is going on globally. Such imperialistic models, including those for culture generally (Dorfman and Mattelart 1975), tend to concentrate on consumption, and to miss production and the circulation of product. As fellow travellers in post-Marxism and inheritors of Adorno and Horkheimer, these models tend to assume that the text is a Trojan horse for the uncritical consumption of ideology.

I am not trying to bypass and ignore either effects or ideology, in some kind of postmodern sleight-of-hand. One may still argue for concern about the reach of global corporations and the possible effects of globally circulating texts. But such concerns have also to take account of audience theories, of context, of an increasingly complex flow of cultural products.

Herbert Schiller (2000), in referring to new technologies and 'new global alliances' talks about control of information, asserts that 'the world information order remains for the large part still America'. Still, one would have to say that assessment of the effects of control of information flow or of textual production also has to be evaluated in terms of the production of meaning – of understanding at the point of reception. It is not the quantity of material which the USA exports that counts, it is what the receiving cultures make of it, what they do with it in their heads.

Mackay (2000) uses Held's three categories of critical interpretation to expound different views of globalization and imperialism. In terms of globalism he refers to the point that 'the vast and intrusive presence of US cultural goods seems undeniable' (Mackay 2000: 63). He says that from this perspective, whatever global culture is, it does not draw in an even or uniform way on the global diversity of cultures. But then the traditionalist argument would be that one can see conservative forces in culture which support, for instance, home programming. Television and especially the press are both consumed dominantly as national product. Regulatory practices reinforce this 'traditionalism'. But then he speaks for the more optimistic views of the transformationalists, who would talk up the complexity of global flows, the fact that most nations are not culturally homogenous anyway, and the fact that these flows (and imports) interact to produce new forms of media text. And of course there is the question of how national and local audiences read imported texts anyway, perhaps reading against the grain of apparent ideological dominance.

David Rothkopf (2000) argues for cultural imperialism, though he does not see this as being entirely dominated by the US media owners. He points out that soap operas from Latin America do well in Russia. Nevertheless he also acknowledges US power. He sees the control of global markets by (media) corporations as a done deal. 'The global marketplace is being institutionalised through the creation of a series of multi-lateral entities that establish common rules for international commerce.'

Rothkopf (2000) makes a near moral argument for global imperialism, referring to cultural divisions which have fuelled war and genocide. Unfortunately, one cannot argue that an American-dominated economic world order would be benign, non-violent or capable of alleviating division on the planet. He may be confusing division with difference, and difference is something which many would wish to preserve and to praise in the context of world media. Once more, globalization of the media is something which is evolving, and monolithic imperialist models seem outdated. Rothkopf (2000) talks about CNN as being a prime source of news in the Middle East. But the beginning of the twenty-first century has seen the inception of Al-Jazeera television news, which is both Arab and pretty independent in its coverage. It became a prime source of news in the war on Iraq in 2003.

In trying to qualify the argument for US imperialism with regard to the media worldwide, I do not want to ignore imposing facts. Herman and McChesney (1999) quote a Disney executive as saying, 'The Disney strategy is to think global, act local.' Ownership and sales fit the strategy, even if one argues about what happens on the cultural ground.

In 2000 the audiovisual trade deficit of Europe with regard to the USA was worth $8.2 billion (Steemers 2004: 40). Also in 2000 US films accounted for 70 per cent of cinema admissions in Europe (Doyle 2002). In the music industry, Polygram, Time Warner, Disney, EMI and Bertelsmann account for 80 per cent of world sales. You will notice that the same names keep coming up. In the film industry, Disney, Time Warner, Viacom (Paramount), Seagram (Universal), Sony (Columbia), Polygram, MGM and News-Corp (Fox) dominate world markets in which non-US revenues represent 65 per cent of their income. Global media ownership is also fairly incestuous – Seagram/Universal owns 15 per cent of Time Warner. Global media ownership is a very big poker game in which entry costs keep out all but the richest players. NewsCorp was big enough to play the game in the USA, and, invoking the principle of synergy, has pieced together film, TV, cable and satellite interests (it owns DirecTV, Echostar and MCI, satellite and cable companies).

So there is a valid question about what space and influence is left either worldwide or locally for smaller companies. One may also ask whether anything like true competition is going to survive on the global media scale. Television news agency business is dominated by Reuters and Worldwide TV News. Advertising is dominated by WPP, Omnicom and Interpublic, who do more business outside the USA than in them.

Herman and McChesney (1999) also comment critically on US attitudes to what constitutes free world trade and legitimate national regulation and protection of culture industries: 'The US government aggressively insists upon a protection of intellectual property that provides maximum income to our industry, while displaying minimal interest in the concerns of anyone else.'

Media global commercialism has become marked by the synergy of mergers and associations between companies, and by the packaging of associated products for multiple audiences. Global consumption has become a five-course meal rather than a snack. In the case of Disney's 1996 ten-year deal with McDonald's worldwide (promoting jointly children's meals and Disney characters and products), we are talking literally about eating as well as cultural consumption. Disney business is not just about film. It owns or controls theme parks, PayTV and a US TV network (control of distribution). It produces soundtracks and TV series, and has controlling interests in relevant distributors. Spin-offs and tie-ins to films make big money. In 1994 Disney's *The Lion King* took $300 million at the box office, but it took $1 billion through spin-offs.

In so far as the imperialism thesis still stands up, one should recognize that it is about more than the commercial imposition of goods on the many by the few, and about more than the covert export of ideology. It covers ways of doing things which in themselves assume ways of thinking about a combination of social relations and commercial practices. Negus and Roman-Velazquez (2000) talk about 'the pressure to conform to a series of aesthetic and commercial agendas, working practices, production routines and working codes'. This is about the corporations imposing their ways of doing things at a local level. It is about their power to allocate resources. It is about the dynamics of volume, where for little extra cost the local producer or market yields a good return on an original investment.

In terms of the 'conventional' media imperialism thesis, McQuail (2000) provides a useful summary of four kinds of effects of globalization:

- Global media promote relations of dependency rather than economic growth.

- The imbalance in the flow of mass media content undermines cultural autonomy or holds back its development.

- The unequal relationship in the flow of news increases the relative global power of large and wealthy news-producing countries and hinders the growth of an appropriate national identity and self-image.

- Global media flows give rise to a state of cultural homogenization or synchronization, leading to a dominant form of culture that has no specific connection with real experience for most people (McQuail 2000).

But one should recognize that there is resistance to forms of imperialism, especially at the level of government and regulation within the nation state. France has a law insisting that at least 40 per cent of pop radio output has to be about French product. Saudi Arabia has banned satellite dishes – though whether this is about freedom of speech rather than freedom of consumption is another matter. If one looks at television schedules in any country, while it is evident that there is a lot of American product, prime time is still dominated by indigenous culture. Leading European TV channels import less than one-third of their programmes from elsewhere, including the USA. Politicians will support, through regulation if necessary, the cultural preferences of those who vote them into power. In any case, genres such as news, chat shows, game shows and sport are usually cheap to generate – at least as cheap as imported product. There is some evidence of critical readings of US product, perhaps of audience pleasures that were not intended by the producers (Liebes and Katz 1993). In this respect one has to beware of generalizing about the global nature of entertainment media, and to recognize that television in particular is rather different from the film industry.

The optimistic Giddens (1999) points to global variations in cultural consumption. There is the huge Latino audience in Los Angeles; the international and dominant Brazilian broadcaster Globo selling programmes to Portugal; the healthy independent hi tech companies and markets in India. One might also add the examples of Grupo Televisa in Mexico, or Zee TV in India, both multimedia broadcasters and international exporters. Giddens (1999: 13) argues that 'local nationalisms spring up as a response to globalising tendencies'. Held (2004) also provides a moderating argument against the thesis that globalization means Americanization. He points out that in 2003 US companies accounted for only one-fifth of world imports and one-quarter of total exports. He also argues that closed domestic markets are worse for consumers, and that overall there is no evidence that developing countries as a whole are losing out in world trade.

So the evidence is that things are not that simple. Certainly the 'developed' world tends to dominate this cultural export business, but it is evident that indigenous cultures do not 'die on their feet', even if they do change. The Japanese export variations on popular music back to the West, with their own slant on, say, punk rock. It does exemplify the fact that the Japanese young are not spending much time on reinforcing traditional and classic Japanese culture. Equally, forms such as Kabuki theatre have not simply disappeared, even if they have become a minority interest, and it may be said that new forms represent a kind of new cultural energy, which is no bad thing.

9 Global genres

In general, comments on media genres concentrate on film and television. They refer to forms such as the action thriller, soaps, news, sport and game shows. Within the imperialistic frame of understanding, much is made of the export of such generic programming, and of the ideologies that may be carried around the world within such texts. While it is true that particular generic material has been especially successful, and while it is interesting that certain genres seem to be popular for many cultures, it is still dangerous to generalize about the transmission of meaning.

One may learn something from looking at points made about the licensing and adaptation of media texts, in respect of TV in particular. Moran (1998) refers to format licensors such as Globo TV and the show *Você Decide!*, and to devisor or producers such as Endemol and the programme *Casualty* when arguing that global texts actually change to meet local cultural conditions. Game shows appear to be especially adaptable. *American Pop Idol* (2004) has spun off its British original, making a celebrity of the imported British judge (Simon Cowell). *Big Brother* – in which contestants are observed in a studio-created house, confined, and voted out by the audience – has versions in many countries, all with different emphases, on, for instance, the relationships between male and female and what is permitted to be shown on screen. The British presenter, Anne Robinson, has taken the game show *The Weakest Link* to the USA (2003) with some success, retaining an emphasis on humiliating the contestants. Once adapted, one may say that such shows reinforce national or local values and identities, not those of the culture of origin. The US syndicated version of the British docu-comedy TV show, *The Office* (2007), is a case in point. The fact that chat shows are common to many TV systems, generically speaking, does not demonstrate that they are part of a global culture.

Global genres do not sell equally well in all countries. For example, it has been impossible to create a successful French soap, let alone one which appeals across Europe. In terms of top-rated programmes in most countries, it is clear that home-grown productions predominate. Where programmes are syndicated, language matters a great deal – dominantly concerning countries which share the English language. But then one also returns to the problem of audience interpretation: a romantic drama does not have the same meaning in every culture. The material can be re-edited in different ways for export to take account of cultural sensibilities and interests.

Perhaps what is more interesting is the process of hybridization, in which generic materials interact and are adapted. There is Tarantino's *Kill Bill* (2003), in which the martial arts meet computer games, with postmodern irony. Japanese game shows have been notorious for an emphasis on physical challenge and suffering, with ritual humiliation. Only recently has the USA made something similar, in *Jackass*, in which painful, absurd and dangerous activities are highlighted – the kind of material that would make *The National Enquirer*.

Steemers (2004) uses the term 'glocalisation' to describe a process by which hybrid forms emerge, adapting to local cultures and preferences: 'glocalization implies the global production of the local and the localization of the global' (Steemers 2004: 17). The selling of programme formats is big business. The British independent TV production company Hat Trick earned £1.1 million from the sales of the programme format for *Have I Got News for You* to seven countries, over five years (Steemers 2004: 39).

Chadha and Kavoori (2005: 97) discuss the national domestication of global TV formats, which they see in positive terms. They talk for example about *Aaj Tak* news in India, and the adaptations that happened as it drew on the CNN/Headline news model. They refer to the programme breaking new ground in local cultural terms, and as a national success, using for instance informal Hindi as one aspect of its presentation. They talk about this and other programmes as transforming the originals into new and local cultural productions.

10 Global audiences

An audience perspective on globalization throws into relief arguments between views which alternatively privilege centralization or localization. On the one hand there are the global texts of multinationals – the latest *Star Wars* movie, or CNN news, or a syndicated TV series. But then different audiences in different locations will read the same material in different ways, mainly because of differing cultural and ideological contexts. To take one obvious example, the reading of a representation of a female body will be different in Muslim cultures from its reading in the USA. The reading may affect perceptions of the motivation, credibility or responsibility of the subject concerned.

Lash and Urry (1994) talk about a contradiction between centralized production and decentralized reception. But one could point out that, apart from the fact that global production is not as centralized as some political economy interpretations would have us believe, reception studies even within national boundaries have shown that audiences are not passive victims of some kind of media textual determinism.

Technology may be global, but there is little or no evidence of anything that one can describe as a global audience or even a global culture. As always, the coherence of audiences as groups melts away when one tries to examine characteristics closely.

There is nothing meaningfully coherent about those watching CNN news in Washington and Jedda at the same time. Indeed it is the differences in reception that are most significant. There are ways in which one may identify global communities, especially in terms of diasporic cultures. Indian families in Britain may watch ZeeTV via satellite or rent videos of Bollywood films, which to some extent link their cultural and media experience with that of communities in India itself. The Internet links religious communities across the world. But again we have to recognize that the context of the experience is different. The participants cannot share the same quality of meaning production that might be the case if they were all living in one place for some time, sharing the same cultural and social rituals. Even websites such as www.eelam.com for worldwide Tamil communities must exist in a tension between shared beliefs and experiences from Sri Lanka, and disparate new contexts and experiences for those logging on.

The fact that television notoriously spills over national boundaries, and may indeed have some effects on its viewers, does not mean that those viewers constitute a coherent group or community, let alone experience a commonality of reactions and effects. So once again what evidence we have is ambivalent. It suggests that even having a worldwide audience sharing the same texts is not the same thing as having a culturally integrated global audience.

Indeed one may return to the anti-globalization argument that national and regional audiences are resistant to texts from elsewhere precisely because of all the nuances of cultural difference. The use of non-verbal and display communication creates problems on a more or less subconscious level. But then there is the level of verbal language and meaning. Translation and dubbing can be difficult to 'accept'. Reading subtitles while hearing another language is also problematic, and this is without the fact that national governments can be resistant to imports on ideological grounds. They may see television as a tool of education and information.

11 Cultures and identities

A globalised culture admits a continuous flow of ideas, information, commitment, values and tastes, mediated through mobile individuals, symbolic tokens and electronic simulations.

(Waters 1995)

Globalization is also unavoidably about cultural interactions and both remaking and reaffirming identities. A positive take on globalization celebrates the hybrid music forms that appear in Brazil as hip hop or drum 'n' bass meets Latin, or the appearance of the telenovella as the form of TV soap is remade. There are simultaneous and apparently contradictory examples of globalization and localization. In north-east Spain both local media and cultural practices affirm more strongly than ever a separate Catalan identity. At the same time, the use of devices such as the ubiquitous mobile phone for social and business use also speaks of a Spanish and indeed a European identity.

There is a lot of truth in Waters' (1995) contention that 'consumption becomes the main form of self expression and the chief source of identity'. Commodification is global. Western corporations have effectively categorized the world as they see it into market areas. One may cite emblematic examples of commodity and identity such as a British TV ad for the Peugeot 205 car (2002–03). In this, one is supposed to be on the streets of an Indian city, where a young Indian guy physically batters and beats his old car into a semblance of the shape of the Peugeot. He wants to achieve cool-ness. He wants to own a cultural icon. It is a Western product. His sense of his culture and identity is very different from that of his grandfather, and yet middle-class Indian urban lifestyle does not simply clone that of Western urban centres. People who can drop in to the new global territory of cyberspace, learn to use the increasingly global language of English, but do not abruptly abandon beliefs and cultural practices.

Daniel Yon (2000), in a study of Canadian high school students and their sense of identity, is in the end quite positive about the influence of the global: 'Globalisation opens up other ways of belonging.' It may 'transcend the idea of an absolutist national identity and culture in favor of a set of experiences that connect them'.

The effects of globalization on cultures are, put simply, complicated and unpredictable. For example, outsourcing of production to the developing world, for media or other industries, may have unexpected effects in terms of gender identity. Just as the telephone exchange and the typewriter gave a non-domestic role to women in the West at the beginning of the twentieth century, so also female factory labour in Asia may be changing women's sense of identity and of their relationship to family and society. Ong (2000) in surveying research into labour in the developing world asserts that 'factory women come to explore new concepts of self, female status, and human worth'.

At the same time as globalization seems to be a threat to the nation state and national identities, there are plenty of examples of how the media are part of new assertions of such identities. Indeed one could say that notions such as British national identity do not actually exist without the media to give them reality. A classic example of this would be the British nation apparently united in mourning by the death of Princess Diana in 1997, but actually only really 'coming together' via television and the press.

Strange things may happen through global technologies such as the World Wide Web. Individuals may play with their online identities even as they join in virtual communities (not least because they are not seen). There are notorious examples discovered of participants changing their genders or their histories. Once more globalization is a process full of contradictions. It both develops communities and identities around the world and can also make them more ambiguous and fluid.

12 Discussion extract

The significant change in the ways in which the public sphere is constituted and functions is partly an effect of the proliferation of global media networks, and partly a simple case of the doxa of globalization and neoliberalism ensuring a 'retreat of the state' from its roles and responsibilities. Now, instead of the notion of public service, governments increasingly rely on the market-driven 'user pays' approach. This is generally articulated in terms of the government's role in promoting the free enterprise of individuals, and importance of capitalism in ensuring wealth and prosperity. It does, however, raise particular problems for the notion of the public sphere, and the public good. Even in a thoroughgoing capitalist system there have always been areas and objects that have not been reducible to market value: those things that are literally priceless, because they cannot be for sale (faith, personal identity, family love), and those things that are only obliquely related to the market (major art works, heritage objects, scientific research). As John Frow writes: 'The political sphere, the sphere of public service, that of art and of some kinds of writing may conform, or may be presumed to conform, to a different logic from that of strict profit maximization' (1997: 131).

But with the substitution of the media sphere for the public sphere we run into the problem of the divided loyalties of the media. On the one hand, and according to their own principles (which are usually articulated in a professional code of ethics), the media are committed to notions such as the truth, accuracy and freedom of speech, the public's right to know, unbiased reporting and independence. These principles supposedly inform all aspects of the journalist's work, including what should constitute news, how it is reported and gathered, and whose opinions are sought and authorized. But on the other hand, they are a business, operating under a model of capitalism that effectively advocates the rejection of the public good in favour of private enterprise. That is, alongside the establishment of the principles of journalistic ethics and practice is the increasing importance of the business of the news. The industrial model of journalism is a quick-turnaround model, a jump-on-the-bandwaggon model, one that relies on soundbites and media panics, and that glosses over alternative points of view in favour of the fashionable one (or the one run by all the other networks). It produces, Shah writes:

> journalism that describes events with little analysis, relies upon polls and statistics to show social trends but without providing historical context, and provides no vehicle of expression for ordinary people at the grass roots level. It is precisely the type of journalism that serves the interests of the owners of the global mass media firms because it avoids asking deeper questions about the exercise of power, the dispensation of social justice, and the prospects for cultural survival (Shah, 2000).

> Schirato, A. and Webb, J. (2003) *Understanding Globalization*. London: Sage.

1   What examples are there of British governments taking a market-driven approach rather than a public service one to the funding and organization of services for the public?

2   What may ideas about commodification have to say about the notion that there are 'things' which remain priceless and not for sale?

3   Do you agree that global media networks have, through the ways that they operate, undermined the ideal of public service and the operation of a public sphere?

4   Have these networks also created the market-driven news that the writers refer to, with the qualities that they describe?

▌ 13 Further reading

Barker, C. (1999) *Television, Globalisation and Cultural Identities*. Buckingham: Open University Press.

Beynon, J. and Dunkerley, D. (2000) *Globalisation: The Reader*. London: Athlone.

Held, D. (ed.) (2000) *A Globalising World: Culture, Economics, Politics*. London: Routledge/Open University.

Herman, E. and McChesney, R. (1999) Global media in the late 1990s, in H. Mackay and T. O'Sullivan (eds) *The Media Reader: Continuity and Transformation*. London: Sage/Open University.

Schirato, A. and Webb, J. (2003) *Understanding Globalisation*. London: Sage.

Glossary

Binary oppositions: appear in texts and in discourses (either implicitly or explicitly) as opposing sets of ideas, characters and plot elements. They are usually framed in terms of the positive and the negative: in effect, that which is approved by the dominant ideology, and that which is not.

Campaign: the organized use of adverts and publicity across media and over a period of time, for the purpose of promoting anything from goods to party political views.

Censorship: the suppression or rewriting of media material by those in power in order to deprive those in subordinate positions of any but a partial set of views which favour the powerful.

Classic realist text: describes the dominant form of narrative in our culture, in which a self-contained diegetic reality is constructed for and by the audience. This reality is bound up with character motivation, denouements at the end of the story, and an acceptance of a representation of time and space which does not match life experience.

Closure: identifies an aspect of popular narratives (classic realist text) in which at the end, problems are resolved, the story is closed off. One may distinguish between this kind of closure and ideological closure where what is shut down by the workings of dominant ideology is the possible range of understandings about the ideological significance of the text as narrative – for example, shutting down ways of understanding how masculinity is represented in a given text.

Code: a systematic combination of signs, bound by conventions or rules. Primary codes include those of speech, non-verbal communication and visual communication.

Cognitive dissonance: describes an inconsistency or disagreement between two things which we believe that we 'know' about the world. Dissonance creates anxiety. Advertising plays on this by inducing a dissonance between that which we know we do, and what we know we believe in (and therefore ought to do). The 'problem' can be resolved by for example, buying the insurance which helps secure our family.

Commodification: the process of creating commodities, of turning everything in our culture into a commodity with a price on it. That price may be more than the 'goods' can possibly be worth in factual terms. See **commodity fetishism**.

Commodities: goods, which may be more than material objects (see **Marxist models**). For example, women may be turned into commodities if they are objectified through visual representations, and then 'sold' to us in an advert. The woman becomes a cultural commodity.

Commodity fetishism: Marxists' views envisage an alienated society dominated by commodity fetishism – the turning of goods such as cars into fetish objects with special meaning (e.g. sexual power), for which we pay far beyond their real material value as objects for transporting people.

Connotation: in semiotics, connotation is the meaning(s) that exist beneath the surface of that which is obviously represented through words or images. Connotations are implicit as much as explicit. They are culturally specific and/or not universal as meanings. See also **denotation**.

Consensus: that 'middle ground' of values and beliefs which it is assumed exist within a society. It implies the virtue of compromise. By definition it marginalizes alternative values and beliefs. See Chapter 8 on News.

Consumption: refers to the process by which texts are decoded and used by people in everyday life, in material terms which suggest that texts (and mass culture) are commodities.

Conventions: permeate the operation, the construction and deconstruction of the various languages which we use. These conventions govern and help make sense of our social lives, the words that we speak, the media texts that we experience. In a popular sense the term is familiar as a way of describing rules for social behaviour. In a formal sense the word has been borrowed into semiotics to describe, for example, the rules underlying the combining of words in terms of what we know as syntax or grammar.

These conventions govern the workings of media languages. There is a kind of 'understanding' between media producers and their audiences which absolutely depends on 'knowing' what these rules are. They are rules which enable us to decode the body language of the performer in a drama. They are rules which enable us to categorize media material by genre, and so adjust our expectations of how it will develop. They are rules about the mode of realism on offer, and therefore how we are to understand material.

Denotation: a semiotic term which describes those signs and meanings which are on the surface of a text, e.g. an image of a cow refers to cows, in the first place. See also **connotation**.

Deregulation: refers to a process which, from the late 1980s onwards, has affected the ownership of media in the USA, Britain and Europe. This process has been marked by various pieces of government legislation which have had the effect of allowing more cross-media ownership and of encouraging more companies to join the media market. It is linked to the arrival of digital media and to changes in broadcasting, in particular. From different perspectives, it has either removed protection from national media, or helped them to compete in a global marketplace. This process has not removed regulations so much as changed them (reregulation).

Determinism/determinist models: in this area one would look at post-Marxist and political economy models. These would argue that there are determining forces at work on the media (essentially economic and market forces): the media then produce the texts influenced by these forces, which in this way go on to work on their audiences. Nevertheless, this position would not see audiences simply as victims of the media. It is a more pessimistic model which explicitly or otherwise retains the notion of ideology at work through the media. The determinist view might well see advertising as the Trojan horse of capitalism in the media sneaking in and endorsing a whole set of values to the advantage of the ideology of capitalism. Advertising is also the engine of media finance, appears as media text and is generally bound up with a dominant ideology. See also **technological determinism**.

Deviancy: identifies social groups (or representatives of these) as varying from norms of appearance, behaviour and attitudes. Deviancy may be glossed in terms which range from eccentricity to criminality. The representation of deviancy occurs through news as much as, say, drama. See also **norms**.

Diaspora: a term used to describe the cultural links and sense of identity that binds a group of people regardless of geographical and political boundaries – as with Jewish people.

Diegesis: describes that self-contained world of the text, whose existence and reality we tacitly agree to accept as, for instance, we watch the average feature film. Non-diegetic material is that which cannot exist in this reality, for example music which has no source in the world of a film.

Difference: a word used formally (and apart from its everyday use) to describe ways in which we fasten on what is dissimilar and contrasting about people and the groups that they belong to. How we are different contributes to your sense of identity. But a sense of difference also contributes to negative representations and stereotypes, and the way that we think about others.

Discourse: discourses are made apparent through particular uses of language to produce particular meanings. They are not peculiar to media. It could be said that myths are some of the meanings which they produce. It can be argued that media by their nature magnify and privilege certain discourses. This is another way of coming to the idea that media emphasize some ways of looking at the world and thinking about it, above others. One example of a discourse is the use of languages relating to babies. This refers not only to words but also to visual language – indeed, to all ways of communicating. The particular use of language is in the ways that we talk about babies. So, for example, words like 'sweet' and 'huggable' and even certain tones of voice are selectively used. The media, especially adverts, magnify such words through pictures which in their language emphasize meanings such as 'adorable', 'to be protected', even 'clean and pure' (which babies without bowel control certainly are not!). Discourses work together. So in the case of babies it can be interesting to see gender discourse in operation when male babies may be called 'a strong little chap' or female babies 'a sweet little thing' when there is no discernible difference other than in genital detail.

Dominant ideology: that kind of ideology, set of values, view of the world and view of power relations in society, which dominates within a given culture. It prevails over other possible views, indeed, makes them difficult (if not impossible) to conceive of.

Dynamic model: see **interactionist models/dynamic models**.

Ethnography: refers to kinds of audience research in which detailed studies are made on a small scale (such as that of the family). Such research may be carried out, for instance, in the family home, and through observations and directed conversations with respondents.

Feminist models: all feminist approaches to media and society pivot on an interest in how gender is represented through the media, in the connections between these representations and gender difference as it is lived in our society. But such approaches may be allied to different critical traditions. For example, a socialist feminist tradition would see gender inequality as a further evidence of ideology in action, of the oppression by the powerful of the powerless – in much the same way that Marx conceived of class oppression. Another strand draws on psychoanalysis, and critiques texts through Freudian or Lacanian readings, for example. In the first case, comment might be made about patriarchal dominance or about fear of female sexuality on the part of males – many Hollywood action films may be read in this way. In the second case, comment might be made about 'the mirror self', about women seeing themselves in media images as being looked at by men. This is about the subordination of women in society. Feminism would relate media representations to social practices, arguing that media narratives tell a story which often supports the idea of patriarchy.

Fourth Estate: a term stemming from the eighteenth century, when it was used by Edmund Burke to identify the new influence of journalists and the press (in addition to the political power of the Commons, the Lords and the bishops).

Frankfurt School: describes a group of intellectuals and critics of society and culture, who originally came together in Frankfurt in the 1930s. These include Walter Benjamin,

Theodor Adorno, Max Horkheimer and Herbert Marcuse, who re-evaluated Marxist critiques, and to some extent criticized what they saw as the negative consequences of the development of mass media culture.

Globalization: refers to a process by which cultural and economic forces have come to operate on global as much as national (or even continental) levels. It is also assumed to refer to the global extension of power of Western corporations and to the increasing homogeneity of product on a global scale. But (see Chapter 10) this interpretation can be questioned.

Hegemony: in the view of Antoni Gramsci hegemony (the invisible exercise of power) is achieved through coercion and consent. The state exercises coercion through various kinds of institution such as the army and the police – a certain kind of law and social order is enforced through the explicit use of material power. But consent is obtained through less obviously instrumental institutions, such as education or the media.

So we acquire a naturalized and dominant view of how things should be, but indirectly, through formal learning and through media consumption. Gramsci also broke with the earlier models by arguing that in fact there is a continuous struggle for the dominance of one set of ideas over another. It may not even be an equal struggle, but it is there. He also proposed that 'intellectuals' were especially important in the struggle because they generated the ideas which inform ideologies. The media are one site for that struggle.

Hermeneutic code: hermeneutics is about the theory and examination of the interpretation of texts. It assumes that texts have an essential meaning which may be discovered through interpretation, and which in that interpretation will reveal a certain view of the world. In Barthes's terms, the hermeneutic code is a structuring of narrative and meaning, which works to stop the text being interpreted in the range of ways that it might be. The code works to force interpretation in a particular way. See **preferred reading**.

Homogenization: describes a process by which the subject is made into a consistent whole. It is often applied to globalization and to that critical view which sees it as reducing media texts to a generalized set of characteristics (and genres), so reducing cultural distinctiveness.

Hyper-reality: refers to a kind of reality in which the simulation becomes the real thing. We, the audience, come to believe that what the media show us is the real thing. Commentators have referred to examples such as television news or the world of celebrity supplanting our sense of real life.

Identity: that sense of self-ness and belonging to a place and a history, belonging with certain others, which gives people a sense of 'who they are'. Identity comprises a mosaic of factors such as family background, sexual orientation and assumptions about personality traits. Identity is also about who we are not, about the dominance and subordination of certain social groups, and that process by which we may see ourselves or be seen as 'the other' (i.e. a subordinated group).

Ideological state apparatus: a phrase devised by Louis Althusser to help explain how institutions operate to promote the dominant ideology. Again, one may see the media as an example of such an apparatus. Education and the family would be other examples. If the media reproduce certain kinds of social relations, and if media consumers see themselves in those relations, then they also see the ideology behind those relations as being acceptable, and they go along with it.

Ideology: refers to that coherent set of beliefs and values which dominate in a society. This does not mean that everyone agrees with them. These are the beliefs of those who have economic, social and material power. Ideology is concerned with social and power relationships between different groups, and the means by which these are made apparent. Ideology is made evident through representations and discourses. Ideology becomes 'the truth' and 'common sense' through a process of naturalization. See also **naturalization**.

Interactionist models/dynamic models: this view of the relationship between media and society is one in which the two elements are seen as being in a dynamic and evolving relationship. It does not take on the deterministic approach of classic Marxism, in which something is done to large groups of people by economic forces or by institutions such as the media. Interactionism is interested in actions carried out by and conducted between people. It may be argued that these interactions give meanings and construct social relations.

Social interaction is a phrase commonly used to describe the complex dynamics of behaviours as between individuals and groups. It is just as clear that there is interactivity between media and media, between media and individual, between media and groups, between people after the media experience, and so on. Interactive or dynamic approaches, together with context, draw out the complexity of exploring influence.

Intertextuality: describes the ways in which texts may refer to one other, especially within genres and across genres. It is about the production of meaning in that we understand one text by being able to refer to another.

Liberal pluralism/liberal pluralist model: this view and this model argues for freedom of the press in particular (as well as other media) and assumes that a belief in freedom is somehow associated with degrees of morality. This position was developed into a further pluralist theory of social responsibility, in which the obligation of the press (media) to be responsible for its utterances and its effects was made explicit.

The principal democratic role of the media, according to the liberal theory, is to act as a check on the state. The media should monitor the full range of state activity, and fearlessly expose abuses of official authority. Only by anchoring the media to the free market, in this view, is it possible to ensure the media's complete independence from government.

(Curran 2000)

Macro and micro media perspectives: these stand for a general categorization of models (and critical views) of the media–society relationship into two kinds of critique. The one set takes a broad view of the relationship between media and society – macro perspectives. They may be interested in culture in general, as much as the media in particular. The other kind of critique – micro perspectives – may bear more directly on text and audience, for example, and be less direct in what they have to say about wider media–society connections. A general debate that is raised by most approaches to media is that which asks whether the media reflect or affect society. This question becomes sharp when, for instance, one is considering representations and the constructed views that these give us of social groups and social relationships.

Marxist models: broadly, Marxist approaches are characterized by a view of media and audience as collective and even coherent entities – mass media, mass audience. The classic Marxist view of the media–audience relationship is dominated by an assumption that the media do things to people. The media are part of capitalism and its interests, and inevitably promote views of the social elite – the ruling class – and promote the dominant ideology which serves to maintain the power of this elite. Capitalist ideology believes in the production and consumption of goods. Media programmes or magazines are examples of such goods. Goods may also be called commodities. Belief in materialism, in the importance of commodities, then affects the way that we value everything else in our lives. Even our social relationships could be valued in terms of these commodities. The process of defining social values and relationships in this way is called **commodification**. The energy which is behind capitalist media industries comes from the force of economic determinism – the behaviour of media institutions is determined by economic factors. The economic base of society is founded on the labour of workers. The media are run in the interests of the wealthy and of wealth creation, which remains the privilege of the few. The media may be seen as part of the Marxist superstructure of society, where ideology is at work. This ideology affects workers and their understanding of the exchange value of their labour and of the goods that they produce.

Marxist views have been much modified over the years, to explain for example why differences in power between social groups are evidently not set in concrete, and do change without revolution (see **hegemony**). They may be related to an argument that control over the means of production and distribution of goods leads to control over the ideas which are (in the case of media) within those goods. It is indisputable that control of media is concentrated in fewer and fewer hands (see Chapter 2). They produce ideas – through representations for instance – about status, power, class, which are made to seem true and valid when they are not. An unequal society is made to seem falsely, and yet naturally, acceptable. The manufacture of this false consciousness is part of the invisible exercise of power – or hegemony.

Mass culture: a phrase used critically (see **Frankfurt School**) to identify the size and number of media products and audiences, based on a system of mass production, controlled by large institutions. The term is used pejoratively, and with the implicit assumption that real art, high culture and individualized production are the opposite of this and are more valuable. Of course, the distinction and the valuation do not necessarily hold true.

Mediation: this is about that inevitable operation and result of media work – that it comes between us and real experience. Therefore, it is not real experience. It is indeed only a representation of that experience. So mediation is inevitable but not obvious. It is not obvious because media in a number of forms (outside broadcasts) pretend to bring us reality – social, material, even truthful. But they do not, not least because they cannot. So any examination of a media text has to work on the knowledge that it is only an artifice. Any consideration of media production has to start with the realization that it is also the process of making an artifice – some kind of illusion.

Mode of address: describes the 'voice' through which any media text addresses or talks to its audience. Most obviously, the audience is addressed not only through chat-show hosts or talk radio jocks, but also through other devices of style and engagement. The mode of address sets up a relationship between the text and the audience.

Modes of narrative: refers to the variety of narrative approaches that we may recognize, characterized by factors such as narrative structure (circular narrative) and authorial position (autobiography).

Modes of realism: refers to the variety of approaches to realism which are commonly recognized, along with their sets of conventions (for example, documentary).

Moral panic: describes a collective and anxious response to given social events, as represented through the news media, and so passed on to the audience. Such panics are usually temporary, and are unjustified in their scale of reaction to, for example, kinds of crime or youth behaviour.

Multinationals/multinationalism: describes business corporations (and the move towards their creation) which operate globally across national boundaries, and which dominate industries from mining to media.

Myth/mythologies: ideas about culture and society which are essentially untrue, which are ideological, and which are very influential in the ways that they cause us to make meanings from texts and to think about our worlds. In some ways myths are also kinds of wish-fulfilment – things that we would like to be true. They may also be ideas which do not really work in our interests, but in the interests of those with power – hence the notion that they are ideological. Examples are the myth that certain ethic groups are inherently superior to others, that science is always objective, that the best male is the strong, silent male.

Narrative: is about the representation of a structured reality which organizes place, events, characters, into a kind of order which makes it believable, and which gives rise to kinds of understanding and meaning about the world. It is what we refer to as 'the story', but is, for instance, about far more than just the plot. We make narratives through our engagement with media texts: they do not pre-exist, even though we are prone to believe that narratives exist independently of the teller, the telling and the audience (see also Chapter 2).

Narrowcasting: describes specialized media output for niche audiences (usually with reference to broadcast media).

Naturalization: refers to a process by which certain kinds of meaning are made to seem natural and common sense and true, even though they are not. Ideological positions are accepted because they are naturalized. Discourses incorporate naturalized meanings. The very idea of 'common sense' is itself a discourse, and so has become naturalized into some kind of benchmark for the validity of beliefs and values.

Norms: those kinds of social behaviour and belief which are understood to be 'normal' within a society, and so are held to be acceptable. What counts as 'normal' will differ over time, and from one group to another. See also **deviancy**.

Paradigm: out of semiotics, this term describes our understanding of sets of signs as belonging together – the alphabet. Conventions organize such signs into a code – rules of spelling.

Pluralism/pluralist models: the optimism of the pluralist model extends to the notion of a variety of institutions producing a variety of products for a variety of audiences. In some cases a market model is invoked which is essentially self-regulating. In other cases it is accepted that the intervention of some regulation is needed to maintain this pluralism. In any case, the media provide opportunities to obtain information and to enjoy leisure. Pluralism would suggest that the media serve us by providing a variety of information and entertainment which represents a variety of points of view.

Political economy models: the political economy model is one which is concerned with ways in which the media exercise power over the society of which they are a part, and with the regulation and sources of that power. When applied to media, it is a view which (as with Marxism) proposes economic determinism in some form. It argues that the power and interests of the media corporations work against the interests of their audiences. This power is enhanced by global concentration of control of media. Consequently choice diminishes: 'One can think about political economy as the study of the social relations, particularly the power relations, that mutually constitute the production, distribution and consumption of resources' (Mosco 1996).

Murdock and Golding (2000) identify three core tasks of political economy in practice:

- To examine the production of meaning as an exercise of power by institutions.

- To approach textual analysis in terms of how institutions/production structure the discourses which inhabit texts (as opposed to looking at texts in isolation).

- To deal with ideas about consumption in terms of a debate between sovereignty or struggle. This is in effect to look at the impact on audiences of institutions and their operations; at how far audiences have any power in this relationship. It is to contest culturalist views of audience autonomy in dealing with texts.

Political economy perspectives: see **political economy models**.

Polysemy: literally means 'many signs', and refers to that quality of visual texts in particular, in which the image is packed with a variety of signs, and so with a range of meanings. It links with the fact that visual texts may be more complex and less specific in their meanings than are written texts.

Popular culture: commonly used to refer to a culture 'of the people', and often conflated with mass culture. It becomes problematic when one questions how 'popular' is defined in terms of something being generally attractive to an audience, and how 'the people' are defined when one has such a variety of audiences within society.

Postmodernism: this is concerned with the text (and not only media texts). It takes a positive view of the active audience having control of the text, and of the making of meanings. It is absorbed with form, fascinated by irony and it is squarely interested in popular culture, in one camp or the other – for example, John Fiske (1989) writing about jeans, or Barbara Creed (2002) writing about cyberstars in film. It is characterized by a reaction against modernist interests in structures, in the big picture, in effects analysis. The view taken is that any possible relationship between media and society as a whole is so complex in its range of variables that nothing meaningful can be said about it. What relationships there are, work on a tighter level. The text and the audience are predominant. Postmodernism rejects teleology, or certainties about how society works – there are no absolute truths or meta-narratives (or overarching explanations about how society operates).

Preferred reading: this is that reading of or meaning to a text which is the dominant one. It is preferred because the text is so encoded through its conventions that this meaning is chosen by the audience above others. It is the meaning which the producer or encoder of the text would prefer the reader or audience to take from that text.

Reception studies: this kind of audience study examines the relationship between particular texts and specific audiences. These approaches also concentrate on the idea of context: the environment in which the reading of the text takes place. This environment – physical and cultural – may affect how a text is read or used. The emergence of interest in audience studies in the 1980s and in the idea of the active audience, naturally led to interest in the context in which the audience may read, watch and listen.

Regulation: refers to those mechanisms, formal or informal, legal or economic or political, through media production and output is controlled and constrained. It defines how media may (as much as may not) operate.

Representation: refers to a process through which the media bring us constructions; manufacture versions of events, people and experiences. The nature of these constructions is predicated on beliefs and values – ideological positions. Representations – of different social groups, for example – are by definition untruthful, though not necessarily lacking any truth at all. Manufacturing representations is what media do. Critical interest is in how this happens, what is produced, how it may affect the conceptions of the audience.

Semiotics/semiotic analysis: this is about the study and analysis of signs. The assumption is that all forms of communication are composed of signs. The purpose of the analysis is to identify signs, to consider possible meanings, to consider how those meanings are generated and how some meanings may be privileged above others.

Sign: in general, anything may be a sign if society agrees that it has a meaning. Specifically, semiotics tends to talk about signs which compose languages. Signs do not have any particular meanings attached to them (though it is often wrongly assumed that they do). Signs stand for something else. In this sense one might say that they are the raw material of representations, in that they help construct that 'something else', and suggest ideas about it. Signs may be iconic (look directly like what they suggest), or indexical (refer indirectly to what they suggest, as smoke refers to fire), or symbolic (are not direct at all, as in the case of writing). See also **signification**, **signified** and **signifier**.

Signification: refers to that process through which meaning is generated by the use of signs.

Signified: the part of 'sign' which identifies a meaning. It is that meaning or mental concept to which the sign refers. All signs have many possible meanings, according to other signs used around them, among other factors. The interesting question is why some meanings are selected when we make sense of signs, and others are ignored.

Signifier: part of the concept of 'sign' which identifies the fact that it has potential meaning – in a context. The signifier makes a word or a flick of the eyebrow active. We know from acquiring language that someone raising an eyebrow at us means something. We do not immediately know what it means – recognition, scepticism and so on.

Sociolinguistics: the study of language use in relation to social interaction.

Structuralism: this has a great deal to do with semiotic analysis in particular. Verbal and visual texts are understood as sets of signs organized according to conventions or rules. These signs, ranging from the spoken word to the camera shot, are combined to produce meanings shared between the producer and the audience. To this extent it might be said that the text is the interface between the institutional producers and the audience. Key debates revolve around how far meanings may be embedded in the text by producers so that texts can only be read one way, and how far the ambiguity of signs, especially in visual media, actually allows the audiences to make alternative or even oppositional readings to the one which is apparently to be preferred above all others.

Structuralist principles extend to narrative analysis, and ideas that there are organizing principles behind any 'story' in any medium. So, the notion of the classic realist text proposes that all conventional stories take the protagonist through difficulties which have to be overcome, until all is resolved at the end and order is restored. Discourse analysis is also structuralist to an extent: a discourse, or dominant set of meanings about the given subject, may be recognized through sets of oppositions – for example, opposing themes, or characters or sets of beliefs or even symbols. These oppositions – the negative and the positive – make clear in this 'either/or' structure what it is that we should approve or disapprove of – what it ideologically acceptable or not.

Syntagm: in semiotic terms, this is a string of signs within a code which add up to a recognizable small unit of meaning – a phrase in verbal language, or a sequence in film television codes (and narratives).

Technological determinism: describes that belief that technology determines certain kinds of development, possible social, but usually understood in terms of what shapes the growth of media.

Transmission models: these see meanings as being something which are sent out through media of communication, from institutions of the media. This simplistic notion of broadcasting messages as packages finds little favour in critical circles nowadays.

Writerly and readerly texts: phrases used by Barthes (1972) to identify the relative accessibility of meanings in texts. The former are those examples where the reader has to work on the signs of the texts to make sense of the writer's intentions (because they may not be so easy to understand). The latter are easy to understand for the reader (for example, genres) because the use of 'language' is unambiguous and familiar.

References

Adorno, T. (1991) *The Culture Industry*. London: Routledge.

Adorno, T. and Horkheimer, M. (1973) *The Dialectic of Enlightenment*. London: Allen Lane.

Alasuutari, P. (ed.) (1999) *Rethinking the Media Audience*. London: Sage.

Allan, S. (1997) News and the Public Sphere, in M. Bromley and T. O'Malley (eds) *A Journalism Reader*. London: Routledge.

Allan, S. (1999) *News Culture*. Buckingham: Open University Press.

Allan, S. (2004) *News Culture*, 2nd edn. Maidenhead: Open University Press.

Allen, M. (1998) From Bwana Devil to Batman Forever: Technology in Contemporary Hollywood Cinema, in S. Neale and M. Smith (eds) *Contemporary Hollywood Cinema*. London: Routledge.

Althusser, L. (1969) *For Marx*. Oxford: Blackwell Verso.

Althusser, L. (1971) *Lenin, Philosophy and Other Essays*. London: New Left Books.

Andersen, R. (1995) *Consumer Culture and Television Programming*. Oxford: Westview.

Ang, I. (1991) *Desperately Seeking the Audience*. London: Routledge.

Appadurai, A. (1993) Disjunction and Difference in the Global Cultural Economy, in P. Williams and L. Chrisman (eds) *Colonial Discourse and Post-Colonial Theory*. London: Harvester Wheatsheaf.

Appadurai, A. (2007) Disjunction and Difference in the Global Economy, in S. During, *The Cultural Studies Reader*, 3rd edn. Abingdon: Routledge.

Atton, C. (2002) *Alternative Media*. London: Sage.

Bakardjieva, M. (2005) *Internet Society: The Internet in Everyday Life*. London: Sage.

Bakhtin, M. (1968) *Rabelais and his World*. Cambridge, MA: MIT Press.

Bandura, A. (1973) *Aggression: A Social Learning Analysis*. Englewood Cliffs, NJ: Prentice-Hall.

Bandura, A., Ross, D. and Ross, S.A. (1963) Imitation of Film-Mediated Aggressive Models. *Journal of Abnormal and Social Psychology*, 67(6): 601, 607, reprinted in J. Bryant and D. Zillmann (eds) (1994) *Media Effects: Advances in Theory and Research*. Hillsdale, NJ: Lawrence Erlbaum.

Barker, C. (1999) *Television, Globalization and Cultural Identities*. Buckingham: Open University Press.

Barker, M. and Petley, J. (eds) (2001) *Ill Effects*, 2nd edn. London: Routledge.

Barnard, S. (2000) *Studying Radio*. London: Arnold.

Barsam, R. (1974) *Non Fiction Film*. London: Allen & Unwin.

Barthes, R. (1973) *Mythologies* (trans. A. Lavers). London: Granada.

Barthes, R. (1977) *Image, Music, Text* (trans. S. Heath). London: Fontana.

Baudrillard, J. (1988) *Selected Writings* (ed. M. Poster). Cambridge: Polity.

Baudrillard, J. (1995) *The Gulf War Did Not Take Place*. Bloomington, IN: Indiana University Press.

Bayton, M. (1997) Women and the Electric Guitar, in S. Whiteley (ed.) *Sexing the Groove: Popular Music and Gender*. London: Routledge.

BBC Trust (2007) *From Seesaw to Wagon Wheel: Safeguarding Impartiality in the 21st Century*. London: BBC Trust.

Bennett, A. (2001) *Cultures of Popular Music*. Buckingham: Open University Press.

Bennett, A., Shank, B. and Toynbee, J. (eds) (2006) *The Popular Music Studies Reader*. Abingdon: Routledge.

Berger, J. (1972) *Ways of Seeing*. London: BBC.

Beynon, J. (2002) *Masculinities and Culture*. Buckingham: Open University Press.

Beynon, J. and Dunkerley, D. (2000) *Globalisation: The Reader*. London: Athlone.

Bignell, J. (2002) *Media Semiotics*, 2nd edn. Manchester: Manchester University Press.

Bignell, J. (2004) *An Introduction to Television Studies*, 2nd edn. Abingdon: Routledge.

Bird, S.E. and Dardenne, R.W. (1997) Myth, Chronicle and Story: Exploring the Narrative Qualities of News, in D. Berkowitz (ed.) *The Social Meanings of News*. London: Sage.

Blain, N. and Boyle, R. (1998) Sport as Real Life: Media Sport and Culture, in A. Briggs and P. Cobley, *The Media: An Introduction*. Harlow: Addison Wesley Longman.

Bolter, J. and Grusin, R. (2000) *Remediation: Understanding New Media*. Cambridge, MA: MIT Press.

Bordwell, D. (1988) *Narrative in the Fiction Film*. London: Routledge.

Born, G. and Hesmondhalgh, D. (eds) (2003) *Western Music and its Others*. London: University of California Press.

Bourdieu, P. (1984) *Distinction*. Cambridge, MA: Harvard University Press.

Boyd-Barrett, O. and Rantanen, T. (eds) (1998) *The Globalisation of News*. London: Sage.

Boyle, K. (2005) *Media and Violence*. London: Sage.

Boyle, R. and Haynes, R. (2000) *Power Play: Sport, the Media, and Popular Culture*. Harlow: Pearson Education.

Brackett, D. (2002) Musical Meaning: Genres, Categories and Crossover, in D. Hesmondhalgh and K. Negus (eds) *Popular Music Studies*. London: Arnold.

Brierley, S. (1995) *The Advertising Handbook*. London: Routledge.

Briggs, A. and Cobley, P. (eds) (2002) *The Media: An Introduction*, 2nd edn. Harlow: Addison Wesley Longman.

Bromley, M. and O'Malley, T. (eds) (1997) *A Journalism Reader*. London: Routledge.

Brooker, W. and Jermyn, D. (eds) (2003) *The Audience Studies Reader*. London: Routledge.

Brookes, R. (2002) *Representing Sport*. London: Arnold.

Brookes, R. and Holbrook, B. (1998) Mad Cows and Englishmen, in C. Carter, G. Branston and S. Allan (eds) *News, Gender and Power*. London: Routledge.

Brown, M.E. (1990) *Television and Women's Culture: The Politics of the Popular*. London: Sage.

Buckingham, D. (2000) *After the Death of Childhood: Growing Up in the Age of Electronic Media*. Cambridge: Polity.

Buckingham, D. (2003) *Media Education: Literacy, Learning and Contemporary Culture*. Cambridge: Polity.

Buckingham, D., Davies, H., Jones, K. and Kelley, P. (1999) *Children's Television in Britain*. London: British Film Institute.

Burns, T. (1977) *The BBC: Public Institution and Private World*. London: Macmillan.

Burton, G. (1999) *Media and Popular Culture*. London: Hodder & Stoughton.

Burton, G. (2000) *Talking Television: An Introduction to Television Studies*. London: Arnold.

Burton, G. (2002) *More Than Meets the Eye: An Introduction to Media Studies*, 3rd edn. London: Arnold.

Burton, G. and Dimbleby, R. (2006) *Between Ourselves: An Introduction to Interpersonal Communication*, 3rd edn. London: Hodder Arnold.

Byron, T. (2008) *Safer Children in a Digital World: Report of the Byron Review*. London: Department for Children, Schools and Families and Department for Culture, Media and Sport.

Cappella, J. and Jamieson, H. (1997) *Spiral of Cynicism, the Press and the Public Good*, 2nd edn. Oxford: Oxford University Press.

Carter, C. and Weaver, C.K. (2003) *Violence and the Media*. Buckingham: Open University Press.

Castells, M. (1997) *The Power of Identity: The Information Age: Economy, Society and Culture* (vol. 2). Oxford: Blackwell.

Castells, M. (2002) *The Internet Galaxy*. Oxford: Oxford University Press.

Chadha, K. and Kavoori, A. (2005) Globalization and National Media Systems, in J. Curran and M. Gurevitch (eds) *Mass Media and Society*, 4th edn. London: Arnold.

Chomsky, N. (1989) *Necessary Illusions*. London: Pluto Press.

Cohen, S. (1973) *Folk Devils and Moral Panics*. London: Paladin.

Cohen, S. (1991) *Rock Culture in Liverpool*. Oxford: Clarendon Press.

Cohen, S. and Young, J. (eds) (1973) *The Manufacture of News*. London: Constable.

Congdon, T. (1995) The Multimedia Revolution and the Open Society, in T. Congdon, A. Graham, D. Green and B. Robinson, *The Cross Media Revolution: Ownership and Control*. London: John Libbey.

Connell, R. (1995) *Masculinities*. Cambridge: Polity.

Corner, J. (1996) *The Art of Record*. Manchester: Manchester University Press.

Corner, J. and Pels, D. (eds) (2003) *Media and the Restyling of Politics*. London: Sage.

Cornford, J. and Robins, K. (1999) New Media, in J. Stokes and A. Reading (eds) *The Media in Britain: Current Debates and Developments*. London: Macmillan.

Cottle, S. (ed.) (2003) *Media Organisation and Production*. London: Sage.

Creed, B. (2002) The Cyberstar, Digital Pleasures and the End of the Unconscious, in G. Turner (ed.) *The Film Cultures Reader*. London: Routledge.

Cronin, A.M. (2000) *Advertising and Consumer Citizenship*. London: Routledge.

Croteau, D. and Hoynes, W. (1997) *Media Society: Industry, Images, and Audience*. London: Pine Forge Press/Sage.

Cullen, R. (2001) Addressing the Digital Divide, *Online Information Review*, 25(5), in E. Devereux (2003) *Understanding the Media*. London: Sage.

Cumberbatch, G. (1989) *The Portrayal of Violence in BBC Television*. London: BBC.

Cumberbatch, G. and Howitt, D. (1989) *A Measure of Uncertainty: The Effects of the Mass Media*. London: John Libbey.

Curran, J. (1996) The New Revisionism in Mass Communication Research: A Reappraisal, in J. Curran, D. Morley and V. Walkerdine (eds) *Cultural Studies and Communications*. London: Arnold.

Curran, J. (2000) Rethinking Media and Democracy, in J. Curran and M. Gurevitch (eds) *Mass Media and Society*, 3rd edn. London: Arnold.

Curran, J. (2002) *Media and Power*. London: Routledge.

Curran, J. (2006) Cultural Theory and Market Liberalism, in J. Curran and D. Morley (eds) *Media and Cultural Theory*. London: Routledge.

Curran, J. and Gurevitch, M. (eds) (1996) *Mass Media and Society*, 2nd edn. London: Arnold.

Curran, J. and Gurevitch, M. (eds) (2000) *Mass Media and Society*, 3rd edn. London: Arnold.

Curran, J. and Gurevitch, M. (eds) (2005) *Mass Media and Society*, 4th edn. London: Arnold.

Curran, J. and Seaton, J. (1997) *Power Without Responsibility: The Press and Broadcasting in Britain*, 5th edn. London: Routledge.

Curran, J., Gurevitch, M. and Wollacott, J. (eds) (1977) *Mass Communication and Society*. London: Arnold.

Curran, J., Morley, D. and Walkerdine, V. (eds) (1996) *Cultural Studies and Communications*. London: Arnold.

Danesi, M. (2006) *Brands*. Abingdon: Routledge.

Das, D. (2000) Local Memoirs of a Global Manager, in P. O'Meara, H.D. Mehlinger and M. Krain (eds) *Globalisation and the Challenges of a New Century*. Bloomington, IN: Indiana University Press.

Davies, N. (2008) *Flat Earth News*. London: Chatto & Windus.

Davis, A. (2007) *The Mediation of Power: A Critical Introduction*. Abingdon: Routledge.

Deacon, D., Pickering, R., Golding, P. and Murdock, G. (1999) *Researching Communications*. London: Arnold.

Department for Culture, Media and Sport (DCMS) (2001) *Creative Industries Mapping Document*. London: DCMS, available at www.culture.gov.uk/reference_library/publications/4632.aspx

Department of National Heritage (1994) *The Future of the BBC: Serving the Nation, Competing World-wide*. London: HMSO.

Devereux, E. (2003) *Understanding the Media*. London: Sage.

Dickinson, R., Harindranath, R. and Linne, O. (eds) (1998) *Approaches to Audiences: A Reader*. London: Arnold.

Dorfman, A. and Mattelart, A. (1975) *How to Read Donald Duck: Imperialist Ideology in the Disney Comic*. New York: International General.

Dougary, G. (1994) *The Executive Tart and Other Myths*. London: Virago.

Doyle, G. (2002) *Understanding Media Economics*. London: Sage.

Du Gay, P. (ed.) (1997) *Production of Culture/Cultures of Production*. London: Sage.

Du Gay, P., Hall, S., Janes, L., Mackay, H. and Negus, K. (1997) *Doing Cultural Studies*. London: Sage.

Dunning, E. (2002) Figurational Contributions to the Sociological Study of Sport, in J. Maguire and K. Young (eds) *Theory, Sport and Society*. Oxford: Elsevier.

During, S. (2005) *Cultural Studies: A Critical Introduction*. London: Routledge.

Ellis, J. (1992) *Visible Fictions*. London: Routledge.

Ellis, J. (1999) Television as Working Through, in J. Gripsrud (ed.) *Television and Common Knowledge*. London: Routledge.

El-Nawawy, M. and Iskandar, A. (2002) *Al-Jazeera*. Cambridge, MA: Westview.

Ewen, S. (1977) *Captains of Consciousness*. New York: McGraw-Hill.

Ewen, S. (1988) *All Consuming Images: The Politics of Style in Contemporary Culture*. New York: Basic Books.

Fairclough, N. and Wodak, R. (1997) Critical Discourse Analysis, in T. Dijk (ed.) *Discourse as Social Interaction*. London: Sage.

Falk, P. (1996) The Benetton-Toscani Effect, in M. Nava, A. Blake, I. MacRury and B. Richards (eds) *Buy this Book: Studies in Advertising and Consumption*. London: Routledge.

Ferguson, R. (1998) *Representing Race*. London: Arnold.

Feshback, S. and Singer, R. (1971) *Television and Aggression: An Experimental Field Study*. San Francisco, CA: Jossey-Bass.

Feuer, J. (1992) Genre Study and Television, in R. Allen (ed.) *Channels of Discourse Reassembled*. London: Routledge.

Feuer, J. (1995) Narrative Form in American Network Television, in O. Boyd-Barrett and C. Newbold (eds) *Approaches to Media: A Reader*. London: Arnold.

Fiske, J. (1987) *Television Culture*. London: Methuen.

Fiske, J. (1989) *Understanding Popular Culture*. London: Routledge.

Fiske, J. (1994) Television Pleasures, in D. Graddol and O. Boyd-Barrett (eds) *Media Texts: Authors and Readers*. Clevedon: Multilingual Matters/Open University.

Flournoy, D. and Stewart, R. (1997) *CNN: Making News in the Global Market*. Luton: University of Luton Press/John Libbey Media.

Foucault, M. (1987) *The Use of Pleasure*. London: Penguin.

Fowles, J. (1996) *Advertising and Popular Culture*. London: Sage.

Franklin, B. (2008) Newszak: Entertainment Versus News and Information, in A. Biressi and H. Nunn (eds) *The Tabloid Culture Reader*. Maidenhead: Open University Press.

Freedman, J.L. (2002) *Media Violence and its Effect on Aggression*. Toronto: University of Toronto Press.

Frith, S. (1992) The Industrialisation of Popular Music, in J. Lull (ed.) *Popular Music and Communication*, 2nd edn. London: Sage.

Frith, S. (1993) Popular Music and the Local State, in T. Bennett, S. Frith, L. Grossberg, J. Shepherd and G. Turner (eds) *Rock and Popular Music*. London: Routledge.

Frith, S. (2000) Power and Policy in the British Music Industry, in H. Tumber (ed.) *Media Power, Professionals and Policies*. London: Routledge.

Frow, J. (1997) *Time and Commodity Culture: Essays in Cultural Theory and Postmodernity*. Oxford: Clarendon Press.

Fuchs, C. (2008) *The Internet and Society*. Abingdon: Routledge.

Furst, L. (ed.) (1992) *Realism*. London: Longman.

Galtung, J. and Ruge, M. (1970) The Structure of Foreign News, in J. Tunstall (ed.) *Media Sociology*. London: Constable.

Gans, H. (1980) *Deciding What's News*. New York: Vintage.

Garnham, N. (1997) Political Economy and the Practice of Cultural Studies, in M. Ferguson and P. Golding (eds) *Cultural Studies in Question*. London: Sage.

Garnham, N. (2000) *Emancipation, the Media and Modernity*. Oxford: Oxford University Press.

Garofalo, R. (1986) How Autonomous is Relative: Popular Music, the Social Formation and Cultural Struggle. *Popular Music*, 6(1), in D. Hesmondhalgh and K. Negus (eds) (2002) *Popular Music Studies*. London: Arnold.

Gauntlett, D. (1995) *Moving Experiences: Understanding Television's Influences and Effects*. London: John Libbey.

Gauntlett, D. and Hill, A. (1999) *Television Living: Television, Culture and Everyday Life*. London: Routledge.

Geraghty, C. (1996) Feminism and Media Consumption, in J. Curran, D. Morley and V. Walkerdine (eds) *Cultural Studies and Communications*. London: Arnold.

Gerbner, G., Gross, L., Morgan, M. and Signorelli, N. (1986) Living with Television: The Dynamics of the Cultivation Process, in J. Bryant and D. Zillman (eds) *Perspectives on Media Effects*. Hillsdale, NJ: Lawrence Erlbaum.

Giddens, A. (1990) *The Consequences of Modernity*. Cambridge: Polity.

Giddens, A. (1999) *Runaway World*. London: Profile Books.

Gillespie, M. (ed.) (2005) *Media Audiences*. Maidenhead: Open University Press.

Gilroy, P. (1996) British Cultural Studies: The Pitfalls of Identity, in J. Curran, D. Morley and V. Walkerdine (eds) *Cultural Studies and Communications*. London: Arnold.

Gitlin, G. (1980) *The Whole World is Watching: Mass Media in the Making and Unmaking of the New Left*. Berkeley, CA: University of California Press.

Goldlust, J. (1987) *Playing for Keeps: Sport, the Media and Society*. Melbourne: Longman Cheshire.

Goldman, R. (1992) *Reading Ads Socially*. London: Routledge.

Goldman, R. and Papson, S. (1998) *Nike Culture*. London: Sage.

Goldsmiths Media Group (1999) A Radical Political Economic Approach: Central Issues, in J. Curran (ed.) *Media Organisations in Society*. London: Arnold.

Goodwin, A. (1992) Rationalisation and Democratisation, in J. Lull (ed.) *Popular Music and Communication*. London: Sage.

Gorn, G. and Goldberg, M. (1980) Children's Responses to Repetitive Television Commercials. *Journal of Consumer Research* 6: 421–4.

Gough-Yates, A. (2003) *Understanding Women's Magazines*. London: Routledge.

Graddol, D. and Boyd-Barrett, O. (eds) (1994) *Media Texts: Authors and Readers. A Reader*. Clevedon: Multilingual Matters/Open University.

Gramsci, A. (1971) *Selections from the Prison Notebooks*. London: Lawrence & Wishart.

Green, D. (1995) Preserving Pluralism in a Digital World, in T. Congdon, A. Graham and D. Green, *The Cross Media Revolution: Ownership and Control*. London: John Libbey.

Gripsrud, J. (2000) Tabloidisation, Popular Journalism, and Democracy, in C. Sparks and J. Tulloch (eds) *Tabloid Tales: Global Debates over Media Standards*. Oxford: Rowman & Littlefield.

Gripsrud, J. (2002) *Understanding Media Culture*. London: Arnold.

Grossberg, L., Wartella, E. and Whitney, D.C. (1998) *Media Making: Mass Media in Popular Culture*. London: Sage.

Gunter, B. (1985) *Dimensions of Television Violence*. London: Gower.

Gunter, B. (1995a) *The Representation of Women on Television*. London: John Libbey.

Gunter, B. (1995b) *Television and Gender Representation*. London: John Libbey.

Gunter, B. and Furnham, A. (1998) *Children as Consumers: A Psychological Analysis of the Young People's Market*. London: Routledge.

Gunter, B., Oates, C. and Blades, M. (2005) *Advertising to Children on Television*. Mahwah, NJ: Lawrence Erlbaum.

Hall, M.A. (1996) *Feminism and Sporting Bodies*. Champaign, IL: Human Kinetics.

Hall, S. (1980) Encoding/Decoding in Television Discourse, in S. Hall, D. Hobson, A. Lowe and P. Willis (eds) *Culture, Media, Language*. London: Hutchinson.

Hall, S. (ed.) (1997) *Representation: Cultural Representations and Signifying Practices*. London: Sage/Open University.

Hall, S., Clarke, J., Critcher, C., Jefferson, T. and Roberts, B. (1978) *Policing the Crisis*. London: Macmillan.

Hallam, J. with Marshment, M. (2000) *Realism and Popular Cinema*. Manchester: Manchester University Press.

Halliday, M.A.K. (1996) Language as Social Semiotic, in P. Cobley (ed.) *The Communication Reader*. London: Routledge.

Hamilton, J.T. (1998) *Channelling Violence: The Economic Market for Violent Television Programming*. Princeton, NJ: Princeton University Press.

Haraway, D. (1990) A Manifesto for Cyborgs: Science, Technology and Socialist Feminism, reprinted in G. Kirkup, L. Janes, K. Woodward and F. Hovenden (eds) (2000) *The Gendered Cyborg: A Reader*. London: Routledge.

Harrison, J. (2000) *Terrestrial TV News in Britain: The Culture of Production*. Manchester: Manchester University Press.

Harrison, J. (2006) *News*. Abingdon: Routledge.

Hartley, J. (1982) *Understanding News*. London: Methuen.

Hawkes, T. (1977) *Structuralism and Semiotics*. London: Methuen.

Hebdige, D. (1979) *Subculture: The Meaning of Style*. London: Methuen.

Held, D. (ed.) (2000) *A Globalising World: Culture, Economics, Politics*. London: Routledge/Open University.

Held, D. (2004) *The Global Covenant*. Cambridge: Polity.

Herbert, J. (2000) *Journalism in the Digital Age*. Oxford: Focal Press.

Herman, E. and McChesney, R. (1997) *The Global Media: The New Missionaries of Corporate Capitalism*. London: Cassell.

Herman, E. and McChesney, R. (1999) Global Media in the Late 1990s, in H. Mackay and T. O'Sullivan (eds) *The Media Reader: Continuity and Transformation*. London: Sage/Open University.

Hesmondhalgh, D. (2002) *The Cultural Industries*. London: Sage.

Hesmondhalgh, D. (2007) *The Cultural Industries*, 2nd edn. London: Sage.

Hesmondhalgh, D. and Negus, K. (eds) (2002) *Popular Music Studies*. London: Arnold.

Hill, A. (2007) *Restyling Factual TV*. Abingdon: Routledge.

Hobson, D. (1982) *Crossroads: The Drama of a Soap Opera*. London: Methuen.

Hoggart, R. (1957) *The Uses of Literacy*. Harmondsworth: Penguin.

Hoggart, S. (1995) *The Way We Live Now: Dilemmas in Contemporary Culture*. London: Chatto & Windus.

Hoggart, S. (2003) *Everyday Language and Everyday Life*. Edison, NJ: Transaction.

Holland, P. (1998) The Politics of the Smile: Soft News and the Sexualisation of the Popular Press, in C. Carter, G. Branston and S. Allan (eds) *News, Gender and Power*. London: Routledge.

Horne, J. (2006) *Sport in Consumer Culture*. Basingstoke: Palgrave Macmillan.

Horvát, J. (2001) American News, Global Audience, in T. Sylvia (ed.) *Global News: Perspectives on the Information Age*. Ames, IA: Iowa State University Press.

Houlihan, B. (ed.) (2008) *Sport and Society*. London: Sage.

Howarth, D. (2000) *Discourse*. Buckingham: Open University Press.

Hughes, P. (2007) Texts and Textual Analysis, in E. Devereux (ed.) *Media Studies: Key Issues and Debates*. London: Sage.

Jameson, F. (1990) *Late Marxism: Adorno, or, the Persistence of the Dialectic*. London: Verso.

Jameson, F. (1991) *Postmodernism, or the Cultural Logic of Late Capitalism*. London: Verso.

Jameson, F. (1992) Reification and Utopia in Mass Culture, in F. Jameson, *Signatures of the Visible*. London: Verso.

Jameson, J. (1998) *The Cultural Turn: Selected Writings on the Postmodern*. London: Verso.

Jamieson, K. and Campbell, K. (2001) *The Interplay of Influence: News, Advertising, Politics and the Mass Media*, 5th edn. Belmont, CA: Wadsworth/Thompson Learning.

Jarvie, G. (2006) *Sport, Culture and Society*. London: Routledge.

Jenkins, H. (1992) *Textual Poachers*. London: Routledge.

Jenkins, H. and Thorburn, D. (eds) (2003) *Democracy and New Media*. Cambridge, MA: MIT Press.

Jensen, K. (ed.) (1998) *News of the World: World Cultures Look at Television News*. London: Routledge.

Jhally, S. (1990) *The Codes of Advertising: Fetishism and the Political Economy of Meaning in the Consumer Society*. London: Routledge.

John, D.R. (1999) Children's Knowledge and Understanding of Advertising, in M.C. Macklin and L. Carlson (eds) *Advertising to Children, Concepts and Controversies*. London: Sage.

Johnson, F. (1996) Cyberpunks in the White House, in J. Dovey (ed.) *Fractal Dreams: New Media in Social Context*. London: Lawrence & Wishart.

Johnson, F. and Young, K. (2002) Gendered Voices in Children's Television Advertising. *Critical Studies in Media Communication*, 19(4): 461–80.

Jones, J.P. (2004) *Fables, Fashions and Facts about Advertising*. London: Sage.

Jones, T. (2003) *The Dark Heart of Italy*. London: Faber & Faber.

Kane, M.J. and Greendorfer, S.L. (1994) The Media's Role in Accommodating and Resisting Stereotyped Images of Women in Sport, in P.J. Creedon (ed.) *Women, Media and Sport: Challenging Gender Values*. London: Sage.

Katz, E. (1996) And Deliver Us from Segmentation. *Annals of the American Academy of Political and Social Science*, 546(1): 22–33.

Katz, E. and Lazarsfeld, P.F. (1995) Between Media and Mass/The Part Played by People/The Two Step Flow of Mass Communication, in O. Boyd-Barrett and C. Newbold (eds) *Approaches to Media: A Reader*. London: Arnold.

Kay, T. and Jeanes, R. (2008) Women, Sport and Gender Inequity, in B. Houlihan (ed.) *Sport and Society*. London: Sage.

Keane, J. (1991) *The Media and Democracy*. Cambridge: Polity.

Kenway, J. and Bullen, E. (2001) *Consuming Children: Education, Entertainment, Advertising*. Buckingham: Open University Press.

Key, W. (ed.) (1989) *The Age of Manipulation*. Lanham, MD: Madison.

Kline, S. (1993) *Out of the Garden: Toys and Children's Culture in the Age of Television Marketing*. London: Verso.

Kruse, H. (1999) Gender, in B. Horner and T. Swiss (eds) *Key Terms in Popular Music and Culture*. Oxford: Blackwell.

Lacey, N. (2000) *Narrative and Genre*. Basingstoke: Palgrave.

Langer, J. (1998) *Tabloid Television: Popular Journalism and the 'Other News'*. London: Routledge.

Larsen, M.S. (1997) The Rise of Professionalism: A Sociological Analysis, in D. Berkowitz (ed.) *The Social Meanings of News*. London: Sage.

Lash, S. and Urry, J. (1994) *The Economics of Signs and Space*. London: Sage.

Laughey, D. (2007) *Key Themes in Media Theory*. Maidenhead: Open University Press.

Lax, S. (2000) The Internet and Democracy, in D. Gauntlett (ed.) *Web Studies*. London: Arnold.

Lee, Martyn J. (1993) *Consumer Culture Reborn: The Cultural Politics of Consumption*. London: Routledge.

Lee, Min-Yang (2006) The Internet in E-Government in Taiwan, in K. Voltmer (ed.) *Mass Media and Political Communication in New Democracies*. Abingdon: Routledge.

Leiss, W., Kline, S., Jhally, S. and Botteril, J. (2005) *Social Communication in Advertising*, 3rd edn. London: Routledge.

Lent, J.A. (1998) The Animation Industry and its Offshore Factories, in G. Sussman and J. Lent (eds) *Global Productions*. Cresskill, NJ: Hampton.

Liebes, T. and Katz, E. (1993) *The Export of Meaning: Cross Cultural Realities of Dallas*, 2nd edn. Cambridge: Polity.

Lister, M., Dovey, J., Giddings, S., Grant, I. and Kelly, K. (2003) *New Media: A Critical Introduction*. London: Routledge.

Livingstone, S. (1990) *Making Sense of Television: The Psychology of Audience Interpretation*. Oxford: Pergamon.

Livingstone, S. (1996) On the Continuing Problem of Media Effects, in J. Curran and M. Gurevitch (eds) *Mass Media and Society*, 2nd edn. London: Arnold.

Livingstone, S. (2002) *Young People and New Media*. London: Sage.

Longhurst, B. (1995) *Popular Music and Society*. Cambridge: Polity.

Longhurst, B. (2007) *Popular Music and Society*, 2nd edn. Cambridge: Polity.

Lull, J. (ed.) (1992) *Popular Music and Communication*, 2nd edn. London: Sage.

Lyotard, J.-F. (1984) *The Postmodern Condition: A Report on Knowledge* (trans. G. Bennington and B. Massumi). Manchester: Manchester University Press.

McChesney, R.W. (2003) Corporate Media, Global Capitalism, in S. Cottle (ed.) *Media Organisation and Production*. London: Sage.

Macdonald, M. (2003) *Exploring Media Discourses*. London: Arnold.

McGowan, K (2007) *Key Issues in Critical and Cultural Theory*. Maidenhead: Open University Press.

McGregor, B. (1997) *Live, Direct and Biased? Making Television News in the Satellite Age*. London: Arnold.

Mackay, H. (2000) The Globalisation of Culture?, in D. Held (ed.) *A Globalising World: Culture, Economics, Politics*. London: Routledge/Open University.

Mackay, H. and O'Sullivan, T. (eds) (1999) *The Media Reader: Continuity and Transformation*. London: Sage/Open University.

McKinnon, K. (2003) *Representing Men: Maleness and Masculinity in the Media*. London: Arnold.

Macklin, M.C. and Carlson, L. (eds) (1999) *Advertising to Children: Concepts and Controversies*. London: Sage.

McLuhan, M. (1994) *Understanding Media: The Extensions of Man*. London: Routledge.

McLuhan, M. and Fiore, Q. (1967) *The Medium is the Message*. London: Penguin.

McNair, B. (1998) *The Sociology of Journalism*. London: Arnold.

McNair, B. (2003) *News and Journalism in the UK*, 4th edn. London: Routledge.

McNair, B. (2007) *An Introduction to Political Communication*, 4th edn. Abingdon: Routledge.

McQuail, D. (1977) The Influence and Effects of Mass Media, in J. Curran, M. Gurevitch and J. Wollacott (eds) *Mass Communication and Society*. London: Arnold.

McQuail, D. (2000) *McQuail's Mass Communication Theory*, 4th edn. London: Sage.

McRobbie, A. (1994) *Postmodernism and Popular Culture*. London: Routledge.

Maguire, J. (1999) *Global Sport: Identities, Societies, Civilisations*. Cambridge: Polity.

Maguire, J. and Young, K. (eds) (2002) *Theory, Sport and Society*. Oxford: Elsevier.

Majors, R. (2001) Cool Pose: Black Masculinity and Sports, in S. Whitehead and F. Barrett (eds) *The Masculinities Reader*. Cambridge: Polity.

Maltby, R. (1995) *Hollywood Cinema*. Oxford: Blackwell.

Manning, P. (2001) *News and News Sources: A Critical Introduction*. London: Sage.

Margolis, M. and Resnick, D. (2007) How the Net Will Not Contribute to Democracy, in R. Negrine and J. Stanyer (eds) *The Political Communication Reader*. Abingdon: Routledge.

Mattelart, A. (1991) *Advertising International: The Privatisation of Public Space* (trans. M. Chanan). London: Routledge.

Maxwell, I. (2002) The Curse of Fandom: Insiders, Outsiders and Ethnography, in D. Hesmondhalgh and K. Negus (eds) *Popular Music Studies*. London: Arnold.

Metz, C. (1974) *Film Language: A Semiotics of the Cinema*. New York: Oxford University Press.

Metz, C. (1982) *Psychoanalysis and the Cinema: The Imaginary Signifier*. London: Macmillan.

Meyer, T.P. (1976) The Impact of 'All in the Family' on Children. *Journal of Broadcasting*, 20(1): 23–33.

Middleton, R. (1990) *Studying Popular Music*. Buckingham: Open University Press.

Miège, B. (1989) *The Capitalization of Cultural Production*. New York: International General.

Miller, T., Lawrence, G., McKay, J. and Rowe, D. (2001) *Globalization and Sport*. London: Sage.

Mistry, R. (n.d.) *From 'Hearth and Home' to a Queer Chic: A Critical Analysis of Progressive Depictions of Gender in Advertising*, available at www.theory.org.uk/mistry.htm (accessed 9 January 2010).

Moran, A. (1998) *CopyCat TV: Globalisation, Programme Formats and Cultural Identity*. Luton: University of Luton Press.

Morley, D. (1989) Changing Paradigms in Audience Research, in E. Seiter, H. Borchers, G. Kreutzner and E. Warth (eds) *Remote Control: Television, Audiences and Cultural Power*. London: Routledge.

Morley, D. (1992) *Television Audiences and Cultural Studies*. London: Routledge.

Morley, D. (1996a) Postmodernism: The Rough Guide, in J. Curran, D. Morley and V. Walkerdine (eds) *Cultural Studies and Communications*. London: Arnold.

Morley, D. (1996b) Populism, Revisionism and the 'New' Audience Research, in J. Curran, D. Morley and V. Walkerdine (eds) *Cultural Studies and Communications*. London: Arnold.

Mosco, V. (1996) *The Political Economy of Communication*. London: Sage.

Mulvey, L. (1989) *Visual and Other Pleasures*. London: Macmillan.

Murdock, G. and Golding, P. (2000) Culture, Communications and Political Economy, in J. Curran and M. Gurevitch (eds) *Mass Media and Society*, 3rd edn. London: Arnold.

Murdock, G. and Golding, P. (2005) Culture, Communications and Political Economy, in J. Curran and M. Gurevitch (eds) *Mass Media and Society*, 4th edn. London: Arnold.

Myers, G. (1999) *Adworlds*. London: Arnold.

Nava, M., Blake, A., MacRury, I. and Richards, B. (1996) *Buy This Book: Studies in Advertising and Consumption*. London: Routledge.

Neale, S. (1995) Questions of Genre, in O. Boyd-Barrett and C. Newbold (eds) *Approaches to Media: A Reader*. London: Arnold.

Neale, S. (2000) *Genre and Hollywood*. London: Routledge.

Negrine, R. (1994) *Politics and the Mass Media in Britain*, 2nd edn. London: Routledge.

Negrine, R. and Stanyer, J. (eds) (2007) *The Political Communication Reader*. Abingdon: Routledge.

Negus, K. (1992) *Producing Pop*. London: Arnold.

Negus, K. (1996) *Popular Music in Theory*. Cambridge: Polity.

Negus, K. (1999) *Music Genres and Corporate Cultures*. London: Routledge.

Negus, K. and Roman-Velazquez, P. (2000) Globalisation and Cultural Identities, in J. Curran and M. Gurevitch (eds) *Mass Media and Society*, 3rd edn. London: Arnold.

Neuman, R. (1991) *The Future of the Mass Audience*. New York: Cambridge University Press.

Newcomb, H. and Hirsch, P. (1984) Television as a Cultural Forum, in W. Rowland and B. Watkins (eds) *Interpreting Television*. Beverly Hills, CA: Sage.

Norris, P., Curtice, J., Sanders, D., Scammell, M. and Semetko, H. (2007) The Effects of Newspapers, in R. Negrine and J. Stanyer (eds) *The Political Communication Reader*. Abingdon: Routledge.

O'Barr, W.M. (1994) *Culture and the Advertisement: Exploring Otherness in the World of Advertising*. Oxford: Westview.

Ofcom (2008) *New News, Future News*. London: Ofcom. Available at www.ofcom.org.uk/research/tv/reports/newnews/ (accessed 17 December 2009).

O'Meara, P., Mehlinger, H.D. and Krain, M. (eds) (2000) *Globalization and the Challenges of a New Century*. Bloomington, IN: Indiana University Press.

Ong, A. (2000) The Gender and Labor Politics of Postmodernity, in P. O'Meara, H.D. Mehlinger and M. Krain (eds) *Globalisation and the Challenges of a New Century*. Bloomington, IN: Indiana University Press.

Osgerby, B. (2004) *Youth Media*. London: Routledge.

Parkin, F. (1972) *Class Inequality and the Political Order*. St Albans: Paladin.

Paterson, C. (1998) Global Battlefields, in O. Boyd-Barrett and T. Rantanen (eds) *The Globalisation of News*. London: Sage.

Pavlik, J. (2001) *Journalism and the New Media*. New York: Columbia University Press.

Perse, E. (2001) *Media Effects and Society*. Mahwah, NJ: Lawrence Erlbaum.

Peterson, R.A. and Berger, D.G. (1990) Cycles in Symbol Production: The Case of Popular Music, in S. Frith and A. Goodwin (eds) *On Record: Rock, Pop and the Written Word*. London: Routledge.

Philo, G. (1990) *Seeing and Believing: The Influence of Television*. London: Routledge.

Pines, J. (2001) Rituals and Representations of Black 'Britishness', in D. Morley and K. Robins (eds) *British Cultural Studies*. Oxford: Oxford University Press.

Potter, W.J. (1999) *On Media Violence*. London: Sage.

Press, A.L. (2000) Recent Developments in Feminist Communication Theory, in J. Curran and M. Gurevitch (eds) *Mass Media and Society*, 3rd edn. London: Arnold.

Preston, P. (2001) *Reshaping Communications*. London: Sage.

Protess, D.L. (1991) *The Journalism of Outrage: Investigative Reporting and Agenda Building in America*. London: Guilford Press.

Provenzano, E. (1991) *Video Kids: Making Sense of Nintendo*. Cambridge, MA: Harvard University Press.

Putnam, R. (2000) *Bowling Alone: The Collapse and Revival of American Community*. New York: Simon & Schuster.

Radway, J. (1984) *Reading the Romance*. Chapel Hill, NC: University of North Carolina Press.

Real, M. (1989) *Super Media*. London: Sage.

Real, M. (1998) Media Sport: Technology and the Commodification of Postmodern Sport, in L.A. Wenner (ed.) *Media Sport*. London: Routledge.

Reese, S.W. (1997) The News Paradigm and the Ideology of Objectivity, in D. Berkowitz (ed.) *The Social Meanings of News*. London: Sage.

Robinson, L. (2008) The Business of Sport, in B. Houlihan (ed.) *Sport and Society*. London: Sage.

Ross, K. and Nightingale, V. (2003) *Media and Audiences: New Perspectives*. Maidenhead: Open University Press.

Rothkopf, D. (2000) In Praise of Cultural Imperialism, in P. O'Meara, H.D. Mehlinger and M. Krain (eds) *Globalization and the Challenges of a New Century*. Bloomington, IN: Indiana University Press.

Rowe, D. (1999) *Sport, Culture and the Media*. Buckingham: Open University Press.

Rowe, D. (2000) No Gain, No Game? Media and Sport, in J. Curran and M. Gurevitch, *Mass Media and Society*, 3rd edn. London: Arnold.

Rowe, D. (2004) *Sport, Culture and the Media*, 2nd edn. Buckingham: Open University Press.

Ruddock, A. (2001) *Understanding Audiences*. London: Sage.

Sabo, D.F. Jr. and Runfola, R. (eds) (1980) *Jock: Sports and Male Identity*. Englewood Cliffs, NJ: Prentice Hall.

Sanjek, D. (1999) Institutions, in B. Horner and T. Swiss (eds) *Key Terms in Popular Music and Culture*. Oxford: Blackwell.

Scammell, M. (2003) Citizen Consumers, in J. Corner and D. Pels (eds) *Media and the Restyling of Politics*. London: Sage.

Scammell, M. (2007) The Wisdom of the War Room, in R. Negrine and J. Stanyer (eds) *The Political Communication Reader*. Abingdon: Routledge.

Schiller, H. (1996) *Information Inequality: The Deepening Crisis of America*. London: Routledge.

Schiller, H. (2000) Digitised Capitalism: What Has Changed?, in H. Tumber (ed.) *Media Power, Professionals and Policies*. London: Routledge.

Schirato, A. and Webb, J. (2003) *Understanding Globalization*. London: Sage.

Schrøder, K.C. (1999) The Best of Both Worlds? Media Audience Research between Rival Paradigms, in P. Alasuutari (ed.) *Rethinking the Media Audience*. London: Sage.

Schudson, M. (1993) *Advertising, The Uneasy Persuasion*. London: Routledge.

Schuler, D. (2003) Reports of a Close Relationship between Democracy and the Internet Have Been Exaggerated, in H. Jenkins and D. Thorburn (eds) *Democracy and New Media*. Cambridge, MA: MIT Press.

Seymour-Ure, C. (1996) *The British Press and Broadcasting since 1945*. Oxford: Blackwell.

Shah, H. (2000) *Journalism in an Age of Mass Media Globalization*, available at www.scribd.com/doc/2577072/Journalism-in-an-Age-of-Mass-Media-Globalization (accessed 9 January 2010).

Shank, B. (2006) Music, Diaspora and Social Movement, in A. Bennett, B. Shank and J. Toynbee (eds) *The Popular Music Studies Reader*. Abingdon: Routledge.

Shuker, R. (2001) *Understanding Popular Music*, 2nd edn. London: Routledge.

Shuker, R. (2008) *Understanding Popular Music Culture*. Abingdon: Routledge.

Siebert, F., Peterson, T. and Schramm, W. (1956) *Four Theories of the Press*. Urbana, IL: University of Illinois Press.

Silverstone, R. (1994) *Television and Everyday Life*. London: Routledge.

Sinclair, J. (1987) *Images Incorporated: Advertising as Industry and Ideology*. Beckenham: Croom Helm.

Singer, T. (1998) Not So Remote Control. *Sport*, March: 36, quoted in D. Rowe, *Sport, Culture and the Media*, 2nd edn. Buckingham: Open University Press.

Skidmore, P. (1998) Gender and the Agenda, in C. Carter, G. Branston and S. Allan (eds) *News, Gender and Power*. London: Routledge.

Sobchak, T. (1988) The Adventure Film, in W.D. Gehring (ed.) *Handbook of American Film Genres*. Westport, CT: Greenwood.

Sobel, D. (1995) *Longitude: The True Story of a Lone Genius Who Solved the Greatest Scientific Problem of his Time*. New York: Walker.

Soloski, J. (1997) News Reporting and Professionalism: Some Constraints on the Reporting of News, in D. Berkowitz, *The Social Meanings of News*. London: Sage.

Spybey, A. (1996) *Globalisation and World Society*. Cambridge: Polity.

Sreberny, A. (2000) The Global and the Local in International Communications, in J. Curran and M. Gurevitch (eds) *Mass Media and Society*, 3rd edn. London: Arnold.

Sreberny-Mohammadi, A. et al. (1985) [Unesco Report], quoted in K. Jensen (ed.) (1998) *News of the World: World Cultures Look at Television News*. London: Routledge.

Stanyer, J. (2007) *Modern Political Communication*. Cambridge: Polity.

Stead, D. (2008) Sport and the Media, in B. Houlihan (ed.) *Sport and Society*. London: Sage.

Steemers, J. (2004) *Selling Television*. London: British Film Institute.

Steinem, G. (1995) Sex, Lies and Advertising, in R. Andersen, *Consumes Culture and Television Programming*. Oxford: Westview.

Sterling, C. (2000) US Communications Industry Ownership and the 1996 Telecommunications Act, in H. Tumber (ed.) *Media Power, Professionals and Policies*. London: Routledge.

Stevenson, N. (1995) *Understanding Media Cultures*. London: Sage.

Stevenson, N. (2002) *Understanding Media Cultures*, 2nd edn. London: Sage.

Stokes, J. and Reading, A. (eds) (1999) *The Media in Britain: Current Debates and Developments*. London: Macmillan.

Street, J. (1999) Remote Control? Politics, Technology and 'Electronic Democracy', in H. Mackay and T. O'Sullivan (eds) *The Media Reader: Continuity and Transformation*. London: Sage/Open University.

Street, J. (2001) *Mass Media, Politics and Democracy*. Basingstoke: Palgrave Macmillan.

Street, J. (2003) Celebrity, in J. Corner and D. Pels (eds) *Media and the Restyling of Politics*. London: Sage.

Sturken, M. and Cartwright, L. (2001) *Practices of Looking*. Oxford: Oxford University Press.

Tellis, G.J. (2004) *Effective Advertising*. London: Sage.

Terranova, T. (2004) *Network Culture: Politics for the Information Age*. London: Pluto.

Thompson, E. and Laing, A. (2003) The Net Generation: Children and Young People, the Internet and Online Shopping. *Journal of Marketing Management* 19(3–4): 491–512.

Thompson, J. (1990) *Ideology and Modern Culture*. Cambridge: Polity.

Thompson, S. (2002) Sport, Gender, Feminism, in J. Maguire and K. Young (eds) *Theory, Sport and Society*. Oxford: Elsevier.

Thornton, S. (2006) Understanding Hipness, in A. Bennett, B. Shank and J. Toynbee (eds) *The Popular Music Studies Reader*. Abingdon: Routledge.

Thussu, D. (2000) *International Communication*. London: Arnold.

Thwaites, T., Davies, L. and Mules, W. (2002) *Tools for Cultural Studies*, 2nd edn. Melbourne: Macmillan.

Tolson, A. (1996) *Mediations: Text and Discourse in Media Studies*. London: Arnold.

Tomlinson, A. (1999) *The Game's Up: Essays in the Cultural Analysis of Sport, Leisure and Popular Culture*. *Popular Cultural Studies*: 15. Aldershot: Ashgate.

Tomlinson, A. (2001) Sport, Leisure and Style, in D. Morley and K. Robins (eds) *British Cultural Studies*. Oxford: Oxford University Press.

Tomlinson, J. (1997) Internationalism, Globalisation and Cultural Imperialism, in K. Thompson (ed.) *Media and Cultural Regulation*. London: Sage/Open University.

Tomlinson, J. (1999) Cultural Globalisation: Placing and Displacing the West, in H. Mackay and T. O'Sullivan (eds) *The Media Reader: Continuity and Transformation*. London: Sage/Open University.

Toynbee, J. (2000) *Making Popular Music*. London: Arnold.

Toynbee, J. (2002) Mainstreaming, from Hegemonic Centre to Global Networks, in D. Hesmondhalgh and K. Negus (eds) *Popular Music Studies*. London: Arnold.

Tuchman, G. (1976) Telling Stories. *Journal of Communication* 26: 93–7, reprinted in J. Curran and M. Gurevitch (eds) (2000) *Mass Media and Society*, 3rd edn. London: Arnold.

Tuchman, G. (1995) The News Net, in O. Boyd-Barrett and C. Newbold (eds) *Approaches to Media: A Reader*. London: Arnold.

Tumber, H. (ed.) (2000) *Media Power, Professionals and Policies*. London: Routledge.

Van Loon, J. (2008) *Media Technology: Critical Perspectives*. Maidenhead: Open University Press.

Van Zoonen, L. (1994) *Feminist Media Studies*. London: Sage.

Van Zoonen, L. (1998) One of the Girls? The Changing Gender of Journalism, in C. Carter, G. Branston and S. Allan (eds) *News Gender and Power*. London: Routledge.

Volkmer, I. (1999) *CNN: News in the Global Sphere*. Luton: University of Luton Press.

Voltmer, K. (ed.) (2006) *Mass Media and Political Communication in New Democracies*. Abingdon: Routledge.

Von Feilitzen, C. (1998) Media Violence: Four Research Perspectives, in R. Dickinson, H. Harindranath and O. Linne (eds) *Approaches to Audiences: A Reader*. London: Arnold.

Von Ginneken, J. (1998) *Understanding Global News: A Critical Introduction*. London: Sage.

Walker, D. (2000) Newspaper Power: A Practitioner's Account, in H. Tumber (ed.) *Media Power, Professionals and Policies*. London: Routledge.

Warshow, R. (1970) *The Immediate Experience*. New York: Atheneum.

Waters, M. (1995) *Globalisation*. London: Routledge.

Watt, S., Lea, M. and Spears, R. (2002) How Social Is Internet Communication?, in S. Woolgar (ed.) *Virtual Society? Technology, Cyberbole, Reality*. Oxford: Oxford University Press.

Wayne, M. (1994) Television, Audiences and Politics, in S. Hood (ed.) *Behind the Screens: The Structure of British Television in the 1990s*. London: Lawrence & Wishart.

Webster, F. (1999) What Information Society?, in H. Mackay and T. O'Sullivan (eds) *The Media Reader: Continuity and Transformation*. London: Sage/Open University.

Wernick, A. (1991) *Promotional Culture: Advertising, Ideology, and Symbolic Expression*. London: Sage.

Westerbeek, H. and Smith, A. (2003) *Sport Business in the Global Marketplace*. Basingstoke: Palgrave Macmillan.

Whiteley, S., Bennett, A. and Hawkins, S. (2004) *Music, Space and Place: Popular Music and Cultural Identity*. Aldershot: Ashgate.

Williams, K. (2003) *Understanding Media Theory*. London: Arnold.

Williams, R. (1974) *Television, Technology and Cultural Form*. London: Fontana.

Williamson, J. (1978) *Decoding Advertisements*. London: Marion Boyars.

Woodward, K. (ed.) (1997) *Identity and Difference*. London: Sage.

Yon, D. (2000) *Elusive Culture: Schooling, Race and Identity in Global Times*. New York: State University of New York Press.

Young, B.M. (1990) *Television Advertising and Children*. Oxford: Clarendon Press.

Selected websites

This list of websites is intended to provide you with starting points for research into media, but it does not cover all possible topics. The range is across institutional sites and academic sites; I have added a comment in each case. These were all accessed in January 2010. If your favourites are not on this list, this may be something I should know, or it could be that I had repeated problems with accessing these websites. There are of course any number of business or company sites which you can search for by name, such as Hollywood majors or newspapers.

Advertising Standards Authority

http://asa.org.uk

An industry site concerned with advertising, including codes of practice and downloadable material.

Association of Teacher Websites

www.byteachers.org.uk

This site provides connection between websites and starting point for searches.

Audit Bureau of Circulations

www.abc.org.uk

An industry site concerned with the press, which includes latest circulation figures.

BARB (Broadcasters' Audience Research Board)

www.barb.co.uk

This site provides some free information about viewing figures and patterns, as well as offering an academic subsite. It supplies links to other useful sites such as Thinkbox (http://thinkbox.tv/).

BBC

www.bbc.co.uk

Much information about the corporation, as well as many links to its various channels, and to specific programmes: needs to be browsed.

The Bookseller

www.thebookseller.com

An online magazine about the book industry, providing items such as links to news about the trade and charts of popular publications.

BRAD (British Rate and Data)

www.bradinsight.com

A professional site offering media news links. You will need institutional access to get at much real data about the media and their consumption.

British Film Institute

www.bfi.org.uk

Useful links to other sites concerned with film industry and film study, and sub-sites for books and journals.

Campaign

www.campaignlive.co.uk

The online version of the magazine for the marketing industry, it is lively and current.

Campaign for Press and Broadcasting Freedom

www.cpbf.org.uk

The main benefit of this website lies in its database of articles: it also provides information about the work of the organization.

Cineuropa

www.cineuropa.org

An industry front for European film

Film Education

www.filmeducation.org

A useful wide range of resources and connections, covering many topics.

Internet Movie Database

www.imdb.com

This provides a wealth of information and comment on films and film makers.

ITV

www.itv.com

This provides useful background on the commercial television giant.

Media and Communications Studies Site (University of Aberystwyth)

www.aber.ac.uk/media

Run by Daniel Chandler, this has a considerable collection of material, covering a great range of topics such as media influence, gender and ethnicity, though perhaps uneven in its usefulness.

Media Guardian

www.guardian.co.uk/media

The *Guardian* newspaper's site provides a useful range of current material about the media and media events, including a compilation of the *Guardian*'s own articles.

Media Theory Site

www.theory.org.uk

David Gauntlett's site, now maintained by the Communications and Media Research Institute (CAMRI), University of Westminster, contains a mixture of reviews and articles; it is strong in some areas, such as identity and gender, and offers some essays and dissertations.

New Media Studies
www.newmediastudies.com
David Gauntlett's site relating to new media includes reference to resources, articles, reviews and more.

Ofcom (Office of Communications)
www.ofcom.org.uk
Ofcom is the UK regulator for broadcast media and telecommunications; its website offers codes of practice and accounts of research carried out, among other things.

PopCultures.com: Sara Zupko's Cultural Studies Center
www.popcultures.com
This has useful links, general references, reviews, accounts of theorists and useful papers.

RAJAR (Radio Joint Audience Research)
www.rajar.co.uk
This provides news and listening figures, among other useful detail, about UK radio stations and audiences.

UK Media Team
www.mediadesk.co.uk
Part of the EU media programme, this provides information about, for example, training, as well as links to other sites.

Undercurrents
www.undercurrents.org
An important alternative news provider, which is counter-establishment and pro the environment, among many issues. Apart from news you do not see, it offers useful publications and DVDs.

Voice of the Shuttle (VoS: University of California)
http://vos.ucsb.edu
This site provides information on an eclectic range of topics: it has useful links to other US sites.

Index

MEDIA AND THEIR PUBLICS

Michael Higgins

This accessible and thought-provoking book provides a critical insight into the relationship between the media and the public. It examines the way in which the public is represented, referred to and portrayed in the media, and how the media acts or speaks on the public's behalf.

The first part explores the political side of the relationship between the media and the public. This includes interesting discussion of advocacy in political interviews and the discursive arrangement of political discussion programmes.

The second part of the book examines a range of discourses outside of the political realm. Michael Higgins looks at the construction of ordinariness, authenticity and public legitimacy, the relationship between institutional and media expertise, and the exercise of public decency. He argues that what unites the relationships between media and forms of public are their concern with wider issues of politics, governance, and cultural influence.

The author offers a range of illustrative examples of broadcasting from US, Australian and British contexts, providing students with a rage of engaging international examples with which to draw comparisons and compare their own media experiences. Each chapter includes recommended texts for further reading and questions for discussion.

The Media and Their Publics is an essential text for students and researchers in media studies, cultural policy and political communications.

Contents: *Acknowledgements - Issues of the public - The construction of the political public - The political public and its advocates - The political public take the stage - The construction of the cultural public - Cultural publics and participation - The construction of expertise in the media - Rethinking media publics - Key figures and their thoughts - References - Index.*

2008   192pp

978-0-335-21929-2 (Paperback)   978-0-335-21930-8 (Hardback)

KEY THEMES IN MEDIA THEORY

Dan Laughey

"**Key Themes in Media Theory** *is wonderfully wide-ranging and deservedly destined to become a key text for students of Media Studies*."

Professor John Storey, University of Sunderland, UK

- What is media theory?
- How do media affect our actions, opinions and beliefs?
- In what ways do media serve powerful political and economic interests?
- Is media consumerism unhealthy or is it empowering?

Key Themes in Media Theory provides a thorough and critical introduction to the key theories of media studies. It is unique in bringing together different schools of media theory into a single, comprehensive text, examining in depth the ideas of key media theorists such as Lasswell, McLuhan, Hall, Williams, Barthes, Adorno, Baudrillard and Bourdieu.

Using up-to-date case studies the book embraces media in their everyday cultural forms – music, internet, film, television, radio, newspapers and magazines - to enable a clearer view of the 'big picture' of media theory. In ten succinct chapters Dan Laughey discusses a broad range of themes, issues and perspectives that inform our contemporary understanding of media production and consumption. These include:

- Behaviourism and media effects
- Feminist media theory
- Postmodernity and information society
- Political economy
- Media consumerism

With images and diagrams to illustrate chapter themes, examples that apply media theory to media practice, recommended reading at the end of every chapter, and a useful glossary of key terms, this book is the definitive guide to understanding media theory.

Contents: *List of figures and illustrations - Acknowledgements - What is media theory? - Behaviourism and media effects - Modernity and medium theory - Structuralism and semiotics - Interactionism and structuration - Feminisms and gender - Political economy and postcolonial theory - Postmodernity and information society - Consumerism and everyday life - Debating media theory - Glossary - References.*

2007   248pp

978-0-335-21813-4 (Paperback)   978-0-335-21814-1 (Hardback)